Gun Violence, Disability and Recovery

Cate Buchanan, Editor

Further endorsements for *Gun Violence, Disability and Recovery*

"I was shot at Virginia Tech on 16 April 2007. It was the most terrifying nine minutes of my life, and I still carry three bullets in my body as a constant reminder of that day. I was lucky to be living in a country where health and social services are relatively functional. I got support. It is our collective responsibility to ensure other survivors get the support they need and to demand greater accountability in the global arms trade. This book helps us understand what survivors of gun violence in various contexts are up against."
Colin Goddard, Brady Campaign to Prevent Gun Violence, USA

"Through my life experience as a person with a disability, my work and activism, I have met so many people impaired and traumatised from gun violence in Guatemala. Advocating for our rights is an ongoing struggle—particularly for women. Books such as this one, giving international exposure to the issue, are an important contribution to improving awareness of the human rights of people experiencing disability."
Sylvia Quan, Disability Ombudsman, Guatemala

"The reality of survivors of gun violence—my reality—is so often lost in narrow political and economic interests. This volume gives me hope that attention to life after gun violence will begin to receive long overdue attention, and contribute to the long haul effort of improving services for survivors as well as working towards accountability about the arms trade." **Shelley Barry,** filmmaker, South Africa

"*Gun Violence, Disability and Recovery* is a sobering reminder of our responsibility towards the many men and women, families and communities who deal with the long term consequences of gun violence. States have made great progress at the multilateral level by adopting the *Convention on the Rights of Persons with Disabilities* in 2006. Let us now connect these commitments to our broader efforts to tackle the consequences of armed violence at the local level."
Luis Alfonso De Alba, Ambassador of Mexico to the United Nations

"Gun violence is a major cause of acquired impairment in many countries, and this will always be traumatic for the individuals concerned. We must ensure that all people with disabilities, regardless of cause, receive rehabilitation and support to enable them to participate in their societies and achieve a good quality of life. This book is an important step forward to achieving that goal."
Tom Shakespeare, Norwich Medical School, University of East Anglia, UK

"My only child Justin, was 19 with an amazing future ahead of him. Justin was shot to death in Toronto on 23 June 2001. A huge part of me died with him. Violence tears at the fabric of society, creates hopelessness, fear and despair and threatens our future. It destroys the sense of community on which family and social wellbeing depend. I am so very grateful for this publication which will help to raise awareness about the devastating effects of gun violence and help promote mutual efforts to end it." **Audette Shephard**, United Mothers Opposing Violence Everywhere, Canada

"This vivid collection brings out of the shadows and into the light the true costs of gun violence in the world today. Through the eyes of survivors, we are confronted with the many policy gaps we need to address to prevent further firearms-related human rights violations."
Barbara A. Frey, Director, Human Rights Program, University of Minnesota, USA and former UN Special Rapporteur on the prevention of human rights violations committed with small arms and light weapons (2002-2006)

"The Philippines has a high gun homicide rate and weak gun controls. How many more people survive their injuries? As is the case in so many other countries, we do not know. The plight of survivors is the hidden face of gun violence. The value of this book is that it no longer allows us to ignore this issue."
Jasmin Nario-Galace, Philippines Action Network on Small Arms

"Gun violence and its consequences represent one of the most serious challenges for governments and communities. As a surgeon, I see firsthand the devastating impacts, leaving individuals and families with enormous health and social challenges. This book helps all of us better understand the realities, and informs our actions to address the challenges."
Carlos Rissa, School of Medicine and Health Sciences, Tecnológico de Monterrey University, Mexico

"The 2006 *Convention on the Rights of Persons with Disabilities* was a landmark achievement. Its provisions are potentially transformative if effectively implemented, providing forms of protection for survivors of violence by explicitly recognising the right to rehabilitation and access to health care; measures to promote justice and affirming participation in decision-making. This is all the more necessary as the 2013 *Arms Trade Treaty* makes no mention of assistance to survivors of gun violence. This book is required reading for anyone concerned about the impact of gun violence on human rights and the role of law in providing protection."
Janet E. Lord, Burton Blatt Institute, Syracuse University; Harvard Law School Project on Disability, USA

"This valuable book helps us understand aspects of gun violence that have been long overlooked. Gun violence is a public health issue. A clinical care and rehabilitation issue. It is also a human rights issue. States—and others—have legally binding human rights obligations to take effective measures to prevent such violence and, where it occurs, to address its repercussions. Obligations, as well as opportunities for action, are carefully described across this volume, offering policymakers and practitioners alike an important resource."
Paul Hunt, Professor of Law, Essex University, UK and UN Special Rapporteur on the Right to the Highest Attainable Standard of Health (2002-2008)

"The costs of violence are far greater than the numbers of lives lost, or the dry calculations of economic losses. This volume helps focus attention on the less visible, but perhaps much greater, psychological and social consequences of the deliberate harm humans inflict on each other. It provides researchers and advocates with much to consider."
Keith Krause, Graduate Institute of International and Development Studies, Geneva and Programme Director, Small Arms Survey, Switzerland

"This important volume looks at the spectrum of gun violence, including what happens after a shot has been fired. Coming through emergency surgery can be harrowing, but for survivors that is only the beginning. Gun violence must be prevented. But if it isn't, then this book shows us how to relieve some of the suffering it brings."
Charles Mock, Professor of Surgery, University of Washington, USA

"This important collection challenges us to think about how survivors of guns and their families live after a shooting, with gender factored in every step of the way. We are prompted to consider if we are accurately calculating the longitudinal costs of a shooting, and especially whether we know enough about the gendered costs of caregiving. We presently pay little attention to the full costs of gun violence that are shared variously by survivors, their families, overburdened health systems, and inadequate legal responses. Those concerned with gender justice have much to gain from this collection, and much work to do."
Vanessa Farr, Editor, *Sexed Pistols: The gendered impacts of small arms and light weapons* (2009)

"One of the great contributions of *Gun Violence, Disability and Recovery* is that it consistently pays attention to the psychological consequences of gun violence, which receive scant attention yet have multiple impacts on individuals, families and communities alike. Highlighting the mental health dimensions so richly, along with actions for policymakers and practitioners, is both welcome and long overdue."
Thomas Elbert, President, Vivo International, Germany

"What a timely contribution this is to a most urgent debate. The United Nations has pressed to "improve the effectiveness of armed violence prevention and reduction policies and programmes through investments in the production, analysis and use of evidence." We underlined that "effective approaches to armed-violence prevention and reduction will require investments [...] in high-quality data-gathering and analysis capacities." And this is precisely what we're getting with this comprehensive work by the Surviving Gun Violence Project."
Daniël Prins, Chief, Conventional Arms Branch, UN Office for Disarmament Affairs

"The moving profiles and testimonies in this book provide insights into the personal dimension of gun violence that statistics, necessary as they are, could never describe. After reading them one is forced to contemplate again that perhaps the most compelling fact concerning gun violence is that it is so preventable. This book should act as a catalyst for policy makers, advocates, researchers, and others to press forward ever more earnestly with the urgent task of limiting gun violence."
Richard J. Brennan, Director, Emergency Risk Management and Humanitarian Response, World Health Organization

"Every year, hundreds of thousands of victims of gun violence, together with their families, experience the real costs of the availability and misuse of arms in our communities. For these victims to attain their basic human rights, so often denied them, we need a better understanding of their predicament, challenges and needs. *Gun Violence, Disability and Recovery*, with its comprehensive overview and analysis, will critically inform our efforts to develop and implement better policies and practices to enhance the realisation of the rights of survivors of armed violence, including implementation of the *Arms Trade Treaty*."
Espen Barth Eide, former Minister of Foreign Affairs, Norway

Contents

Acknowledgements

Respect and appreciation are extended to the survivors of gun violence who so willingly and generously gave their time to this book by writing text, peer reviewing chapters, fact checking, and providing contacts and suggestions. The telling and re-telling of traumatic and intensely personal moments in your lives is not without complications and cost. It has been an honour to work with you to bring your experiences and ideas to light.

Thank you to: Adam (Somalia); Ahmad (Somalia); anonymous (Haiti); Association of Widows of Urban Bus Drivers/Asociación de Viudas de Pilotos Urbanos (Guatemala); Shelley Barry (South Africa); Neville Beling (South Africa); Zilla Beling (South Africa); Carol Bell (South Africa); Ben (USA); Mary Leigh Blek, Million Mom March (USA); Christine Buchanan (South Africa); Vinicio Cabrera, Transitions Foundation (Guatemala); Adelma Cifuentes (Guatemala); Pam Crowsley (South Africa); Danilo (El Salvador); Thembani Dyule (South Africa); Ronnie Fakude (South Africa); Julia Farquharson (Canada); Michelle Fernando (Australia); Alex Gálvez, Transitions Foundation (Guatemala); Manolo García (Guatemala); Colin Goddard, Brady Campaign to Prevent Gun Violence (USA); Joan Howard (Canada); Bill Jenkins, National Gun Victims Action Council (USA); Jorge (Guatemala); Lomeruka Kristen (Uganda); Juan Miguel, Transitions Foundation (Guatemala); Suela Lala (Albania); Oscar Manios and family (Colombia); Félix Omar Morataya, Homies Unidos (El Salvador); Neena Ningombam (India); Luis Orosco (Guatemala); Mark Roberts (South Africa); Luis Romero, Homies Unidos (El Salvador); Louise Russo (Canada); Audette Sheppard, United Mothers Opposing Violence Everywhere (Canada); Lorraine Small (Canada); Javed Tak, Humanity Welfare Organisation (India); and Vera and Wellington (Brazil).

Thank you to all the book contributors and peer reviewers (listed at the end of each piece in the book), who provided a diverse array of input from all points of the globe and across dozens of disciplines.

Thank you to the Government of Norway which provided support to the Surviving Gun Violence Project to develop the book.

For their consistent encouragement, ideas and support, appreciation goes to: Annette Bailey, Sheree Bailey, Michael O'Connell, Vanessa Farr, Jemima Garcia-Godos, Nora Groce, Thilo Kroll, Jim Mercy, Antonia Potter-Prentice, Pilar Reina, Christian Holmboe Ruge, Aleema Shivji, Sky Starr, and Fiona Stephenson.

Thanks very much to Helaine Boyd, who came in at the last leg of the process, and provided invaluable fact checking, drafting, and support with communications work.

To the editing team extraordinaire: Rebecca Peters, Mireille Widmer, and Emile LeBrun. Your individual and collective contributions, unique experiences and perspectives, significantly sharpened all elements of the book. Thank you for your professional commitment and for your love and friendship over the lengthy gestation period of this book.

Finally, to my family who have been entirely supportive and encouraging: Denise Buchanan, Neil Buchanan, Pam Kowal, Paul Kowal, Ariel Grace and Marley— thank you.

Cate Buchanan

Dedication

This book is dedicated to those whose
lives have been changed in an instant
by gun violence.

Foreword

Gun violence takes the lives of hundreds of thousands of men, women, and children every year. Many millions more survive with injuries, psychological trauma, and/or impairments. Yet when States debate the weapons trade—typically only focussing on the illicit aspect—little is said about the people whose lives are ended or forever altered by their misuse.

In 2008 I was placed in an induced coma after being shot two times in the back, with one bullet 2 mm from my spinal cord. By some miracle no organs were damaged but I live with the scars, and permanent nerve and tissue damage. If I had not been airlifted to Australia for emergency medical treatment I would have suffered more permanent damage, demonstrating the critical importance of timely medical care and quality rehabilitation.

This book is timely and important because the international community is not properly addressing this issue. Even the small arms control community lags behind on attention to those who are shot and injured. I find this striking given the importance of victim assistance in other weapons control processes, notably the effort to end the use of anti-personnel landmines, in which victim assistance has become a central pillar of "mine action". Addressing the suffering of affected communities is also central to the 2008 *Convention on Cluster Munitions*.

Looking around at other international frameworks, albeit of a non-binding nature, the 2006 *Geneva Declaration on Armed Violence and Development* has done much to advance a people-focussed agenda on armed violence. It can provide a framework for addressing the rights and needs of the millions whose lives have already been affected by gun violence, and who are yet to be heard. The *Oslo Commitments on Armed Violence* also provides an important entry point for further future policy efforts.

The core message of *Gun Violence, Disability and Recovery* is that survivors of gun violence have needs that must be addressed. More than needs, they have rights: the right to the best attainable standards of health, the right to live independently, and the right to participate fully in all aspects of life. These rights have implications for specific services, as well as for the broader social environment in which survivors live.

Much is already being done on the ground to fulfil these rights. Some States support modern health and rehabilitation institutions, impose high standards of training for health professionals, have social security schemes to sustain livelihoods, promote the integration of persons with disabilities, and have adopted comprehensive normative frameworks. Civil society actors have also organised to provide support—psychological, legal, and economic—to vulnerable survivors and their families. International cooperation and assistance programmes are increasingly directed at States or regions where needs are great but resources are scarce. This is all very encouraging.

But we can do better.

The great value of this publication is that it shows us how. It draws on the expertise of a wide range of contributors from relevant professions—physiotherapists, nurses, gender specialists, disability rights experts, trauma surgeons, rehabilitation practitioners, lawyers, and advocates—from all corners of the globe. Country case studies and thematic chapters combine to highlight good practices and identify gaps in research, programmes, and services, or norms and policies.

There is something in this volume for all of us: researchers and activists, policymakers and practitioners, whether we live or work in conflict-affected areas or regions "at peace", and whatever the resources at hand or the capacity of the State.

I commend the Government of Norway for supporting the Surviving Gun Violence Project, an initiative that is long overdue and much needed. This first significant piece of work compels all of us to engage and find ways to ensure that the ideas and recommendations contained in these pages are discussed, debated, and included in policy and programming. It is time that survivors of gun violence take centre stage.

José Ramos-Horta
Nobel Peace Prize Laureate (1996) and President of Timor-Leste (2007-12)
UN Under-Secretary-General/Special Representative of the Secretary-General for Guinea-Bissau (2013—)

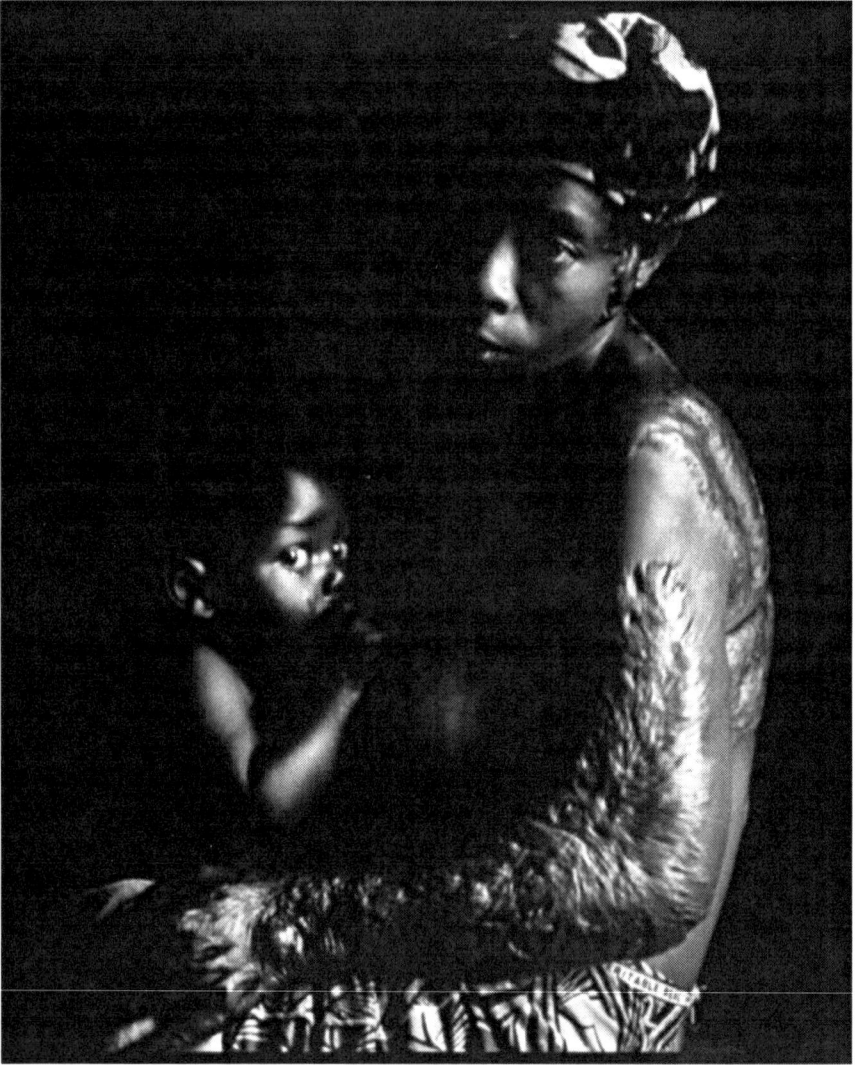

In Goma, Maombi, 26 years old, was living in a camp for internally displaced people when she suffered third degree burns during a violent gang rape. At the time she was pregnant. Her children were playing while her husband and youngest child were with her in their tent. Six men, wearing military uniforms, used knives to tear through the fabric of the tent. Her husband ran away. Three men stayed outside the tent. Inside, one held a gun to her four-year-old child's head and warned that if either cried they would be killed. At some point Maombi lost consciousness. The men then set the tent on fire. Maombi survived, but with severe burns, her child died. "When my mind came back it is after two weeks... they informed me the baby died in the fire... I feel like death." Her husband then abandoned her. Unable to work due to the scar tissue damage, she is raising her four surviving children by begging. Some 250,000 women have endured sexual violence during the Democratic Republic of Congo's civil war. (Image: Robin Hammond/Panos, May 2010)

1 Introduction

Acquiring an impairment or disability as a result of gun violence—whether intentional, self-directed, or accidental—can occur in a wide range of settings, from quiet suburban streets to conflict zones.[1] A child is caught in crossfire on the way to school; someone is robbed at gunpoint while working in their shop; a civilian is shot and sexually violated whilst fleeing a civil war; a political activist is detained at gunpoint and tortured; a young woman is paralysed after being shot by her former boyfriend; a teenager's suicide attempt results in severe life-long impairment.

Gun Violence, Disability and Recovery explores a range of issues related to the aftermath of gun violence: physical injuries and psychological trauma; impairment and disability; rehabilitation and recovery; victimisation and victims' rights; with a strong commitment to highlighting gender dimensions. The book focuses on the lives and experiences of gun violence survivors, as well as affected families and caregivers, with the aim of identifying ways to improve their prospects for full recovery and inclusion in their communities and societies.

Surviving gun violence is not yet established as a field in its own right for enquiry, policy, or programming, and responses to address survivors' rights and needs are often haphazard. This book is a contribution to elaborating coherent and comprehensive norms and interventions. It offers a multi-disciplinary analysis of what happens to people once they are shot or threatened at gunpoint. It brings the perspectives of various professions—victims' rights specialists and advocates, health personnel, criminologists, economists, social workers, gender experts, and others—together with those who have been shot and those who provide care to loved ones with long-term impairments as a result of gun violence. This is the first time these diverse viewpoints and experiences have been combined in one resource.

A global issue

Gun violence is a serious problem in many parts of the world. Millions of people are directly and indirectly affected by the injuries, trauma, grief, and loss from gun-related violence, including murders, suicides, kidnappings, armed robberies, intimidation, and accidents. Key facts include:

- Lethal violence claims some 526,000 lives each year, including 396,000 intentional homicides, 55,000 direct conflict deaths, 54,000 "unintentional" homicides, and 21,000 killings during policing or security interventions. About half of all lethal violence is due to guns.[2]
- Almost all of these deaths (90%) occur in non-war settings.[3] Many are likely nations affected by violent crime, with weak law enforcement and justice systems.

- According to the Small Arms Survey, some 2-7 million people could be living with the consequences of firearm injuries sustained in settings outside of armed conflicts.[4]
- The World Health Organization (WHO) estimates that 50-80% of traumatic deaths happen before arrival at hospital in low and middle income settings; thus effective first response trauma care stands to "substantially reduce death and disability following injury."[5]
- Global estimates of firearm stocks are around 875 million small arms, with standards to regulate and diminish stocks varying dramatically among and within nations.[6]
- Nearly 75% of the world's small arms (650 million) are in the hands of civilians, including gangs (2-10 million), private security companies (1.7-3.7 million), and non-state armed groups (1.1-1.8 million).[7]

In the United States of America (USA), the estimated cost of gun-related violence (including psychological costs and reduced quality of life) has been calculated at USD100 billion per year.[8] Brazil spends an estimated 0.5% of its annual gross domestic product—USD10 billion—responding to armed violence; Colombia about 1%, some USD4 billion.[9] But these calculations may not adequately factor in the costs of lengthy recovery processes, given that so little is known about the long-term health and social impacts.

While governments at every level of society are obliged to develop violence prevention and gun control policies, prevention is not the main focus of this book. Instead, it explores what happens to people once they have been shot or intimidated; who cares for them if they cannot fully care for themselves; what impacts this has on families and communities; and what core responses are needed at local, national and global levels.

Counting survivors

Survivors greatly outnumber people killed by armed violence, but estimates of the ratios vary and are highly context-specific. The WHO estimates that violence (with and without weapons) results in more than 16 million injuries requiring medical attention each year.[10] Further, the WHO notes that violence, including homicide, suicide, and other injuries, account for 9% of global mortality and are a leading cause of impairment and resulting disability.[11]

Injuries (of all types, including violence, road trauma, and occupational injuries) account for approximately 17% of the global burden of disease in adults aged 15-59.[12] Some 90% of the burden of injury occurs in low and middle income countries (LMIC).[13] However, specific information on gun injuries is scarce. In the USA—with advanced trauma care capacity, good data collection, and high rates of gun violence—it was estimated in 2001 that for every firearm fatality, three people with non-fatal gun injuries were treated in hospital emergency rooms; many more stayed away from hospitals, increasing the estimate to possibly six non-fatal injuries per fatality.[14] Data from 2011 from the Centers for Disease Control and Prevention revealed that 31,672 people died by gunshot in the USA; more than twice as many (73,505) were treated in hospital emergency rooms for non-fatal firearm injuries.[15]

One of the challenges in understanding the scale of gun-related victimisation, which largely relies on hospital data collection techniques, is that many people are not treated in hospital-for example, those avoiding being arrested who seek alternative forms of medical "care"; those experiencing psychological trauma months or years later who present to different parts of a health care system, if at all. Further, gun-related victimisation is often lost or inadequately noted in incident recording processes—for example, when a gun is used as an enabling "tool" to perpetrate sexual violence at gunpoint but is never fired and the misuse of the weapon not accurately recorded.

What happens after someone is shot and becomes impaired? Significant gains in understanding the prevalence of impairment and the experience of disability in recent years allow us to note that:

- Approximately 15% of the world's population lives with impairment and disability.[16]
- If families are included, approximately two billion people are directly affected by impairment and disability.[17]
- Living with disability increases the risk of living in poverty.[18]
- People with impairments are particularly susceptible to co-morbidities, compounded by unequal access to health care, further imperiling their health status.[19]
- Acquired impairments in low and middle income countries typically occur from extremity injuries, and in high-income countries from spinal and head injuries.[20]
- In 62 countries no rehabilitation services are available.[21]
- In many low and middle income settings, only 5-15% of people with impairments can obtain assistive devices.[22]

Elements and contents of the book

This volume contains thematic and country-focussed chapters. The book's components chart issues arising over time for survivors of gun violence, from the immediate aftermath of an injury to long-term rehabilitation to social protection, normative frameworks, and services available in selected countries. The diversity of country foci illustrate responses in a variety of cultural and socio-economic contexts. Shorter "Spotlight sections" provide reflections from diverse individuals as well as analysis of events and processes. These often take a deeper look at a programme, service, or significant event. Table 1 provides an overview of the main themes across the book and examples of where the reader can find a focus on such themes.

All elements of the book give voice to the experiences of survivors and their families, as well as experts in health, victims' rights advocacy, social work, gender, and criminal justice. These testimonies attest to the difficult path survivors undergo to reconstruct an identity and reclaim a place in society. They are significant and ought not to be dismissed as having no policy or research value.

Table 1. Main themes and foci covered across the book

Theme/focus	Where to find it in the book
Perspectives from survivors	Profiles and content in the chapters: India; South Africa; Canada; Somalia; Guatemala; Rehabilitation and Recovery
	Spotlights sections: Vera and Wellington (Brazil); Spinal cord injury in Haiti; Danilo and the ISRI Rehabilitation Centre (El Salvador); Suela Lala (Albania); Ronnie Fakude (South Africa); Lomeruka Kristen (Uganda); New Year's Eve in Colombia; Neville Beling (South Africa); Norwegian State Response to the 22 July 2011 Attacks; Mental Illness Provisions in Gun Laws; Quality Rehabilitation and Links to Violence Reduction; Surviving the Lusignan Massacre in Guyana; Gun Violence and Masculinity
Perspectives from health, justice and social work professionals	Chapters: India; Guatemala; Canada; South Africa; Traumatic Injuries; Evolution of Victims' Rights and International Standards; Rehabilitation and Recovery
	Spotlights: Paying for Gun-related Impairment in the United States; Rehabilitation and Violence Reduction; New Year's Eve in Colombia; Spinal Cord Injury in Haiti; El Salvador Gun Tax and Victims' Services
Government policy responses	Chapters: India; South Africa; Guatemala; Somalia; Canada; Social Protection
	Spotlights: El Salvador; Norway; Colombia's Victims' Law; Guyana; Mental Illness Provisions in Gun Laws
Examples of reparation and compensation schemes	Chapters: Canada; India; Somalia; Victims' Rights; Social Protection
	Spotlights: Norway; Colombia Victims' Law; Assistance to Survivors and Clauses in Peace Agreements
Caregiving	Chapters: Canada; India; South Africa; Rehabilitation and Recovery; Conclusion and Recommendations
	Spotlights: Vera and Wellington
International standards and principles	Chapters: Victims' Rights and Annex 1, International Standards Relevant to Survivors of Gun Violence; Social Protection
	Spotlights: Colombia's Victims' Law; Clauses in Peace Agreements; El Salvador

Peer support	Chapters: Guatemala; Canada; Rehabilitation and Recovery
	Spotlights: United States; Rehabilitation and Violence Reduction
Gender (which is mainstreamed across all elements; these elements have a particularly prominent focus.)	Chapters: Canada; India; Somalia; South Africa; Guatemala
	Spotlights: Gun Violence and Masculinity; Rehabilitation and Violence Reduction; United States
Rehabilitation	Chapters: Guatemala; South Africa; India; Rehabilitation and Recovery
	Spotlights: Vera and Wellington; Spinal Cord Injury in Haiti; Danilo and ISRI; United States; Suela Lala; Lomeruka Kristen; Rehabilitation and Violence Reduction
Physical trauma	Chapters: Guatemala; Traumatic Injuries; Rehabilitation and Recovery
	Spotlights: New Year's Eve in Colombia; Norway; Neville Beling; United States
Psychological trauma	Chapters: Canada; Somalia; South Africa; Rehabilitation and Recovery
	Spotlights: Danilo; Guyana; Neville Beling; Lomeruka Kristen; Ronnie Fakude; Rehabilitation and Violence Reduction; Mental Illness Provisions in Gun Laws; Vera and Wellington, Norway
Role of civil society	Chapters: Guatemala; Somalia; South Africa; India; Victims' Rights
	Spotlights: Guyana; Rehabilitation and Violence Reduction
Victims' rights	Chapters: Guatemala; South Africa; Canada; India; Victims' Rights and Annex 1
	Spotlights: Norway; Guyana; United States; El Salvador; Colombia Victims' Law; Mental Illness Provisions in Gun Laws
Examples of good practice	Chapters: Guatemala; South Africa; Canada; India; Somalia; Rehabilitation and Recovery; Traumatic Injuries; Victims' Rights; Social Protection
	Spotlights: United States; El Salvador; Norway; Rehabilitation and Violence Reduction; Danilo and ISRI

Disability rights	Chapters: India; South Africa; Guatemala; Rehabilitation and Recovery; Social Protection; Victims' Rights and Annex 1
	Spotlights: Haiti; Suela Lala; Danilo; Ronnie Fakude
Social protection	Chapters: Canada; Guatemala; South Africa; India; Social Protection
	Spotlights: Danilo; Ronnie Fakude; United States; Norway
Secondary survivors	Chapters: Canada; Guatemala; Victims' Rights
	Spotlights: Norway; Vera and Wellington; Neville Beling; Guyana; Mental Illness Provisions in Gun Laws
War affected people and communities/ armed conflict specific	Chapters: India; Somalia; Rehabilitation and Recovery; Victims' Rights and Annex 1; Social Protection; Traumatic Injuries
	Spotlights: Colombia's Victims' Law; Haiti; Clauses in Peace Agreements; El Salvador
Perpetrators	Chapters: Canada; India; Guatemala; Somalia; South Africa; Victims' Rights
	Spotlights: United States; Gun Violence and Masculinity; Danilo; Vera and Wellington; Rehabilitation and Violence Reduction
Annex 1: International Standards Relevant to Survivors of Gun Violence	Linked to the chapter, Evolution of Victims' Rights and International Standards. The annex provides a summary of 56 international instruments and standards relevant to the rights of survivors of gun violence.

Responses to a complex reality

For survivors of gun violence, whether permanently impaired or not, the road to recovery is often long and arduous. Recovery encompasses navigating the realities of trauma, impairment, status change in communities, regaining a sense of self, independence (where possible), or acceptance of dependence.

While much of this transformation rests on the shoulders of survivors themselves, this book illustrates how the dedication of loved ones, supporters, professionals, and the wider society are also necessary in recovery processes.

One important point the book makes is that these many pieces of the recovery "puzzle" rarely fit together neatly. Individual health facilities are not typically well networked with each other, so their division of labour is suboptimal. First responders sometimes do not have access to important information and may not direct victims to appropriate facilities and services. Emergency care personnel need to have an understanding of rehabilitation in order to minimise the risk of additional impairment. Health personnel must also understand the psychological trauma associated with violence, so that specialist care can be called in if necessary. The same is true of police and legal professionals, who otherwise risk exacerbating secondary trauma for survivors. If impairment cannot be prevented, service providers must be prepared to accompany and support individuals through a rehabilitation process, including long-term needs, such as assistance to gain alternate or additional employment and educational skills. Limited resources must be spread along this continuum in the most efficient way. A recurring theme in the book is the challenges survivors face in trying to secure support (services, livelihood related) in a disconnected system.

For the "joining up" of systems and policies to occur, relevant actors must somehow be coordinated. Harmonising assistance and policies is the responsibility of States, even if the services themselves might be delivered by the private sector, local communities, civil society, and international organisations. Normative frameworks (laws, policies) are needed to guarantee human rights, set priorities, and build service delivery capacities. Of course, civil society plays important roles, especially in contexts where governments are stretched thin or incapable of responding. The book focuses on all these aspects.

A note on terminology

Terminological precision proved to be a challenge in the development of this book. We have tried to be transparent with respect to the debates over different terms, and offer the reader text that is accessible, jargon-free, and appropriately referenced. Some key terms are explained in Box 1.

Box 1: Terms, concepts and definitions

Victims and survivors
Across the book the following terms are generally used: "victims" of gun violence for people who have died from gunshot wounds; and "survivors" usually refers to those who have lived through gun-related injury or trauma.

The definitions of "victims" and "survivors" draws on the 1985 UN *Declaration of Basic Principles of Justice for Victims of Crime and Abuse of Power*. Put more formally, survivors of gun violence are persons who, individually or collectively, have suffered harm, including physical or mental injury (violently acquired impairment/s), emotional suffering, economic loss or substantial diminution of their fundamental rights due to the misuse of small arms or light weapons. A person is considered a survivor or a victim regardless of whether the perpetrator is identified, apprehended, prosecuted or convicted, and regardless of the familial relationship between the perpetrator and the victim. The term also includes, where appropriate, the immediate family or dependants of the direct victim and persons who have suffered harm in intervening to assist victims in distress or to prevent victimisation.[23]

We recognise that this usage is not universal, even among affected persons. For example, international discussions and research on weapons control typically apply the term "victims" to people injured or traumatised by violence as well as those who have died. Further, in policy documents the status of victim is often stereotypically attributed to "women, children, and the elderly"—conflated in one sentence as though they were a homogenous group. In criminal justice and health advocacy, the word "survivor" is considered to a more empowering terms than "victim". Many individuals use the phrase "from victim to survivor" (or even, from "survivor to thriver") to describe the continuum of their journey toward recovery. Because of space considerations, this book does not address the varying theories and concepts of victimhood and victim identity. These are, however, important discussions.[24]

Primary and secondary survivors

"Primary survivors" are people who have been directly victimised (i.e. shot or otherwise directly physically or psychologically harmed by violence); "secondary survivors" include those who witnessed the violence, as well as family members grieving the loss of murdered loved ones or caring for the primary survivors.[25] The concept of secondary survivors also acknowledges the pain, humiliation, and ostracism that family members and loved ones can experience because of a relative's action(s) or experiences. Secondary survivors are frequently overlooked but can experience multiple health, social, and economic consequences. There is little understanding of the onset, duration, and varied manifestations of trauma and anxiety that secondary survivors may experience. This can include loss of confidence, employment challenges, well-being, and fragmented/fractured family connections. Vivo International has noted that secondary survivors often "show the after-effects of violent acts and constitute a much larger group than the one traditionally considered by policy makers."[26]

Disability and impairment

In this book, the term "disability" refers not to an attribute of a person with an impairment or injury, but rather to the negative interactions this person may have with society and environment.[27] "Impairment" is a problem or alteration in physical or mental function resulting in a limitation or restriction or perhaps a difficulty in independent living. The book has tried to pay attention to external factors perpetuating disability, respecting the view that "...Injustices occur when disability is over-medicalised. Seeing difficulties purely as individual problems can ignore structural issues that contribute to health status such as poverty, environmental barriers, and social exclusion."[28] Many gun injuries result in permanent impairment, either physical, mental, or both. A person's experience of impairment is uniquely personal, affected by their economic status, gender, spiritual beliefs, capacity to adapt, and other factors: two people with similar impairments may have vastly different experiences and encounter disability in divergent ways.

Victimisation[29]

Victimisation refers to the process by which an individual or group of individuals are negatively affected by some form of intimidation, harm, or violence. Related to violence, victimisation can be inflicted by another person (interpersonal) or through the power of an entity (e.g. police services and security agencies), or self-inflicted. The latter is also referred to as "auto-victimisation" and includes self-destructive behaviours including suicide.[30]

Secondary victimisation refers to the effects of inappropriate or insensitive behaviour towards survivors or grieving families, such as when police officers adopt a demeaning attitude, or ask insensitive or inappropriate questions.

Victimology

Victimology is the study of victims and victimisation.[31] It builds on criminology by examining effects rather than causes. Three broad types of suffering are important to note: material, personal, and intangible.[32] Material suffering involves the loss of personal property (e.g. by destruction or confiscation). Personal suffering refers to harm to life, body, or liberty. In situations of armed conflict this harm can occur both during and outside combat situations. Intangible suffering refers to the loss or lack of opportunities and invisible trauma such as post-event or post-traumatic shock. These forms of suffering call for different approaches to policy, support and services, involving choices with complex ethical, socio-political and resource challenges.

Transitional justice
Transitional justice measures are designed to establish or re-establish democratic rule of law, typically in the wake of violent conflict. These can include truth seeking and remembering (e.g. truth commissions, memorials, documentation), criminal prosecutions, reparations (see below), and institutional reforms (e.g. attention to representativeness; vetting and dismissal of compromised personnel and/or human rights abusers in government agencies) to support or enhance transitions from periods of violence, war, repression, or instability.[33] Such measures include a mixture of formal/informal, judicial, and non-judicial methods and processes.

Reparations
Reparations refer to acts or processes of making amends for moral or legal crimes. The 2005 UN *Basic Principles and Guidelines on the Right to a Remedy and Reparation for Victims of Gross Violations of International Human Rights Law and Serious Violations of International Humanitarian Law* affirmed that effective reparations contain five core elements: restitution, compensation, rehabilitation, satisfaction (with process, and/or access or disclosure of truth), and non-repetition (Principles 19-23). Reparations can include apologies and acknowledgement of harm or indignity; repair or return of physical belongings; and financial compensation for past and future lost earnings, stolen or misappropriated funds, payment for services (medical, psychological, rehabilitation, care etc.). "Remedy" and "redress" are also terms used to denote reparations.[34]

Rehabilitation
In the health, medical, and disability communities, the term "rehabilitation" is associated with physical recovery from an incident or event that has led to change of form, function, or ability. In human rights and legal communities, it often implies a political transformation of individuals and entities (e.g. armed groups, corrupt institutions), typically as part of a transitional political process such as an end to violent conflict. In this book we have tried to be clear about how the term is used in specific chapters. Important work is underway to extend understanding of rehabilitation.[35]

Gun violence and armed violence
As this book focuses solely on gun violence, the term "gun violence" predominates. Where the term "armed violence" is used, it is to recognise broader forms of violence committed with weapons, of which gun violence is one type.[36] Survival from injuries caused by other so-called conventional weapons (such as landmines, bombs, and unexploded ordnance) is extensively covered elsewhere.[37] However, the issues, concepts, and proposals in this book are of relevance to those with an interest in, or responsibility for, responding to the rights of survivors of violence and weapons-related assistance more broadly.

Standards and normative frameworks

At the national level, laws are needed to protect the rights of survivors in dealing with the criminal justice system, as well as facilitating and regulating social protection and disability rights. One of the pressing policy tasks is to generate guidance for States on what an effective mix of laws and policies entails. The book provides some initial thoughts in this regard with country case studies outlining the state of key national legislation and policy, while thematic chapters provide "food for thought" on normative issues and good practice.

In an effort to achieve further coherence, an increasing number of States have adopted National Action Plans (NAPs) to determine the legislative, administrative, and institutional changes needed to respond to the crisis of small arms proliferation, or to the scourge of landmines and other conventional weapons. To date over 30 countries have developed a NAP or report on violence and health.[38] NAPs can facilitate an assessment of gaps in emergency response systems, trauma care, mental health support, rehabilitation, and human rights. States are also developing NAPs and domestic laws to implement the 2006 *Convention on the Rights of Persons with Disabilities* (CRPD), regarded as a landmark treaty powerfully fusing human rights, development, and socio-political objectives.[39] The CRPD is particularly significant because systemic laws to address disability discrimination remain a global challenge.[40]

At the global level, over recent decades, significant paradigm shifts have occurred in the area of disability rights, particularly with the advent of the CRPD. Progress has been made on conceptual, terminological, and standards fronts. These shifts reflect a rights-based approach to understanding and acting on reducing the experience of disability.[41] This has important implications for gun violence survivors.

Opportunities for normative development also exist in arms control and disarmament processes, but in the recent decade of intensive focus on the arms trade, little consideration has been given to survivors. The small arms control agenda has instead focused almost exclusively on the weapons themselves (tracking, control, and management). The centre of gravity has shifted in recent years towards a broader focus on armed violence reduction and prevention, with a concomitant increased focus on human suffering as a rationale for identifying solutions to violence.[42] Yet recent norms, both "soft" (e.g. the 2006 *Geneva Declaration on Armed Violence and Development*) and "hard" (e.g. 2013 *Arms Trade Treaty*) have been developed without a dedicated focus to the rights and needs of survivors of armed violence.

Outside the domain of arms control there are a number of relevant norms for survivors of gun violence—notably with the establishment of international standards in the areas of criminal justice and human rights. The book contains an annex that surveys many of the relevant international standards and laws, and how they may be relevant to policymaking on surviving gun violence (see Annex 1: International Standards Relevant to Survivors of Gun Violence).

Improving responses

What else stands in the way of appropriate support to survivors of gun violence? Lack of resources is a major obstacle. This volume highlights promising approaches, particularly from under-resourced contexts and low and middle income countries. However, financial resources are not everything. Two other ingredients are needed for proper planning and good practice: reliable information and political will.

Reliable information is necessary to accurately direct support. Yet a recurring challenge in developing the book was the lack of reliable information about types of survivors, their socio-economic status, the circumstances and characteristics of injuries and resulting impairments, interactions with health care and legal systems, as well as the recovery process. Information is also lacking on caregiving, psychosocial needs, and secondary survival. The data that do exist are not necessarily adequately shared and used, even though information and tools developed in one field could benefit others. For example, victimisation surveys, often developed to improve the operations of law enforcement agencies, can yield important insights for other relevant service providers.

In many countries conceptual challenges abound, further inhibiting the necessary linkages across public policy concerns; disability is still characterised largely as a medical problem with outdated terminology and concepts underpinning regulations and laws; gun violence is misunderstood or narrowly defined to be solely a manifestation of the illegal trade in weapons.

This also means listening to the experiences of survivors. Importantly, recovery and rehabilitation cannot be reduced to an easily charted, single-track road along which survivors can be sped. Whatever systems are in place to support gun violence survivors must be capable of accommodating variations in individual pathways to recovery. The perspectives of survivors in this volume bear testament to this diversity.

Once information and resources are at hand, political will is needed to enact legislation, policies, and procedures, and to ensure that these are properly implemented. Even in contexts where legislation is appropriate, implementation often falls short. The book offers suggestions for where policy and practice can be improved in accordance with international good practice (see the Conclusion and Recommendations, and Box 4: Pointers for Strengthening Policy and Programming for Survivors of Violence and Crime, in the chapter, Evolution of Victims' Rights and International Standards).

Advocating for survivors of violence and crime

Survivors of gun violence face specific obstacles, chief among them the complexity of the care they often require, psychological trauma, and social discrimination. Recovery from an act of violence, a fundamental breach of social norms, arguably differs from that of an accident. Why, then, is their collective voice generally so weak? Several reasons are suggested across the book, including the complex and contentious nature of perpetrators who are also victims. In many contexts where justice is slow and corrupt, paralysis following involvement in gun violence and gang activity is seen as a punishment and little consideration is given to the individual's on-going rights and needs. Second, the impairments resulting from gun violence may make it difficult to be involved in advocacy—for example, the ability to engage in public processes may be curtailed by limited access to transport, and difficulty in speaking or writing. Third, many survivors may not wish to draw attention to themselves because of stigma and fear of further violence.

Yet survivors have benefited broadly from progress in two specific fields: the rights of crime victims in judicial processes (including in post-war, transitional justice contexts), and disability rights. This book therefore pays close attention to these socio-political processes at global and national levels.

Disability rights advocacy is a hard-won success story, though much more remains to be done globally. This advocacy community brings together people experiencing disability regardless of the cause or nature. Indeed, how a person became impaired loses significance over time, compared to the daily struggle of living with disability, discrimination, and lack of access to public facilities and work opportunities.

Victims and survivors of crime have come forward in many countries to reshape policies and services that are more responsive, humane, and effective. Victims' rights movements gained prominence in the 1970s, followed by the first advocacy organisations calling for procedural rights and welfare needs of crime victims in the 1980s. While these gains benefited all victims of crime, they directly concern gun violence survivors. In the mid-1990s, the field of transitional justice began to expand with the movement towards an International Criminal Court and increasing gains in the realm of people-centred international law and practice related to armed conflict, crimes against humanity, and genocide.

Methodology for developing the book

Considerable effort was invested to ensure that as many perspectives and specialisations as possible are reflected in this book. To facilitate an inclusive process, a call for contributions was disseminated widely in English, French, and Spanish on a range of listservs and websites in November 2011. The response was most positive; many of the elements of the book stem from this call. Each element was then developed into an outline with the contributor(s), who were often teamed up to work with others wishing to contribute on similar topics. After in-house editing and drafting, text was peer reviewed by numerous experts in mental health, trauma care, gun policy, gender, caregiving, amongst many other fields. This review process refined the chapters immensely. Contributors and reviewers are listed at the end of each piece.

Survivors of gun violence contributed in a range of ways: through chapter design, interviews, reflections on their personal experiences, suggestions for other contacts, and peer reviews of text (see the acknowledgments list). Many people writing and reviewing gave their time and energy freely, for which we are extremely grateful. This contribution of valuable time and diverse expertise strengthened the book immensely. Those supported to write did so with funds from the Norwegian Ministry of Foreign Affairs.

The book development team undertook content editing, fact checking, conceptual framing, and redrafting across the various elements of the volume. Through to the end of August 2013, we have worked to ensure that the content is accurate.

Gender

The need for a dedicated gender focus ought not to require detailed argument. Put simply: men and boys are acutely vulnerable to, and highly involved in gun violence, and women and girls are largely responsible for their care once injured. Violence is among the leading causes of death for people aged 15-44 years worldwide, accounting for 14% of deaths among males and 7% of deaths among females in this age group.[43] Across all settings (high-middle-low income, war-torn, peaceful or countries in transition), males dominate firearm-related death and injury whether interpersonal, self-directed or accidental. For example, over 90% of gun-related homicide victims are male.[44] Of those who commit suicide with a gun, 88% are men.[45]

Women and girls require particular attention when conceptualising responses, because of a) disproportionate sexual and gender-based violence at gunpoint, and b) the low socio-political status of women in many contexts.[46] Violence against women is acutely exacerbated by weapons availability and misuse, with women at great risk of death and injury where a violent partner has access to a gun.[47] Caregiving responsibility post-injury falls largely to women and girls—mothers, wives, sisters, partners—limiting their opportunities to engage in economic activities, and often contributing to the deterioration of their own health.[48]

To build on these understandings, gender concerns are highlighted or noted in every element of the book; language is gender-inclusive; and caregiving is emphasised as a fundamental overlooked and feminised socio-economic reality resulting from gun violence. The views of women are prominently included as contributors and peer reviewers.

Data

Reliable data was the single biggest methodological challenge in developing this book. Detailed data is in fact absent on a range of indicators relevant to surviving gun violence. Action-oriented research is required to move beyond incidental information to focused research that can inform policy, programming, monitoring and evaluation. The small arms issue and the broader discussions on armed violence have led to hundreds of data collection initiatives over the past decades. These much-needed efforts to track and count the guns and their impacts have however rarely included information on survivors. Given the data needs, *Gun Violence, Disability and Recovery* includes a call to adapt existing information collection efforts, as well as those being formulated, to include better collection of data on post-hospital injury and impairment (see the Conclusions and Recommendations section). It is also critical that mixed methods are used to generate data to the highest standards: quantitative studies that track prevalence and incidence, complemented by qualitative studies that gauge opinions, choices, and outcomes. Another area of need is guidance for researchers and analysts in the area of armed violence prevention and small arms control on how to engage with the politics of disability and ethical and inclusive research practices.[49]

Some funds were made available for primary research to contribute to this volume, covering mainly interviews or analysis of existing data rather than collection of new data. Time did not permit the type of studies necessary to uncover long-term consequences, health and social outcomes, and choices. Some issues are thus illustrated through interviews and other secondary evidence. We hope the book will spark interest and support for further research.

Conclusion

Survivors of gun violence and caregivers are often voiceless in decisions that directly affect their future. Violence prevention and reduction initiatives, peace and security research, and development and human rights processes should look for inclusion points for survivors. This means not only engagement at the local level but also involvement in collective advocacy, research, and policymaking. If it is successful, this volume will provide the reader with a better understanding of the multiple and interconnected facets of the experience of surviving gun violence. This collection aims to rally attention and stimulate conversations all over the world between survivors, government officials, disability rights, health, and violence reduction experts, criminal justice specialists, gender activists, and many others. In the process, it seeks to inspire, constructively provoke, enquire, and bear witness to the realities of surviving gun violence.

References

[1] The Introduction was written by Cate Buchanan and Mireille Widmer. Additional input was received from Emile LeBrun and Rebecca Peters.

[2] Geneva Declaration Secretariat, *Global burden of armed violence: Lethal encounters* (Geneva: Geneva Declaration Secretariat, 2011). This estimate is based on an average count of violent deaths each year between 2004 and 2009. Most of the data is derived from incident reporting systems and databases, which typically yield conservative estimates.

[3] Geneva Declaration Secretariat (2011), p. 44.

[4] A. Alvazzi del Frate and L. De Martino, "Non-lethal Firearm Violence," *Research Notes*, Number 32, July (Geneva: Small Arms Survey, 2013), p. 3.

[5] World Health Organization, *Small arms and global health* (Geneva: WHO, 2001), p. 22. See also C. Mock, "Trauma mortality patterns in three nations at different economic levels: implications for global trauma system development," *Journal of Trauma* 44 (1998), pp. 804-12.

[6] Small Arms Survey, *Small Arms Survey 2007: Guns and the City* (Cambridge, UK: Cambridge University Press, 2007), p. 39.

[7] A. Karp, *Estimating Civilian Owned Firearms* (Geneva: Small Arms Survey, 2011), p. 1.

[8] P.J. Cook and J. Ludwig, *Gun violence: The real costs* (Oxford: Oxford University Press, 2000); T.R. Miller and M.A. Cohen, "Costs of gunshot and cut/stab wounds in the United States, with some Canadian comparisons," *Accident Analysis and Prevention* 29/3 (1997), pp. 329-341. For more on the USA, also see: Institute for Economics and Peace, *The Economic Costs of Containing Violence,* Institute for Economics and Peace submission to the Global Thematic Consultation on Conflict, Violence and Disaster and the Post-2015 Development Agenda (Sydney: IEP, 2013).

[9] Geneva Declaration Secretariat, *More Violence, Less Development: Examining the relationship between armed violence and MDG achievement* (Geneva: Geneva Declaration Secretariat, 2010). Also see, H. Waters et al, *The economic dimensions of interpersonal violence* (Geneva: World Health Organization, 2004).

[10] World Health Organization, *Preventing violence and reducing its impact: how development agencies can help* (Geneva: WHO, 2008).

[11] This includes all deaths from violence, not only gun-related mortality. World Health Organization, *Injury: A leading cause of the Global Burden of Disease* (Geneva: WHO, 2000). Available at: www.whqliboc.who.int/publications/2002/9241562323.pdf Accessed 5 July 2013.

[12] World Health Organization, *The Global Burden of Disease: 2004 Update* (Geneva: WHO, 2008). The term "burden of disease" indicates the gap between actual and ideal health status. It is measured in disability adjusted life years (DALY), a combination of years of life lost due to premature mortality and time lived in less than full health.

[13] C. Mock, J. Lormand, J. Goosen, M. Joshipura and M. Peden, *Guidelines for essential trauma care* (Geneva: World Health Organization, 2004).

[14] J. Bonderman, *OVC Bulletin, Working with Victims of Gun Violence,* United States Department of Justice, Office of Justice Programs (Washington DC: Office for Victims of Crime, 2001).

[15] Centers for Disease Control and Prevention, "Injury Prevention & Control: Data & Statistics". Available at: www.cdc.gov/injury/wisqars/ Web page updated 17 December 2012. Accessed 12 July 2013.

[16] World Health Organization and World Bank, *World Report on Disability* (Geneva: WHO, 2011), p. 29.

[17] UN Enable, "Relationship between development and human rights". Available at: www.un.org/disabilities/default.asp?id=1568 Accessed 12 July 2013.

[18] A. Elwan, *Poverty and disability: A survey of the literature,* Social Protection Discussion Paper Series No. 9932, Social Protection Unit, Human Development Network (Washington DC: World Bank, 1999). Also see, N.E. Groce and J-F. Trani, "Millennium Development Goals and people with disabilities," *The Lancet* 374/9704 (2009), pp. 1800-1801.

[19] World Health Organization and World Bank (2011); M.A. Stein, P. Stein, D. Weiss and R. Lang, "Health care and the UN Disability Rights Convention," *The Lancet* 374/9704 (2009), pp.1796-98.

20   C. Mock, J. Lormand, J. Goosen, M. Joshipura and M. Peden (2004), p. 4.

21   South-North Centre for Dialogue and Development, *Global Survey on Government Action on the Implementation of the Standard Rules on the Equalization of Opportunities for Persons with Disabilities* (Amman: South-North Centre for Dialogue and Development, 2006), p. 32.

22   *Assistive Devices/Technologies: What WHO is doing* (Geneva: World Health Organization, undated). Available at: www.who.int/disabilities/technology/activities/en

23   This definition, drawing on the language of the Declaration, has also been used in United Nations, *International Small Arms Control Standards*, Series 02 - Concepts, Policies and Strategies, Module 02.10: "SALW Control in the Context of Preventing Armed Violence", Version 2.3, October 2010 (forthcoming).

24   See various chapters in S.G. Shoham, P. Knepper and M. Kett (Eds), *International handbook of victimology* (Boca Raton: CRC Press, 2010); C. Fernandez de Casadevante Romani, *International law of victims* (Heidelberg: Springer, 2012); E. Bouris, *Complex political victims* (Connecticut: Kumarian Press, 2007); P.E. Rock, "Society's Attitude to the Victim," In E. Fattah (Ed), *From Crime Policy to Victim Policy* (London: Macmillan, 1986).

25   Useful analysis can be found in R. Condry, "Secondary victims and secondary victimization," In S.G. Shoham, P. Knepper and M. Kett (Eds), *International handbook of victimology* (Boca Raton: CRC Press, 2010), pp. 219-250.

26   Centre for Humanitarian Dialogue, *Trauma as a consequence—and cause—of gun violence,* Background paper No. 1 commissioned from Vivo International (Geneva: HD Centre, 2006), p. 2.

27   World Health Organization and World Bank (2011), p. 4.

28   T. Shakespeare, "Disability and the training of health professionals," *The Lancet* 374/9704 (2009), p. 1815.

29   Description of victimisation and victimology draws on input from Michael O'Connell, Commissioner for Victims' Rights, South Australia.

30   E.A. Fattah, *Understanding Criminal Victimisation* (Toronto: Prentice Hall, 1991), p. 9.

31   See a range of views: H. von Hentig, *The Criminal and his Victim: Studies in the Socio-biology of Crime* (New Haven: Yale University Press, 1948), pp. 3-18; B. Mendelsohn, "The Origin of the Doctrine of Victimology," *Excerpta Criminal* 3 (1963), pp.239-244; H. Weir, "The Nature and Concerns of Victimology," In *Victimology: Book 1* (Adelaide: Adelaide Institute of TAFE, 1991), pp. 8-11; M. O'Connell, "Victimology: A social science in waiting?" *International Review of Victimology* 15 (2008), pp. 91-103; S. Garkawe, "Revising the Scope of Victimology—How Broad a Discipline Should it Be?" *International Review on Victimology* 11 2/3 (2004), pp. 275-294; R.D. Knudten, "The Scope of Victimology and Victimisation: Towards a Conceptualisation of the Field," In S. Ben David, and G.F. Kirchhoff (Eds), *International Faces of Victimology* (Mönchengladbach: World Society of Victimology Publishing, 1992), pp. 43-51.

32   J. Elster, *Closing the Books: Transitional Justice in Historical Perspective* (Cambridge: Cambridge University Press, 2004).

33   See the work of REDRESS, the International Center for Transitional Justice, UN Rule of Law website (unrol.org); C.L. Sriram, J. García-Godos, J. Herman, and O. Martin-Ortega (Eds), *Transitional justice and peacebuilding on the ground—Victims and excombatants* (London: Routledge, 2012); N. Roht-Arriaza and J. Mariezcurrena (Eds), *Transitional Justice in the Twenty-First Century. Beyond Truth Versus Justice* (Cambridge: Cambridge University Press, 2006).

34   C. Evans, *The right to reparation in international law for victims of armed conflict* (Cambridge: Cambridge University Press, 2012), p. 13.

35   For example see: REDRESS and the Essex Transitional Justice Network, *Rehabilitation as a form of reparation: Opportunities and challenges*, Workshop Report (UK: REDRESS, 2010). Also, M. Berghs, *War and embodied memory: Becoming disabled in Sierra Leone* (Surrey: Ashgate, 2012); E. Martz (Ed), *Trauma Rehabilitation After War and Conflict: Community and Individual Perspectives* (New York: Springer, 2010).

36   The Geneva Declaration definition states: "Armed violence is the intentional use illegitimate force (actual or threatened) with arms or explosives, against a person, group, community, or state, that undermines people-centred security and/or sustainable development." Geneva Declaration Secretariat, *Global burden of armed violence* (Geneva: Geneva Declaration Secretariat, 2008), p. 2.

[37] For example, Geneva International Centre for Humanitarian Demining, *Assisting landmine and other ERW survivors in the context of disarmament, disability and development* (Geneva: GICHD, 2012); Cluster Munition Coalition and International Campaign to Ban Landmines, *Connecting the dots: Detailed guidance, Victim assistance in the Mine Ban Treaty and the Convention on Cluster Munitions and in the Convention on the Rights of Persons with Disabilities* (Geneva: CMC and ICBL, 2011); Handicap International, *Lessons Learned Workshop: A review of assistance programs for war wounded and other persons with disabilities living in mine-affected countries* (Paris: Handicap International, 2004).

[38] Some 30 States have developed these plans thus far including but not limited to: Australia, Belgium, Costa Rica, France, Jordan, Macedonia, Malaysia, Mexico, Mongolia, Nepal, Romania, Russia, South Africa, Sri Lanka, Thailand, and the United Kingdom. Email communication between Cate Buchanan and Chris Mikton, World Health Organization, Violence and Injury Prevention team, 7 March 2013.

[39] See Annex 1 for details of signatures and ratifications.

[40] In July 2013 Cate Buchanan and Sheree Bailey estimated some 84 States have disability rights specific law/s in place. This was drawn from data at: UN Enable reporting on CRPD ratifications into domestic laws and the Country Laws Index of the Disability Rights Education and Defense Fund. Web page http://dredf.org/international/lawindex.shtml Accessed 31 July 2013. Thanks to Marianne Schulze for her assistance. Also see: M.A. Stein, P. Stein, D. Weiss and R. Lang (2009).

[41] World Health Organization and World Bank (2011); T. Shakespeare, *Disability rights and wrongs* (London: Routledge, 2006); UK Department for International Development, *Disability, poverty and development* (London: DFID, 2000).

[42] See for example: Action on Armed Violence, *Victims and survivors of armed violence: Responding to rights and needs*, Background paper for Oslo Conference on Armed Violence and Development, 20-22 April 2010 (UN Development Programme and Norwegian Ministry of Foreign Affairs, 2010).

[43] World Health Organization, *World Report on Violence and Health: Summary* (Geneva: WHO, 2002), p. 1.

[44] World Health Organization, *World Report on Violence and Health* (Geneva: WHO, 2002), pp. 274-275.

[45] Small Arms Survey, *Small Arms Survey: Rights at Risk* (Oxford: Oxford University Press, 2004), p.178.

[46] M. Vlachova and L. Biason, *Women in an insecure world: Violence against women, facts, figures, analysis* (Geneva: Geneva Centre for the Democratic Control of Armed Forces, 2005).

[47] Intimate partner violence is actual or threatened physical or sexual violence or psychological and emotional abuse directed toward a spouse, ex-spouse, current or former boyfriend or girlfriend, or current or former dating partner. Intimate partners may be heterosexual or of the same sex. Source: National Center for Injury Prevention and Control, *Injury Fact Book, 2001-2002* (Atlanta: Centers for Disease Control and Prevention, 2001).

[48] International Committee of the Red Cross, *Women and War: Health fact sheet* (Geneva: ICRC, 2001); E. Esplen, *Gender and Care, Overview Report*, BRIDGE, Institute of Development Studies (Brighton: BRIDGE, 2009).

[49] Guidance can be found in a range of sources: C. Barnes and G. Mercer, "Breaking the Mould? An introduction to doing disability research," In C. Barnes and G. Mercer (Eds), *Doing Disability Research* (Leeds: The Disability Press, 1997); M. H. Rioux, "New research directions and paradigms: Disability is not the measles," In M.H. Rioux and M. Bach (Eds), *Disability is not the measles: New research paradigms in disability* (Ontario: Roeher Institute, 1994); T. Shakespeare (2006); E. Stone and M. Priestley, "Parasites, Pawns and Partners: Disability Research and the Role of Non-Disabled Researchers," *The British Journal of Sociology* 47/4 (1996); M. Smyth and G. Robinson (Eds), *Researching Violently Divided Societies: Ethical and Methodological Issues* (Tokyo/London: UN University Press and Pluto Press, 2001); P. Connolly, *Ethical principles for researching vulnerable groups*, Commissioned by the Office of the First Minister and Deputy First Minister (University of Ulster, 2003).

"People who live after being shot often find
themselves re-routed away from a normal path,
always conscious that there is another road somewhere else,
the one they should be on, the one that leads to safety."

Gail Bell, shot in the back aged 17.

Shot: A personal response to guns and trauma,
(Sydney: Picador, 2003).

SPOTLIGHT SECTION
Vera and Wellington (Brazil)

One Saturday in January 2008, my son Wellington and I went to party at a friend's house in Realengo, the neighborhood in northern Rio de Janeiro where we live. He was 19 years old at the time. When it was time to go, we left the party separately. I had been home for more than half an hour when I heard gunshots. Shootings used to happen quite regularly in Realengo, where rival drug gangs and police are in regular conflict. But when the phone rang I never imagined the shots I had heard would change my family's life forever. Wellington had been hit by a stray bullet.

Wellington: "I had walked [my girlfriend] to the front door and started walking home. That is when I heard the shots, and before I knew it I was on the ground. I blacked out and only woke up a few days later in the hospital."

During the long hours of surgery we had no sense of the extent of his injuries. I feared for his life. He came out of the second surgery in an induced coma that lasted five days. Some doctors had already given up on him. I never lost hope.

In the hospital we were approached by a police officer. For getting caught in the crossfire, my son was suspected of involvement in the drug trade. With no criminal background, my son was summoned to give a statement as soon as he was released from hospital. To this day, nobody has confessed to shooting my son, nor been investigated or charged.

Wellington: "When I woke up I couldn't feel my legs. I noticed that I was handcuffed to the bed and there was a police officer by my side. I was very distressed and started hitting myself. The police officer explained to me what had happened…. I had not only lost all feeling in my legs, but I was also considered a criminal."

The family has tried to move on, but I was unable to do so. I spent ten years of my life savings and took two months off work as a cleaner to care for him. Every day I would get up, wash his hospital sheets, take some fruit, and head to the hospital to spend afternoons with him. All he did was cry.

Wellington: "While I was hospitalised I cried a lot. Sometimes I was outraged and they would sedate me two or sometimes three times a day, so I would sleep."

After two weeks the chief of surgery told me that Wellington would never walk again, though another doctor said there was still a chance. What I really wanted was to take him home. But because of the inefficient public healthcare system it took three months to schedule the necessary examination for his release from hospital.

His return home was filled with challenges. My husband and I gave up our room for him. Nobody showed us what to do with Wellington's feeding tube, advised us about the implications of his colostomy, or told us how to manage pressure sores.

We learned the hard way. Wellington had many infections, underwent two more surgeries, and had to take a lot of antibiotics before we figured out how to care for him properly. We could really have used advice as we lacked all knowledge and resources to cope with his paraplegia.

Our life changed a lot. Although he was 19, Wellington was still in school when he was shot. Mobility and accessibility issues prevented him from going back to school. He gave up his dream of joining the army. He was only given a month of weekly sessions with a psychologist at the state hospital. Wellington stopped going after he left hospital because of lack of transport to get to the sessions.

Wellington used to be a calm boy. He liked going out with his girlfriend, going to the movies and spending time with friends. Four years later, he spends the whole day lying down, alternating between moments of rage and depression.

For myself, I had just earned my high school degree and dreamed of going to university. But I had to give that up. Today I spend my time working and caring for Wellington. I have to rely on my oldest daughter and my nine-year old niece to make sure he is never home alone. My niece is the one who helps him overcome the physical challenges of accessing the cyber café where he likes to surf the Internet.

There are no more weekends at the beach or family visits. In fact, because of his mobility problems, we rarely go out anymore. Our only distraction is the church we started to attend after Wellington's injury and its enormous consequences.

I would really like him to have physiotherapy. I managed to register him with the Association for Children with a Disability. That was when we discovered that the terrible smell from his body was caused by the pressure sores that we subsequently began to treat. Only after he is fully cured can he start physiotherapy.

The Association gave us information about his nutrition. After the colostomy, nobody in the hospital explained that Wellington would lose nutrients more rapidly than a healthy person. We had to begin legal proceedings to ensure that the government provided his food concentrate (Sustagen) which is guaranteed in situations where people cannot afford medication or nutrition support. We had signed up for this support, but it is not always available.

We have adapted to our new reality. To cover all the expenses I rely on the help of my entire family and work colleagues. Our dreams are tied to his wellbeing. I am very hopeful that he will be able to get physiotherapy and walk again. It would be wonderful if he could go back to school, but the schools nearby are not accessible and lack the necessary infrastructure like lifts or ramps. He first needs to become more independent.

Wellington: "I would like to work so I can occupy my mind, go back to school, and lead a normal life. And who knows, perhaps someday even go out on the street without depending on other people."[1]

References

[1]   Told to Ilona Szabó de Carvalho and Monica Viceconti in Realengo, Rio de Janeiro, Brazil in March 2012.

SPOTLIGHT SECTION
El Salvador Gun Tax and Victims' Services

With one of the world's highest rates of gun violence, El Salvador has the opportunity to become a leader in assistance to survivors. Existing mechanisms in the Salvadoran health and justice systems could be adapted to provide support and rehabilitation to people injured or traumatised by gun violence.

El Salvador's rate of homicide was 66/100,000 in 2010, or more than 4,000 deaths per year, of which 77% are committed with guns.[1] Thousands more are seriously wounded by gunshot each year.[2] Assaults constitute the largest single cause of death among men (more than heart disease or motor vehicle crashes), and a major cause of spinal injury.[3]

Recognising that the proliferation of guns, like alcohol and tobacco, is damaging to health, the Government has created an innovative scheme to raise funds for health care from the sale of these products. Guns and ammunition, alcoholic beverages and tobacco products are taxed at 10%, and 35% of this revenue (about USD24 million in 2011) goes to an agency called FOSALUD (Fondo Solidario para la Salud or Health Solidarity Fund).

Established in 2005, FOSALUD now employs over 2,400 people providing a range of services to complement the public health system, including after-hours services at 149 health centres in remote communities, plus border health centres, maternity homes, women's and children's health services, smoking cessation clinics, an emergency medical centre, two clinics for partner and family violence and sexual assault survivors, and 49 ambulances. In 2010 these services provided over 2 million instances of health care including medical and dental appointments, family planning, prenatal checks, pap smears, HIV tests, baby health checks, emergency medical care and counselling, and smoking cessation treatments. In cases of gender-based violence and sexual assault, FOSALUD staff work closely with police, the offices of the public prosecutor and forensic medicine, as well as NGOs.

FOSALUD also runs public awareness campaigns against tobacco and alcohol, and most recently a campaign warning of the danger to children posed by fireworks and other explosives. These campaigns are conducted under Objective IV of the law that created the agency: "It is necessary to put in place measures to prevent the use and consumption of substances that are noxious to human beings, and to count on adequate resources to deal with the illnesses and medical emergencies caused by the consumption or use of products that are noxious and dangerous to the health of the population."

Notably absent from the agency's programmes is any campaign or service explicitly related to the misuse of firearms, the third category of product whose taxes finance FOSALUD. Although survivors of gun violence may benefit from the partner and family violence clinics, ambulances, emergency medical care and counselling, they are not identified as a target group; nor does the word "firearm" appear in any FOSALUD policy documents.[4]

Dr Cristina Vega, a senior official at FOSALUD, is conscious of the omission. She identified several obstacles to the development of programmes or campaigns on the theme of gun violence. Resources are stretched already, so adding new activities is challenging. Pushing up FOSALUD's share of the tax revenue on alcohol, tobacco and firearms would help; most Salvadorans would be surprised to learn that FOSALUD receives only 35% of this revenue at present.

The tax from guns and ammunition account for only 1% of FOSALUD's income; about USD357,000 in 2012.[5] Dr Vega believes the low figure reflects the poor state of regulation: "In some places it costs more to buy a tin of baby formula than a box of bullets—that tells you something about how weak the gun control system is."[6] Unlike alcohol and tobacco, whose regulation involves the Ministry of Health, guns fall under the dominion of the Ministry for Defence, with which FOSALUD has no relationship.

FOSALUD would like to see stronger regulation and better enforcement of the gun law—in order to increase the taxes collected, but mainly to prevent some of the thousands of gunshot deaths and injuries suffered each year in El Salvador. FOSALUD works with NGOs lobbying for alcohol and tobacco control, but has not been part of public campaigns on gun control. In 2012 it planned to begin working with youth groups and the Ministry of Education on youth violence prevention and building a culture of peace.

Asked what assistance FOSALUD might provide to survivors of gun violence if funding were available, Dr Vega pointed out that physical therapies and rehabilitation are the responsibility of ISRI (Instituto Salvadoreño de Rehabilitación Integral or Salvadoran Institute for Rehabilitation). However, FOSALUD could provide psychosocial support. She said the same comprehensive approach should apply to gunshot victims as for gender-based violence and sexual assault cases, involving a range of agencies and services (including ISRI).

FOSALUD could also run public awareness campaigns on the risks associated with firearms ownership or activities like firing into the air. Dr Vega remarked, "Violence in El Salvador is such a daily occurrence that it has become invisible. People don't notice unless a member of their own family is shot, or unless the shooting is on a scale that is out of the ordinary. The press also plays a role in desensitising the population, by giving the impression that violence is normal."

Victim Care Unit, Ministry of Justice
Another promising source of assistance for survivors is the Victim Care Unit (Dirección de Atención a Víctimas) in the Salvadoran Ministry of Justice and Public Safety. Created in 2011, the Unit has five staff: a coordinator, a lawyer, a sociologist,

a psychologist and a communications specialist. It also operates a telephone support service to callers who dial 1-2-3. The objectives are to make available comprehensive legal and psychosocial support to victims and survivors of crime, promote social restitution and prevent further victimisation (for example in revenge attacks).

The Unit's services are available to victims of any crime, violent or not, and regardless of whether a criminal prosecution is under way. (This is significant because many Salvadorans lack confidence in the justice system and are not prepared to report a crime to the police. In the past, victims who did not formally report a crime were unable to seek help from the State.) If a prosecution is underway, the Unit provides information, advice and support to the victims during the process, hoping to restore their faith in the overstretched justice system. The Justice Ministry has a separate service providing protection to victims or other witnesses deemed to be in danger because of their involvement in prosecutions. Participating in the protection programme may create additional fear and anxiety, and the Victim Care Unit also assists in these cases.

Although the Unit supports victims of any crime, specific protocols are being developed for six types of events: extortion, robbery, intimidation, rape, family violence and trafficking in people. In addition, Director Fátima Ortiz de Zelaya hopes to develop two more areas of work: crimes against children and gun violence.

The Unit itself provides some counselling, but its primary method of operation is identifying, referring and coordinating support for crime victims from a range of other agencies—generally NGOs—with relevant expertise and experience. For example, victims of family violence are referred to organisations specialising in this field. The Unit also provides training for family law judges and police, and this training includes a specific focus on firearms.

The Unit has experience of helping crime victims who have also committed crimes—a common scenario among young men in El Salvador. For example, former gang members assisting police with information may also have survived violence by other gang members or by the police. In such cases, aid is restricted to medical referrals and psycho-social support, and excludes legal assistance. "Our interest is in the person as a victim, not in the trial or the sentence," said Ortiz.[7]

An example of a person assisted was a man who sold second-hand cars from home, who had been kidnapped and assaulted at gunpoint by criminals initially posing as customers. He was rescued by police and is cooperating with the prosecution of the perpetrators. The Victim Care Unit is supporting him through this process and also providing counselling after his ordeal. "He has been totally traumatised and does not want to return to selling cars. He's frightened of anyone who knocks on his door. But that is how he supports his family," explained Ortiz. The goals are to help this survivor recover his ability to work, prevent further attacks on him and his family, and to avoid them seeking revenge by further violence.

One obstacle is a lack of specialised assistance in the non-government sector for different types of crime victims. There are many organisations dedicated to helping survivors of family violence, but very little available for people affected by other crimes. The Victim Care Unit hopes to help NGOs to develop the necessary skills to provide high quality psychosocial care for a wider range of victims and survivors.

"We hope that NGOs can fill that gap one day. There are lots of agencies helping women who are victims of domestic violence, but not for gun violence if the perpetrator is not your partner—yet there are thousands and thousands of cases every year. We hope we can develop information about this type of crime and the assistance required, and eventually generate solutions, even if it is in the civil society sector. Of course governments are averse to forming new units or new services, so we hope NGOs will develop which can cooperate with us," commented Ortiz.

Contributors: Rebecca Peters, independent consultant and Senior Associate with the Surviving Gun Violence Project.

Peer review was provided by **Emperatriz Crespín**, International Physicians for the Prevention of Nuclear War (El Salvador).

References

1   United Nations Office on Drugs and Crime, *2011 Global Study on Homicide: Trends, Context, Data* (Vienna: UNODC, 2011), pp.93, 114.
2   Reliable statistics for non-fatal firearm injuries in El Salvador are not available, but health officials maintain the numbers are very high.
3   M. Acosta, M. Sáenz, B. Gutiérrez and J.L. Bermúdez, "Sistema de salud de El Salvador," *Salud Pública de México* 53/ supl2 (2011), pp. 188-5196. Available at: http://bvs.insp.mx/rsp/_files/File/2011/vol%2053%20suplemento%202/14Salvador.pdf Accessed 14 October 2012.
4   Partner and family violence services and mental health care were specifically excluded from FOSALUD's mandate when the agency was created, but those exclusions have now been abolished. See Centre for Humanitarian Dialogue, *Surviving gun violence in El Salvador: a tax on firearms for health,* Background paper No. 3 (Geneva: HD Centre, 2007), p.7. Available at: http://survivinggunviolence.org/topic/armed-violence/surviving-gun-violence-in-el-salvador-a-tax-on-firearms-for-health/ Accessed 10 November 2012.
5   The breakdown is 44% from beer, 33% cigarettes, 22% other alcoholic beverages and 1% guns and ammunition.
6   Interview by Rebecca Peters with Dr Cristina Vega in San Salvador, 15 December 2011.
7   Interview by Rebecca Peters with Fátima Ortiz de Zelaya in San Salvador, 14 December 2011.

Mark Chilutti (left), Ismael Vasquez and Joe Davis, all paralysed as a result of gun violence, lead a protest march against gun violence, up Broad Street in Philadelphia, USA. (Image: Mark Stehle/AP, October 2007)

2 Evolution of Victims' Rights and International Standards

Introduction

Historically, victims and survivors of crime, violence and injustice have been side-lined in criminal justice processes the world over. Even when the notion of individual human rights started appearing in Western thinking in the early 20th Century, the first application of rights were extended to the accused, with guarantees of due process and the rule of law. The idea that victims may also have, and could indeed benefit from a set of rights, has only gained solid currency in the last few decades.

As such the rich field of victims' rights provides a critical lens from which to better understand the rights of survivors of armed violence. This is all the more important as attention to survivors of armed violence lies at the intersection of several issues where significant policy development has occurred in recent years: disability rights, sustainable development, gender justice and violence prevention. Each of these domains has its own body of international standards and agreements, whether legally binding or not, and many of these standards can be invoked to deliver on the rights and needs of survivors and to reduce gun violence. The discussion about what standards and conceptual frameworks are pertinent for survivors and victims of armed violence is long overdue, as opportunities for coherent policy development continue to be missed. Over the last two decades of research and advocacy on regulating the arms trade and tackling gun violence, this has been a missing piece of the policy "puzzle".

Building clearer understanding on normative obligations, and gaps, is vital for more coherent policy development at both national and international levels. This chapter first reviews attempts to define the notion of "victim". It then looks at how victims' rights have gradually been won at the national level, before being enshrined in some key international instruments. The next section examines what such rights actually entail, from procedural rights (to be kept informed and heard in criminal justice processes) to substantive rights (to reparation), noting on-going tensions between the rights of victims and those of perpetrators. A further section is devoted to the aftermath of armed conflict, overviewing international law, practice and policy.

In addition to the content of the chapter, an annex provides a schema for categorising existing international standards across six thematic areas: 1) human rights; 2) war and armed conflict; 3) social protection and livelihoods; 4) criminal justice systems; 5) crime prevention; and 6) disarmament and weapons control. Some 56 standards are then briefly summarised for their relevance for survivors of gun violence (see Annex 1: International Standards Relevant to Survivors of Gun Violence). The chapter also contains a set of pointers for policymakers and practitioners to consider (see Box 4: Pointers for Strengthening Policy and Programming for Survivors of Violence and Crime).

Section 1: Key concepts

The meaning of a "victim" has been hotly debated, and a range of terms apply to different moments or perspectives on an act of crime or violence.[1] Someone who has suffered direct harm from crime or abuse is a "primary victim"; while a person bereaved by the murder or disappearance of a family member is regarded as a "secondary victim". When a primary or secondary victim experiences further trauma in the pursuit of justice or health care, due to inappropriate responses or treatment by officials, this may be called "secondary" or "re-victimisation". One who helps in the immediate aftermath of an incident is often termed a "Good Samaritan". A person or a business suffering losses as a result of an incident can also be regarded as a victim. In addition, the citizens and taxpayers who bear the costs of responding to violence and crime in the health and criminal justice systems may be regarded as tertiary victims.

Victimologists, government officials, and victims' rights advocates reached a consensus on a definition in the 1985 UN *Declaration of Basic Principles of Justice for Victims of Crime and Abuse of Power* (Declaration). It defined a victim in terms of harm suffered, rather than in a strict legal sense. For instance, in homicide cases, the person is the deceased, yet the harm is also endured by the deceased's family and social network.[2]

Article 1 defines victims as: "persons who, individually or collectively, have suffered harm, including physical or mental injury, emotional suffering, economic loss or substantial impairment of their fundamental rights, through acts or omissions that are in violation of criminal laws operative within Member States, including those laws proscribing criminal abuse of power."

Article 2 adds: "A person may be considered a victim, under this Declaration, regardless of whether the perpetrator is identified, apprehended, prosecuted or convicted and regardless of the familial relationship between the perpetrator and the victim. The term 'victim' also includes, where appropriate, the immediate family or dependants of the direct victim and persons who have suffered harm in intervening to assist victims in distress or to prevent victimization."

This book—and this chapter—use the terms "survivors" and "victims" interchangeably. Refer to Box 1 in the Introductory chapter for further detail on terminology.

The Declaration is an aspirational document with the status of "soft law"; it is a politically rather than legally binding instrument. For example, it calls upon—but does not oblige—States and national institutions, and those who work in such entities, to regard survivors of crime with respect and compassion and to facilitate their access to justice and practical, medical and other assistance. With no enforcement mechanisms, there are limitations as to how far States can be pressed to implement the Declaration; and the expectations that surrounded its adoption have not always been fulfilled. Many people want what is promised; many have come to expect it; and, too many find the promise is just that—a promise.[3]

Nonetheless, the Declaration has value as a set of universally agreed principles. It expanded the international discourse on the rights of crime victims, and has become a blueprint or framework for policy guidance, informing legislation, programme design and service provision at local, national and international levels.

The 1998 *Rome Statue of the International Criminal Court* (ICC) has also prompted significant developments in the area of victims' rights.[4] Two decades after the Declaration, came another major normative advance, the 2005 UN *Basic Principles and Guidelines on the Right to a Remedy and Reparation for Victims of Gross Violations of International Human Rights Law and Serious Violations of International Humanitarian Law* (Basic Principles).[5] With a focus on situations of systemic human rights abuse and armed conflict, these Principles use the same definition of victim(s) as the Declaration, and further develop other important concepts such as reparation and compensation (discussed in Section 3).

Harm-oriented definitions are also common in regional and national law.[6] Notably the "victim" definitions in international instruments law do not distinguish between so-called conventional crimes and those of gross violations of international human rights law.

Section 2: Evolution of victims' rights—Key advances
Victims' rights have increased exponentially in recent decades at the national level, as well as in international law. Yet implementation challenges remain. This section provides an overview of the evolution of standards and good practice. It is not exhaustive and summarises developments thematically.

National organisations and services
In the 1970s, several social movements coalesced in response to the lobbying of survivors of crime and violence. In particular, feminist movements campaigning for rape crisis centres and refuges for women and children escaping violence in the home pushed forward victims' services and policies.[7] This was observable in countries as diverse as the former Yugoslavia, Malaysia, the United States, Australia and Japan, for example. These services often began in the non-government sector and without government funds.

From this, national victims' rights organisations started to emerge. In 1973 the first national conference on assistance was held in the USA, sowing the seeds for the establishment in 1975 of the National Organization for Victim Assistance.[8] In the United Kingdom volunteers offered support to victims of crime; and the aggregate of these modest organisations became the National Association of Victim Support Schemes (later Victim Support UK). Services for female survivors of sexual assault and family and partner violence were set up in the early 1970s in Australia, and in 1979 the Victim Support Service was founded by families bereaved by homicide. This organisation was one of the founders of a regional organisation, Victim Support Australasia. At around the same time in Canada, the victims' rights movement began to exert pressure on the federal and provincial governments to invest in programmes of services for victims (some of these are detailed in the Canada chapter).[9]

Feminist mobilisation led to innovations such as female officers staffing police stations. In 1985 in Sao Paulo, Brazil, the first such station was established in recognition of the negative bias many women experienced from police when they attempted to report violence.[10] Since then other nations have followed suit, including Argentina, Costa Rica, India, Pakistan and the Philippines.[11] Police stations also began to create victim care units and liaison officers. These have now become a common feature of police services in many countries.[12]

Some victim support programmes have been accused of "facilitating criminal justice functioning" rather than easing pain and suffering.[13] In fact, they probably do both.

In the early 1980s, victim advocacy organisations started to gain prominence. Especially in common law countries with adversarial criminal justice systems, survivors of violence and crime began to assume important roles beyond being solely witnesses. The North American victims' movements pursued victims' rights in court proceedings (procedural rights), whereas the British and Australian movements tended initially to focus on addressing victims' welfare needs.

Meanwhile, in other regions of the world, there was a greater reliance on informal systems of support or assistance. Many Asian countries, for example, provided private forms of victim assistance founded on "non-monetary familial social services", in contrast to Western welfare state approaches.[14] With time and significant socio-political change (including transitions to multi-party democracy and increasingly independent justice systems), concern for victims' rights emerged in Thailand, the Philippines and Indonesia, amongst other nations and regions. Globally, legal and service improvements are mainly attributable to activism by affected individuals and NGOs, rather than being State-led.[15] Some governments have responded to such activism; in 2006 the Indonesian President led the establishment of a national agency for the protection of witnesses and victims.[16]

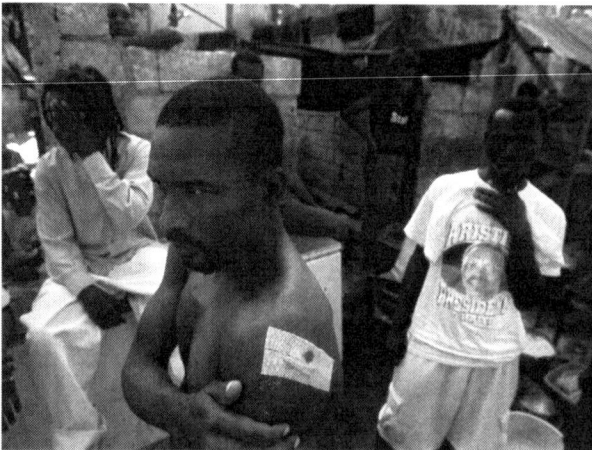

A man shows his bullet wounds received during a gun fight in Marttisant in Port-au-Prince. (Image: Ramon Espinosa/AP, 23 January 2007)

Gauging the opinions of survivors of crime and violence

Asking the opinions of victims of crime and violence can, and indeed should, inform public policy. Data on crime was collected in Belgium, France and England in the 1830s; however, it was not until the 1960s that regular crime surveys were conducted.[17] Victim surveys and research on the nature of crime resulted in an array of recommendations for legislative and administrative reforms across the globe.[18] The first national crime survey in the USA was conducted in 1966 and reported in 1967.[19] Results revealed that nearly half of crime was not reported to police. In 1972 the US Bureau of Justice Statistics then developed the annual household National Crime Victimization Survey.

In 1988/9, global level victimisation trends began to be compared through national survey data.[20] These have since become an important element in the victimology "toolkit", revealing that despite high demand for specialised help, many survivors of crime and violence do not receive such services. Almost half of respondents surveyed from Africa and Latin America, for example, would have appreciated specialised support post-victimisation.[21] National and city-level surveys are now commonly used to better understand perceptions and experiences of crime and violence. Crime observatories also collect victimisation data.[22]

Innovations in criminal justice processes

Victimisation surveys and the growing pressure of victims' movements eventually led to changes in criminal justice laws. From the late 1970s, the rights of those affected by crime and violence began to be included in both procedural and substantive legal and policy frameworks.

On a procedural level, victims' rights can include guarantees of respectful treatment by criminal justice institutions. The right to information often translates into an obligation for the State to keep victims informed of key steps in the proceedings. Other rights include the right to be heard (such as through the provision of impact statements); and more rarely, the right to be consulted on sentencing, predominantly in jurisdictions that use restorative justice principles.[23] Recognising that people may experience difficulties in participating in these processes (e.g. due to the effects of the crime they experienced), specialised services may be set up to accompany them throughout the proceedings. One example is the Victim Care Unit within the El Salvador Ministry of Justice (see the El Salvador Spotlight).

Advances have also been made in rights of witnesses to crimes, including better information provision, psychological accompaniment, and protection.[24]

National inquiries have helped spur innovation. In the USA, the 1982 President's Task Force on Victims of Crime made over 60 recommendations for the criminal justice system, health and welfare, and other agencies and services. These recommendations sought to make the criminal justice system and personnel more "victim friendly" and to expand services, especially government-funded compensation schemes. This process moved the US Congress to enact the 1982 *Victim and Witness Protection Act*, providing protections for witnesses and allowing victim impact statements to be lodged pre-sentence in federal criminal prosecutions. Also in 1982, California's legislature ratified a *Bill of Rights for Victims of Crime*;

this was significantly expanded in 2008 with the passing of "Marsy's Law", which amended the state constitution and provided 17 specific rights and standards for victims.[25] Almost every state in the US has now passed victims' rights legislation. In 2004, the US Congress also enacted victims' rights law for federal offences.

In 1985, almost simultaneously to the adoption of the Declaration; the Council of Europe approved a Recommendation on the Position of the Victim in the Framework of Criminal Law and Procedure.[26] However, other regions lagged behind Europe. To support international implementation, the United Nations developed guidance manuals in the late 1990s, further stimulating debate, policy and programming.[27]

Some countries have made constitutional changes to include a focus on victims' rights. Brazil—in the post-dictatorship era—has fundamental individual and collective rights and duties stated in its Constitution, including guarantees on access to justice and fair treatment; certain offences such as torture, terrorism and other heinous crimes are now considered non-bailable, thus affording some protection to victims and witnesses. South Africa also has victims' rights entrenched in its Constitution as well as in the Service Charter for Victims of Crime (see the South Africa chapter).[28] In Thailand constitutional protections arguably extend to victims of crime. In a criminal case, for instance, an injured person has the right to protection, treatment and compensation from the State, as provided in law.[29]

Elsewhere, national normative development has occurred in policy and legislation. In Australia a national framework for the rights of victims was agreed in 2013 (see Box 1: Developments of victims' rights standards in Australia). Korea has integrated forms of victims' rights into law and practice.[30] Singapore now has some victim-related laws (e.g. provision for impact statements) and practices (e.g. limited consultations with survivors regarding prosecutorial decisions).[31] Likewise, amendments to Chinese law have integrated victims' participatory rights into the justice system.[32] Since 2004 the Japanese Diet has passed laws that, among other advances, strengthen procedural rights for victims, especially the right to participate in key decisions that affect them.[33] Survivors have been given status as a party in criminal proceedings and the right to legal representation. There is also a national plan (required by the law) that governs the implementation of victims' rights and the administration of a victim assistance programme.[34]

Box 1: Development of victims' rights standards in Australia

In 1985, the Attorney-General for South Australia promulgated the country's first declaration on victims' rights. Since then every state and territory has introduced a similar declaration or charter, and in 1993 the Standing Committee of Australia's Attorneys-General endorsed a national charter. In 2005 Australia's Federal Attorney-General joined counterparts from other Commonwealth nations in approving a *Statement of Basic Principles of Justice for Victims of Crimes*. Australia reaffirmed this in 2011.[35]

In 2013, all state and territory Attorneys-General, sitting as the Standing Council on Law and Justice, approved the *National Framework on Rights and Services for Victims of Crime*.[36] Thus, although Australia does not have a national or federal office for victims of crime (such as in the USA) to co-ordinate, improve or be accountable for the implementation of victims' rights and provision of assistance, it now has a national framework. The emphasis is on strengthening rights, first by enshrining standards in law, and second by establishing implementing bodies to respond to grievances.

As one example of good practice, the Commissioner for Victims' Rights, South Australia, is an independent statutory officer whose role is likened to a crime-victims' Ombudsman. Commissioners have also been appointed in the Australian Capital Territory, New South Wales and Western Australia, and a proposal to establish a similar position exists in Victoria.[37]

Compensation schemes

On a substantive level, the most significant right gained by victims has been reparations (discussed in further detail in Section 3), of which one element is compensation for loss.

The first State-led compensation scheme was established in New Zealand in 1963. This was followed by government-funded crime victim compensation schemes in the United Kingdom, several states in the USA and Australia, typically with funding from central revenue.[38] There are now schemes in Hong Kong, Japan, Korea, the Philippines, Taiwan, Thailand, several Indian states and China (for victims of abuse of power) as well as Indonesia (for survivors of certain human rights abuses).[39] The Western schemes were generally driven by notions of benevolence and the social contract between the State and its citizens. Those in Asia were motivated by largely ineffective efforts at offender restitution.[40]

By the end of the 1980s all nations in the European Union (EU) had at least minimal State-funded victim compensation schemes in accordance with the 1983 *European Convention on the Compensation of Victims of Violent Crimes*[41] and affirmed in 2004 with the EU Directive Relating to Compensation to Crime Victims.[42]

The execution of offender-paid compensation (also known as restitution) leaves much to be desired; and this can be a complicated way to pursue justice for victims of violence and crime.[43] Compensation orders are often not enforced; and offenders frequently cannot pay or pay by instalments, thus the compensation process takes a long time, leading to dissatisfaction or a sense of injustice among victims.[44]

Several Latin American countries have introduced government-funded victim compensation for specific purposes. Brazil has a scheme for next of kin of "disappeared" persons and victims of torture during the military regime in the 1980s.[45] Colombia has a law in place since 2011 for victims of the internal armed conflict; it does not compensate victims of non-conflict-related violent crime (for more detail see the Spotlight section on the Colombia Victims' Law). In 2012, Mexico passed a law to compensate those affected by organised crime.[46]

The debate on government-funded compensation continues in South Africa (see the South Africa chapter) and in India several state-based schemes are limited to survivors of terrorism and insurgency (see the India chapter).[47] Israel is one of the few nations in the Middle East that operates a formal compensation scheme for victims of terrorism and their dependants. Payments include a bereavement benefit to cover the expenses incurred during *shiva* (the seven-day mourning period observed by members of the Jewish faith).[48] However, in some regions compensation may be part of customary law even when it is not formalised in the criminal justice code (see the Somalia chapter for a description of such a system).

Specialised services

The nature and type of services available to victims tend to mirror the national political, cultural and social structures. Funding availability, infrastructure and the legitimacy of victims' groups vary widely among countries. Victims' movements and demands are typically shaped in reference to the quality of services offered. Government responses and assistance programmes began to expand post-1985. The first schemes were typically welfare or response focussed (e.g. payment of medical expenses, reimbursement for loss of income and funeral expenses). Specialist services began targeting assistance to people requiring highly specific support, for example, survivors of torture who have relocated to another country.

In some countries victim services have prospered because of government intervention, whereas in other countries government investment has focussed more on attempts to re-educate and reintegrate offenders.[49] In fact these two aspects of criminal justice are not mutually exclusive.

Philanthropic organisations (charities, grant-giving entities etc.), often driven (and partly funded) by survivors themselves, have been established in many countries.[50] Across the globe, this activism frequently drove the evolution of "care and share", self-support organisations. Advocates urged governments to assume a more central role in the provision of assistance.

Over time there has been a move away from volunteer contributions to the professionalisation of such services and advocacy. A wide range of disciplines are now typically involved: psychologists, psychiatrists and other mental-health personnel attend to emotional and psychological harm; social workers provide case management support; rehabilitation experts provide post-injury or trauma therapy; legal advocates offer advice in preparing for court cases and impact statements. In many nations, volunteers (who may or may not be professionally trained) work with affected individuals and families. Lay peer-based support can also have an important place in the recovery process, as well as enabling services to run on limited funding. For those traumatised and impaired by violence, peer support processes can also have beneficial outcomes for reducing social isolation, increasing independence and confidence to manage health conditions and social engagement (see the Rehabilitation and Recovery chapter for further detail, as well as the chapter on Guatemala highlighting the work of the Transitions Foundation in this area). While attention must be paid to accountability and other standards, appropriately managed volunteer contributions to victim services can have a positive effect to repair social cohesion; typically undermined by violence and crime.[51]

Funding methods

Innovation in government funding of services is another important development—and challenge. Sometimes a victims-of-crime levy is payable for certain offences, in addition to the fixed penalties paid by the offender in fees or fines. In South

Australia, someone caught speeding is issued with a fine which once paid then includes a contribution to the Victims of Crime Fund. The Fund is used to pay for compensation, assistance programmes and other initiatives, including the salary of the Commissioner for Victims' Rights.[52]

Another option is for a portion of court fines to be directed to services for survivors (see Canada chapter for detail on this). Funds may also be raised from the sale and seizure of criminal assets; and money recovered from convicted offenders can fund compensation for their victims (an unusual example is described in the Canada chapter in the profile on Louise Russo). In El Salvador, the taxes from gun sales support health programmes (though ironically not direct services to survivors of gun violence), see the Spotlight on El Salvador.[53]

Challenges

Victims' rights gained significant global recognition in 1985 with the adoption of the Declaration, but application of its standards has been uneven. Some States still do not have adequate legislation to frame the rights of survivors of crime, repression and violence. Even when legislation exists, implementation is often lacking or lagging, because the necessary services do not exist, resources are inadequate, or simply because information about services and justice processes has not reached potential beneficiaries.

The connection of support services to formal justice processes raises challenges, as access to such services depends on the existence of an open criminal case (under investigation or in court). When cases close, for example when a perpetrator is sentenced, victims may find themselves abruptly disconnected from the help they had previously received. For traumatised survivors of violence, it is essential to ensure a transition between judicial-related victim services and broader programmes of support.

A third challenge is the delicate balance to strike between victims and perpetrators. Both groups have rights, which in theory do not detract anything from the other. However politically, the two sets of rights are not easily compared. Debates about perpetrators having more rights than victims and survivors developed in the 1970s— and continue in many places. Clear distinctions between "innocent" victims and "guilty" perpetrator can be a key determinant of public attention and resources. Related specifically to gun violence, as many survivors are young men, often involved in or proximate to criminal activity, policymakers can be reluctant to direct resources and rights to those who are often said to "deserve their injuries".[54]

In exceptional circumstances, due to a major violent incident, victims' rights may be improved as demonstrated in the Norwegian State response to the July 2011 massacre (see Spotlight on Norway). Where mass violence turns into armed conflict, victim rights are typically addressed through transitional justice mechanisms. Innovations in the methods to establish truth and seek justice in the wake of violent conflict and repression are explored in detail in Section 3.

Finally, further international normative development is required to give greater legal standing to the 1985 Declaration. Some effort has been mobilised in this regard, with the World Society of Victimology, Tilburg and Tokiwa University's respective International Victimology Institutes putting forward a draft convention to give the Declaration treaty status.[55] Arguments in favour of a global treaty include the increased visibility it would provide for the rights of survivors of crime and violence; it would be "hard law" that applies greater pressure on States to act; and a range of State agencies (e.g. courts, police) would have further requirements to take victims' rights seriously. Importantly a treaty would also provide mechanisms to hold States accountable through monitoring and reporting on implementation.

Section 3: Victims' rights in the aftermath of repression and armed conflict

International attention to victims' rights in the context of war and armed conflict has developed as a distinct focus. Post-war or post-dictatorship, victim-centred approaches to justice seek accountability for human rights violations. This "transitional justice" focuses on both judicial and non-legalistic ways that societies emerging from authoritarian rule and/or armed conflict can deal with past abuses and human rights violations.[56] Although victims' rights include access to justice and truth, in transitional justice these rights tend to be associated in particular with reparations, one mechanism that is perceived to substantively address survivors' needs (see also, Box 2: General Comment 3 on the right to redress).[57]

This section will first examine how victims' rights have been addressed in the contexts of repression and armed conflict. It will then review the main transitional justice mechanisms devised to uphold victims' rights, namely criminal accountability (prosecutions and trials), truth-seeking initiatives, reparations, vetting, and amnesties.[58] Reference will be made to relevant international norms wherever they exist. These mechanisms are not mutually exclusive, and are often used in combination.

International criminal justice

International criminal accountability for serious breaches of international law was introduced by the Nuremberg and Tokyo Trials in 1945-1946. What started as a victors' process of retribution has increasingly provided political space for the human rights of survivors of organised violence, repression and armed conflict. Modern international tribunals include the special courts for the former Yugoslavia and Rwanda, established in 1993 and 1994 respectively by the UN. These were followed by tribunals for Sierra Leone, Cambodia and Bosnia and Herzegovina, as well as international involvement in the courts of Timor-Leste. Increasingly, serious breaches of international law are also tried under domestic jurisdictions of third party States under the principle of universality. Victims' rights are approached differently in all these jurisdictions.

The best-known international tribunal is the International Criminal Court (ICC) in The Hague, Netherlands, established by the 1998 *Rome Statute of the International Criminal Court,* which entered into force in 2002. The ICC is an independent, permanent court that tries persons accused of core international crimes: genocide, crimes against humanity, war crimes and acts of aggression.[59] The ICC's Rules of Procedure define victims as those who suffered harm resulting from crimes within the jurisdiction of the Court (Rule 85).[60] Victims have rights including access to justice, information and participation in court proceedings. The ICC has the power to order an individual to pay reparation to another—a significant development in international law. The Court may lay down the principles for reparation for victims (Rules of Procedure, Article 75). A Trust Fund for Victims has the mandate to implement Court-ordered reparations awards and to provide general assistance to individuals and their communities. Such assistance has included reconstructive surgery and health-related rehabilitation; counselling and vocational training; a village savings and loan association; psychological support, physical rehabilitation and material support for survivors of sexual violence in the Democratic Republic of the Congo and Northern Uganda; and construction of wheelchair ramps at health centres.[61]

The victim-centred perspective of the ICC can also be observed in its organisational structure. Within the ICC Registry, the Court established the Victims Participation and Reparations Section, with a mandate to inform people about their rights and enable their participation in proceedings. A separate Victims and Witnesses Unit provides support and protection to witnesses and victims appearing before the Court, as well as to their families. The independent Office of Public Counsel for Victims assists with legal representation. These units pay particular attention to the needs of children, women, the elderly, persons living with disability and those who have experienced sexual violence. This is in recognition that such people often experience disproportionate victimisation in contexts of armed conflict due to their lower social and political status (e.g. women and girls), or their reliance on others (e.g. children). However there are significant challenges including funding sustainability and processing times of applications.[62]

The institutionalisation of victims' rights in the work of the ICC has had a strong effect on national and hybrid tribunals, by protecting the right to remedy as well as promoting accountability.[63]

Box 2: General Comment 3 on the right to redress

General Comment 3 (GC3) was issued in 2012 by the UN Committee on the 1984 *Convention Against Torture and Other Cruel, Inhuman or Degrading Treatment or Punishment* (CAT).[64] It provides clarification on the right to redress, specifically regarding Article 14 of the CAT, which addresses States' obligations in this area. Article 14 requires State parties to "ensure in its legal system that the victim of an act of torture obtains redress and has an enforceable right to fair and adequate compensation, including the means for as full rehabilitation as possible. In the event of the death of the victim as a result of an act of torture, his [sic] dependents shall be entitled to compensation."

General Comments (GCs) are issued by experts who comprise committees with oversight on UN conventions, providing clarity on treaty implementation. They reflect developments in some, but not necessarily all, States parties' interpretation of specific treaty provisions. General Comments do not have legal effect on States obligations, but often express some sort of majority expectations to how certain provisions should be interpreted. As such, they can have a significant influence on the implementation practice of States parties (and other treaty implementation actors).

Importantly GC3 defines "victim" using the 1985 Declaration definition and also refers to the use of the term "survivors" as preferable in some contexts. Employing this definition allows a focus on family members and other secondary survivors. The Comment refers to redress as containing five core elements, which are articulated in the 2005 Basic

Principles: restitution, compensation, rehabilitation, satisfaction, and guarantees of non-repetition. Thus, GC3 affirms key definitions in two leading instruments related to the rights of survivors of violence and crime, either missing from, or poorly developed, in the CAT.

For those interested in improvement of standards and services for survivors of violence and repression, GC3 represents a significant development, providing conceptual (and thus legal) clarity in key areas: the responsibility of the State to provide rehabilitation regardless of its resource levels; elucidation of the components comprising redress; obligations of a substantive nature (actual services provided to an individual, or their family, following victimisation) and those of a procedural nature (legal and institutional responses).[65]

GC3 states that "the restoration of the dignity of the victim is the ultimate objective in the provision of redress" (para. 4). It applies a victim-oriented approach, affirming the importance of participation in the selection of rehabilitation services. GC3 clarifies State obligations, noting the central responsibility to ensure obstacles, such as statutes of limitations, amnesties or grants of immunity for torture or ill-treatment do not hinder individuals (and their families) ability to obtain redress.

GC3 also places the onus of the provision of rehabilitation services back to the State, an area which NGOs have been particularly active, in the absence of government-led or funded services. The Comment insists that rehabilitation services "should be holistic and include medical and psychological care as well as legal and social services" (para. 11) and not be dependent on survivors being involved in formal justice processes (para. 15).

The Comment further explains that Article 14 extends to refugees, asylum-seekers, stateless persons and individuals tortured in States not party to the CAT and that such persons are entitled to protection and rights once they enter a State party. It also reiterates the importance of careful attention to gender-based violence (also explored in GC2 of the Committee), a focus notably absent from the CAT. In 2013 the UN Human Rights Council agreed a resolution affirming the content of GC3. It is the most prominent reference to date by the Human Rights Council to the right and need for rehabilitation services as part of States' obligations to provide redress to victims of torture and ill-treatment.[66]

Truth and reconciliation commissions

Truth seeking initiatives have a different focus. Rather than punishing perpetrators, as with traditional or formal retributive justice processes, the aim is to achieve societal healing through fact-finding, bearing witness, recognition of past abuse and memorialising. In communities affected by long-term violent conflict, restorative justice processes may enable victims and perpetrators to grapple with legacies of mass abuse in ways that criminal prosecutions alone cannot. The best known example is the South African Truth and Reconciliation Commission (1996-2003). There have been over 30 truth commissions, including those established in Argentina, Guatemala, Peru, Timor-Leste, Morocco, Liberia, Haiti, and other nations.[67] National human rights commissions may serve similar fact-finding purposes. Truth-telling processes have had problematic elements, especially in relation to full or partial amnesty for perpetrators (for example in South Africa, Colombia, Chile, Guatemala, and Argentina). Other challenges include the management of expectations of those telling their experiences, often for the first time, and minimising secondary victimisation.

Reparations

Reparations provide concrete remedies for victims. They may be material (e.g. money) or symbolic (e.g. apologies, monuments or ceremonies) or operational (e.g. the restoration of legal rights, rehabilitation programmes). Aside from references to compensation or reparation in peace agreements, two major developments in international law have dealt with reparations: the International Criminal Court and the 2005 UN *Basic Principles and Guidelines on the Right to a Remedy and Reparation for Victims of Gross Violations of International Human Rights Law and Serious Violations of International Humanitarian Law.*[68]

The Basic Principles were adopted by the General Assembly in 2005, after seven years of development.[69] The principal obligation is for States to "provide reparation to victims for acts or omissions which can be attributed to the State and constitute gross violations of international human rights law or serious violations of international humanitarian law" (Principle 15). The right to remedy has two aspects: the procedural right to justice and the substantive right to redress for injury suffered due to act(s) in violation of international law.[70]

Reparation includes five core concepts: restitution, compensation, rehabilitation, satisfaction, and guarantees of non-repetition (Principles 19-23). Restitution aims to restore, where possible, the individual to the original situation before violations were committed, addressing mainly personal but also material suffering (for example, return of property). Compensation is for damage that can be economically assessed and provided to the claimant/s. Rehabilitation involves wide ranging health and psychological care (see Box 2 on the right to redress for more on rehabilitation, as well as the chapter on Rehabilitation and Recovery).[71] Measures for satisfaction include cessation of violations, truth seeking, the search for the disappeared, the recovery and the reburial of remains, public apologies, judicial and administrative sanctions and commemoration, as well as human rights training. Non-repetition involves structural policy change to strengthen human rights, the rule of law, security system transformation, judicial independence, etc. These concepts have informed the development of specific measures for reparation in the aftermath of war.

The Basic Principles have been influential in several Latin American countries when authorities were drawing up legislation on reparation for victims. In Colombia, the former National Commission for Reparation and Reconciliation followed the forms of reparations defined in the Principles in preparing its own line of implementation (for more detail on Colombia, see the Spotlight on that theme). On several occasions, the Inter-American Court of Human Rights (IACHR) has referred to the Basic Principles in its jurisprudence relating to the award of collective and individual reparation. It is important to note that some of the most influential decisions of the IACHR in the area of reparations pre-date the Basic Principles.[72]

Deciding who can receive reparations has proven to be challenging. For example, in Peru, survivors of the internal armed conflict are entitled to receive reparations from the State (including in the areas of health, education and monetary compensation). To identify who is entitled to these benefits, a National Victims Register (Registro Único de Víctimas) has been established and people can register individual and collective claims. Victims are defined as a person or group of people whose human rights were violated during the armed conflict between April 1980 and November 2000.[73] As in Colombia, India and other countries, members of Peru's insurgent or subversive groups are considered illegitimate and are not included in the National Victims Register and therefore not entitled to any form of reparation.[74]

Box 3: Example of a reparation programme—Chile

In September 1973, the elected government of Chile was overthrown by a military junta led by the army's commander-in-chief, General Augusto Pinochet. The junta appointed Pinochet as president the following year. From 1973 until 1989, thousands of citizens suspected of opposing the regime were arrested, tortured, murdered, and disappeared in one of the most authoritarian military regimes in Latin America. After a 1988 referendum voting Pinochet out of government and elections in 1989, Chile underwent a peaceful transition to democracy. Two years later, a national rehabilitation programme for victims of human rights violations was established—PRAIS (Programa de Reparación y Atención Integral en Salud y Derechos Humanos). The programme was based on the recommendations of the first Chilean Truth and Reconciliations Commission Report, delivered in May 1991.

The programme provides health services to direct victims of repression and their families, including victims of torture, political prisoners, exiles, and people subjected to political persecution, as well as the families of those disappeared and arbitrarily executed. Mental and physical health care and specialised rehabilitation programmes are provided free of charge through the national health care system at all levels, from health posts to national hospitals. During its first ten years, 51,065 people received health assistance through PRAIS.[75] Today there are 29 professional teams across the country providing services to victims, and the programme is fully incorporated into the national health system. PRAIS still stands as one of the most comprehensive health-focussed reparations programmes in the world.

However, PRAIS is not without its shortcomings. In 2002, the organisation REDRESS submitted a petition to the Inter-American Commission on Human Rights on behalf of Leopoldo Garcia Lucero, a then 68 year old Chilean citizen who was detained, brutally tortured and forced into exile to the UK in 1973. At stake is what constitutes effective remedy and full and adequate reparation for victims of torture. Does it include the substantive right to justice (investigating and prosecuting perpetrators)? What is the standard for appropriate monetary compensation: the one applying within the country where the abuse occurred, or should it be adjusted according the country of exile? Are States obliged to provide for medical rehabilitation for citizens living outside their borders, when they have a national programme within borders? The case moved to the Inter-American Court of Human Rights in 2011; a hearing occurred in March 2012 and a decision is expected in the latter half of 2013.[76]

Vetting

Vetting is a procedure specific to post-violence and conflict transitions. It aims to remove individuals involved in past abuses from public administrations—including the police, military and judiciary. Vetting, when implemented appropriately, occurs with clear procedural guidelines including objective and lawful criteria, oversight, and remedies available to those removed from public office and/or charged with past abuses.[77]

Amnesties

By shielding perpetrators from prosecution, amnesties can encourage former perpetrators or combatants to reintegrate society, signal a break from the past, and avoid divisive judicial processes. However, they are sometimes offered at the expense of survivors' right to justice and acknowledgment. To mitigate this risk, amnesties are sometimes conditional—for example in South Africa, amnesty could only be granted to individuals who would fully disclose their past actions in hearings of the Truth and Reconciliation Commission. Furthermore, according to current international standards, amnesties can never be offered to individuals responsible for gross violations of human rights, crimes against humanity, genocide or war crimes.[78]

Peace agreements

Peace talks and agreements provide a critical opportunity for attention and commitment to survivors rights in war-affected contexts. However, most agreements contain only broad declarative clauses of support, with little definition on timeframes or implementation parameters and strategies. Negotiating parties—armed groups, armies and governments—as well as international donors and UN agencies, have a responsibility to ensure that the needs and rights of those injured or impaired in war are included substantively in the outcomes of peace processes. For further detail, see the Spotlight on Assistance to Survivors and Clauses in Peace Agreements.

One of those outcomes is disarmament, demobilisation and reintegration (DDR) processes, particularly reintegration strategies. These processes often see a mismatch between the needs of injured combatants and assistance to injured civilians, leading to inequity in health care, social protection and other forms of assistance.[79] The R in DDR is often underfunded or overlooked in comparison to the D&D elements, regarded as more pressing. Post-war conditions—fractured economies, weak infrastructure, damaged health and education systems—also pose challenges for reintegration. As Handicap International has pointed out, people living with disability in war-torn countries are often very poor and have little education; in addition, "too little market research is done to ensure that the training given is rationally connected to job possibilities in the society at large."[80]

Conclusion

The international trend towards accountability for human rights violations has reinforced people-centred approaches to justice, in terms of process (e.g. participation of victims and survivors in the ICC proceedings) and substance (e.g. reparations). At the same time, States and civil society groups have developed measures to embed the rights of crime victims in national criminal justice processes (e.g. impact statements in court) and to help process trauma and grief (e.g. State-funded services for psychological support).

Despite the growth in laws, policies and assistance programmes to advance victims' rights globally and nationally there is clearly more to be done. Policymaking goals related to survivors of gun violence specifically, and those victimised by violence more broadly, include:

- linking legislative change to practical implementation;
- ensuring synergy between international standards and national legal and policy frameworks;

- actively including survivors of violence and crime in decision-making, service design and justice processes; building survivor-centred elements into armed violence prevention programming;
- reviewing existing practice to discern good and transferable practice; and
- increasing communication between relevant professionals (victimologists, criminologists, psychologists, violence reduction specialists, rehabilitation experts, gender justice advocates, amongst others).

To support these goals, the chapter contains two further elements as "food for thought": Annex 1 reviews 56 international standards and provides a brief summary of their relevance for the development or refinement of normative frameworks; and Box 4 following, concludes the chapter by outlining 14 core considerations for those engaged, or interested in, strengthening policy and programming for those affected by armed violence.

Box 4: Pointers for Strengthening Policy and Programming for Survivors of Violence and Crime

The following points are non-exhaustive and offered to those involved in policy development, programming and service delivery to consider in the course of their work to ensure that:[81]

1. Survivors of violence and crime are treated with compassion and dignity by service providers and State authorities, and in ways respectful of age, sex, gender, ethnic identity, ability and capacity.
2. Timely medical, psychological and rehabilitation services is accessible and affordable, and premised on non-discriminatory service from professional staff and associated volunteers.
3. Information is timely, accessible and comprehensible about rights, services, and criminal justice processes.
4. Competent authority(s) effectively investigate an incident/event in an impartial, non-discriminatory and timely manner and for survivors or appropriate others to be consulted on decisions such as whether to prosecute.
5. Affordable and non-discriminatory legal representation, and active participation in court or penal processes, including the right to appeal judicial decisions, is possible.
6. Safety and protection for individuals, family and other acquaintances involved in criminal justice processes, including witness identity protection, is assured.
7. Privacy of information and identity are respected.
8. Truth recovery and the right to memory are respected.
9. Reparations are accessible, and are proportionate, timely and transparent, including offender-restitution and where an offender is unable to pay restitution, government or other forms of compensation are available.
10. Satisfaction regarding timely conclusion of criminal justice or truth seeking processes including access, is achieved. This includes the possibility for survivors, and appropriate others, to choose alternatives to traditional court-based justice, such as restorative justice.
11. Attention is applied to managing and reducing secondary victimisation experiences resulting from giving witness statements, appearing in court and other processes.
12. The possibility exists to request re-examination of the State's decision not to prosecute a suspected perpetrator.
13. National laws and policies are developed, updated, or appraised according to the minimum standards set down in international human rights and humanitarian law and relevant international standards related to assistance to survivors of violence, crime, repression and armed conflict, in particular but not limited to, the 1985 UN *Declaration*

> *of Basic Principles of Justice for Victims of Crime and Abuse of Power* and the 2005 UN *Basic Principles and Guidelines on the Right to a Remedy and Reparation for Victims of Gross Violations of International Human Rights Law and Serious Violations of International Humanitarian Law.*
>
> 14. Victims and survivors of violence and crime are included and participate in the development of relevant legal frameworks, policies, plans of action and programmes.

Contributors: Cate Buchanan, Director, Surviving Gun Violence Project. **Jemima García-Godos**, Associate Professor, Department of Sociology and Human Geography, University of Oslo, Norway. **Michael O'Connell**, Commissioner for Victims' Rights, South Australia and Secretary-General of the World Society of Victimology. **Mireille Widmer**, Senior Associate, Surviving Gun Violence Project. Editing was also provided by **Rebecca Peters** and **Emile LeBrun**. **Helaine Boyd** provided assistance with fact checking and drafting.

Peer reviews were provided by **Anna Alvazzi**, Research Director, Small Arms Survey (Switzerland); **Sheree Bailey**, independent disability and victim assistance adviser (Australia); **K. Jaishankar**, Department of Criminology and Criminal Justice, Manonmaniam Sundaranar University, and President of the South Asian Society of Criminology and Victimology (India); **Kieran Mundy**, Tokiwa International Victimology Institute (Japan); and **Irvin Waller**, Department of Criminology, University of Ottawa and President, International Organization for Victim Assistance (Canada). Additional thanks to: **Christian Holmboe Ruge**, Director, Humanitarian Disarmament Programme, International Law and Policy Institute (Norway).

References

[1] M. O'Connell, "Who May Be Called a Victim of Crime?" *Journal of the Australasian Society of Victimology* 1/3 (1992), pp. 15-23; M.A. Young, "Survivors of Crime," In D. Sank and D.I. Caplan (Eds), *To be a Victim: Encounters with Crime and Injustice* (New York: Insight Books/Plenum Press, 1991), pp. 27-42; J. García-Godos, "Victim reparations in transitional justice—what is at stake and why," *Nordic Journal of Human Rights* 26/2 (2008), pp. 111-130; C. Fernandez de Casadevante Romani, "The International Categories of Victims," In *International Law of Victims* (Berlin: Springer-Verlag, 2012), pp. 39-61.

[2] Adopted by the UN General Assembly 29 November 1985; A/RES/40/34. Available at: www.un.org/documents/ga/res/40/a40r034.htm Accessed 16 August 2013.

[3] M. O'Connell, "Victims' Rights in International, National and Domestic Law," Unpublished paper presented to the victimology course hosted by Unidad para la Attencion y Reparacion Integral a las Victimas, Javeriana University, Bogota, Colombia, 13 June (2013).

[4] Rule 85, ICC Rules of Procedure and Evidence.

[5] Adopted by the UN General Assembly 16 December 2005; A/RES/60/147. Available at: http://untreaty.un.org/cod/avl/pdf/ha/ga_60-147/ga_60-147_e.pdf Accessed 16 August 2013.

[6] Regional legal instruments such as the European Council Framework Decision of 2001 (2001/220/JHA, 15 March): the Council of Europe Recommendations (Rec(2006)8) of the Committee of Ministers to member states on assistance to crime victims; Directive of the European Parliament and of the Council Establishing Minimum Standards for the Rights, Support and Protection of Victims of Crime (COM (2011) 275); and the 2005 Commonwealth Nations Basic Statement of Basic Principles of Justice for Victims of Crimes, also adopt a harm based approach to defining victim.

[7] W.G. Doerner and S.P. Lab, *Victimology,* 4th ed (New York: Lexis Nexis, 2005).

[8] P.M. Tobolowsky, *Crime Victim Rights and Remedies* (North Carolina: Academic Press, 2001).

[9] I. Waller, *Rebalancing Justice: Rights for Victims of Crime* (United Kingdom: Rowman and Littlefield, 2011); P.E. Rock, "Society's Attitude to the Victim," In E. Fattah, (Ed) *From Crime Policy to Victim Policy* (London: Macmillan, 1986a); P.E. Rock, *A View from the Shadows: The Ministry of the Solicitor General of Canada and the Justice for Victim of Crime Initiative* (Oxford: Oxford University Press, 1986b).

[10] I. Waller (2011), p. 73.

[11] I. Waller (2011). See also United Nations Office for Drug Control and Crime Prevention and the Centre for International Crime Prevention, "Examples of interdisciplinary approaches used to enhance police response," In *Handbook on Justice for Victims of Crime—On the use and application of the Declaration of Basic Principles of Justice for Victims of Crime and Abuse of Power* (New York: UN, 1999), pp. 64-65; W. Chan, (Ed) *Support for Victims of Crime in Asia* (London: Routledge, 2008); H.Q. Giralt, "Costa Rica," In *World Fact-book of Criminal Justice* (Washington DC: Bureau of Justice Statistics, 2004); M. O'Connell, "Police and Victims," Presentation at 13th Asia Post-graduate Course on Victimology and Victim Assistance, National Law University, Delhi, India, 13 August (2013).

[12] For example, in 2006 Canada's Federal-Provincial Task Force created specialist victim units within some police services, staffed by crisis workers. Government of Canada, *History of Victims' Movement* (Ottawa: Government of Canada, 2006). Also see: J. Muir, *Model Victim Service Program for Police Officers* (Ottawa: Canada Solicitor General, Research Division, 1986). Regarding police responses across the globe see also UNODCCP (now the UN Office for Drugs and Crime, UNODC) and the Centre for International Crime Prevention (1999), pp. 64-65.

[13] L.W. Kennedy and V.F. Sacco, *Crime victims in context* (Los Angeles: Roxbury, 1998).

[14] A. Croissant, "Changing welfare regimes in East and Southeast Asia: Crisis, change and challenge," *Social Policy and Administration* 38 (2004), p. 506. Further analysis on the development of victim assistance and rights in Asia can be found in: W. Chan (2008); T. Ota (Ed), *Victims and criminal justice: An Asia perspective* (Tokyo: Keio University Press, 2003); V.S. Malimath, *Report of the Committee on Reforms of the Criminal Justice System* (New Delhi: Government of India, 2003); UNODCCP and the Centre for International Crime Prevention (1999); A. Alvazzi de Frate, *Victims of crime in the developing world*, UNICRI Publication, No. 57 (Rome: UNICRI, 1998).

[15] L. Sebba, "Wither victim policies? A view from the crossroads," In W. Chan (2008), pp. 81-112.

[16] L.P. Siregar, "LPSK works silently to provide effective protection," *The Jakarta Post* 5 November (2012).

[17] Adolphe Quetelet analysed and reported on crime statistics from several countries. For more on his pioneering work in this area see the "Quetelet, Adolphe" Web page at the International Encyclopedia of the Social Sciences of 1968. Available at: Encyclopedia.com Accessed 14 August 2013. Also see: M.R. Gottfredson and M.J. Hindelang, "Sociological Aspects of Criminal Victimization," *Annual Review of Sociology* 7 (1981), pp. 107-128.

[18] R. Block, "Victim—Offender Dynamics in Violent Crime," *Journal of Criminal Law and Criminology* 72/2 (1981), pp. 743-761; R.F. Sparkes, *Research on Victims of Crime: Accomplishments, Issues and New Directions,* Crime and Delinquency Issues: Monograph Series (Maryland: US Department of Health and Human Services, 1982); R.I. Mawby and M.L. Gill, *Crime Victims: Needs, Services, and the Voluntary Sector* (London: Tavistock, 1987).

[19] P. Ennis, *Criminal Victimization in the United States*: *A Report of a National Survey*, President's Commission on Law Enforcement and Administration of Justice (Washington DC: Department of Justice, *1967)*. See also: M.R. Gottfredson and M.J. Hindelang (1981), pp. 107-128; W.G. Skogan, "Reporting crime to the police: The status of world research," *Journal of Research in Crime and Delinquency* 21/ 2 (1984), pp. 113-137.

[20] J. van Dijk, P. Mayhew and M. Killias, *Experiences of crime across the world: Key findings of the 1989 International Crime Survey* (Netherlands: Kluwer Law and Taxation Publishers, 1989). See also: J. van Kesteren and J. van Dijk, "Key victimological findings from the International Crime Victims Survey," In S.G. Shoham, P. Knepper and M. Kett, *International Handbook on Victimology* (Boca Raton: CRC Press, 2010), pp. 151-180.

21 J. van Dijk, "Victim empowerment and support in an international context," *Putting Victims on the Agenda*, Monograph No. 7, Institute for Security Studies (Pretoria: ISS, 1996).

22 For an interactive map of observatories see: http://aoav.org.uk/2013/an-eye-on-violence-monitoring-systems-and-observatories/ Web page updated 11 July 2013. Accessed 31 July 2013.

23 An impact statement is a written or spoken declaration provided to the court by victims or their loved ones, which can be considered in the estimation of "loss" as well as penalties.

24 See for example, 2003 UN *Convention Against Corruption* (Article 32); UN Office on Drugs and Crime, *Justice in Matters involving Child Victims and Witnesses of Crime* (New York: UN, 2009); International Bureau of Children's Rights, *Guidelines on Justice for Child Victims and Witnesses* (Montreal: IBCR, 2003).

25 State of California, Department of Justice, Web page "Victims' Bill of Rights Act of 2008: Marsy's Law." http://oag.ca.gov/victimservices/marsys_law Accessed 28 March 2013. For detailed analysis on this law see I. Waller (2011), pp. 121-124.

26 Recommendation No. R (85) 11. This was followed by two further recommendations in 1987: European Committee on Crime Problems, *Recommendation No. R (87)* 21 on assistance to victim and the prevention of victimisation; European Committee on Crime Problems, Recommendation No. R (87) 19 on the organisation of crime prevention. In 2012, a further affirmation of EU standards was articulated in Directive 2012/29/EU of the European Parliament and of the Council, 25 October 2012, establishing minimum standards on the rights, support and protection of victims of crime, and replacing Council Framework Decision 2001/220/JHA.

27 UNODCCP and the Centre for International Crime Prevention (1999). Available at: www.uncjin.org/Standards/9857854.pdf and UNODCCP and the Centre for International Crime Prevention (1999). United Nations Office for Drug Control and Crime Prevention and the Centre for International Crime Prevention, *Guide for Policy Makers—On the Use and Application of the United Nations' Declaration of Basic Principles of Justice for Victims of Crime and Abuse of Power* (New York: UN, 1999). Available at: www.unodc.org/pdf/criminal_justice/UNODC_Guide_for_Policy_Makers_Victims_of_Crime_and_Abuse_of_Power.pdf

28 See R. Peacock, *Victimology in South Africa* (Pretoria: Van Schaik Publishers, 2013); M. Groenhuijsen, *Objectives of victim assistance: The professionalisation of service providing organisations. A comparison between European experiences and recent developments in South Africa,* Social work practice (Pretoria: South African Department of Welfare, 1998).

29 Section 245 of the 1997 *Constitution of the Kingdom of Thailand*; see also 2001 *Act for the Compensation of Victims and Accused Persons in Criminal Cases Act.* Also see: P. Watanavanich, *The Emergence of Victim's Rights in Thailand: Twenty Years after the U.N. Declaration of Basic Principles of Justice for Victims of Crime and Abuse of Power*, Resource Material Series No. 70, The 131st International Senior Seminar, Visiting Experts Papers, United Nations Asia and Far East Institute for the Prevention of Crime and the Treatment of Offenders (2006). Available at: www.unafei.or.jp/en glish/pdf/RS_No70/No70_05VE_Watanavanich.pdf Accessed 28 March 2013. K. Kittayarak, *Restorative Justice: The Thai Experience*, Resource Material Series No. 63, The 123rd International Senior Seminar, Visiting Experts Papers, United Nations Asia and Far East Institute for the Prevention of Crime and the Treatment of Offenders (2003). Available at: www.unafei.or.jp/english/pdf/RS_No63/No63_13VE_Kittayarak1.pdf Accessed 28 March 2013.

30 C. Kyoon Seok, *The Current Situation of Measures for Crime Victims in the Korean Criminal Justice System,* Resource Material Series No. 081, The 144ᵗʰ International Senior Seminar, Visiting Experts Papers, United Nations Asia and Far East Institute for the Prevention of Crime and the Treatment of Offenders (2010). Available at: www.unafei.or.jp/english/pdf/RS_No81/No81_10VE_Seok.pdf Accessed 28 March 2013.

31 M. Hor, "Clashing conceptions of the victim's role in Singapore's criminal process," In W. Chan (2008), pp. 207-221; T. Ota, "The development of victim support and victim rights in Asia," In W. Chan (2008), pp. 113-148.

32 G-F Jin, *The Protection and Remedies for Victims of Crime and Abuse of Power in China*, Resource Material Series No. 70, The 131st International Senior Seminar, Visiting Experts Papers, United Nations Asia and Far East Institute for the Prevention of Crime and the Treatment of Offenders (2006). Available at: www.unafei.or.jp/english/pdf/RS_No70/No70_15PA_Jin.pdf Accessed 28 March 2013.

33 T. Ota, "A new horizon of victim support in Japan," In W. Chan (2008), pp. 240-261; see also T. Ota (2003); J. Dussich and K. Kiyoko, "Victim Assistance in Japan: History, Culture and Programmes" In P.C. Friday and G.F. Kirchhoff (Eds), *Victimology at the Transition: From the 20th to the 21st Century: Essays in Honor of Hans Joachim Schneider* (Monchengladbach: Shaker Verlag, 2000).

34 Crime Victim Policy Promotion Council, *The Crime Victim Basic Plan* (Tokyo: Cabinet Office, 2005).

35 Commonwealth *Statement of Basic Principles of Justice for Victims of Crimes.* Available at: www.thecommonwealth.org/shared_asp_files/uploadedfiles/6297EFD0-B74B-4106-AD88-D3E4E75F18A9_ANNEX-VictimStatement.pdf Accessed 28 March 2013. Also see: S.B. Garkawe and M. O'Connell, "The need for a federal, Australia-wide approach to issues concerning crime victims," *Current Issues in Criminal Justice* 18/3 (2007), pp. 488-493.

36 Available at: www.lawlink.nsw.gov.au/lawlink/victimservices/ll_vs.nsf/vwFiles/SCLJ_Framework-2013-16.pdf/$file/SCLJ_Framework-2013-16.pdf Accessed 16 August 2013.

37 The Secretary for the Department of Justice in Victoria and the Victims of Crime Coordinator in Queensland play key roles in this regard in lieu of formal independent positions.

38 The United Kingdom includes England, Scotland, Wales and Northern Ireland. The latter has a separate victim compensation scheme.

39 T. Ota (2003); T. Ota, In W. Chan (2008), pp. 113-148; F. Atty, "The Anti-Rape Law of 1997," *Criminal Law and Litigation and Labor Law*, 25 September (2006); V.S. Malimath, *Report of the Committee on Reforms of the Criminal Justice System* (New Delhi, Government of India: 2003); S.P. Singh Makkar and G. Lyallpuri, "Victimisation: State Responsibility in India," Presentation at the 8th International Symposium on Victimology, Adelaide, 21-26 August (1994), p. 2; K. Kittipong, *A brief outline of the current situation on the protection of victims of crime in Thailand*, Visiting Experts' Papers, The 123rd International Senior Seminar, Resource Material Series No. 63, United Nations Asia and Far East Institute for the Prevention of Crime and Treatment of Offenders (2005); G-F. Jin, *The protection and remedies for victims of crime and abuse of power in China*, The 131st International Training Course, Resource Material Series No. 70, United Nations Asia and Far East Institute for the Prevention of Crime and Treatment of Offenders (2006).

40 T. Ota, In W. Chan (2008), pp. 113-148.

41 *European Convention on the Compensation of Victims of Violent Crimes*, Strasbourg, 24. XI. CETS 116 (1983). Entered into force in 1988. At 16 August 2013; 25 ratifications and 8 signatories. See: http://conventions.coe.int/Treaty/Commun/QueVoulezVous.asp?NT=116&CM=8&CL=ENG Accessed 16 August 2013.

42 Council Directive 2004/80/EC of 29 April 2004 relating to compensation to crime victims. Available at: http://eur-lex.europa.eu/LexUriServ/LexUriServ.do?uri=CELEX:32004L0080:EN:HTML Accessed 16 August 2013.

43 M.E.I. Brienen and E.H. Hoegen, *Victims of Crime in 22 European Juridictions: The Implementation of Recommendation 85 (11) of the Council of Europe on the Position of the Victim in the Framework of Criminal Law and Procedure* (Tilburg: Wolf Legal Productions, 2000). Also see: Project Victim Support Europe, *Implementation of the EU Framework Decision on the standing of victims in the criminal proceedings in the Member States of the European Union* (Lisboa: Associação Portuguesa de Apoio à Vítima, 2009). Available at: http://ec.europa.eu/justice/news/consulting_public/0053/project_victims_europe_final_report_en.pdf Accessed 16 August 2013.

44 Irvin Waller outlines seven steps of survivors of crime to secure reparations, compensation being one element. Waller inverts findings from the US, which are globally applicable, of common obstacles in this area. See I. Waller (2011) pp. 97-113.

45 R.M. Latore, "Coming Out of the Dark: Achieving Justice for Victims of Human Rights Violations by South American Military Regimes," *Boston College International Comparative Law Review* 25/419 (2002), pp. 419-448; B. Hamber, "Living with the legacy of impunity: lessons for South Africa about truth, justice and crime in Brazil," *Latin American Report* 13/2 (1998), pp. 4-16.

46 H. Stone, "Mexico and Colombia Victims Laws: Broad Enough to Bring Justice?" *InSight Crime*, 25 February (2013). Available at: www.insightcrime.org/news-analysis/comparing-mexico-colombia-victims-law Accessed 28 March 2013. BBC News, "Mexico passes law to

47 compensate victims of crime," 30 April (2012). Available at: www.bbc.co.uk/news/world-latin-america-17902965 Accessed 31 July 2013.

47 A useful overview of standards and key challenges in the area of crime victims is to be found in K. Chockalingam, *Measures for crime victims in the Indian criminal justice system*, Resource Material Series No. 081, The 144th International Senior Seminar, Visiting Experts Papers, United Nations Asia and Far East Institute for the Prevention of Crime and the Treatment of Offenders (2010). Available at: www.unafei.or.jp/english/pdf/RS_No81/No81_11VE_Chockalingam.pdf Accessed 28 March 2013.

48 For a discussion on victims' rights more broadly, see: U. Yanay and T. Gal, "Lobbying for rights: Crime victims in Israel," In S.G. Shoham, P. Knepper and M. Kett (2010), pp. 373-396.

49 M.A. Young, "Towards a New Millennium in Victim Assistance," In C. Sumner, M. Israel, M. O'Connell and R. Sarre (Eds), *International Victimology: Selected Papers from the 8th International Symposium on Victimology,* Conference Proceedings (Canberra: Australian Institute of Criminology, 1996), pp. 233-240; H. Reeves, "The Growth of Policies and Services for Victims of Crime in the UK, 1974-1994," In M. O'Connell, (Ed) *Challenges and Directions in Justice Administration* (Adelaide: Institute of Justice Studies, 2001), pp. 149-60; J. Taylor and D. Smith, "Victim Impact Statements: History and Use in New Zealand," Presentation at the 8th International Symposium on Victimology, Adelaide, 21-26 August (1994).

50 See for example: H. Reeves, "The Growth of Policies and Services for Victims of Crime in the UK, 1974-1994," In M. O'Connell, (Ed) *Challenges and Directions in Justice Administration* (Adelaide: Institute of Justice Studies, 2001), pp. 149-160; M. Maguire and J. Shapland, "The Victims' Movement in Europe," In A.J. Lurigio, W.G. Skogan and R.C. Davis (Eds), *Victims of Crime: Problems, Policies and Programs* (California: Sage, 1990) pp. 205-225. M.A. Young, "Present and future developments in victim services and victims' rights: a view from the United States," In C. Wing-Cheony (Ed) *Support for victims of crime in Asia* (United Kingdom: Routledge, 2008), pp. 325-349; Victorian Community Council Against Violence, *Victims of Crime: Inquiry into Services* (Melbourne: VCCAV, 1994); Justice Strategy Unit, *Review on Victims of Crime—Report One* (Adelaide: Attorney General's Department, South Australia, 1999); R. Peacock (Ed), *Victimology in South Africa* (Hatfield: Van Schaik Publishers, 2012).

51 R. Condry, "Secondary victims and secondary victimization," In S.G. Shoham, P. Knepper and M. Kett (2010), pp. 219-249.

52 The Victims of Crime Fund has other revenue sources: consolidated revenue; a percentage of money paid as court ordered fines; money recovered from convicted offenders after the state has paid compensation; and money derived from the sale of confiscated criminal assets.

53 Centre for Humanitarian Dialogue, *Surviving gun violence in El Salvador: a tax on firearms for health,* Background paper No. 3 (Geneva: HD Centre, 2007).

54 Comment made in a discussion between Cate Buchanan and a Latin American government official, New York, July 2006.

55 S. Garkawe, "The need for a victims' convention," *The Victimologist* 9/2 (2005), pp. 4-5; see also "Recommendation to acknowledge 25th anniversary of the UN Declaration of Basic Principles of Justice for Victims of Crime and Abuse of Power, and establish an Expert Group to report to the UN Commission of Crime Prevention and Criminal Justice in 2011", 12th United Nations Congress on Crime Prevention and Criminal Justice, A/CONF.213/NGO/11; J. Dussich, "Introductory Comments—History of the draft Convention and Introduction of the draft UN Resolution for a Convention on Justice and Support for Victims of Crime and Abuse of Power," *The Victimologist* 13/2 (2010), pp. 4-6; M. O'Connell, "Cloaking the truth—ex post facto the UN Declaration of Basic Principles of Justice for Victims of Crime and Abuse of Power," *The Victimologist* 13/2 (2010), pp. 6-7. The draft text is available at: www.worldsocietyofvictimology.org/publications/Draft%20Convention.pdf Accessed 31 July 2013

56 According to the UN, the field of transitional justice "comprises the full range of processes and mechanisms associated with a society's attempts to come to terms with a legacy of large-scale past abuses, in order to ensure accountability, serve justice and achieve reconciliation. These may include both judicial and non-judicial mechanisms, with differing levels of international involvement (and none at all) and individual prosecutions, reparations, truth-seeking, institutional reform, vetting and dismissals, or a combination

thereof." See: Report of the UN Secretary-General, *The rule of law and transitional justice in conflict and post-conflict societies,* S/2004/616, 23 August (2004), para. 8.

[57] J. García-Godos, and C.L. Sriram, "Introduction," In C.L. Sriram, J. García-Godos, J. Herman, and O. Martin-Ortega (Eds), *Transitional Justice and Peacebuilding on the Ground—Victims and Excombatants* (London: Routledge, 2012).

[58] See also the work of REDRESS, the International Center for Transitional Justice, UN Rule of Law site (unrol.org).

[59] See Annex 1 for ratification and signature details. Regarding acts of aggression, these will not be prosecuted until at least the start of 2017 following a delay mechanism agreed at the 2010 ICC Review Conference at which, after lengthy negotiations, States agreed this amendment to the core crimes to be investigated, would come into force one year after ratification by 30 States parties or a vote by two-thirds of States parties is secured. For more detail see the Coalition for an International Criminal Court, Web page "The Crime of Aggression" www.iccnow.org/?mod=aggression Accessed 18 July 2013.

[60] "For the purposes of the Statute and the Rules of Procedure and Evidence: a) "Victims" means natural persons who have suffered harm as a result of the commission of any crime within the jurisdiction of the Court, b) Victims may include organizations or institutions that have sustained direct harm to any of their property which is dedicated to religion, education, art, or science, or charitable purposes, and to their historic monuments, hospitals and others places and objects for humanitarian purposes." The definition has also been interpreted to include deceased people, who are advocated for in ICC processes. For more detail see, H. Olasolo, *Essays on International Criminal Justice* (Portland: Hart Publishing, 2012).

[61] For more examples, see www.trustfundforvictims.org/projects

[62] Victims' Rights Working Group, *The implementation of victims' rights before the ICC: Issues and concerns presented by the Victims' Rights Working Group on the occasion of the 10th session of the Assembly of States Parties, 12-21 December 2011.*

[63] There are two ways this could be linked. Firstly through the concept of "positive complementarity", a term used to refer to assistance offered by the Court to States on how to proceed with investigations of international crimes domestically. Secondly, a more general way to establish an effect is to refer to national processes where victims' rights have assumed an important role, even in the absence of direct assistance from the ICC. For example, Argentina's tribunals over the past ten years, the Fujimori trials in Peru, and the most recent Rios Montt trial in Guatemala. In all these trials, international standards are being applied, in particular those regarding core international crimes. See: S. Carsten, "Complementarity: a tale of two notions," *Criminal Law Forum* 19 (2007), pp. 87-113; C. Collins, L. Balardini and J-M. Burt, "Mapping perpetrator prosecutions in Latin America," *International Journal of Transitional Justice* 7/1 (2013), pp. 8-28; J-M. Burt, "Guilty as charged: The trial of former Peruvian President Alberto Fujimori for human rights violations," *International Journal of Transitional Justice* 3/3 (2009), pp. 384-405.

[64] Available at: www2.ohchr.org/english/bodies/cat/docs/GC/CAT-C-GC-3_en.pdf Accessed 8 August 2013. See Annex 1 for signature and ratification details. Information on the Committee and previous General Comments available at www.ohchr.org/EN/HRBodies/CAT/Pages/CATIndex.aspx Accessed 8 August 2013.

[65] For further thinking in this area see: REDRESS and the Essex Transitional Justice Network, *Rehabilitation as a form of reparation: Opportunities and challenges*, Workshop Report (UK: REDRESS, 2010); P. De Greiff (2006).

[66] Adopted by UN Human Rights Council 12 April 2013; A/HRC/RES/22/21. Resolution 22/21— Torture and other cruel, inhuman or degrading treatment or punishment: rehabilitation of torture victims. Available at: http://ap.ohchr.org/documents/alldocs.aspx?doc_id=21560 Accessed 20 August 2013.

[67] For further detail see: P. Hayner, *Unspeakable Truths: Transitional Justice and the Challenge of Truth Commissions,* 2nd edition (New York: Routledge, 2011); M. Valiñas and K. Vanspauwen, "Truth-seeking after violent conflict: experiences from South Africa and Bosnia and Herzegovina," *Contemporary Justice Review* 12/3 (2009), pp. 269-287. Also see: United Nations, *The rule of law and transitional justice in conflict and post-conflict societies: Report of the Secretary-General,* S/2004/616, 23 August (2004).

68   A third process could be added to the list, involving the elaboration of the "Articles on Responsibility of States for internationally wrongful acts" adopted by the UN General Assembly 12 December 2001; A/RES/56/83, which also include the issue of reparation. See: www.un.org/ga/search/view_doc.asp?symbol=A/RES/56/83&Lang=E Accessed 16 August 2013. The Articles will not be discussed here, as they refer to responsibility between States, not between States and individuals. See: J. García-Godos (2008).

69   UN General Assembly Resolution 60/147 of 16 December 2005. For background see: D. Shelton, *Remedies in International Human Rights Law*, 2nd edition (Oxford: Oxford University Press, 2005); T. Van Boven, *Basic Principles and Guidelines on the Right to a Remedy and Reparation for Victims of Gross Violations of International Human Rights Law and Serious Violations of International Humanitarian Law* (United Nations Audiovisual Library of International Law, 2010).

70   Principle 11 notes: "remedies for gross violations of international human rights law and serious violations of international humanitarian law include the victim's right to the following as provided for under international law: equal and effective access to justice; adequate, effective and prompt reparation for harm suffered; and, access to relevant information concerning violations and reparation mechanisms."

71   For further analysis on rehabilitation after war see: E. Martz (Ed), *Trauma Rehabilitation After War and Conflict: Community and Individual Perspectives* (Portland: Springer, 2010); M. Berghs, *War and Embodied Memory: Becoming Disabled in Sierra Leone* (Surrey, UK: Ashgate: 2012).

72   Among these are the Velásquez-Rodríquez case judgement on compensation (1989), the Loayza Tamayo case decision on reparations (1998), and the Castillo Páez case judgement on reparations (1998). See: A.J. Carrillo, "Justice in Context: The Relevance of Inter-American Human Rights Law and Practice to Repairing the Past," In P. De Greiff (Ed), *The Handbook of Reparations* (Oxford: Oxford University Press, 2006), pp. 504-538.

73   Law No. 28592 of 2005, Ley que crea el Plan Integral de Reparaciones—PIR, Lima, Peru.

74   During the armed conflict, there were two active subversive groups in Peru, Sendero Luminoso (Shining Path) and Movimiento Revolucionario Túpac Amaru. See: International Center for Transitional Justice, *Reparations in Peru: From Recommendations to Implementation* (New York: ICTJ, 2013).

75   A. Minoletti, "Atención de salud mental a personas afectadas debido a la represión política ejercida por el Estado en los años 1973-1990," In E. Lira and G. Morales (Eds) *Derechos humanos y reparación: Una discusión pendiente* (Santiago: LOM Ediciones, 2005), p. 74.

76   See REDRESS Web page "Leopoldo Garcia Lucero v. Chile". Available at: www.redress.org/case-docket/leopoldo-garcia-lucero-v-chile?utm_source=smartmail&utm_medium=email&utm_campaign=REDRESS+Reparation+News+April+2013   Accessed   18 August 2013.

77   R. Duthie, "Introduction," In A. Mayer-Rieckh and P. de Greiff (Eds), *Justice as Prevention: Vetting Public Employees in Transitional Societies*, (New York: Social Science Research Council and International Center for Transitional Justice, 2007), pp. 17-38.

78   Office of the High Commissioner for Human Rights, *Rule-of-Law tools for post-conflict states: Amnesties* HR/PUB/09/1 (Geneva: United Nations, 2009).

79   C. Buchanan and J. Chavez, "Guns and violence in the El Salvador peace negotiations," *Negotiating Disarmament Case Study,* No. 2 (Geneva: Centre for Humanitarian Dialogue, 2008).

80   Handicap International, *Lessons Learned Workshop: A review of assistance programs for war wounded and other persons with disabilities living in mine-affected countries* (Paris: Handicap International, 2004), p. 14.

81   For further consideration of key principles in this area see: I. Waller (2011). Importantly, Waller provides model legislation for those working to strengthen legislative standards; P. Connolly, *Ethical principles for researching vulnerable groups*, University of Ulster, Commissioned by the Office of the First Minister and Deputy First Minister (2003); the two publications from UNODCCP and the Centre for International Crime Prevention (1999); Geneva International Centre for Humanitarian Demining, *Assisting landmine and other ERW survivors in the context of disarmament, disability and development* (Geneva: GICHD, 2012); Handicap International (2004).

SPOTLIGHT SECTION
Colombia's Victims' Law

In 2011 with the agreement of the *Ley de Víctimas y de Restitución de Tierras* (Victims' Law), the Colombian Government took a historic step in recognising the victims of the long running armed conflict.[1] The product of a broad, and contested, political process, the law is evidence of Colombia's strengthening democracy moving a step forward in recognising the needs and rights of victims of conflict-related violence.[2] It recognises, for the first time, State responsibility for the consequences of the internal war which has lasted more than four decades, and in which millions of citizens have suffered extrajudicial execution, forced disappearance, torture, forced displacement, sexual violence, and other forms of harassment and intimidation.[3]

Colombia already had a law to assist displaced persons, (Law 387 of 1997); but the transitional justice framework of this new law goes much further.[4] It aims to provide not only basic assistance, but also broad measures for compensation and land restitution.[5]

Article 3 invokes the term "victims" broadly, and includes people who have been killed as well as survivors:

- "any persons who have individually or collectively suffered damage as a result of violations of International Humanitarian Law or severe and manifest violations of the norms of International Human Rights, which occurred in the context of the internal armed conflict.
- the spouse, permanent partner, same sex partner, first degree relative or executor of the estate of the direct victim, when that person has died or disappeared; or in the absence of these, second-degree relatives.
- persons who have suffered damage when they intervened to help a victim in danger, or to prevent victimisation."

It also states a victim is "independent of whether the perpetrator of the violation has been identified, caught, prosecuted or sentenced, and regardless of any relationship that may exist between the perpetrator and the victim." The law covers victims of abuses committed by government forces as well as by non-state armed groups.[6] Members of illegal armed groups are not eligible for assistance, unless they were aged under 18 at the time when the violation occurred. Members of state security services are also ineligible.

The law specifically excludes people who have suffered damage as a result of "ordinary crimes"—i.e. acts not related to the conflict. This excludes many victims and survivors of gun violence: deaths associated with armed conflict represented only 11-13% of gun deaths between 2003 and 2008.[7]

Article 3 also specifies that financial compensation will only be paid for violations occurring in the context of armed conflict after 1 January 1985. Survivors who suffered from similar violations before that date are only entitled to know the truth and receive symbolic reparation, as well as guarantees that the violations will not recur.[8] Controversially, restitution of land applies only to people who suffered violations after 1 January 1991.[9]

Protesters carry burning crosses during a march to remember victims of political violence in Bogota. (Image: Fernando Vergara /AP, 6 March 2008)

Since becoming operational on 1 January 2012, the Government has delivered over 800,000 hectares (ha) of land and expects to deliver over 130,000ha more to about 10,000 dispossessed farmers in 2012; a total of 3.5 million hectares will be delivered by 2014.[10] The law also seeks to establish a right of return for about four million survivors who were forcibly displaced.[11] Some six million hectares of abandoned or usurped land could be redistributed as a result.[12]

While reparation processes typically come at the end of a conflict, Colombia—where the internal armed conflict continues—is an exception. This poses challenges for the implementation of the law. In addition to ongoing violence by armed groups, some of it deliberately directed at survivor claimants, organised crime is rising, increasing the overall levels of violence and insecurity.[13] Preventing the internal armed conflict from deteriorating further while delivering on the law's land restitution component will be a major challenge.[14]

Several peace processes have failed in the past. The Government of Juan Manuel Santos (2010-14) is making a new attempt to bring an end the armed conflict in Colombia and peace negotiations began in October 2012. If a final peace agreement is achieved, the Victims' Law should be amended accordingly.

Transitional justice processes are usually politically and institutionally complex and lengthy. At an operational level, the challenges are considerable. The procedures for claiming benefits are set out in supplementary legislation, Regulation 4800.[15] People must register with a new agency called the Victim Support and Reparation Unit (Unidad para la Atención y Reparación Integral a las Víctimas). For land restitution, an independent agency called the Management and Restitution Unit (Unidad para la Gestión y Restitución de Tierras) was created.[16] It conducts a review to determine and eventually deliver the appropriate land titles. However, claims can be complex and involve multiple and conflicting parties; and there are cases where titles remain unclear or cannot be established. In cases of financial compensation, the maximum payment is 40 times the minimum monthly wage per person, or the equivalent of about USD12,000.[17] In 2012, (first year of implementation), some 157,840 Colombians were compensated. It had been expected the number would be in the order of 130,000. For 2013, it is anticipated another 150,000 people will be compensated.[18]

This ambitious and comprehensive new law must also be set in the wider context of Colombian society, which remains severely affected by underdevelopment, income inequality, and the use of violence to address diverse grievances and interests. Breaking the historical reliance on armed violence and authoritarian political practices is essential to building strong social and institutional foundations, and promote the social inclusion and development needed to implement this law.

Contributors: Pilar Reina, Research Assistant, Small Arms Survey (Switzerland). **Rebecca Peters, Cate Buchanan** and **Emile LeBrun** edited the text and provided additional drafting.

Peer reviews were provided by **Matthias Nowak**, Associate Researcher, Small Arms Survey (Switzerland); **Jemima García-Godos**, Associate Professor, Department of Sociology and Human Geography, University of Oslo (Norway); **Elisa Gilgen**, former Senior Researcher, Small Arms Survey (Switzerland); **Katherine Aguirre**, Research Assistant, Small Arms Survey (Switzerland).

References

1   The Victims' Law (Ley 1448) was approved by the Congress of Colombia on 24 May 2011 and signed by President Juan Manuel Santos on 10 June. Available in Spanish at: www.leydevictimas.gov.co/#!__normatividad Accessed 28 May 2013. For a detailed account of the evolution of this law, see, C. Evans, "Case study: reparations in Colombia," In *The right to reparation in international law for victims of armed conflict* (Cambridge: Cambridge University Press, 2012), pp. 203-222.
2   See the press release by the Senate of Colombia, "Plenaria del Senado aprobó sin contratiempos la Ley de Víctimas," 25 May (2011). Available at: www.senado.gov.co/sala-de-prensa/noticias/item/11960-plenaria-del-senado-ya-aprobo-187-articulos-de-la-ley-de-victimas-/-nuevo-avance Accessed 28 May 2013. Also informed by a telephone interview by Pilar Reina with Camilo Sanchez, researcher at DeJusticia Center for Law, Justice and Society, and Professor of Law at the Universidad National de Colombia in Bogota on 3 March 2012.
3   The NGO REDEPAZ suggests that about 5 million survivors have been affected by the internal armed conflict between 1964 and 2006. See D. Otero, *Los costos de la guerra* (Bogota: REDEPAZ, 2007). REDEPAZ refers to Colombia as "a country of victims" because more than

10% of Colombians have been directly affected as a consequence of the armed conflict. See: REDEPAZ, *Víctimas del conflicto armado en Colombia: Perfil, escenarios, autores y hechos* (Bogota: REDEPAZ, 2008), p. 8. Available at: www.redepaz.org.co/IMG/pdf/VICTIMAS_DEL_ CONFLICTO_ARMADO_EN_COLOMBIA-2.pdf Accessed 28 May 2013. Also see International Center for Transitional Justice, *'Voices of Dignity': Victims Rights in Colombia*, video and photo galleries at http://ictj.org, released December 2012. Accessed 28 May 2013.

4 Law 387 of 1997 establishes measures for the prevention of forced displacement, care, protection, settlement and socio-economic stabilisation of people displaced by violence. The Act, however, addresses the problem of displacement as an issue of public order, rather than acknowledging State responsibility for IDPs needs, compensation, the right to due process and accountability and the right of return. The Victims' Law includes these foci. Available in Spanish at: www.secretariasenado.gov.co/senado/basedoc/ley/1997/ ley_0387_1997.html Accessed 28 May 2013. Regarding transitional justice: Transitional justice practices were introduced in Colombia through Law 975 of 2005, known as the *Law of Justice and Peace*, which regulated the demobilisation of illegal armed groups (paramilitaries and guerrillas) and the promotion of victims' rights and accountability. Partial amnesties and reduced sentences to members of illegal armed groups who had committed human rights violations during their time in combat would be provided in exchange for their demobilisation, participation in a semi-judicial process, information/ truth about crimes committed, and the provision of assets for victims' reparations. See: J. García-Godos and K.A. Orgaland Lid, "Transitional Justice and Victims' Rights before the End of a Conflict: The Unusual Case of Colombia," *Journal of Latin American Studies* 42 (2010), pp. 487-516.

5 It includes measures on psychosocial support, financial compensation, training and career support. It promises satisfaction in the search for truth and justice, by seeking to restore the dignity of victims and survivors and raise awareness of what happened to them. It also guarantees that the human rights violations will not recur.

6 Ministry of Justice website, "Ley de Víctimas y Restitución de Tierras" response to the question 'Who is a victim?' Available in Spanish at: www.leydevictimas.gov.co/#!__ quien-es-victima Accessed 28 May 2013. This point is not explicitly stated in the law itself, but was confirmed by staff of Senator Juan Cristo, one of the principal sponsors of the law. Email correspondence between Pilar Reina and Lucas Urdaneta, member of the Legal Support Unit for Senator Juan Cristo, 26 June 2012.

7 S. Granada, J. Restrepo and A. Vargas, "El agotamiento de la política de seguridad: evolución y transformaciones recientes en el conflicto armado colombiano," In J. Restrepo and D. Aponte (Eds), *Guerras y violencias en Colombia: herramientas e interpretaciones* (Bogota: Centro de Recursos para el Análisis de Conflictos, 2009), p. 68.

8 Symbolic reparation refers to measures that seek "to ensure the preservation of historical memory, the non-repetition of victimising events, public acceptance of the facts, public forgiveness and restoring the dignity of the victims" (Article 141).

9 Article 75. Camilo Sanchez stressed that fixing the dates of 1985 and 1991 generated heated debate, since it excluded survivors who were forcibly displaced earlier. Telephone interview on 3 March 2012.

10 Revista Semana with EFE and SIG, *Santos: la restitución de tierras deja a las Farc sin discurso*, 28 January (2012). Available at: www.semana.com/nacion/santos-restitucion-tierras-deja-farc-discurso/171183-3.aspx Accessed 20 April 2012. See also press release by the Senate of Colombia, "Doce preguntas fundamentales de la ley de víctimas," 24 April (2012). Available at: www.senado.gov.co/sala-de-prensa/ noticias/item/11618-doce-preguntas-fundamentales-de-la-ley-de-victimas/informe-especial?tmpl=component&print=1 Accessed 29 May 2013. Note: these figures contain some uncertainty because many dispossessed farmers do not have proper land ownership titles and many indigenous and Afro-Colombian communities own land collectively.

11 While there is international agreement that Colombia has one of the world's largest populations of internally displaced people, the numbers tend to differ among national and international sources. The UN High Commissioner for Refugees put the figure at up to 3.4 million (cumulative since 1997): UNHCR, *2012 UNHCR country operations profile—Colombia*. Available at: www.unhcr.org/cgi-bin/texis/vtx/page?page=49e492ad6 Accessed 29

May 2013. Conversely, national estimates put the number as high as 5 million: C.A. Torres and J.E. Vargas, "Housing for displaced population in Colombia. Public policy and law enforcement recommendations," *Revista Invi* 66/ 24 (2009), pp. 24-86. The latter is similar to the estimate used by NGOs: ABColombia, *Returning Land to Colombia's Victims* (London: ABColombia, 2011), pp. 1-12.

[12] The Commission to Monitor Public Policies on Forced Displacement states that between 1980 and July 2010, 6.6 million hectares of land were abandoned or usurped. However, the National Movement of Victims against State Crime claims the area is more than 10 million hectares. ABColombia (2011), p. 2.

[13] Groups called "armies against land restitution" have killed at least 17 local political leaders since the Congress approved the Law in May 2011. See A. Molano, "La amenaza de los ejércitos anti-restitución," *El Tiempo,* 31 March (2012). Available at: www.elespectador.com/ impreso/judicial/articulo-335700-amenaza-de-los-ejercitos-antirrestitucion Accessed 29 May 2013.

[14] The Law takes into account that the number of victims will increase, and they will need to be given the same recognition and benefits as those previously affected. Interview with Camilo Sanchez, 3 March 2012.

[15] Decreto Reglamentario 4800 de 2011 establishes the Unit and details the survivors' rights and obligations and the administrative procedures that should be followed (Title I and II). Available at: www.vertice.gov.co/Portals/o/Documentos/Decreto%204800%20de%202011. pdf Accessed 28 May 2013.

[16] Title IV, Chapter II of Decreto Reglamentario 1448 of 2011, created a legal process to restore and formalise the return of land return to those registered since 1 January, 1991. See http:// restituciondetierras.gov.co/?action=index Accessed 21 November 2013.

[17] Decreto Reglamentario 4800 de 2011, Article 149.

[18] It is expected that the Special Administrative Unit, in charge of administering compensation to survivors, will coordinate efforts with the Land Restitution Unit to address collective compensation and rehabilitation efforts. This would first target ethnic communities or members of unions, as they have been subjected to years of systematic violence. See EFE "Colombia planea reparar en 2013 a 150,000 víctimas del conflicto," *El Tiempo* 28 February (2013). Available at: www.eltiempo.com/archivo/documento/CMS-12626079. Accessed 28 May 2013.

SPOTLIGHT SECTION
Assistance to Survivors and Clauses in Peace Agreements

How do peace negotiators and mediators in peace processes deal with the issue of assistance to survivors in the aftermath of armed conflict? Some 356 peace agreements dated 1921 onwards were reviewed in 2008 assessing clauses related to, among other concerns, victims and survivors of war-related violence and trauma.[1] The preliminary review reveals that the needs of injured former combatants garner more attention than civilians; even then references are skeletal with a mere 20 peace agreements including clauses focussed on this group of war-affected individuals. The research noted transitional justice provisions—truth seeking processes, reparations schemes, memorials—however for the purposes of this Spotlight, the focus is on other pertinent themes including broader attention to injured civilians; scope of assistance provisions; ambiguous language; psychological trauma; dependants; non-discrimination; and funding mechanisms.[2] Some references to reparations are noted across these themes given the significance of the concept for advancing the rights of victims of war and repression.[3]

Broader focus on civilians
A singular focus on former combatants in peace agreements is discriminatory when civilians have been equally affected. Encouragingly, some agreements explicitly recognise this. As an example, the 1992 El Salvador Chapultepec agreement states that the National Reconstruction Plan shall include "programmes for the war-disabled... among the civilian population."[4] Similarly, a 1993 Rwanda peace agreement with the Rwandan Patriotic Front commits the parties to "set up a programme of assistance to the victims of war (both civilian and military) and of social strife encountered since the outbreak of the war, to the physically handicapped, orphans, widows and widowers."[5] The 2002 Burundi peace agreement with the National Council for the Defense of Democracy-Forces for the Defense of Democracy (CNDD-FDD) calls for "particular attention" to combatants and civilians impaired by war-related violence,[6] and the 2003 Democratic Republic of the Congo (DRC) Sun City Agreement refers to both civil and military war-affected individuals.[7] Internally displaced people and refugees are infrequently singled out for assistance.[8]

Scope of assistance
Some agreements do not specify the type of assistance to be provided—which can alternately be frustrating, as well as an opportunity for wide ranging responses. In Sierra Leone, for example, the 1999 peace agreement required the Government to "design and implement a programme for the rehabilitation of war victims", without specifying any parameters.[9] In Liberia, the 2003 peace agreement stated that the "NGTL [National Transitional Government of Liberia] in formulating and implementing

programs for national rehabilitation... shall ensure that the needs and potentials of the war victims are taken into account and that gender balance is maintained in apportioning responsibilities for program implementation."[10]

Some agreements provide more detail, often related to medical care, recognising that people experiencing disability require more than immediate medical care. A 1993 Rwandan peace agreement provides that "the handicapped or invalid shall take advantage of special programmes designed for socio-economic integration. They shall fall under the responsibility of the Secretariat of State for Rehabilitation and Social Integration as soon as possibilities of their integration will have been identified."[11] A 1996 Guatemalan agreement also calls for "specific priority attention" to be given to people with impairments and injuries, among others, in reintegration programmes. The agreement recognised that: "The integration of this group is a more complex matter, because of the personal and social impact of their disability", and states that these special sub-programmes will "provide proper professional care for their rehabilitation and access to education and training so that they can be genuinely integrated into social and productive life in decent conditions."[12]

Psychological trauma

Armed violence does not only have physical consequences; psychological damage is a common, though overlooked, consequence.[13] Few peace agreements recognise the issue of trauma as an impact of war that also needs to be addressed, and those that do generally limit wording to calls for psychosocial assistance.[14] Some positive examples nonetheless exist. The 2003 DRC Sun City Agreement included an appeal to donors for the creation of "strategic centres for psychological assistance and treatment for traumatised persons as well as centres for psychological rehabilitation", and further called to "set up psychological rehabilitation centres for women, girls, children and all other traumatised persons."[15] The 2006 Darfur Peace Agreement allows compensation claims for people who "have suffered harm, including physical [or] mental injury", and states that compensation could include "rehabilitation including medical and psychological care."[16] Finally, in 2007 and 2008, Uganda peace agreements foresaw a policy for the support and rehabilitation of victims, including special assistance programme for "traumatized children", and provided for a special fund for the payment of reparations to "victims of the conflict", a category that specifically notes children with war-related trauma.[17]

Dependants

The reality of remaining dependants is also poorly covered, included in about a dozen peace agreements, in general terms.[18] Some agreements however include specific references to financial aid. In Nicaragua, monthly pensions were granted to widows and orphans of the armed resistance.[19] In El Salvador, social security was offered to "families of combatants who have died", and reference is made to a National Reconstruction Plan to include provisions for the "relatives of victims among the civilian population."[20] In Afghanistan, a specific fund was provided to assist "families and dependents of martyrs and victims of the war."[21] As already noted, the Uganda settlement provides for a reparations fund to "victims of the conflict", which include "child-headed households, orphans... widows, [and] female-headed households."[22]

Non-discrimination

To ensure the principle of non-discrimination is realised in practice, care is required to ensure that language specifying assistance to people whose injuries or impairments are due to war-related violence, is placed within the wider context of addressing the needs and rights of all people living with disability. This has yet to become a consistent reference point in peace agreements. The 2003 DRC Sun City Agreement stands out by calling on the government to "define a coherent policy for... people living with a handicap... and for war invalids (civil or military)."[23]

Funding mechanisms

Calls for assistance have a greater chance of implementation if adequate funding and monitoring mechanisms are also provided. The 1996 Sierra Leone agreement provides that the Committee for Demobilisation and Resettlement shall "raise resources internationally" for the rehabilitation of war-affected people, and the 1999 agreement states that the proceeds from the transactions of gold and diamonds shall feed into a fund for the "compensation of incapacitated war victims."[24] The 2002 Burundi peace agreement with CNDD-FDD calls on the international community for assistance.[25] The 2001 Bonn agreement for Afghanistan sets up a "fund to assist... the war disabled."[26] A 2008 Uganda peace agreement provides for a special fund for the payment of reparations to "victims of the conflict."[27]

In conclusion, there is considerable room for strengthening language on survivor related-references in peace agreements, as a starting point for more coherent policy and programming following war and repression. Two points seem most pressing: a) ensuring reference to international standards, in particular the 1985 UN *Declaration of Basic Principles of Justice for Victims of Crime and Abuse of Power;* 1998 *Rome Statue of the International Criminal Court;* 2005 UN *Basic Principles and Guidelines on the Right to a Remedy and Reparation for Victims of Gross Violations of International Human Rights Law and Serious Violations of International Humanitarian Law;* and the 2006 UN *Convention on the Rights of Persons with Disabilities,* and b) agreeing text which assigns leadership to relevant State agencies, and other pertinent actors (civil society, donors), to make tangible gains for all people experiencing disability, in particular those who have suffered permanent injury and trauma from conflict-related violence.

Contributors: Cate Buchanan and **Mireille Widmer**, Surviving Gun Violence Project.

References

[1]   Over 2006-2007, Mireille Widmer and Cate Buchanan, in the context of their work in the former Arms Programme of the Centre for Humanitarian Dialogue, undertook projects supported by the Government of Norway on survivors of armed violence and weapons-management in peace agreements. This included an experts meeting, briefing papers, reflection pieces, research on trends in peace agreements and a set of background papers (focussed on surviving gun violence in El Salvador and Burundi; DDR and disability; and trauma—all available at www.survivinggunviolence.org in the e-resources section). This Spotlight is an updated excerpt from an unpublished review of 356 peace agreements in English, French and Spanish ranging from the 1921 Convention between Finland and

Sweden to the 1 March 2008 Addendum to the Cessation of Hostilities agreement between Uganda and the Lord's Resistance Army. The review was undertaken by Mireille Widmer and Sarah Parker, with supplementary input from Cate Buchanan. The text was revised in July 2013. The overall study will be finalised over 2014/15.

[2]   For further detail on transitional justice provisions in agreements see: C. Evans, *The right to reparation in international law for victims of armed conflict* (Cambridge: Cambridge University Press, 2012); C. Bell, *Peace agreements and human rights* (Oxford: Oxford University Press, 2000); J. García-Godos, "Victim reparations in transitional justice—what is at stake and why," *Nordic Journal of Human Rights* 26/2 (2008), pp. 111- 130; and the work of the University of Ulster, INCORE and the Transitional Justice Institute in developing the Transitional Justice Peace Agreements Database. Available at: www.peaceagreements. ulster.ac.uk/

[3]   Other issues of relevance, though not covered here, include medical care particularly in provisions related to cantonment and demobilisation conditions, disability pensions and other allowances or forms of social protection, and eligibility for integration into new armed and police services.

[4]   Chapultepec Agreement, 16 January 1992.

[5]   Protocol of Agreement on Power-Sharing within the Framework of a Broad-Based Transitional Government between the Government of the Republic of Rwanda and the Rwandese Patriotic Front, 9 January 1993.

[6]   Ceasefire Agreement between the Transitional Government of Burundi and the Conseil National pour la Défense de la Démocratie—Forces pour la Défense de la Démocratie, 2 December 2002.

[7]   Inter-Congolese Negotiations: The Final Act (The Sun City Agreement), 2 April 2003.

[8]   General Peace Agreement for Mozambique, 4 October 1992; Protocol of Agreement between the Government of Rwanda and the Rwandese Patriotic Front on the Repatriation of Rwandese Refugees and the Resettlement of Displaced Persons, 9 June 1993.

[9]   Peace Agreement between the Republic of Sierra Leone and the Revolutionary United Front of Sierra Leone (RUF/SL) also referred to as the Lome Agreement, 7 July 1999.

[10]   Comprehensive Peace Agreement Between the Government of Liberia and the Liberians United for Reconciliation and Democracy (LURD) and the Movement for Democracy in Liberia (MODEL) and Political Parties, 18 August 2003.

[11]   Protocol of Agreement between the Government of the Republic of Rwanda and the Rwandese Patriotic Front on the Integration of the Armed Forces of the Two Parties, 3 August 1993, art. 158.

[12]   Agreement on the Basis for the Legal Integration of Unidad Revolucionaria Nacional Guatemalteca (URNG), 12 December 1996, art. 12 and 50-51.

[13]   Centre for Humanitarian Dialogue, *Trauma as a consequence—and cause—of gun violence,* Background paper No. 1 commissioned from Vivo International (Geneva: HD Centre, 2006).

[14]   See Acuerdo Final Gobierno Nacional- Ejército Popular de Liberación (Colombia), 22 January 1991; Acuerdo Final entre el Gobierno Nacional y el Partido Revolucionario de los Trabajadores (Colombia), 25 January 1991; Acuerdo Final entre el Gobierno Nacional y el Movimiento Armado Quintin Lame (Colombia), 27 May 1991; Acuerdo Político Final Gobierno Nacional Corriente de Renovación Socialista/CRS (Colombia), 9 April 1994.

[15]   Inter-Congolese Negotiations: The Final Act (The Sun City Agreement), 2 April 2003.

[16]   Darfur Peace Agreement, 5 May 2006.

[17]   Agreement on Comprehensive Solutions, 2 May 2007; Implementation Protocol to the Agreement on Comprehensive Solutions, 22 February 2008.

[18]   The 1990 Tocontin Agreement in Nicaragua grants assistance to "injured orphans and widows" (The Tocontin Agreement, 23 March 1990); the 1991 Colombia agreement with the PRT gives attention to relatives of victims of violence (Acuerdo Final entre el Gobierno Nacional y el Partido Revolucionario de los Trabajadores, 25 January 1991); in Guatemala, particular emphasis was placed on protecting female-headed families and widows and orphans (Agreement on the Resettlement of Population Groups Uprooted by the Armed Conflict, 17 June 1994); Sudan agreements provide for assistance for the rehabilitation of "widows, orphans and other war victims" (The Sudan Peace Agreement, 21 April 1997; Protocol between the Government of the Sudan and the Sudan People's Liberation

Movement on Power Sharing, 26 May 2004; Protocol between the Government of Sudan and the Sudan People's Liberation Movement on the resolution of Conflict in Southern Kordofan/Nuba Mountains and Blue Nile States, 26 May 2004; Darfur Peace Agreement, 5 May 2006); a 2006 Nepal agreement makes provisions for the "relief and resettlement of family members who have died, disappeared or been disabled due to the conflict" (Decisions of the Seven Party Alliance—Maoist Summit Meeting, 8 November 2006).

[19] The Managua Protocol on Disarmament, 30 May 1990.

[20] New York Agreement, 25 September 1991; Chapultepec Agreement, 16 January 1992.

[21] Agreement on Provisional Arrangements in Afghanistan Pending the Re-establishment of Permanent Government Institutions (Bonn Agreement), 5 December 2001.

[22] Implementation Protocol to the Agreement on Comprehensive Solutions, 22 February 2008.

[23] Inter-Congolese Negotiations: The Final Act (The Sun City Agreement), 2 April 2003.

[24] Abidjan Peace Agreement, 30 November 1996; Lomé Peace Agreement, 7 July 1999.

[25] Ceasefire Agreement between the Transitional Government of Burundi and the Conseil National pour la Défense de la Démocratie-Forces pour la Défense de la Démocratie, 2 December 2002.

[26] Agreement on Provisional Arrangements in Afghanistan Pending the Re-establishment of Permanent Government Institutions (Bonn Agreement), 5 December 2001.

[27] Implementation Protocol to the Agreement on Comprehensive Solutions, 22 February 2008.

SPOTLIGHT SECTION

Norwegian State Response
to the 22 July 2011 Attacks

At 15.27 on 22 July 2011, Anders Behring Breivik detonated a huge homemade bomb inside a van he had parked outside Oslo's central government building. The bomb devastated the tall building, which housed the Prime Minister's office and other ministries, as well as the adjacent government office buildings. The explosion shattered windows all over central Oslo. After the detonation 32 year old Breivik, dressed as a police officer, travelled to the inland island of Utøya, some 45 minutes away, claiming he had been sent out to assess the security situation following the explosion in Oslo. The island, measuring some 500m x 300m, is owned by the youth wing of the Norwegian Labour Party, and for decades has hosted a political summer camp for Party members. There were 564 persons on the island, mainly youth aged 13-25, when Breivik landed.

Breivik was armed with a Glock 17 semiautomatic pistol and a Ruger Mini 14 semi-automatic rifle; he carried extra loaded magazines for both weapons, and several hundred rounds of 9mm Parabellum and 223 Remington ammunition. Hollow-tipped bullets were deliberately chosen to cause maximum damage and large exit wounds blazed a path of internal damage. (See the Box on wound ballistics in the Traumatic Injuries chapter for more detail.)

His first action at Utøya at 17.20 was to shoot dead the woman running the camp, known in the Labour movement as Mother Utøya. In the following hour he walked around and shot 129 people. Breivik was arrested on Utøya by a special forces police team at 18.37. He did not attempt to resist arrest.

The bomb blast left eight people dead and 30 physically injured; at Utøya 69 people were murdered and 60 seriously injured. Several of the injured have permanent impairments, including amputations of arms and legs as well as brain damage and long-term, possibly permanent, memory loss. More than 100 people sustained smaller physical injuries and several hundred more are regarded as psychologically traumatised.

Immediate response from the State

The emergency responses to the two attacks were completely different. The bombsite was in the centre of Oslo, right next to the central fire station and with several hospitals close by. Trained paramedics, fire brigades, police, doctors and nurses were on the site promptly. The blast took place on a Friday afternoon during the summer vacation period, so there were relatively few people in and around the government complex, compared to a normal working day.

Utøya, by contrast, was marked by chaos, breakdown of communications and lack of coordination between response services. The police response was particularly slow and inefficient. The island is only accessible by boat, the crossing measuring about 500m at the shortest point. The report of the Government-appointed "22/7 Commission" later revealed that while the emergency telephone system more or less collapsed under pressure, the police wasted crucial time getting to the island, and while armed, stayed on the landside observing the situation even when boats where available. As more than 20 people were murdered in the final 15 minutes of the massacre, the decisions taken by the police had devastating consequences. The tactical response police team (Beredskapstroppen/Delta) arriving an hour after Breivik started shooting was the first outside assistance received by the people at Utøya. The Commission concluded: "The authorities' ability to protect the people on Utøya Island failed. A more rapid police operation was a realistic possibility. The perpetrator could have been stopped earlier on 22 July."[1]

Meanwhile the young people at Utøya had to take care of themselves as best they could. Several hundred escaped by swimming in the 16°C water, and tourists camping on the other shore used their own boats to pick them up, risking their own lives in the process. Several ambulances were on the shore, but were not allowed by the police to park at the jetty, since the area was "not secure"; so the tourists and individual medics established a makeshift reception area and had to walk the injured survivors up to the "secure area". However, after that point the response was effective, and the intensive care units saved the lives of all admitted, except one person, from both attacks.

Intermediate responses from the State
In Norway the responsibility for care and rehabilitation of all trauma victims lies with the municipalities, while the funding for these services is allocated from a combination of local, regional and state budgets. Survivors of violence have the right to seek financial compensation through a State-funded mechanism (Voldsoffererstatning). In the case of a victim who dies, the surviving relatives may be eligible for compensation. The compensation may cover loss of present and future income, expenses stemming from the injury, travel and other expenses. Survivors may also be eligible to receive special compensation for long-lasting medical injuries and certain non-economic damages.

A survivor of violence has the right to be represented in the trial of the perpetrator, through an "assistance-lawyer"—to avoid revictimisation and to be recognised as having a stake in the process beyond being a mere witness. This lawyer participates in the formal proceedings, and can ask questions of the defendant as well as witnesses.

In the weeks following the attacks there was a strong focus on, and recognition of, the victims—those who had been killed and those who survived. The Government organised a national mourning service, funeral costs were covered and government officials participated in the funerals. An independent commission was established to investigate all aspects of the attacks, including the official responses. The upper limit for victim compensation was raised from NOK3.2 million (USD524,000) to NOK4.7 million (USD770,000). Municipal psychosocial rehabilitation services were asked to prioritise the survivors of the attacks. With the majority of the victims and survivors being young, schools and universities were asked to prioritise attention to the needs of survivors, ranging from deferred exams to counselling services. Despite this support, there are indications that survivors attending courses have significantly underperformed. In addition, relatives of victims established a national peer support group which has become recognised as speaking for the victims and survivors.[2]

During the trial
The trial of Anders Breivik started in Oslo on 16 April and lasted for 10 weeks—the largest single trial in the history of Norway. Court cases are typically available to the public. The live reporting of this case were restricted, however steps were taken to ensure that as many people as possible could follow the proceedings. There were live transmissions to 17 courthouses around Norway to make the trial accessible to survivors outside Oslo. A total of 166 assistance lawyers represented the survivors, and three of them coordinated and followed the proceedings daily. The court took care to protect the dignity of the survivors who testified, as well as of the victims who died. The court case was structured so that every single murder was dealt with, every casualty was named and identified, and their injuries and cause of death were presented individually. A pathologist used a mannequin to illustrate the injuries. At the end of each presentation, the assistance lawyers read out some text describing the victim, including his or her aspirations in life.

Survivors who testified could ask that the defendant not be present during their testimony. During testimonies from survivors and presentations on the deaths, the court days were shortened to reflect the gravity of the information presented.

The meticulous approach of the court, combined with the clear central role given to victims and survivors, gave an extra dimension to the national process of coming to terms with this tragedy, beyond the dispensing of justice. Most survivors who testified referred to the importance of the court case as providing closure and a step towards rebuilding their own lives. For many this included seeing the perpetrator eye-to-eye, in the structured setting of the court. Some chose to address him directly in their testimony. Media coverage has centred on the resilience, collective solidarity and sheer courage demonstrated by the Utøya youths, and it was this message rather than the violence committed on 22 July that dominated the discourse.

Reflections
The bomb attack and Utøya massacre were completely unprecedented; one has to go back to World War II to find armed violence at a similar level in Norway. Over the past decades the annual number of homicides has been around 25-30, mostly by stabbing. Since 1980 there have been two bomb attacks, with one casualty. The attacks shook the foundations of Norwegian society and the State. Since the perpetrator was immediately apprehended and freely admitted to the violence, Norway escaped the traumatic experience of a long and potentially fruitless search for the culprit. The focus could instead be placed on managing the national trauma and putting the machinery of justice to work.

As noted, severe shortcomings affected the State's emergency response to the mass shooting at Utøya. However, after the attacks, both the short and medium term responses by the State improved. Perhaps inevitably there were some exceptions: with the large number of victims and survivors, and a mainly decentralised public health system, some individuals did not receive the assistance to which they were entitled or was necessary to their recovery process.

The attacks resulted in greater public recognition of victims of armed violence, their needs and their rights. The central role of the victims in the court case is a landmark in the Norwegian justice system. It highlighted the wide variation of support needs within a heterogeneous group of survivors. Some have taken on strong identities as both victims *and* survivors—in a media-savvy way, others in a more low-key fashion. Some chose to stay away from the public eye to cope in their own way. Many are clearly traumatised. One survivor who published a book about the massacre and often commented on the trial in the international media was charged with, and admitted to, brutally assaulting two persons in a bar in November 2011. The assault took place the same day the person had seen Breivik in a pre-trial court meeting.

However, while direct victims were acknowledged and supported, this was not the case of the ordinary civilians who risked their own lives to assist the young people fleeing Utøya before the police took control. While their heroic actions have been praised in the media and in speeches, the State took a long time to recognise that they may be traumatised and deeply affected as well. In June 2012, 19 individuals, mainly tourists and locals from the area, where awarded the official "medal for brave deed/act" (*medaljen for edel dåd*) for their actions at Utøya. The medal is rarely awarded in Norway.

Eirin Kristin Kjær, 20 years old, was shot four times while trying to protect some younger friends. Part of "One Day in History", portraits of young people who survived the massacre at Utøya, 22 July 2011. (Image: Andrea Gjestvang/Moment, 2013)

Anders Behring Breivik was convicted on 24 August, 2012. The court declared him sane and responsible for his actions and a danger to society. He received the maximum penalty of 21 years, with the option of additional protective detention, and will probably never leave prison.

Survivors continue to piece together their lives. Just after 17.30, Eirin Kristin Kjær was shot four times in the stomach, armpit, arm and knee while protecting younger friends. Reflecting on her recovery: "Sometimes it bothers me that I can be so functional, like everybody else. This happened to me and I'm just like any other 21-year-old girl... [but] it's like a movie. I see all the faces, the blood, the injuries, but I cannot connect with it emotionally. I don't understand that it is what happened to me."[3]

In September 2013, four survivors, and Labour Party members, were elected to the national parliament. They were among 33 candidates who survived the attacks and campaigned for political office.

Contributor: **Christian Holmboe Ruge**, Director, Humanitarian Disarmament Programme, International Law and Policy Institute, Norway.

References

[1] *Norges offentlige utredninger, Rapport 22-juli-kommisjonen,* Preliminary English version of selected chapters, Oslo, 13 August (2012), p. 11.
[2] See http://22juli.info for more information.
[3] M. Townsend, "Utøya: after the massacre," *The Observer* 28 April (2013). Available at: www.guardian.co.uk/artanddesign/2013/apr/28/utoya-after-the-massacre-photographs Accessed 30 April, 2013.

"Indeed, the most intense feeling we know of, intense to the point of blotting out all other experiences, namely, the experience of great bodily pain, is at the same time the most private and least communicable of all."

Hannah Arendt

The Human Condition (Chicago: The University of Chicago Press, 1998).

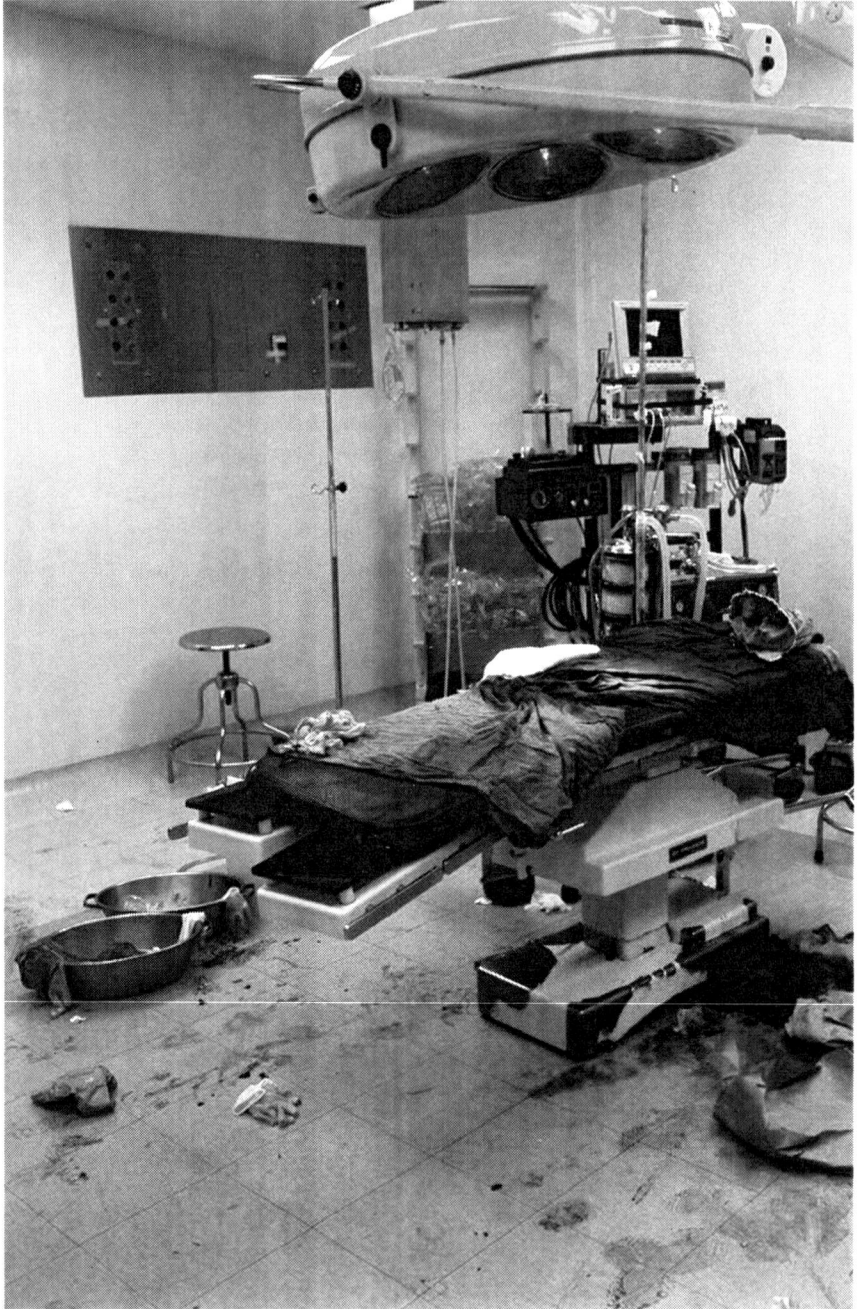

An operating room after a three-hour surgery on a man with gunshot wounds, who later died at the San Juan de Dios hospital in Guatemala City, Guatemala. (Image: Rodrigo Abd/AP, 5 May 2010)

3 Traumatic Injuries

Introduction
This chapter provides an overview of medical experiences and good practice in care (pre—and in-hospital) of traumatic injuries caused by gun violence. It examines some concepts in the science of ballistic injury and reviews contemporary approaches to the effective management of gunshot wounds, including standards for the care of the injured. Focus is also cast on specific topics: the experience of a trauma surgeon in Jamaica and low-cost first response possibilities.

Section 1: Understanding trauma
It all happens in a split second. A bullet is shot, lashing through the air, and penetrates the skin. It can dramatically change a life—if it does not end it. This section looks at the damage bullets can cause after they penetrate the skin and the chain of actions that is then necessary, very quickly, to save a life or a limb, prevent or minimise impairment, and limit suffering. It presents an ideal case scenario, but also recognises the reality in most of the world, where resources are scarce and services are poor.

Trauma in the context of this chapter is defined as the injuries—physical and physiological—due to the effects of bullets on the human body. These include injuries to the skin, soft tissues and bones, neurological damage, as well as the effects on the vital internal organs. The physiological effects include blood-loss and the inflammatory response as the body attempts to reduce the impact of the injury.[1] Psychological "trauma" or mental health effects, is not the topic of this chapter, but is covered in the chapter on Rehabilitation and Recovery.

The trauma spectrum varies from minor injuries (tissue abrasions, small lacerations) treated with simple wound care, to moderate or severe injuries involving damage to bones, nerves or organs that require admission to specialised critical care units and repeated surgical and reconstructive procedures.[2] In low to middle income countries (LMICs) such as South Africa, the relative distribution of all traumatic injuries (including firearm injuries) is reported to be one death for every four severely injured persons, and another 20 with minor injuries.[3] Mortality due to traumatic injuries could be 2.5 to six times higher in LMICs than in high income settings. The difference is due to scarcity of resources and the ineffective organisation of emergency response systems.[4]

The immediate response to firearm injuries is highly dependent upon the location and circumstances of the incident. If the incident occurs in an urban environment, police or emergency medical services generally arrive at the scene relatively promptly. By contrast, in rural areas such services rarely arrive in a timely manner. Depending on the capacity of the emergency system, health care professionals or community members may be involved in transportation to health care facilities.

Box 1. Profile: Trevor McCartney

Kingston, the capital of Jamaica, has experienced a steady increase in gun violence over the past 20 years. With a population of 2.87 million people, Jamaica is estimated to have a homicide rate of 52.1 per 100,000.[5] The global average homicide rate is estimated at 6.9 per 100,000.[6]

The typical survivor of gunshot injuries undergoes several surgical procedures, including staged repair of injuries with multiple blood transfusions, a prolonged stay in the intensive care unit, and another lengthy stay in the general wards. This extended period in hospital creates an economic burden, not only for the hospital, but also for the victim's immediate family and community. Surgery on gunshot victims often involves multiple organs. My team and I place particular emphasis on assessment and stabilisation of the cardiopulmonary systems, which may include emergency room surgery. The support of the anaesthetic and intensive care staff is crucial in the continued care of the victim.

The length of time taken by the procedures results in longer waiting time for other patients, some of whom have life-threatening conditions.[7] In my clinic, one in three patients scheduled for surgery is postponed or significantly delayed as a result of surgery on victims of gunshot injuries.

Over the period 2000-09, Jamaica averaged over 1,000 gun deaths annually, peaking at 1,681 in 2009.[8] Some 1,100 to 1,500 survivors present to the emergency room each year.[9] On average we succeed in saving the lives of 85% of these patients; the remainder die mainly from brain injuries (10%) or major vascular damage (5%).

Most victims of gun violence are adult males; many are involved in gang warfare or the illicit drug trade. Innocent bystanders also get caught in crossfire. Gun violence has an impact not only on the victims and their families, but also on the people involved in attempting to save them. Survivors of gunshot injuries need counselling, both in hospital and after discharge, and the psychological health of the medical team must also be monitored.

Community initiatives involving the police, social workers, and violence prevention committees have resulted in a significant reduction in gun violence in certain areas. In South Central Clarendon parish, the May Pen Hospital experienced a 36% reduction in the annual number of people with gunshot injuries, from 76 to 49 cases over the four years 2007-10.[10] The initiative included the use of geographic information systems technology to identify gun violence "hot spots", and work with the police and peacebuilding organisations to support community action in those areas. Interventions included sporting and cultural events, grief counselling, health services, training programmes, job placement, and local governance strengthening activities. These initiatives are being replicated in other highly volatile communities, but data are not yet available to evaluate outcomes.

Ideally, in a well-developed emergency system, a patient will be appropriately classified at the site of the incident according to the severity of their injuries, treated en route by a trained ambulance crew, and transported to the correct level of care facility. Appropriately trained medical, nursing and ancillary practitioners will ensure early diagnosis and timely surgical intervention.

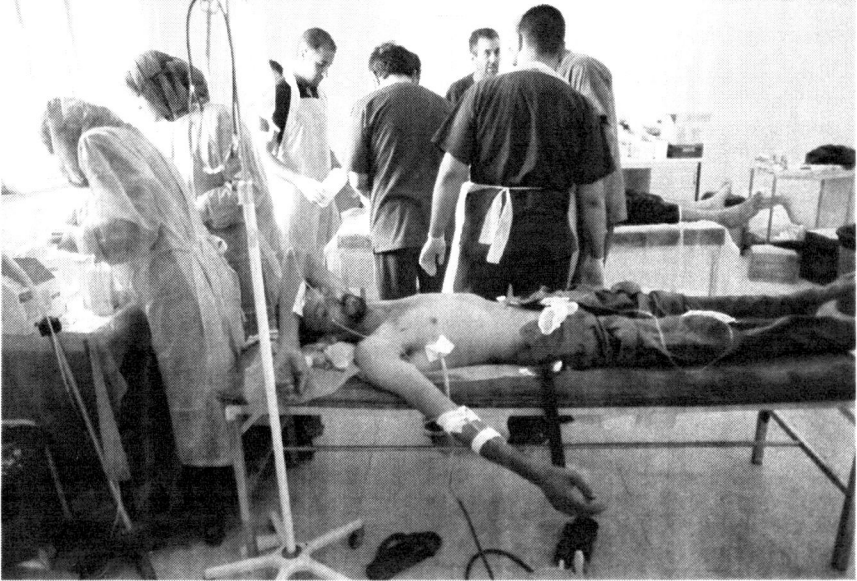

A Libyan rebel fighter paralysed from the waist down by a gunshot wound to his spine lies in the operating room at the Bir Muammar Hospital on the outskirts of Zawiyah. (Image: Bob Strong/ Reuters, 15 August 2011)

This goal is not always accomplished in LMICs, where ambulances may be limited to urban areas and their crews do not always have advanced training. Instead, especially in rural areas, it may be up to the family to load the injured person into a vehicle and transport them directly to the nearest (often inadequately equipped) health care facility. One South African study revealed that up to 40% of trauma patients arrive at hospital in their own vehicle or other mode of transport.[11] In other LMICs this figure may be up to 90%.[12] This course of action may be beneficial if the patient is delivered to an appropriate care facility, because waiting for emergency medical services may result in higher blood loss at the scene.[13] However, these transport methods increase the likelihood of the patient ending up in a low-level clinic which cannot perform surgery—thus requiring a further transfer, delaying surgery and increasing the likelihood of permanent impairment or death. The development of cost-effective trauma systems in LMICs can mitigate such events by ensuring that patients are taken immediately to the most appropriate facility (see Box 2).[14]

Box 2: First responders[15]

Significant advances in trauma care in recent decades have demonstrated the potential to reduce fatalities and level of impairment; however, these advances remain limited to particular settings such as high income nations, some urban areas in LMICs, or military hospitals.[16] Studies and programmes in a number of countries have shown that low cost, sustainable improvements can be made to health care through training of first responders, and through better organisation of existing resources and equipment.[17] First responders include those most often proximate to injury incidents such as taxi and truck drivers, shopkeepers, and bar workers; as well as those who may attend an injured person such as community health workers, traditional healers, or pharmacists.

According to the World Health Organization, 50-80% of traumatic deaths in LMICs happen before hospital arrival and effective pre-hospital trauma care can "substantially reduce death and disability following injury."[18] One study found that pre-hospital trauma care can be improved by training those most likely to first arrive at the site of an injury incident.[19] For example, in Ghana, training long distance truck drivers (often first on the scene of road accidents) in basic emergency trauma care helped to bolster the weak emergency medical services and improve survival rates. In Kurdistan and Cambodia, where many people are injured by landmine explosions, significant improvements in emergency trauma care resulted from increased training and the provision and reorganisation of supplies and equipment. In these settings, while ambulances still remained unavailable, death rates among injured people fell from 40% to 9% due to training of first responders and advanced training in trauma care to existing medical staff.[20] Adapting this to gun violence could involve training of people in key occupations in violence "hot spots" such as shopkeepers in violence-prone neighbourhoods, and bus and taxi drivers.

People injured by gunshots are often admitted to a general ward after chest, abdominal, or orthopaedic surgery. More serious injuries may require more specialised care, including admission to critical care units for advanced clinical procedures like mechanical ventilation or the use of special intravenous medications to maintain stability of blood pressure and heart contraction.

Shortfalls in resources for trauma care may lead to lives lost that could otherwise have been saved, or to the risk of temporary or permanent impairment (for more detail see the Rehabilitation and Recovery chapter as well as the Spotlight, Quality Rehabilitation and Links to Violence Reduction). Delays in surgery for a patient with an abdominal gunshot wound can lead to infection or death. Failure to provide early external oxygenation to a patient who has been shot in the head can lead to brain damage.

In the longer term, a lack of assistive devices such as wheelchairs or suitable beds and chairs, combined with poor access to rehabilitation, leads to pressure sores, systemic infection, and premature death. While developed countries have the luxury of well-established rehabilitation services, health professionals in LMICs face a daily dilemma in providing care to patients once the acute hospital care has been completed. Due to the scarcity of residential rehabilitation facilities, acute care beds remain occupied with patients who need physical, occupational, speech therapy and rehabilitation after spinal cord, orthopaedic, or brain injury caused by gunshot wounds.

Section 2: Key developments and standards in the area of trauma[21]

The right to health is a fundamental human right recognised in the 1948 *Universal Declaration of Human Rights*, and the 1966 *International Covenant on Economic, Social, and Cultural Rights*.[22] This right is also guaranteed in times of war: the four Geneva Conventions of 1949 guarantee adequate care to the wounded and sick, whether combatants or civilians (see Annex 1 for further detail on international standards).[23]

Obligations for States deriving from the right to health were detailed in 2000 by the Committee on Economic, Social, and Cultural Rights through General Comment No. 14.[24] It stipulates: "The realisation of the right to health may be pursued through numerous, complementary approaches, such as the formulation of health policies, or the implementation of health programmes developed by the World Health Organization (WHO), or the adoption of specific legal instruments." It further states four characteristics that health systems must fulfil in order for States to live up to their obligations: availability, accessibility, acceptability, and quality.

States therefore have a responsibility for normative action, which encompasses trauma care. Adequate regulation and policies can ensure that health facilities and services for survivors of gun violence are available in sufficient quantity, accessible—known, within safe physical reach, affordable, and treating survivors without discrimination—culturally acceptable and of good quality. Attention to trauma care pursues three objectives in particular:[25]

- Life-threatening injuries are appropriately and promptly treated, in accordance with appropriate priorities, so as to maximise the likelihood of survival;
- Potentially disabling injuries are treated appropriately, so as to minimise functional impairment and to maximise the return to independence and to participation in community life; and
- Pain and psychological suffering are minimised.

To assist States—and Ministries of Health in particular—in formulating adequate norms and policies, in 2004 the WHO developed guidelines for essential trauma care.[26] The guidelines focus on low-cost improvements, so as to be relevant in virtually every setting. They were followed in 2005 by the WHO guidelines on pre-hospital trauma care systems.[27] Then in 2007, the World Health Assembly—the governing body of the WHO—adopted resolution 60.22 spelling out concrete steps for States to strengthen their trauma care services.[28] In 2009 the WHO also organised a Global Forum on Trauma Care with the goal of promoting greater political commitment to affordable and sustainable improvements in trauma care.[29] In 2013, the WHO launched the Global Alliance for Care of the Injured (GACI). Spearheaded by the Governments of Romania, Brazil, Mozambique and Thailand and the WHO, GACI aims to mobilise attention and support to governments to improve care of the injured through systematic provision of essential trauma services.[30]

Norms and policies provide guidance as well as regulation of health personnel. Laws and regulations must define the level of training required to exercise medical professions. This includes both basic education and continuous or post-graduate training. In terms of continuous education, a variety of courses are available worldwide, such as the Advanced Trauma Life Support course promulgated by the American College of Surgeons; or countries may develop their own curricula based on their specific needs.[31] The creation of professional associations can be encouraged, as they play a role in promoting self-regulation and continuous training (see Box 3).

Norms and policies must also focus on institutions and services.[32] Through central planning, the state must decide which facilities will play what roles in an organised system of trauma management. The necessary resources (human and physical) to fulfil these roles must be specified. The agreed division of responsibilities should then be supported by a system of hospital inspections and related accreditation. The state should also facilitate systems of medical audits or peer review processes in order to verify and improve the quality of health care delivered by institutions.[33] Inspections and audits can be delegated to professional bodies, although in low or middle income countries the State will often need to provide necessary initial resources to set up such programmes. Adequate data collection systems are essential, both to enable audits, and to verify whether recommendations were implemented. Importantly, the state should also set up adequate financial mechanisms to ensure that a core set of trauma and emergency-care services are accessible to all people who need them.[34]

Finally, norms and policies must focus on systems and procedures.[35] This can involve the designation of trauma centres mentioned above, and ensuring adequate agreements are in place for referrals and inter-hospital transfers. Efficient communication systems should be set up to alert emergency services, preferably with a universal access number. In less-resourced areas with no formal emergency medical services, access to pre-hospital first aid can be improved through training and equipping fire service personnel and police, as well as commercial drivers or other members of the public who commonly come into contact with the injured.[36] Systems of pre-hospital triage can also improve pre-hospital care.

Box 3. Setting standards: The role of the Trauma Society of South Africa

The Trauma Society of South Africa (TSSA) provides a good example of inter-disciplinary cooperation essential for strengthening trauma care systems. It engages paramedics; nurses from emergency centres, intensive care unit and operation theatres; and doctors from emergency medicine, surgery, orthopaedics, intensive care and post-acute care in one professional body with a common objective—prevention, training, and optimal care of the injured. In 1992 the TSSA produced guidelines for staffing, equipment, audit and quality assurance within the confines of cost efficiency and availability. In that same year TSSA brought to South Africa the Advanced Trauma Life Support training programme. This was followed in 1999 by the Definitive Surgical Trauma Care programme developed by the International Association for Trauma and Surgical Intensive Care to enhance evidence-based care. In 2011 the TSSA published its criteria for the accreditation of trauma centres, covering staffing, equipment, and facility and the processes for establishing cost-effective trauma systems. This collaborative effort with the Emergency Medicine Society of South Africa, Emergency Nurses Society of South Africa and Critical Care Society of Southern Africa will enable the establishment of more formal trauma systems across the country.[37]

Section 3: Essential elements of a trauma care system

The greatest advances in trauma surgery, especially for ballistic injuries, were made during the major wars of the 20th century. Compared to World War I, mortality during World War II was reduced by the use of antibiotics and blood transfusions. During the Korean and the Vietnam wars, the concept of emergency medical services came to fruition with the introduction of Mobile Army Support Hospitals, which provided initial surgical care next to the battlefields. These types of first response care services significantly raised survival rates. Advances in medical technology and practice meant that blood vessel repairs started to replace routine amputation for limb vascular injury.[38]

Outside the context of war, high rates of gun crime in Central and South America, South Africa and USA have led to the development of "damage control surgery"— early surgical repair of vital organs including the use of devices such as the "Bogota Bag" to stabilise the patient and buy time before the main surgical intervention. This entails stitching a plastic sheet into the abdominal wall rather than closing the abdomen in unstable gunshot injuries (for more on wound ballistics, see Box 4).[39]

Clinical policies and protocols for the care of injuries to different organ systems are regularly updated and disseminated by professional medical societies at national and regional levels.[40] Many aspects of the internationally accepted management strategies for gunshot patients have been guided by studies undertaken in high crime contexts. These include studies of initial fluid resuscitation (the use of less drip fluid, early surgery, and early blood transfusion); early primary repair of cranial (head), abdominal, and chest injuries; conservative management of bullet wounds of the abdomen without the need for surgery, management of jaw and facial injuries, as well as associated airway problems; and the timing of nerve injury repair.[41]

Political oppression and armed violence have also been catalysts for innovation in trauma care. In South Africa, advances were stimulated by injuries resulting from the political and civil unrest and the border war during the apartheid era. Innovations also included the evolution of professional bodies such as national trauma societies which work with government and other key actors in developing policy guidance. In Mexico and Colombia the high numbers of people injured in the "war on drugs" have led to quality improvement being prioritised in trauma and emergency care.[42]

Box 4: Wound ballistics[43]

Ballistics is the study of firearm projectiles, their transit, and consequent impacts on materials and objects. Terminal ballistics is the study of the damage caused to the target tissues and other objects. The proliferation of military weaponry and ammunition in the hands of civilians means that emergency and trauma professionals increasingly need to be familiar with the science of wound ballistics.[44]

The velocity, shape, mass, consistency, calibre, distance travelled, and interaction that a bullet has with materials such as glass and clothing all contribute to its wounding potential.[45] There are three types of bullets: full metal jacket (lead shape covered with copper, cupronickel, or steel), semi-jacketed (partially covered), and unjacketed (without cover). Under the Geneva Conventions, "it is prohibited to employ weapons, projectiles, and material and methods of warfare of a nature to cause superfluous

---

injury or unnecessary suffering."[46] Conventional military ammunition is typically full metal jacketed: designed for penetration, it does not expand significantly upon body impact. Semi-jacketed or unjacketed bullets have been shown to cause greater damage, resulting in the highest energy transfer from bullet to tissue with lead fragmentation (every fragment having the same amount of potential energy for damage). These bullets are designed to maximise tissue damage and organ injury. For this reason, the use of semi-jacketed or unjacketed bullets is prohibited by military personnel.

Bullets do not cause sterile wounds, despite the high heat and gases involved in their propulsion. They can force bacteria and pieces of bone or debris deep into tissues, so wound care must be meticulous to avoid infection.

Trauma care is largely about secondary prevention—preventing further adverse outcomes after a violent event has already occurred. It includes immediate life-saving measures, as well as measures to minimise permanent damage and impairment. Trauma or injury prevention is also part of violence prevention strategies, which directly affect clinical practice by reducing the incidence of trauma.[47] Such upstream prevention seeks to induce behavioural change through appropriate laws, environmental design, security system reform, awareness campaigns, etc., so that injury does not happen in the first place (primary prevention). Both primary and secondary prevention measures aim to reduce the burden of gun violence.

An audit of existing systems, facilities and staff will provide data to develop cost-effective systems that improve overall health care for all trauma patients, including gunshot survivors. Drawing on a range of sources, the basic needs of health care services and facilities dealing with gunshot injuries can be summarised, from a range of guidelines and reflections on good practice, as follows:[48]

Relating to strengthening system response and human capacity:

- Protocols of care based on international evidence-based methodologies;
- Systems for delivering specialised multi-disciplinary care;
- Trained medical staff able to perform surgery to stop bleeding and contamination;
- Trained surgical nursing staff and allied health professionals (physiotherapy, occupational therapy, etc.);
- Rehabilitation services, both inpatient and outpatient;
- Counselling for patients following a violent incident, and also to support staff mental health and wellbeing in stressful work environments;
- Internal audit and quality assurance programmes to measure the quality of care provided and enable improvements; and
- Ongoing educational opportunities to ensure staff remain competent.

Relating to technical capacity:

- Pre-hospital services for all forms of trauma, equipped with essential medical resuscitation and immobilisation equipment. These may be a formal service like ambulances, or informal, based for example on taxis,

where less equipment will be available. The essential point is that they
should be integrated into the greater emergency care system;

- Emergency call centres to enable early and rapid dispatch, with universal access numbers across the country;
- Access to surgical and medical critical care facilities, either immediately on-site or after transfer to a higher level of care;
- Emergency hospitals with sufficient space and access points, with rapid access to definitive care operation rooms and post-operative care facilities;
- Equipment to manage problems with the airways, to maintain the supply of oxygen to the lungs.
- Equipment to drain the chest cavity if there is bleeding in or leaking of air into the cavity;
- Ventilation devices for timely management of lung injury and prevention of secondary neurological injury due to the lack of oxygen delivery to the brain;
- Drugs for the management of physiological changes due to blood loss (e.g. to maintain cardiac contraction and blood pressure), monitoring devices for coagulation disorders, safe blood products and intravenous fluids to maintain the pressure inside blood vessels;
- Equipment to keep trauma victims warm, reducing the complications associated with hypothermia;
- Modern imaging facilities for X-rays, ultrasound, and computerised tomography;
- Appropriate immobilisation equipment for fractures to prevent unnecessary deformities; and
- Appropriate beds, mobility aids and other devices to prevent secondary complications and impairments.

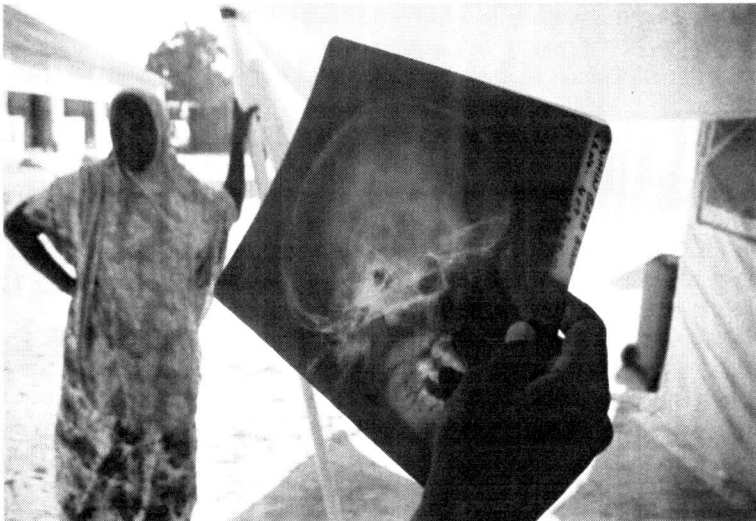

A doctor at the African Union peacekeeping hospital holds up an x-ray scan of a patient injured by fighting in Mogadishu, Somalia. (Image: Siegfried Modala, April 2010)

Including trauma and rehabilitation in violence prevention programming
Numerous initiatives are underway globally to "map" armed violence at the national and sub-national level, but these rarely appear to include a focus on trauma systems and rehabilitation services. The goal of such initiatives is to develop evidence-based approaches to reduce gun violence; therefore it is critical that a serious focus be directed to non-fatal injuries. Donors and violence reduction practitioners can be particularly engaged in this regard. Mental health services, typically overlooked as part of recovery from gun violence, also need to be included (see the chapter, Rehabilitation and Recovery for further detail). Performance improvement strategies for trauma systems based on international guidelines should also be included in such audits.[49]

Conclusion
Trauma care is far more than just the provision of ambulances or hospital facilities. It involves a commitment to scientific trauma surgery, modern operative techniques, research to improve policy and practice and audits of local practice assessed against international standards. It requires the development of systems of care based on methods that are cost-effective as well as relevant to the social and cultural context of the country. Trauma care requires a commitment by health ministries to establish prevention and response programmes to reduce the numbers of violent deaths and respond to survivors of violence.

The burden of disease and injury caused by gun violence can only be mitigated through a combination of primary prevention, including normative action (legislation and enforcement) and secondary prevention including service provision and comprehensive systems of care. This requires a multi-sector response including medical, police, justice, community development and other government ministries, making a committed effort to work together. It also requires cooperation to ensure that health systems are robust and able to withstand the pressures that gun violence creates in terms of diversion of limited material and human resources. Those working to stem gun violence should ensure that trauma systems are included in policy and programming as an essential part of reducing the impacts of such violence, particularly the extent of impairment and disability.

Contributors: **Timothy Hardcastle**, trauma surgeon, University of KwaZulu-Natal, President of the Trauma Society of South Africa and Deputy Director of the Trauma Unit, Inkosi Albert Luthuli Central Hospital, Durban. **Andres M. Rubiano**, neurosurgeon, critical care physician and Chief of Trauma and Emergency Services at Neiva University Hospital in Huila, Colombia; Associate Professor at the South Colombian University, Neiva; Chair of the Pan-American Trauma Society's Prehospital Trauma Care Committee; Advisor to the World Health Organization Trauma and Emergency Care Committee. **Cate Buchanan**, **Rebecca Peters** and **Mireille Widmer** undertook further drafting and editing. Additional editing was provided by **Emile LeBrun**.

Box contributors: **Cate Buchanan**, Director, Surviving Gun Violence Project; **Trevor McCartney**, Medical Chief of Staff, University of the West Indies (UWI), Mona Campus, Associate Senior Lecturer in Surgery at UWI, Deputy Dean of the Faculty of Medicine UWI Mona and Chief Operating Officer of the University Hospital of the

West Indies (Jamaica); **David Skinner**, Trauma Fellow, University of KwaZulu-Natal, Durban (South Africa).

Peer reviews were provided by **Jacques Goosen**, Head of Trauma Unit, Charlotte Maxeke Academic Hospital (South Africa); **Thilo Kroll**, Co-Director, Social Dimensions of Health Institute, University of Dundee and St. Andrews (Scotland); **Scott Sasser**, Centers for Disease Control and Prevention and Director, International Programs, Department of Emergency Medicine, Emory University School of Medicine (USA); **Aleema Shivji**, independent consultant (UK). Additional thanks to: **Charles Mock**, Professor of Surgery and Epidemiology, Harborview Injury Prevention and Research Center, University of Washington (USA); **Carlos Arreola Rissa**, School of Medicine and Health Sciences, Tecnológico de Monterrey University (Mexico); and **Elizabeth Ward** and **Tiffany Liscombe**, Violence Prevention Alliance Jamaica (Jamaica).

References

[1] I. Greaves, K. Porter and J. Garner, *Trauma Care Manual* (Oxford: Oxford University Press, 2008).

[2] A. Nicol and E. Steyn (Eds), *Oxford Handbook of Trauma* 2nd Ed (Cape Town: Oxford University Press Southern Africa, 2010).

[3] M. Peden and A. Butchart, "Chapter 24, Trauma and Injury" In N. Crisp (Ed), *South African Health Review* (1999). Available at: www.healthlink.org.za/uploads/files/chapter24_99.pdf Accessed 10 May 2012.

[4] C.N. Mock, G.J. Jurkovich, D. Nii Amon Kotei, C. Arreola Risa and R.V. Maier, "Trauma mortality patterns in three nations at different economic levels: Implication for global trauma system development," *Journal of Trauma* 44 (1998), pp. 804-812; C.N. Mock, J.D. Lormand, J. Goosen, M. Joshipura and M. Peden, *Guidelines for Essential Trauma Care* (Geneva: World Health Organization, 2004).

[5] United Nations Office on Drugs and Crime, *Global Study on Homicide: Trends, Contexts, Data* (Vienna: UNODC, 2011), p. 93.

[6] United Nations Office on Drugs and Crime (2011), p. 19.

[7] E. Ward, T. McCartney, D.W. Brown, A. Grant, A. Butchart, M. Taylor and the Technical Working Group for the Costing Study (P. Bhoorasingh, H. Wong, C. Morris, A.M. Deans-Clarke, J. East, C. Valentine, S. Dundas and C. Pinnock), "Results of an exercise to estimate the costs of interpersonal violence in Jamaica," *West Indian Medical Journal* 58/5 (2009), pp. 447-451.

[8] Jamaica Constabulary Force, "Annual Reports 2001-2010," *Jamaica Constabulary Statistical Division* (Jamaica: Statistical Division, Constabulary Force).

[9] E. Ward, T. McCartney, S. Arscott-Mills, N. Gordon, A. Grant, A.H. McDonald and D.E. Ashley, "The Jamaica Injury Surveillance System: a profile of the intentional and unintentional injuries in Jamaican hospitals," *West Indian Medical Journal* 59/1 (2010), pp. 7-13.

[10] Emergency room data from May Pen Hospital 2007-10 provided by Dr Elizabeth Ward, April 2012.

[11] M. Strydom, "Ambulance transport of trauma cases in the Cape Metropole," *Trauma Review* 3/1 (1995), pp. 7-8.

[12] B.S. Roudsari, A.B. Nathens, P. Cameron, I. Civil, R.L. Gruen, T.D. Koepsell, F.E. Lecky, R.L. Lefering, M. Liberman, C.N. Mock, H.J. Oestern, T.A. Schildhauer, C. Waydhas and F.P. Rivara, "International comparison of prehospital trauma care systems," *Injury* 38/9 (2007), pp. 993-1000; K. Nielsen, C. Mock, M. Joshipura, A.M. Rubiano, A. Zakariah and F.P. Rivara, "Assessment of the status of prehospital care in 13 low- and middle-income countries," *Prehospital Emergency Care* 16/37 (2012), pp. 381-389; C.N. Mock, K.E. Adzotor,

E. Conklin, D.M. Denno and G.J. Jurkovich, "Trauma outcomes in the rural developing world: Comparison with an urban level I trauma center," *Journal of Trauma* 35 (1993), pp. 518-523.

[13] D. Demetriades, L. Chan, E. Cornwell, H. Belzberg, T.V. Berne, J. Asensio, D. Chan, M. Eckstein and K. Alo, "Paramedic vs private transportation of trauma patients: Effect on outcome," *Archives of Surgery* 131/2 (1996), pp. 133-138.

[14] T.C. Hardcastle, "The 11-P's of an Afrocentric trauma system for South Africa," *South African Medical Journal* 101 (2011), pp. 160-162; C.N. Mock et al (2004); S. Sasser, S. M. Varghese, A. Kellermann and J.D. Lormand, *Prehospital trauma care systems* (Geneva: World Health Organization, 2005); H.T. Stelfox, M. Joshipura, W. Chadbunchachai, R.N. Ellawala, G. O'Reilly, T.S. Nguyen and R.L. Gruen, "Trauma quality improvement in low and middle income countries of the Asia-Pacific region: A mixed methods study," *World Journal of Surgery* 36/8 (August 2012), pp. 1978-1992.

[15] Contributed by Cate Buchanan, Surviving Gun Violence Project.

[16] A.R. Harris, S.H. Thomas, G.A. Fisher and D.J. Hirsch, "Murder and medicine. The lethality of criminal assault 1960-1999," *Homicide Studies* 6/2 (2002), pp.128-166.

[17] See C. Mock, C. Julliard, M. Joshipura and J. Goosen, *Strengthening care for the injured: Success stories and lessons learned from around the world* (Geneva: World Health Organization, 2010); C. Mock, C. Arreola-Risa, and R. Quansah, "Strengthening care for injured persons in less developed countries: a case study of Ghana and Mexico," *Injury Control and Safety Promotion* 10 (2003), pp. 45-51; Centers for Disease Control and Prevention, Factsheet, "Strengthening global injury care: Innovative strategies and sustainable solutions." Available at: www.cdc.gov/traumacare/pdfs/Global_Trauma_factsheet-a.pdf Accessed 14 November 2012.

[18] World Health Organization, *Small arms and global health* (Geneva: WHO, 2001), p. 22. See also C.N. Mock et al (1998).

[19] C.N. Mock, M. Tiska, M. Adu-Ampofo and G. Boakye, "Improvements in pre-hospital trauma care in an African country with no formal emergency medical services," *Journal of Trauma* 53/1 (2002), pp. 90-97.

[20] H. Husum, M. Gilbert, T. Wisborg, Y. Van Heng and M. Murad, "Rural prehospital trauma systems improve trauma outcome in low-income countries: A prospective study from North Iraq and Cambodia," *Journal of Trauma* 54/6 (2003), pp. 1188-1196.

[21] Contributed by Mireille Widmer, Surviving Gun Violence Project.

[22] *Universal Declaration of Human Rights* (1948), Article 25.1: "Everyone has the right to a standard of living adequate for the health and wellbeing of himself and his (sic) family…"; International Covenant on Economic, Social and Cultural Rights (1966), Article 12.1: "the right of everyone to the enjoyment of the highest attainable standard of health…"

[23] Geneva Convention I Article 15; Convention II Article 18, Convention III Article 30, Convention IV Article 16, 18. See also International Committee of the Red Cross, *Rules for behaviour in combat* (Geneva: ICRC, 1987).

[24] United Nations Economic and Social Council, "The rights to the highest attainable standard of health", *General Comment No. 14 (2000)*, E/C.12/2000/4, 11 August (2000).

[25] C.N. Mock et al (2004), p. 11.

[26] C.N. Mock et al (2004). See also Y. Holder (Ed), *Injury surveillance guidelines* (Geneva: World Health Organization, 2001); M.F Hazinski, "Part 1, Executive summary: 2010 International consensus on cardiopulmonary resuscitation and emergency cardiovascular care science with treatment recommendations", *Circulation* 122/Suppl 2 (2010), pp. S250-S275.

[27] S. Sasser et al (2005).

[28] World Health Assembly, *Health systems: emergency care systems*, WHA60.22, 23 May (2007).

[29] World Health Organization, *Global Forum on Trauma Care, Rio de Janeiro, 28-29 October 2009, Meeting Report*. Available at: www.who.int/violence_injury_prevention/services/traumacare/global_forum_meeting_report.pdf Accessed 21 September 2012.

[30] See www.who.int/violence_injury_prevention/services/gaci/en/index.html Accessed 20 August 2013.

[31] C.N. Mock et al (2004), pp. 60-64.

[32] C.N. Mock et al (2004), pp. 72-75.

[33] C.N. Mock et al (2004), pp. 64-69.

[34] World Health Assembly, *Health systems: emergency care systems*, WHA60.22, 23 May (2007), Article 2.10.

[35] C.N. Mock et al (2004), pp. 75-78; S. Sasser et al (2005), particularly pp. 17-18.

[36] S. Sasser et al (2005).

[37] T.C. Hardcastle, E. Steyn, K. Boffard, J. Goosen, M. Toubkin, A. Loubser, D. Allard, S. Moeng, D. Muckart, P. Brysiewicz, L. Wallis and Trauma Society of South Africa, "Guideline for the assessment of trauma centres for South Africa," *South African Medical Journal 101* (2011), pp. 189-194.

[38] N.M. Rich, "Vascular trauma historical notes," *Perspectives in Vascular Surgery and Endovascular Surgery* 23/1 (2011), pp. 7-12.

[39] See: K.D. Boffard, "Chapter 4, Damage Control Surgery," In K.D. Boffard (Ed), *Manual of Definitive Surgical Trauma Care,* 3rd Ed (London: Hodder-Arnold, 2011); I. Greaves, K. Porter and J. Garner (2008).

[40] See: the Brain Trauma Foundation (www.braintrauma.org); the International Association for Trauma Surgery and Intensive Care (http://iatsic.org/index.html); the American College of Surgeons Committee on Trauma (www.facs.org/trauma/index.html); the Pan-American Trauma Society (www.panamtrauma.org); the Australasian Trauma Society (www.traumasociety.com.au/); the South African Trauma Society (http://traumasa.co.za/); the European Society for Trauma and Emergency Surgery (www.estesonline.org/); the American Association for the Surgery of Trauma (www.aast.org/Default.aspx).

[41] For example: D.L. Clarke, S.R. Thomson, D.J. Muckart and P.A. Neijenhuis, "Universal primary colonic repair in the firearm era," *Annals of the Royal College of Surgeons of England* 81/1 (1999), pp. 58-61; T.E. Madiba, S.R. Thomson and N. Mdlalose, "Penetrating chest injuries in the firearm era," *Injury* 32/1 (2001), pp. 13-16; T.C. Hardcastle, "Unusual management of a complex pancreaticoduodenal injury: case report and brief literature overview, *Journal of Trauma* 68/2 (2010), pp. E42-E43; J.A. Omoshoro-Jones, A.J. Nicol, P.H. Navsaria, R. Zellweger, J.E. Krige, and D.H. Kahn, "Selective non-operative management of liver gunshot injuries," *British Journal of Surgery* 92 (2005), pp. 890-895; P.H. Navsaria, S. Edu and A.J. Nicol "Civilian extraperitoneal rectal gunshot wounds: surgical management made simpler," *World Journal of Surgery* 31/6 (2007), pp. 1345-1351; E.E. Lutge, "The epidemiology and cost of trauma to the orthopaedic department at a secondary-level hospital," *South African Journal of Surgery* 43/3 (2005), pp. 74-77.

[42] C. Mock et al (2010).

[43] Contributed by Dr David Lee Skinner, Trauma Fellow, University of KwaZulu-Natal, Durban, South Africa.

[44] C. Giannou and M. Baldan, *War Surgery: Working with limited resources in armed conflict and other situations of violence, Volume 1* (Geneva: International Committee of the Red Cross, 2009).

[45] R.A. Santucci and Y.J. Chang, "Ballistics for physicians: Myths about wound ballistics and gunshot injuries," Journal of Urology 171 (2004), pp. 1408-1414; M.L. Fackler, "Civilian gunshot wounds and ballistics: dispelling the myths," *Emergency Medicine Clinics of North America 16/1* (1998), pp. 17-27.

[46] Protocol Additional to the Geneva Conventions of 12 August 1949, and relating to the Protection of Victims of International Armed Conflicts (Protocol I), 8 June 1977. Part III: Methods and means of warfare - Combatant and prisoner-of-war status. Section I - Methods and means of warfare. Article 35 - Basic rules.

[47] G.R. Kellerman (Ed), *Preventing injuries and violence: a guide for ministries of health* (Geneva: World Health Organization, 2007); World Health Organization, *Preventing violence: a guide to implementing the recommendations of the World Report on Violence and Health* (Geneva: WHO, 2004).

[48] C.N. Mock et al (2004). Also see: C. Mock et al (2010); R. Saadia, "Organisation of hospital responses for the trauma epidemic," *British Medical Bulletin*, 55/4 (1999), pp. 767-784; T.C. Hardcastle (2011); Committee on Trauma, American College of Surgeons, *Resources for*

the *Optimal Care of the Injured Patient: 1999 Update* (Chicago, Illinois: American College of Surgeons, 1999); C. MacFarlane, "Aide memoir for the management of gunshot wounds," *Annals of the Royal College of Surgeons of England*, 84/4 (2002), pp. 230-233; S. Sasser et al (2005); C. Giannou and M. Baldan (2009).

[49] C. Mock, C. Julliard, S. Brundage, J. Goosen and M. Joshipura, *Guidelines for trauma quality improvement programmes* (Geneva: World Health Organization, 2009); D. Sethi, S. Marais, M. Seedat, J. Nurse and A. Butchart, *Handbook for the documentation of interpersonal violence prevention programmes*. (Geneva: World Health Organization, 2004).

"Much of what low income countries need to do to prevent deaths occurring soon after injury is well within reach of these economies—they are simple and relatively inexpensive interventions which are not being instituted yet. And most don't require surgeons—but first aiders, nurses, drivers."

Olive Kobusingye, trauma surgeon and violence prevention advocate, Uganda, 2005

SPOTLIGHT SECTION
New Year's Eve in Colombia

On New Year´s Eve 2012, I was on call for neurosurgery at the local hospital in Neiva, serving a large community of five departments/states in southern Colombia. Patients come from rural and urban areas. At midnight I finished the family dinner, kissed my wife and went to bed, because I have learned what lies ahead on such a night.

At 1am on January 1, the hospital emergency room (ER) staff contacted me because three gunshot victims had arrived, a father and his two sons. Two days previously, the father had an argument with his neighbour. They insulted and threatened each other, but both families helped calm down the situation. On New Year´s Eve, shortly after midnight, the neighbour knocked on the family door, and right in the middle of their celebrations, opened fire with a .38 calibre weapon. Father and sons were injured. In worst condition was the 22 year old son, who suffered cranial, heart, left lung and left thigh bullet wounds.

Driving to the hospital, I looked around—at the fireworks, people dancing, and cars and motorcycles filling the streets. I thought: Welcome, 2012!

When I arrived at the hospital, my colleagues were working madly. There had been car and motorcycle crashes, stab wounds and gun violence. My patient, Oscar Manios, was the first head injury of the year—too early. Oscar had gunshot wounds to the temporal, parietal and occipital left cerebral lobes, the parts of the brain responsible for language, body sensations, memory and visual processes (Picture 1).

I went straight to the operation room (OR). Trauma surgeons were at work on heart, lung and thigh injuries, so I talked briefly with the family. The father and other son were already in the ER, the father wounded in the hand and the older brother with gunshots to the leg and abdomen, waiting to go after his brother to the OR. I explained to them how critical the situation was, including the possibility of death if we did not open the skull. As soon as the other injuries were repaired, I started with the brain surgery.

This young man had a severe brain injury with intracranial bleeding, bone fragments, bullet fragments and cerebral tissue damage. I took out half of the cranial vault (the frontal, temporal and parietal left bones) as a preventive measure to control inflammation of the brain after the surgery (Picture 2). The left side of his skull was removed; bleeding was controlled and the membranes that normally cover the brain were left opened; then the skin was closed to prevent infection. The skull bones were stored in a hospital freezer; if the patient survived, I would put them back later.

Two hours later, the injury was mostly repaired. By 7am I was out of the OR and the patient was taken to the intensive care unit (Picture 3). Next in the queue was his brother.

By the time I got back to the ER, at least 10 more patients were being treated for abdominal and extremity injuries (three due to gunshots, waiting for OR). I reviewed three more head injury cases due to motorcycle crashes and left work at 8:30am on 1 January 2012.

As I drove home, people were coming home from parties in their cars and on motorcycles, outside their homes, all dressed up and still drinking. I thought about the very different New Year's Eve I had just been a part of, all preventable and a drain on health resources. When I arrived home, my neighbour, a wine glass in hand, greeted me: "Good morning Doc, Happy New Year! How was your party last night?" I just smiled and said, "Happy New Year, my friend, the party was really crazy."

Contributor: Andres M. Rubiano, neurosurgeon, critical care physician and Chief of Trauma and Emergency Services at Neiva University Hospital in Huila, Colombia; Associate Professor at the South Colombian University in Neiva; Chair of the Pan-American Trauma Society's Prehospital Trauma Care Committee; Advisor to the World Health Organization Trauma and Emergency Care Committee.

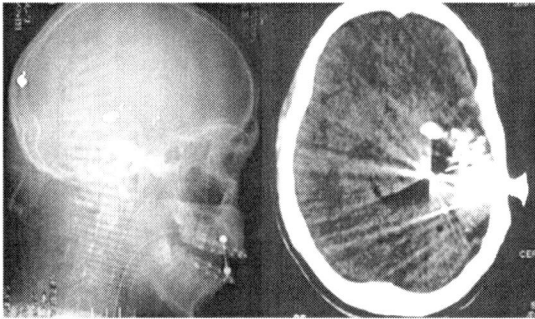

Picture 1

Skull X-ray and computed tomography of the brain of Oscar Manios, age 22

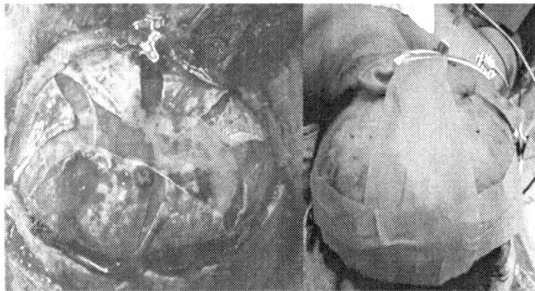

Picture 2

The left side of the skull was removed

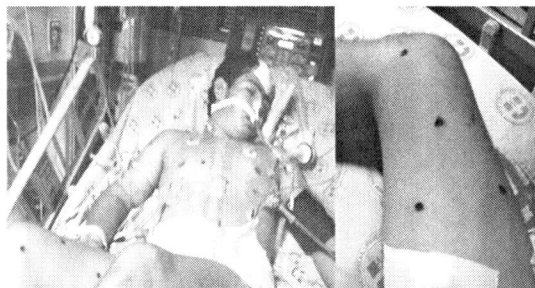

Picture 3

Recovering from multiple gunshot wounds in the Intensive Care Unit.

Picture 4

The patient and his mother, 20 days after surgery and before his skull bones were put back in place. He was discharged from hospital with a speech comprehension disorder and a light right side muscle weakness. This story had a happy ending because the shooting occurred near a fully equipped trauma center. However, in rural areas of low and middle income countries, many gunshot victims have no access to specialised trauma hospitals or clinics.

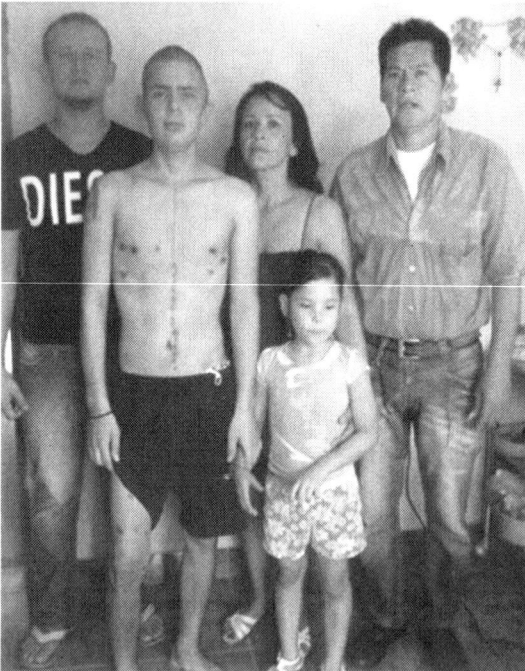

Picture 5

The Manios family two months later. They paid USD1000 for Oscar's treatment while insurance paid USD15,000. Post-discharge rehabilitation and medication were further costs to the family.

Collected by police over the past ten years, 36,000 illegal guns are held in this deposit in Bogota, Colombia. The captain reports that they receive about 150 guns every day, and that about 50% are made in North America. (Image: Heidi Schumann, 2006)

Protais Mbonimumpa, 38 years old, on his tricycle at his vegetable and fruit shop in Bujumbura, Burundi. Seven years ago he was shot and permanently injured in the leg by a thief in his home. Protais struggled to provide a living for his wife and six children. He already had this shop but couldn't go to rural Bujumbura where he used to buy his goods. After receiving a tricycle from Handicap International he is now mobile enough to purchase produce himself. (Image: Dieter Telemans/Panos, 2009)

4 Rehabilitation and Recovery

Introduction

The nature of rehabilitation for individuals with acquired impairments as well as the conceptual understanding and framing of disability have changed profoundly in recent decades. In the past, rehabilitation was equated mainly with efforts to address an individual's impairments through specific medical and physical therapies. Over time, it has become widely recognised that rehabilitation must also include environmental modifications and socio-political change to shift attitudes, maximise independence and ensure equal participation in social, cultural, political and economic life. This reflects a shift away from a medical to a human rights based understanding of disability.

For survivors of gun violence, a multi-disciplinary approach to rehabilitation is an essential part of the recovery process and should begin as soon as possible after injury. It "can improve health outcomes, reduce costs by shortening hospital stays, reduce disability, and improve quality of life."[1] Rehabilitation services, if high standard, will be made up of multi-disciplinary health professionals including physical medicine and rehabilitation doctors and nurses, social workers, psychosocial and mental health practitioners; physical, speech, cognitive and other therapists; as well as access to assistive devices and environment modification.

This chapter provides an overview of some key issues related to the rehabilitation of survivors of gun violence with physical and/or psychological impairments. It reviews the phases and components of rehabilitation services, focusing on: physical rehabilitation, psychosocial and mental health services, assistive devices and environmental modifications. It highlights some primary barriers to holistic rehabilitation, reviews existing norms, and suggests priorities for improving both policy and practice.[2] Rehabilitation as a form of redress in legal and political processes is explored in further detail in the chapter, Evolution of Victims' Rights and International Standards.

Section 1: Understanding rehabilitation

According to the World Health Organization (WHO) and the World Bank, rehabilitation is "a set of measures that assist individuals who experience, or are likely to experience, disability, to achieve and maintain optimal functioning in interaction with their environments... Rehabilitation measures target body functions and structures, activities and participation, environmental factors, and personal factors."[3]

Rehabilitation is an evolving process. Typically it begins during the acute care phase in the hospital with a focus on preventing and/or minimising impairment, including psychological trauma. It prepares the individual and their family for hospital discharge, with an emphasis on self-management skills. Once at home, the focus is on caregiving arrangements, assistive devices, environmental adaptations and the like. Psychosocial assistance is geared towards enhancing a person's resilience, and processing the trauma of a life-altering event. A comprehensive rehabilitation programme will cover all these phases, and be strongly linked to other services and programmes such as education, vocational training and social protection. In countries affected by war and repression this will also involve criminal justice and truth seeking processes. The latter concepts are discussed in detail in the chapter on Victims' Rights and International Standards.

Appropriate rehabilitation and psychosocial support can assist survivors contending with the short and long-term effects of violence on their lives. Longer-term physical and/or psychological impairments affect functioning and have negative impacts on livelihoods, social inclusion, health outcomes, wellbeing, and economic status. For example, according to the *World Report on Disability*, people living with disability and their families may need to spend more money to achieve a similar standard of living as other families.[4]

Impairment and disability are not one and the same. Whereas the old medical model sought to "cure" the impairment through health and medical interventions exclusively, disability is now understood to derive from an individual's interactions with society and environment more broadly.[5] In the words of the 2006 UN *Convention on the Rights of Persons with Disabilities* (CRPD), disability "is an evolving concept... that... results from the interaction between persons with impairments and attitudinal and environmental barriers that hinders their full and effective participation in society on an equal basis with others."[6]

Rehabilitation examines an individual's functioning (e.g. capacity to communicate or walk), as well as their ability to participate in their family life and community (e.g. take care of family members or go to school). The ultimate goals of rehabilitation are to maximise independence, physical, mental, social and vocational ability, inclusion and active participation of people living with disability—consistent with Article 26 of the CRPD. As a result, rehabilitation will take very different forms, dependent on the social, cultural, political and economic contexts, as well as the type of services that are available and accessible.

Section 2: Rehabilitation during acute hospital care
Rehabilitation during initial hospitalisation focuses primarily on preventing and minimising impairment. Attention is also given to additional health conditions (co-morbidities) that could influence the rehabilitation process. Support is provided to transition the individual into the community, with a focus on self-management skills. This section will look in turn at each of these steps.

Trauma and impairments from gun violence
Injuries from gunshot wounds can have particularly devastating consequences, dependent on factors such as weapon and ammunition type and bullet trajectory. Injuries can be localised or extensive and this lack of predictability is a major medical and rehabilitation challenge. For example, a review of 49 cases of gunshot-induced spinal cord injury in the United States of America (USA) showed that more than half had a single bullet entry while 17% had more than three sites of entry, thus

increasing the clinical complexity.[7] Gun injuries commonly include organ and eye injuries, bone fractures, and vascular damage.[8] In some cases, amputations are necessary, while paralysis and brain injuries are common. People with violently acquired spinal injuries are more likely to experience complete paraplegic injuries than individuals with spinal injuries from other causes.[9] Facial injuries may leave survivors disfigured and require complex dental or facial reconstructive interventions (for further detail see the chapter, Traumatic Injuries).[10]

Evidence from the USA suggests that long-term survival for people with traumatic injuries has increased over the past three decades.[11] However, mortality rates are not equal between developing and developed countries,[12] and recent data suggest that household income may be a determinant of mortality and survival.[13] With appropriate and timely medical and rehabilitation care, improvements in mortality rates can occur in low and middle income countries (LMICs). An example from Gujarat state in India following the 2001 earthquake demonstrates that five-year post-discharge mortality rates in people with spinal cord injuries dropped from 60% to only 4% through participation in a comprehensive hospital and community based rehabilitation programme.[14] As more people survive their injuries (because of improved transport to medical facilities, timely medical care and advances in intensive trauma care) the focus has shifted towards supporting them in their adaptation to a life with permanent impairments. This requires a comprehensive, long-term rehabilitation approach, which also needs to prevent secondary conditions and complications.

Some examples of common primary and secondary impairments resulting from gun violence include:

Primary impairments:

- Physical and/or cognitive limitations due to neurological trauma (such as traumatic brain injury);
- Paralysis due to spinal cord injury;
- Amputation due to the initial injury; and
- Sensory impairments such as blindness and deafness.[15]

Secondary impairments:

- Limb deformation due to poorly-managed neurological injuries;
- Limb paralysis from poorly-managed fractures;
- Amputation due to infection; and
- Organ failure or dysfunction due to paralysis.

Psychological trauma resulting from gun violence is discussed in Section 3.

Preventing permanent impairments

Not all injuries result in permanent or long-term consequences. It is clear that early rehabilitation is essential, as some injuries develop into permanent impairments simply for lack of appropriate, timely and regular care and services. To illustrate this challenge, following the 2011 revolution in Libya, medical staff treating an individual for gunshot wounds did not realise he also had peripheral nerve injuries; by the time the patient was seen by a rehabilitation worker, his muscles had contracted into a permanently distorted position (known as contracture).[16]

Three measures are essential to prevent or minimise physical impairment:

- Positioning and immobilisation (including splinting, plaster casts, fixation devices, and traction) is needed to avoid contracture, secondary nerve damage and potentially lethal pressure sores. Contracture prevention is necessary not only to avoid functional limitations, but in the case of people with amputations, to prepare for prosthetic limb fitting;
- Range of motion and strengthening (movement and exercise) is essential to gain the movement and strength to complete daily and functional activities; and
- Mobility devices (including crutches, prosthetics, wheelchairs) and associated training, are crucial for quick recovery of mobility, which can reduce further complications.

Rehabilitation for gun-related injuries differs qualitatively and quantitatively from approaches directed at survivors of non-violently acquired injuries.[17] The complexity and nature of the injuries associated with gun violence generally necessitates additional and/or more prolonged medical, rehabilitation and psychosocial support. Furthermore, ensuring that rehabilitation and other medical and non-medical services are connected is a major challenge. According to rehabilitation experts for gun violence survivors "the impact of rehabilitation without medical services is much lower than with many other injuries or conditions," particularly due to the prevalence of health factors and high risk of complications requiring medical intervention.[18] For example, in some cases, rehabilitation can only have full benefit if carried out alongside reconstructive surgery. On the other hand, preventable impairments may develop simply for lack of an appropriate diagnostic and referral system towards rehabilitation services.

Dealing with co-morbidities and complications

The injury(s) may not be the only source of concern: other concomitant medical conditions may also affect the recovery process, as can complications from the initial injury. For survivors with spinal cord injuries, a comprehensive multi-disciplinary rehabilitation programme will also include bowel and bladder management, skin care, and pain management. In addition, drug and substance abuse, as well as emotional trauma, must also be managed alongside the rehabilitation associated with the physical injuries.[19] Individuals, particularly women and girls, threatened or attacked with weapons, especially in conflict zones, may also have suffered sexual violence, which requires separate but simultaneous support and management.

For patients with violently acquired injuries, the most immediate medical challenges are pain and infections.[20] If infection risk and chronic pain are not managed effectively, they interfere with day-to-day activities, and inhibit effective social reintegration.[21] For a person with amputation, this could impact their ability to use a prosthetic device. A violently caused spinal cord injury has been identified as a principal risk factor for long-term medical complications, such as pressure ulcers, respiratory problems, and autonomic dysreflexia, a life-threatening condition.[22]

A number of other factors are associated with complications in the outpatient stage of recovery, including injury duration, functional independence at discharge, post-injury (or pre-existing) drug and alcohol abuse, medication management, and injury completeness. The most important factors are level of functional impairment and—in the case of spinal injury—injury completeness, i.e. whether there is a full paralysis below the level of injury.[23]

Pre-discharge: teaching self-management

The disabling consequences of gun violence only become fully apparent when the person leaves the inpatient care setting. Rehabilitation personnel typically need to teach survivors and their caregivers' self-management skills to maintain good health, maximise mobility and function, use assistive technologies, navigate the environment, and access social and vocational support.

In an active conflict or other humanitarian context, immediate priority rests on increasing basic independence and mobility to ensure the person can flee from on-going or renewed violence, navigate a temporary or altered environment such as a camp, and access essential humanitarian assistance such as food, water and temporary latrines.

For people with spinal cord injuries, avoiding pressure sores and infections of the urinary tract or respiratory system is a critical challenge. Poor housing conditions, limited personal assistance and scarce opportunities for health monitoring compound the challenge. Bladder catheters are a case in point. In many contexts, the high cost of health care and supplies may lead individuals to reuse bladder catheters, thus increasing the risk of severe infection and re-hospitalisation. In 2008, the USA Medicare insurance scheme implemented a new policy of paying for single-use catheters to stem the tide of preventable urinary tract infections (see the Spotlight, Paying for Gun-related Impairment in the United States for further detail).[24] In some LMICs, changing catheters is simply not possible; thus the rehabilitation programme must also integrate training on how to safely clean and re-use catheters.[25] Similar issues can occur with needles, dressings, plasters, etc.

The challenges of inpatient rehabilitation, and the shrinking length of hospital stays in many countries, mean there are fewer opportunities to familiarise patients with self-management and navigating their immediate environment (e.g. houses, schools and work-places that have lots of stairs and are not wheelchair friendly), and an inaccessible external environment (i.e. transport and public walkways).[26] This also affects the capacities of their caregivers, who are unlikely to receive training or support in day-to-day care requirements.

Successful discharge from hospital needs to be connected to appropriate community-level care in order to continue provision of appropriate rehabilitation services, mitigate complications, and focus on inclusion and the removal of social and environmental barriers. Section 4 will look at returning to the community in more detail.

Timing of discharge

The progress and success of rehabilitation tends to be assessed on short-term, functional outcomes over qualitative outcomes and typically does not include prospective, context-sensitive outcomes, thus missing critical elements that can affect health, wellbeing and participation.[27] Considerable emphasis is placed on attaining functional gains—moving, eating, dressing, and washing—with the fewest resources and in the shortest time possible.[28] While this approach saves initial costs, it may have costly consequences for both individuals and health care systems. Short-term functional gains, which are measurable at discharge from hospital, may not necessarily translate into good self-management and sustainable rehabilitative success; early discharge may also raise the risk of costly re-hospitalisations.[29]

The average length of stay for inpatient rehabilitation has steadily decreased in the USA; it is currently around 30 days for spinal cord injuries at most rehabilitation centres.[30] Between 1974 and 1994 the average length of stay in inpatient rehabilitation in the USA decreased by 57% from 127 to 56 days.[31] This trend is unlikely to be restricted to the USA. In the UK, in 2009 the average length of stay ranged between 65 and 140 days.[32] Rising health care expenditures, exacerbated by large aging populations in most countries, have refocused rehabilitation from the inpatient to the outpatient sector, but many countries lack the infrastructure or the economic resources to provide continuous rehabilitative support.[33] In crisis contexts, overwhelmed hospitals may have no choice but to discharge patients early to free up beds for new or more severe casualties.

Independent living in the community is not an option for many gun violence survivors because assistance and support is often expensive or unavailable. In many countries, a person may return home, but to sub-optimal living conditions with high dependency on others for care, poor access to community level services, and numerous barriers to participation in community life. Safety is another particular concern. Survivors of gun violence may choose not to return to the environment where they were shot, out of fear that they may get killed, or concern that family members may become targets of violence. In the USA, for example, young people may find the only accessible and safe care setting to be a nursing home, which is neither socially—nor age—appropriate. One study found that in the past decade, adults aged 30-65 were the fastest-growing population in US nursing homes.[34]

The loss of mobility, hearing, or eyesight—or the inability to respond quickly to threats—makes some survivors especially vulnerable. They may also decide that they do not want to "burden" their family, "choosing" institutionalisation if alternatives are not available.

"Since I've been in a wheelchair, I don't feel comfortable. I can't protect my family the way I would if I wasn't in the chair. It's not the way I would protect them. I don't feel comfortable having my daughter and my son grow up in that bullshit." (Jackson, aged 34, paraplegia from gun violence, Washington, DC.)[35]

Section 3: Dealing with psychological trauma

A number of psychological problems such as flashbacks, self-destructive or suicidal behaviours, nightmares, fear, disturbances to mood or sleeping and eating patterns, psychosomatic changes, aggression, or memory and concentration problems also result from gun-related trauma.[36] This can act to reduce self-esteem and cause alienation from friends and family. Yet mental health consequences associated with gun violence (and trauma in general) are often underestimated and undiagnosed.[37] This may result from poor understanding of the subject, or cultural barriers to discussing mental health and wellbeing.

Mental health problems associated with traumatic exposure include depression, anxiety and post-traumatic stress disorder (PTSD).[38] An accurate diagnosis is essential to ensure provision of appropriate treatment and services.[39] Mental illness can result in receiving poorer health care service due to stigma and misdiagnosis. Poor understanding of mental illness by health workers may also lead to inappropriate assumptions influencing diagnosis and treatment, which in turn can result in an increased risk of secondary complications from a gunshot injury.[40]

Psychological trauma may be linked to gun violence directly, or to other instances of violence surrounding victimisation at gun point, thus when dealing with the traumatic effects of gun violence it is important to take the whole context into consideration. For example, a survivor in the recent Libyan revolution explains that being shot multiple times was only one part of the torture he experienced. He was also blindfolded, tied up, locked in a container and beaten with a machete at gun point; all equally terrifying.[41]

Witnesses to gun violence may also be deeply affected, as may those threatened by a weapon without it being fired. Rapid screening and early interventions are essential to correctly identify people requiring specialised interventions and/or longer-term support. Psychological impacts may not occur immediately after the traumatic event; thus a long-term strategy is necessary to identify and address trauma.

For people with permanent impairments, adapting can be challenging, and lead to psychological difficulties. It means not only learning to live in an altered body, but also creating a new identity, self-image and role in society.[42] Studies of war veterans' experiences suggest that this transition is often challenging, and can result in impaired psychological functioning, a focus on physical losses and dependency on others.[43]

Impacts on men, women, boys, and girls appear different. Men and boys are the majority of those killed and injured by guns. However, for women and girls, gun violence is often accompanied by intimidating behaviour such as gun "brandishing", coercion at gun point and sexual violence, and support to them must take these experiences into account.[44] Cultural barriers can also limit the type and impact of support provided. For example, in conservative cultures, men may not be able to visit their wives in hospital, cutting off vital support necessary to process trauma associated with a violent injury.

Where trauma has affected large swathes of a population (i.e. violent conflict), many people affected by these traumatic events exhibit resilience, and are able to process their experience once order has been restored (in the case of collective violence), or through primarily social interventions (e.g. dissemination of key survival information, restarting schools, revival of pre-existing social support groups, or support to local communal healing practices).[45] A subsection of the affected population may require more focused psychosocial interventions and a smaller number may require specialised psychological or psychiatric support in order to overcome psychological and mental health impacts affecting ability to function.[46] Where the trauma has been significant, the number of people requiring specialised psychosocial, psychological or psychiatric support can indeed be substantial. This is another area with limited evidence, making it difficult to ascertain the prevalence of short and long-term traumatic impacts of gun violence. Timely assessment to identify people requiring different levels of support, and ensure they can subsequently access relevant services, is therefore required.

Psychosocial and mental health services

Appropriate mental health and psychosocial services for survivors are often unavailable and sometimes when available do not meet the needs of those seeking or needing help. Where services exist, they are often specialised, focusing on more obvious groups requiring such assistance (for example, for female victims of gender-based violence). The issues associated with cumulative trauma and the difficulties associated with treatment are often inadequately understood and provided.[47] Furthermore, mental health services are often based in institutions, even though community-based support is generally preferable.[48]

The type of support required depends on the level of trauma and may range from social interventions to specialised psychiatric care. More specialised care tends to focus on counselling and treating specific mental health problems, while psychosocial support emphasises increasing the resilience of people to deal with subsequent traumatic events, supporting social cohesion, and instilling positive coping mechanisms.[49]

Psychosocial support can assist people in coping with the impact of violence on their lives by focusing on their abilities and emotional resources. In particular it can reduce the risk of a survivor becoming a perpetrator in the future.[50] For some, life post-injury may be seen as a "wake-up call", a turning point or a key moment in identity transformation.[51]

Such support may involve a number of techniques, and may target survivors individually, or in groups, either with other survivors or other people with disabilities. Peer mentoring and support groups are a particularly useful tool which provides a space for survivors to share experiences, become empowered, and learn from each other.[52] Peer support is also a process that can help to foster a sense of community between participants, support positive health outcomes, reduce social isolation (for illustration of the role of peer support initiatives see the Spotlights on the USA and Quality Rehabilitation and Links to Violence Reduction as well as the Guatemala chapter for the work of the Transitions Foundation).[53]

Survivors' environments (e.g. the pressure of poverty, or living in an unsafe neighbourhood) can also affect their ability to overcome the trauma associated with their injury or impairment.[54] War also disrupts social support structures and access to care. As one example, in the Libyan conflict of 2011, hospital-based psychosocial support was severely curtailed because survivors were sometimes treated in medical facilities run by an opposing faction; this made them reluctant to speak freely about their mental health and emotions.[55] Uneven service provision can result in certain groups of people receiving preferential treatment, or survivors being supported in isolation from other persons with disabilities and/or injuries. This has occurred in South Sudan where ex-combatants were treated separately from other persons with similar injuries, thereby excluding them from some peer support activities.[56]

Section 4: Returning to the community

Article 19 of the CRPD mandates people-centred assistance services be provided in the community, rather than institutionalised settings. It is essential that appropriate services be available and accessible for people when they leave hospital. These services must be adapted to the nature and severity of the injury, as well as to the setting into which the individual returns. Community-level support for survivors is an essential component of rehabilitation and may take many forms: visits to outpatient clinics, home visits, peer support groups, and community-based rehabilitation are some prime examples.

For survivors with permanent impairments, long-term physical rehabilitation services will likely be required to prevent development of further co-morbidities and possible death from infection, pressure sores, or the like. Infection care regimes, self-management and caregiver skills development, assistive device provision, access to affordable medicines and pain control are some of the key focus areas upon return to the community. The success of rehabilitation is a function not only of individual and injury characteristics but also of the dismantling of societal and environmental barriers. Thus, the rehabilitation process at community level must focus on going to school or work and participation in community life, focusing on such aspects as physical accessibility, self-esteem building, and breaking down discriminatory attitudes.[57]

Two recent studies of people with gun-related spinal cord injuries demonstrated that rehabilitation outcomes can be undermined by a lack of support at home (e.g. fragmented, unstable families), material resources (e.g. low income), and negative attitudes by the injured individual toward engagement with the rehabilitation process and the professionals involved in it (e.g. resistant, unengaged in the process).[58] The extent of rehabilitative support needs is clearly linked to the complexity of the injury situation and the existence of co-morbid conditions such as drug and substance addiction.[59]

Rehabilitation must also take into account the survivor's socio-economic position. For example, the most likely survivor of a gunshot injury in the USA is a young, unmarried African American male who has not completed high school and is unemployed.[60] These facts must be considered in the design of appropriate rehabilitation programmes along with the socio-political context in which interventions are to take place (see the Spotlights, Quality Rehabilitation and Links to Violence Reduction and Paying for Gun-related Impairment in the United States, for further detail).

In Cité Soleil, a renowned "red zone" in Port au Prince, Haiti, for example, rehabilitation services are inaccessible as service providers are unable to visit, and survivors frequently unable to leave, due to the violent gang-controlled nature of the area. In other areas, men, women and children experiencing disability find that poverty, stigma, the local terrain and lack of appropriate transportation has made rehabilitation facilities virtually impossible to access (for further analysis, see the Spotlight, Spinal Cord Injury in Haiti).

Caregiving

Trusted and reliable personal assistance is often crucial to maintain health, prevent secondary health problems, promote access to vocational training, and enable social integration. Personal assistance may come in the form of family or community members, or trained professionals. With the latter requiring skilled staff and strong social welfare programmes or heavy out-of-pocket expenses, access is a major issue, particularly in LMICs.

In inner-city neighbourhoods blighted by violence or rural locations affected by armed violence, family bonds may be broken, communities shattered by violence, and support services for survivors rudimentary. Mothers, wives, girl-children, grandparents, aunts, and siblings are often the principal assistance providers to injured survivors. In most cultures, domestic responsibilities fall on female family members; caring for an injured relative generally falls within this category. When demands are high, children (particularly girls) may also have to shoulder some (or much) of the burden of caregiving.[61]

Livelihood and lifestyle adaption to provide care can translate into lost economic or educational opportunities, as well as emotional stress, reduced wellbeing, and burnout.[62] Respite care—by other family members, community groups and/or professionals—is essential to avoid burnout and other negative consequences of full-time caregiving. In most cultures, domestic responsibilities fall on female family members; caring for an injured relative generally falls within this category. When demands are high, children (particularly girls) may also have to shoulder some (or much) of the burden of caregiving.[63] Caregivers may struggle with challenges related to their own health, education, well-being, ability to perform paid work, and care of children or elderly family members.

Assistive devices and environmental adaptations

Technological solutions have an increasingly important place in the toolkit of environmental adaptation and personal assistance. Wheelchair accessible footpaths and products such as stair or bath lifts and smart home safety monitoring systems remain the ideal, but one that not many can afford, even in high-income countries. Even a basic wheelchair or prosthetic device—essential for basic mobility—is out of reach for many survivors. (See the Spotlight Danilo and the ISRI Rehabilitation Centre in El Salvador for more on this theme.) In LMICs the situation is daunting: only 5-15% of people living with disability can access assistive devices.[64] Such assistive technologies often carry a high price tag and are rarely covered by health insurers (for those who have such coverage).[65]

Public or social housing is also less likely to be appropriately modified to meet accessibility requirements, either for structural reasons (e.g. stair-lifts cannot be fitted or doorways are too narrow to allow for wheelchair access) or lack of legislation and its enforcement. While legislation and enforcement may be quite variable, in many instances private landlords are under no obligation to make potentially costly modifications. Without such modifications, opportunities for independent living can be significantly curtailed.[66] The situation is amplified during war or in countries recovering from conflict, where the infrastructure, and its accessibility, is severely compromised.

In many countries, information, funds and access to repair or replacement services can be major obstacles. Even where financial assistance is available, the paperwork involved can be prohibitive. As stated by John: "I have to go through all this paperwork to just get a ramp or a new chair. I have to go through questions from the insurance company: Do you need a new chair? I have to prove to them that the problem is so great that they need to change it." (Aged 39, paraplegia from gun violence, Washington DC.)[67]

For effective barrier breakdown, adaptations must also be made to the wider environment. For example, an affordable and accessible transport infrastructure is critically important for community integration.[68] In neighbourhoods with high crime rates and/or in states of decay, safe and accessible public transport routes (including accessible footpaths, walking and cycling paths) and transit services are less likely to be found.[69] Overcrowding and discrimination are often challenges, particularly in LMICs where disability rights legislation is often weak or non-existent and there are competing priorities for scarce resources. Where they exist, specialised para-transit services may not always be reliable and as flexible as needed. The lack of access to transportation may in turn preclude a return to education, employment, or medical and therapy appointments. This has been the case for Wellington in Rio de Janeiro, who was not able to attend much-needed sessions with a psychologist simply due to a lack of transport (see the Spotlight, Vera and Wellington in Brazil).

While most countries have some policies and regulations in place to provide assistance for families, many lack the resources for financial and instrumental family support and home adaptations to maximise supported living in home environments (see the chapter, Social Protection, for further detail).

Box 1. Profile: Ben

My basic concern is with other people. I had a strong family and friends and things like that, but I know there's a lot of people [in a different situation]... Some people I went to rehab with seemed like they fell back. They went back to the same person they were before their injury. A lot of people fell back into the same traps that got them into the situation the first time. They let that consume them. They're on a crash course with themselves... Every individual is different, but my suggestion would be to have better awareness and violence counselling... There needs to be better outreach... First you have to notice where they came from, what kind of lifestyle they led before and what kind of lifestyle they're leading

---

now, and try to solve these issues. Some of it could be positive programmes, things that could help them switch and maintain a positive life, getting through obstacles and being somebody.

Note: Aged 27 at the time of interview in 2003; with paraplegia from gun violence.[70]

Community Based Rehabilitation

Community-based rehabilitation (CBR) is a particularly useful approach for resource-poor contexts. It has followed the shift from an individual medical approach to a more holistic one, and has been redefined as "a strategy within general community development for the rehabilitation, poverty reduction, equalization of opportunities and social inclusion of all people with disabilities."[71] CBR may include: home visits by rehabilitation and mental health workers, support group creation, and the local fabrication of assistive devices or environmental adaptations using low-cost local materials. It is a promising but not yet widespread approach.

The World Health Organization promotes implementation of CBR programmes "...through the combined efforts of people with disabilities themselves, their families, organizations and communities, and the relevant governmental and non-governmental health, education, vocational, social and other services."[72] The 2010 CBR guidelines emphasise community-based inclusive development, focusing on empowerment and mainstreaming of disability and facilitating access to health, education, jobs and social activity.[73] Mainstreaming—ensuring that all services and programmes are disability-inclusive—is central to the successful participation of people with injuries and impairments into society. The CBR approach, while showing success in a number of settings, remains aspirational, as it requires the implementation of long-term processes, and in particular, support from national and local governmental authorities to ensure sustainability.

Even in developed countries, "there are challenges with access to services at the community level" because of low prioritisation and funding, as well as inadequate or under trained staff.[74] This is compounded by wider barriers such as inaccessible transport networks, discriminatory attitudes, etc. Hence peer support and self-help approaches can be critically important in the process of removing barriers and obstacles.

Section 5: Obstacles to rehabilitation

While policies on violence prevention, and protocols for medical management are improving in some contexts, rehabilitation policies and standards are lagging behind as it is rarely regarded a priority. As a result, services that are eminently complementary are not coherently delivered. In many cases this is exacerbated by the uneven distribution of financial and administrative responsibilities across various departments (e.g. health, social care, education).

Where rehabilitation services exist, access remains limited due to:

- Negative attitudes from service providers, transport operators and others to those seeking care, which may create stigma;

- Barriers to access, compounded by a survivors' own resistance to accessing services for fear of being negatively labelled "disabled";
- Limited training and variable standards for rehabilitation workers at all levels from community to hospitals;
- Poor training and awareness on disability and its relationship with injuries by mainstream health and social services personnel;
- Fragmented services and poor referral systems;
- Uneven distribution of services (both in type and location), often with high concentration in urban centres;
- Prohibitive costs;
- Inadequate staffing;
- Inaccessible buildings;
- Communication difficulties; and
- Inaccessible or expensive transportation systems.

A comprehensive multi-disciplinary rehabilitation programme will involve various types of specialised and non-specialised workers. Yet a lack of training programmes and variable training standards are leading reasons why there are inadequate numbers of appropriate rehabilitation staff in many countries. Underlying reasons include basic lack of resources, as well as low prioritisation of disability-specific services more widely. The below example illustrates how some of these barriers can be overcome, even in a very resource-poor context like South Sudan.

Box 2. Health worker training in Jonglei state, South Sudan: An example of good practice

The proliferation of weapons in South Sudan, a context with on-going low-level conflict particularly along borders and between tribes, causes a high level of gun violence related injuries. In a setting with almost non-existent rehabilitation services, the consequences can be dire. In Jonglei state before 2007, people with gunshot wounds were medically stabilised and then discharged home without any rehabilitation. This often resulted in the development of preventable secondary impairments simply for the lack of rehabilitation care.

To overcome this problem and reduce long-term consequences of the injuries, a training programme was set up by Handicap International in a number of hospitals seeing high levels of people wounded from gunshots. The programme operates in partnership with the Ministry of Health and NGO health service providers. Nurses and nursing assistants are sensitised to the disabling consequences of injuries and trained in prevention, assessment, and management of injuries and impairments. The training focuses on basic rehabilitation techniques including essential exercises, positioning to reduce contracture, prescription of mobility devices and pressure sore management. Alongside the nurses training programme, doctors are sensitised on the importance of rehabilitation to facilitate referrals. A community follow-up programme has also been set up to continue care and support once the person is discharged from hospital, both at the level of primary health care centres and at home with caregivers.

Training of nurses on basic rehabilitation measures is important in any context, and becomes essential when specialised rehabilitation services do not exist. Simple measures implemented during the acute phase of an injury can make a major difference in avoiding the development of preventable long-term consequences of injuries.

During armed conflict, services may be unequally available for different fighting factions and populations under their control; and awareness or prioritisation of both the need for rehabilitation and the service options low.[75] For example, people in conflict settings may neglect rehabilitation while they are still caught up in fighting and may not realise or admit they have needs.[76]

Rehabilitation services are rarely connected to other programmes such as education, employment, and social protection. In addition, rehabilitation services face sustainability challenges. Funding for innovative rehabilitation projects may not be sustainable or the effectiveness of interventions is not borne out by empirical evidence. Moreover, multiple understandings of what constitutes "sustainability" may compete with one another.[77] The ultimate rehabilitation goals of increasing inclusion and participation of survivors in their communities will be greatly hindered unless these essential services are strongly inter-linked and sustainable approaches are used.

Apart from the immediate health-related consequences of gun violence, the disabling social impact of limited rehabilitation is considerable. Many young gun violence survivors have not completed high school, had vocational training, or skilled work experience. When returning to their communities after initial trauma care or inpatient rehabilitation, this population has lower post-injury employment and education rates.[78] Pre-injury involvement with the criminal justice system may also preclude social service interventions, inhibiting long-term social integration.[79]

Section 6: Standards and normative frameworks
A number of international standards and protocols mandate or promote the development of, and access to, rehabilitation services. Most are non-binding, resulting in uneven application. Even where they are binding, inadequate implementation and monitoring systems limit their practical application.

For further analysis on rehabilitation in criminal justice and legal contexts, across situations of violent crime as well as armed conflict, see the chapter, Evolution of Victims' Rights and International Standards. Box 2, in that chapter, reflects on the 2012 General Comment issued by the UN Committee on the Convention Against Torture, which provided clarity on the right to redress of which one core element is rehabilitation.

The WHO International Classification of Disability, Function and Health (ICF), and the RIPPH/INDCP Disability Creation Process both adopt the "interaction" model of disability—viewing disability as a dynamic relationship between an individual and their environment.[80] This view also underpins the CRPD. The adoption of the CRPD in 2006 was a pivotal moment in the shift to a human rights-based model towards disability. It recognises that, for people living with disability to fully exercise their rights, barriers must be addressed at both individual and societal levels; for example, guaranteeing access to appropriate services to improve functioning, while also removing barriers within the environment in which the person lives.

The most important binding obligations for States on rehabilitation are associated with the CRPD. The sections of the CRPD relevant to gun violence and/

or rehabilitation services include articles on accessibility (Article 9), freedom from exploitation, violence, and abuse (Article 16), living independently and being included in the community (Article 19), personal mobility (Article 20), and habilitation and rehabilitation (Article 26). For example:

- Article 26 requires States to "organise, strengthen and extend comprehensive habilitation and rehabilitation services and programmes", ensuring programmes are multi-disciplinary and, as also stated in Article 19, provided close to people with disabilities in their own communities;
- Article 16 focuses on people affected by violence, mandating that States "promote the physical, cognitive and psychological recovery, rehabilitation and social reintegration of persons with disability who become victims of any form of exploitation, violence or abuse", in an age—and gender-appropriate manner; and
- Article 32 states a requirement for inclusive international cooperation and development programmes. This places some of the obligation on States providing development assistance.

The 1993 non-binding UN *Standard Rules on the Equalization of Opportunities for Persons with Disabilities* (Standard Rules) precede the CRPD (see Annex 1 for more detail). However, according to a 2005 survey on its implementation, 50% of the respondent countries had no legislation on rehabilitation, and 40% of countries had not established rehabilitation programmes.[81] This confirms that the challenge is not just the creation of legislation, but also its implementation.

A 2005 resolution by the World Health Assembly (WHA) urges States to promote access to rehabilitation services, promote and strengthen community-based rehabilitation programmes, and facilitate access to assistive devices.[82] The WHO developed a five-year action plan (2006-2011), based on the Standard Rules and the 2005 WHA resolution. Further, the revised CBR guidelines launched in 2010 are an example of a concrete outcome of the resolution.

In 2013, a further WHA resolution urged States to implement the CRPD, develop a national disability strategy and plan of action, and improve data collection. States are also encouraged to ensure that mainstream health services are disability-sensitive and provide more support to informal caregivers. The Resolution also tasks the WHO to develop an action plan based on findings from the *World Report on Disability*.[83]

At a more technical level, a number of standards, guidelines and good practices on rehabilitation are emerging, although there remain a number of areas where standards still do not exist. A non-exhaustive list of guidelines that provide practical recommendations includes:

- WHO Community-based rehabilitation guidelines;[84]
- Guidelines on the provision of manual wheelchairs in less resourced settings;[85]
- Guidelines for training personnel in developing countries for prosthetics and orthotics services;[86]

- UN Inter-Agency Standing Committee guidelines on mental health and psychosocial support in emergency settings;[87]
- E-learning modules of the International Spinal Cord Society;[88] and
- The Sustainability Analysis Process: The case of physical rehabilitation.[89]

The WHO released a joint position paper on mobility device provision in 2009. Developed in collaboration with 20 governmental and non-governmental actors, the paper aims to support the implementation of the CRPD with respect to personal mobility.[90] One of the outcomes of this process has been the development of a wheelchair service training package, launched in 2012, which aims to train experts from a range of countries to deliver further training in their home country. This training demonstrates a key shift from simply delivering wheelchairs, to a more comprehensive integrated service approach.[91]

Both the 1997 Anti-Personnel Mine Ban Treaty and the 2008 *Convention on Cluster Munitions* (CCM) provide examples of inclusion of rehabilitation concerns into weapons treaties.[92] Article 6 of the Mine Ban Convention states that "each State Party in a position to do so shall provide assistance for the care and rehabilitation, and social and economic reintegration, of mine victims." The CCM takes a firmer stance: under Article 5 (Victim Assistance) States are obligated to "adequately provide age—and gender-sensitive assistance, including… rehabilitation and psychological support." Development of national laws, policies and action plans, and incorporation of relevant standards and good practices include part of the obligations of this convention. Both treaties have provided the foundation for improvements in victim assistance services and coverage to survivors of those weapons. Although such assistance is now a prominent aspect of both treaty processes, implementation has not been without challenges, with assistance to survivors often overlooked to focus on other obligations such as demining and stockpiling (see Annex 1 for further analysis.) More positively, the push to provide meaningful assistance has engaged States and others (UN agencies, NGOs) to address disability discrimination and increase understanding of psychosocial consequences of violence and trauma.

Conclusion
When framed within the human rights model of disability, rehabilitation focuses on maximising the independence, inclusion and participation of an individual in society by targeting both personal and environmental factors. This is not yet the case. To date, services—where they exist—remain heavily weighted towards individual medical treatment and interventions.

Efforts to improve access to rehabilitation must overcome a number of barriers including negative attitudes, stigma, uneven and inadequate services, limited and variable staff training, and low awareness and prioritisation. For gun violence survivors, early and ongoing rehabilitation is essential to overcome trauma, improve functioning and participation, and limit the development of preventable secondary impairments and conditions.

Although legislation and policies are improving in some settings, major gaps still exist in the content of existing standards, and in their application. Following the adoption of the CRPD and the release of the *World Report on Disability*, now is the time to build on existing standards and ensure implementation. In particular, application of the CRPD at country level through legislation, policies, national strategies and application of technical standards is essential. The development of mainstream and specific services concurrently, inclusion of survivors in the decision-making process, holistic and context-appropriate services, training of rehabilitation and mainstream workers, and increased research and data collection are all priorities.

Contributors: Thilo Kroll, Co-Director, Social Dimensions of Health Institute of the Universities of Dundee and St Andrews, UK. **Aleema Shivji**, Director, Handicap International UK. The views expressed in this chapter are personal and do not officially present or represent those of Handicap International. Additional drafting and editing was undertaken by **Cate Buchanan**, **Rebecca Peters**, **Emile LeBrun** and **Mireille Widmer**.

Peer reviews were provided by **Thomas Elbert**, Professor for Clinical Psychology and Behavioural Neuroscience, Department of Psychology, University of Konstanz; and Vivo International (Germany); **Merle Friedman**, psychologist (South Africa); **Nora Groce**, Director, Leonard Cheshire Disability and Inclusive Development Centre, University College London (United Kingdom); **Tom Shakespeare**, formerly of the World Health Organization Disability and Rehabilitation Team (Switzerland); senior lecturer, Norwich Medical School, University of East Anglia (United Kingdom); and **Fiona Stephenson**, Coordinator, Haiti Spinal Cord Injury Database (Haiti).

References

[1] World Health Organization and World Bank, *World Report on Disability* (Geneva: WHO, 2011), p. 96.
[2] While efforts were made to identify sources of information from different settings, it should be noted that the great bulk of relevant existing literature on gun violence and rehabilitation currently comes from the United States.
[3] World Health Organization and World Bank (2011), pp. 95-96.
[4] World Health Organization and World Bank (2011), p. 43. To note that while the report does confirm the additional costs, it also states that it is extremely difficult to quantify these costs.
[5] M. Oliver, *The Politics of Disablement* (London: MacMillan, 1990); C. Barnes and G. Mercer, "Breaking the Mould? An Introduction to Doing Disability Research," In C. Barnes and G. Mercer (Eds), *Doing Disability Research* (Leeds, UK: The Disability Press, 1997), pp. 1-14; A. Officer and N. Groce, "Key concepts in disability," *The Lancet* 374/9704 (2009), pp. 1795-1796.
[6] The CRPD does not provide a fixed definition of disability, and further goes on to state in Article 1 that impairments may be of a physical, mental, intellectual or sensory nature.
[7] W.O. McKinley, J.S. Johns and J.J. Musgrove, "Clinical presentations, medical complications, and functional outcomes of individuals with gunshot wound-induced spinal cord injury," *American Journal of Physical Medicine and Rehabilitation* 78/2 (1999), pp. 102-107.
[8] W.M. Kaptigau, L. Ke and J.V. Rosenfeld, "Open depressed and penetrating skull fractures in Port Moresby General Hospital from 2003 to 2005," *Papua and New Guinea Medical Journal* 50/1-2 (2007), pp. 58-63.
[9] D.M. Burnett, S.A. Kolakowsky-Hayner, J.M. White and D.X. Cifu, "Impact of minority status following traumatic spinal cord injury," *Neurorehabilitation* 17/3 (2002), pp. 187-194.

[10] L. Colgan and D. Shannon, "Dento-alveolar and facial injury caused by air gun pellets," *Dental update* 37/5 (2010), pp. 323-325.

[11] D.J. Strauss, M.J. Devivo, D.R. Paculdo and R.M. Shavelle, "Trends in life expectancy after spinal cord injury," *Archives of Physical Medicine and Rehabilitation* 87 (2006), pp.1079-85.

[12] A.S. Burns and C. O'Connell, "The challenge of spinal cord injury care in the developing world," *Journal of Spinal Cord Medicine* 35/1 (2012), pp. 1-6.

[13] J.S. Krause, L.L. Saunders and M.J. Devivo, "Income and Risk of Mortality After Spinal Cord Injury," *Archives of Physical Medicine and Rehabilitation* 92/3 (2011), pp. 339-345.

[14] World Health Organization and World Bank (2011), p. 116.

[15] Y.H. Hong and S.K. Mun, "A case of sudden unilateral sensorineural hearing loss with contralateral psychogenic hearing loss induced by gunshot noise," *Military Medicine* 176/10 (2011), pp.1193-1195.

[16] Interview by Aleema Shivji with Pete Skelton, physiotherapist based in Libya with the International Medical Corps, Libya, 30 March 2012.

[17] P. Devlieger and F. Balcazar, "Bringing them back on the right track: Perceptions of medical staff on the rehabilitation of individuals with violently acquired spinal cord injuries," *Disability and Rehabilitation* 32/6 (2010), pp. 444-451; T. Kroll, "Rehabilitative needs of individuals with spinal cord injury resulting from gun violence: The perspective of nursing and rehabilitation professionals," *Applied Nursing Research* 21 (2008), pp. 45-49.

[18] Interview by Aleema Shivji with Chiara Retis, Rehabilitation Technical Advisor with Handicap International Federation, Lyon, France, 28 March 2012.

[19] W.O. McKinley, S.A. Kolakowsky and J.S. Kreutzer, "Substance abuse, violence, and outcome after traumatic spinal cord injury," *American Journal Of Physical Medicine and Rehabilitation* 78/4 (1999), pp. 306-312.

[20] S.H. Kitchel, "Current treatment of gunshot wounds to the spine," *Clinical Orthopaedics and Related Research* 408 (2003), pp. 115-119; W.O. McKinley, J.S. Johns and J.J. Musgrove, "Clinical presentations, medical complications, and functional outcomes of individuals with gunshot wound-induced spinal cord injury," *American Journal of Physical Medicine and Rehabilitation* 78/2 (1999), pp.102-107.

[21] D.D. Cardenas, T.N. Bryce, K. Shem, J.S. Richards and H. Elhefni, "Gender and minority differences in the pain experience of people with spinal cord injury," *Archives of Physical Medicine and Rehabilitation* 85/11 (2004), pp.1774-1781; J.D.R. Putzke, J.S. Richards and M.J. Devivo, "Gunshot versus nongunshot spinal cord injury—Acute care and rehabilitation," *American Journal of Physical Medicine and Rehabilitation* 80/5 (2001), pp.366-370.

[22] See http://en.wikipedia.org/wiki/Autonomic_dysreflexia Web page updated 20 November 2012. Accessed 6 June 2013. E.H. Carillo, J.K. Gonzalez, L.E. Carrillo, P.M. Chacon, N. Namias, O.C. Kirton and P.M. Byers, "Spinal cord injuries in adolescents after gunshot wounds: An increasing phenomenon in urban North America," *Inquiry* 29 (1998), pp. 503-507; W.O. McKinley, A.B. Jackson, D.D. Cardenas and M.J. Devivo, "Long-term medical complications after traumatic spinal cord injury: a regional model systems analysis," *Archives of Physical Medicine and Rehabilitation* 80/11 (1999), pp. 1402-1410.

[23] R.L. Waters, R.H. Adkins, I. Sie and J. Cressy, "Postrehabilitation outcomes after spinal cord injury caused by firearms and motor vehicle crash among ethnically diverse groups," *Archives of Physical Medicine and Rehabilitation* 79 (1998), pp. 1237-1243.

[24] J.A. Saint, D. Calfee, C.P. Kowalski and S.L. Krein, "Catheter-associated Urinary Tract Infection and the Medicare Rule Changes," *Annals of Internal Medicine* 150/12 (2009), pp. 877-884.

[25] A.S. Burns and C. O'Connell, "The challenge of spinal cord injury care in the developing world," *Journal of Spinal Cord Medicine* 35/1 (2012), pp. 1-6; F. Stephenson, "Transforming care for patients with spinal cord injury in Haiti," *Nursing Times* 108 18/19 (2012), pp. 22-23. Available at: www.nursingtimes.net/nursing-practice/clinical-zones/continence/transforming-care-for-patients-with-spinal-cord-injury-in-haiti/5044290.article Accessed 3 December 2012.

[26] S.C. Kirshblum, M.M. Priebe, C.H. Ho, W.M. Scelza, A.E. Chiodo and L.A. Wuermser, "Spinal cord injury medicine—Rehabilitation phase after acute spinal cord injury," *Archives of Physical Medicine and Rehabilitation* 88/3 Suppl 1 (2007), S62-S70.

[27] For example the Functional Independence Measure (FIM).

[28] C.V. Granger, A.K. Karmarkar, J.E. Graham, A. Deutsch, P. Niewczyk, M.A. Divita and K.J. Ottenbacher, "The uniform data system for medical rehabilitation: report of patients with

traumatic spinal cord injury discharged from rehabilitation programs in 2002-2010," *American Journal of Physical Medicine and Rehabilitation* 91/4 (2012), pp. 289-299.

[29] D.D. Cardenas, T.N. Bryce, K. Shem, J.S. Richards and H. Elhefni, "Gender and minority differences in the pain experience of people with spinal cord injury," *Archives of Physical Medicine and Rehabilitation* 85/11 (2004), pp. 1774-1781.

[30] S.C. Kirshblum et al (2007).

[31] I.G. Fiedler, P.W. Laud, D.J. Maiman and D.F. Apple, "Economics of managed care in spinal cord injury," *Archives of Physical Medicine and Rehabilitation* 80/11 (1999), pp.1441-1449.

[32] Spinal Injuries Association, *Preserving and Developing the National Spinal Cord Injury Service: Phase 2—Seeking the evidence* (Milton Keynes: SIA, 2009), p. 19.

[33] V. Riis and M.C. Verrier, "Outpatient spinal cord injury rehabilitation: managing costs and funding in a changing health care environment," *Disability and Rehabilitation* 29/19 (2007), pp.1525-1534.

[34] J. Shapiro, "A new nursing home population: The young," *National Public Radio*, December 9 (2010). Includes data from the US Centers for Medicare and Medicaid Services. Available at: http://n.pr/dPMli3 Accessed 3 December 2012.

[35] Interviews conducted as part of a research study led by Thilo Kroll in Washington DC in 2003.

[36] Centre for Humanitarian Dialogue, *Trauma as a consequence—and cause—of gun violence*, Background paper No. 1 commissioned from Vivo International (Geneva: HD Centre, 2006). See also: D. Summerfield, "The Psychosocial Effects of Conflict in the Third World," *Development in Practice* 1/3 (1991) pp. 159-173; E. Krug, L. Dahlberg, J. Mercy, A. Zwi and R. Lozano, *World Report on Violence and Health* (Geneva: World Health Organization, 2002); T. Calvot, G. Pegon, S. Rizk and A. Shivji, *Practical guideline to implement inclusive mental health and psychosocial supports in emergency and post-crisis contexts* (Lyon: Handicap International, 2013, in press). Most of this section has been drawn with permission from Aleema Shivji's work on psychosocial support with Handicap International, in particular from this last publication.

[37] A. Elwan, *Poverty and disability: a survey of the literature*, Social Protection Unit, Human Development Network (Washington DC: The World Bank, 1999), p. 19. Elwan specifically notes that "estimates of the numbers of people with conflict-related disabilities, where they exist, are likely to underestimate some of the psychological disabilities brought on by conflict-related trauma that often remain undiagnosed and unrecorded."

[38] T.E. Keane, D.J. Brief, E.M. Pratt and M.W. Miller, "Assessment of PTSD and its Comorbidities in Adults," In M.J. Friedman, T.M. Keane and P.A. Resick, *Handbook of PTSD: Science and Practice* (New York: The Guildford Press, 2007); E. Krug et al (2002); Centre for Humanitarian Dialogue (2006).

[39] E. Krug et al (2002); Inter-Agency Standing Committee, *IASC Guidelines on Mental Health and Psychosocial Support in Emergency Settings* (Geneva: IASC, 2007).

[40] T. Shakespeare, L.I. Iezzoni and N.E. Groce, "Disability and the training of health professionals," *The Lancet* 374/9704 (2009), pp. 1815-1816.

[41] Interview conducted in March 2012 with a male survivor of the 2011 Libyan conflict by staff at the International Medical Corps, Libya.

[42] R. Ostrander, "Meditations on a Bullet: Violently Injured Young Men Discuss Masculinity, Disability and Blame," *Child and Adolescent Social Work Journal* 25/1 (2008), pp. 71-84; T. Calvot et al (2013, in press).

[43] T. Tanielian, "Invisible wounds of War. Recommendations for addressing psychological and cognitive injuries," RAND Corporation Testimony Series (Santa Monica: RAND, 2008).

[44] Centre for Humanitarian Dialogue, "Women, men and gun violence: Options for action," *Missing Pieces: Directions for reducing gun violence through the UN process on small arms control* (Geneva: HD Centre, 2005); V. Farr, H. Myrttinen and A. Schnabel (Eds), *Sexed Pistols: The Gendered Impacts of Small Arms and Light Weapons* (Tokyo: United Nations University Press, 2009).

[45] Inter-Agency Standing Committee (2007). Also see: E. Martz (Ed), *Trauma Rehabilitation After War and Conflict: Community and Individual Perspectives* (Portland: Springer, 2010); M. Berghs, *War and Embodied Memory: Becoming Disabled in Sierra Leone* (Surrey, UK: Ashgate: 2012).

46 E. Krug et al (2002); Inter-Agency Standing Committee (2007); T. Calvot et al (2013, in press).

47 M.D. Seery, E.A. Holman and R. Cohen Silver, "Whatever Does Not Kill Us: Cumulative Lifetime Adversity, Vulnerability, and Resilience," *Journal of Personality and Social Psychology* 99/6 (2010), pp. 1025-1041.

48 Inter-Agency Standing Committee (2007).

49 T. Calvot et al (2013, in press); Inter-Agency Standing Committee (2007); Geneva International Centre for Humanitarian Demining, *Assisting Landmine and other ERW Survivors in the Context of Disarmament, Disability and Development* (Geneva: GICHD, 2011).

50 A. Butchart, A. Phinney, P. Check and A. Villaveces, *Preventing Violence: A Guide to Implementing the Recommendations of the World Report on Violence and Health* (Geneva: World Health Organization, 2004), p. 61.

51 On the "wake up call" angle, see: B. Hernandez, "A voice in the chorus: perspectives of young men of color on their disabilities, identities, and peer-mentors," *Disability and Society* 20/2 (2005), pp. 117-133.

52 See the work of the *Disabling Bullet project* in the USA for an example of peer support. See also I. Ljungberg, T. Kroll, A. Libin, S. Gordon, S. Groah and M. Neri, "Using peer mentoring with people with spinal cord injury to enhance self-efficacy beliefs and prevent medical complications," *Journal of Clinical Nursing 20* 3-4 (2011), pp. 351-358.

53 A.S. Burns and C. O'Connell, "The challenge of spinal cord injury care in the developing world," *Journal of Spinal Cord Medicine* 35/1 (2012), pp. 1-6.

54 R. Ostrander (2008).

55 Interview by Aleema Shivji with Joanna Woodrow, physiotherapist speaking about personal and professional experiences in Ireland, Haiti and Libya, London, 4 April 2012.

56 Interview by Aleema Shivji with Chiara Retis, 28 March 2012.

57 V. Riis and M.C. Verrier, "Outpatient spinal cord injury rehabilitation: managing costs and funding in a changing health care environment," *Disability and Rehabilitation* 29/19 (2007), pp.1525-1534.

58 P. Devlieger and F. Balcazar (2010); T. Kroll (2008).

59 N. Cook, "Respiratory care in spinal cord injury with associated traumatic brain injury: bridging the gap in critical care nursing interventions," *Intensive and Critical Care Nursing* 19/3 (2003), pp. 143-153; R.J. Marino, J.F.J. Ditunno, W.H. Donovan and F.J. Maynard, "Neurologic recovery after traumatic spinal cord injury: data from the Model Spinal Cord Injury Systems," *Archives of Physical Medicine and Rehabilitation* 80/11 (1999), pp. 1391-1396; J.C. Farmer, A.R. Vaccaro, R.A. Balderston, T.J. Albert and J. Cotler, "The changing nature of admissions to a spinal cord injury center: violence on the rise," *Journal of Spinal Disorders and Techniques* 11/5 (1998), pp. 400-403.

60 D.M. Burnett et al (2002).

61 World Health Organization and World Bank (2011).

62 International Committee of the Red Cross, *Women and war: Health fact sheet* (Geneva: ICRC, 2001); E. Esplen, *Gender and care, overview report,* BRIDGE, Institute of Development Studies (Brighton: BRIDGE, 2009). Also see: World Health Organization and World Bank (2011); T. Calvot et al (2013, in press).

63 World Health Organization and World Bank (2011).

64 *Assistive Devices/Technologies: What WHO is doing* (Geneva: World Health Organization, undated). Available at: www.who.int/disabilities/technology/activities/en

65 The Institute of Medicine, "Assistive and Mainstream Technologies for People with Disabilities," In *The Future of Disability in America* (Washington DC: IOM, 2007), pp. 183-221.

66 N.K. Purewal, "Paths to Housing Access for the Urban Poor in Amritsar," *Global Built Environment Review* 4/2 (1997), pp. 29-43.

67 Interviews conducted as part of a study led by Thilo Kroll in Washington DC in 2003.

68 P. Loprest and E. Maag, *Barriers to and supports for work among adults with disabilities: results from the NHIS-D* (Washington DC: Urban Institute, 2001).

69 K.M. Neckerman, G.S. Lovasi, S. Davies, M. Purciel, J. Quinn, E. Feder, N. Raghunath, B. Wasserman and A. Rundle, "Disparities in Urban Neighborhood Conditions: Evidence from GIS Measures and Field Observation in New York City," *Journal of Public Health Policy* 30 (2009), pp. 264-285.

70 Interviews conducted as part of a study led by Thilo Kroll in Washington DC in 2003.

71 World Health Organization (2010), p.11.
72 World Health Organization (2010), p. 24.
73 World Health Organization (2010).
74 E-mail correspondence between Aleema Shivji and Dr. Colleen O'Connell, Research Chief at the Stan Cassidy Centre for Rehabilitation, Fredericton, Canada, 18 April 2012.
75 Recently observed in Libya (interview by Aleema Shivji with Pete Skelton, 30 March 2012) and Côte d'Ivoire (information from Handicap International).
76 Interview by Aleema Shivji with Joanna Woodrow, 4 April 2012.
77 K. Blanchett and S. Girois, "Selection of sustainability indicators for health services in challenging environments: Balancing scientific approach with political engagement," *Evaluation and Program Planning* 38 (2013), pp. 28-32.
78 E.H. Carrillo, J.K. Gonzalez, L.E. Carrillo, P.M. Chacon, N. Namias, O.C. Kirton and P.M. Byers, "Spinal cord injuries in adolescents after gunshot wounds: an increasing phenomenon in urban North America," *Injury* 29/7 (1998), pp. 503-507; W.O. McKinley, D. Cifu, L. Keyser-Marcus and K. Wilson, "Comparison of rehabilitation outcomes in violent versus non-violent traumatic SCI," *Journal of Spinal Cord Medicine* 21/1 (1998), pp. 32-36.
79 M.V. Ragucci, M.M. Gittler, K. Balfanz-Vertiz and A. Hunter, "Societal risk factors associated with spinal cord injury secondary to gunshot wound," *Archives of Physical Medicine and Rehabilitation* 82/12 (2001), pp. 1720-1723.
80 Although differences do exist between the two frameworks, both are based on the concept of an interaction between internal (health condition or impairments) and external (social and environmental) factors. World Health Organization, *International Classification of Functioning, Disability and Health (ICF)* (2012). See: www.who.int/classifications/icf/en/ Accessed 3 December 2012.The ICF was endorsed by the 54th World Health Assembly on 22 May 2001 (Resolution WHA 54.21). RIPPH (Réseau international sur le Processus de production du handicap or International Network on the Disability Creation Process), *Disability Creation Process,* RIPPH (2006). See: www.ripph. qc.ca/?rub2=2andrub=6andlang=en Accessed 3 December 2012. The Disability Creation Process (DCP) is commonly referred to by its French translation: PPH (Processus de production du handicap).
81 World Health Organization and World Bank (2011).
82 World Health Assembly, *Disability, including prevention, management and rehabilitation,* WHA58.23, 25 May (2005). Only aspects related to rehabilitation have been highlighted here.
83 World Health Assembly, *Disability,* WHA66.9, 27 May (2013).
84 World Health Organization (2010).
85 World Health Organization, *Guidelines on the Provision of Manual Wheelchairs in Less Resourced Settings* (Geneva: WHO, 2008).
86 International Society for Prosthetics and Orthotics and the World Health Organization, *Guidelines for Training Personnel in Developing Countries for Prosthetics and Orthotics Services* (Geneva: WHO, 2005).
87 Inter-Agency Standing Committee (2007).
88 See www.elearnsci.org
89 See www.sustainingability.org for the guideline, case studies and other resources on sustainability. Also see, K. Blanchett and D. Boggs, *The Sustainability Analysis Process: The case of physical rehabilitation* (UK: Handicap International and the International Centre for Evidence in Disability, 2012.)
90 World Health Organization and USAID, *Joint position paper on the provision of mobility devices in less-resourced settings: a step towards implementation of the Convention on the Rights of Persons with Disabilities (CRPD) related to personal mobility* (Geneva: WHO, 2011).
91 See, World Health Organization, "Wheelchair Service Training Package." Available at: http://who.int/disabilities/technology/wheelchairpackage/en/index.html Accessed 18 April 2013.
92 See Annex 1 for details on signature and ratification, and analysis on relevance to gun violence survival.

SPOTLIGHT SECTION
Spinal Cord Injury in Haiti

Haiti has a thriving gang culture and weak rule of law. A lack of education and legal job opportunities makes gangs attractive options for young people, particularly young men, as a form of employment and "social security". The risks for children are especially high as conventional social structures and protective institutions—schools, families and churches—are often weak in comparison to the attraction of gang life. Children as young as ten years old are reportedly used by armed groups in and around Port-au-Prince to courier drugs, warn members when security forces are conducting operations, carry weapons and intervene in armed confrontations, convey messages, act as spies, collect ransom during kidnapping, and carry out arson attacks or destroy private and public property.[1]

Guns play a prominent role in not only gang violence, but also sexual violence in Haiti. A Médecins Sans Frontières facility in Port-au-Prince provided treatment to 500 survivors of sexual violence between January 2005 and June 2007; 61% of these patients had been threatened with a gun.[2] For one woman's experience of rape and gun violence, see Box 1.

Box 1: Sexual assault and gun violence in Haiti[3]

I was at home one night, in bed. It had been a normal day—hot and humid—and I was very tired. I heard a noise and suddenly a masked man was on top of me. I struggled to get away but he had a gun. I was raped. He then shot me in my left arm and then again in my chest. The man left me for dead. He went through my room and stole things—I don't know exactly what. I just prayed to my God to help me.

The police came and took me to a hospital in Port au Prince, that is all they did. No investigation, nothing. Just took me to the hospital in the back of their van and then left.

I stayed in three different hospitals—they gave me medication to help me sleep as I could not get the vision of the man, the struggle, his smell, out of my mind... I had so many thoughts like this. The noise of the gun going off twice—it was so loud.

I was discharged back home after two months... I was so scared. I thought the thief would return and do it all again. I got flashbacks of his mask, the gunshots and his smell. I just could not sleep or be at peace.

My mother and father are dead. I have a brother who has a small child. It was very difficult and I could not walk any more. I prayed and prayed and waited for God's decision.

My cousin came to talk to me and told me of a clinic and a hospital that help people like me.

I had been in bed all the time, with very bad pain, and I had a big pressure sore. I had nightmares and bad thoughts in the day. My neighbours tried to help me but they were busy and I had no money.

> My cousin took me to the rehabilitation clinic and the doctor and psychologist talked to me—I had not spoken to anyone before and this did help a bit.[4] I was then transferred to the hospital in North Haiti—I have been here for over 6 months.[5]
>
> My future? I do not have any family here. I sometimes speak to my brother on the phone—but he is busy with his kid and work.
>
> I pray a lot. I like to sew and make things. I want to be independent again. But I still can smell him.
>
> I used to want kids… Not now. No, never. I don't like seeing children pretending to play with guns; it scares me. I don't watch violence on television—I just can't watch or hear it.
>
> I still talk to the psychologist and rehabilitation support worker. I don't know what the future will be. I am scared to go home because I think the thief will come back again.
>
> I want to work… But I am a woman and I am in Haiti…
>
> I am now in a wheelchair—I have been shot at and violated. I do not want a boyfriend. I just want peace.

Weak vital and criminal statistics make it difficult to quantify the prevalence of violence in Haiti. The UN Office on Drugs and Crime notes a homicide rate of 6.9 per 100,000 in 2010.[6] If true, this would fall near or even below the world average. But the figures are likely underestimates due to underreporting because of low levels of trust and faith in the police service and fear of gang retribution. A series of three household surveys conducted between 2005 and 2010 indicates a trend of steadily decreasing crime rates between early 2007 (after democratic elections) and 2010, but found that security still ranks highly on people's priorities.[7] Encouragingly, this trend of improving security has continued, at least in the period following the devastating January 2010 earthquake.

Accurate information on the number of guns (legal and illegal) in Haiti is difficult to obtain. In 2011, the UN estimated there were some 205,000 illegal weapons in Haiti, of which 17,000 were held by gangs.[8] The 2010 household survey found that 2.3% of respondent households of the Port-au-Prince area declared owning firearms, which researchers considered reasonably reliable.[9] Those owning firearms reported an average of 2.7 firearms per household. Interestingly, reasons stated for possessing a weapon vary according to socioeconomic status. In densely populated and low income areas, respondents stated "work" as a reason for possession, with at least one adult in these households employed as a security guard or police officer. In contrast, in other areas, the most common reason was "personal protection".

Violently acquired spinal cord injuries in a strained health system

Injuries and impairments from gun violence are common, especially among young men and boys. From October 2010 to May 2012, 44 out of 110 patients with spinal cord injury (SCI), registered at the Healing Hands for Haiti Physical Rehabilitation Clinic in Port au Prince, had sustained spinal cord injuries from the earthquake and 23 resulted from gunshots.

"Jerry", graffiti artist in Haiti. (Image: Courtesy of Fiona Stephenson, 2010)

Data is difficult to collect but continues to be received by the Haiti SCI Working Group (see below). Information gathered so far suggests that from March 2010 to May 2012, 43 out of 292 of identified people with SCIs in other clinics in Haiti were caused by gun violence, compared to 145 caused by the 2010 earthquake. Among patients injured by gun violence, 35 were men aged 19-28 years. The Working Group is hearing of new hospital/clinic referrals (due to gun violence) on a weekly basis.[10]

The country is poorly equipped to deal with such violence. Haiti ranks 158 out of 187 countries on the 2011 Human Development Index.[11] It is estimated that 80% of the population, some 10 million, people live below the poverty line and that unemployment is 40%.[12] The state of the health system further worsened with the January 2010 earthquake. The Pan American Health Organization (PAHO) state that eight hospitals were totally destroyed and 22 seriously damaged.[13]

Haiti's Ministry of Health and Population lost 200 personnel when its' building collapsed and many other health care professionals were affected elsewhere.[14] Adding the October 2010 cholera outbreak, post-trauma care has been directly affected.

Dr Fritzgerald Moise, Orthopedic Surgeon, Traumatologist and Physical Medicine and Rehabilitation specialist states: "Most of our hospitals don't have enough blood supply to cope with the profuse bleeding from gunshot wounds. In these neighborhoods, where the population is malnourished and anaemic, most people get turned away by the blood collection centers when they volunteer to donate some of their blood to help save their loved ones injured accidentally or intentionally. Sometimes precious minutes are wasted in enormous and chaotic traffic jams on their way to the major surgical units."[15]

Clearly, material support is required to (re)build resources in the health sector. Some progress can already be seen. As Dr. Moise further notes: "Major improvements have been seen in the aftermath of the earthquake. The General Hospital of the State University was severely destroyed, but is now in the process of being rebuilt. Hopefully it will be well equipped with proper operating rooms, blood bank, proper imaging lab, and spine stabilization materials, rehabilitation health care professions—nurses, physiotherapists, doctors—and enough ambulances to facilitate transportation of the most urgent cases on time."[16]

Yet equipment and facilities are not the whole story: information and training are equally important and this has become a main focus of the Haiti SCI Working Group.[17] Complex spinal cord injuries are a case in point. Before the earthquake, such injuries were poorly understood or dealt with. Anecdotally, it is believed that most SCI patients admitted to hospital were discharged within a few days or weeks to die at home. Prior to the earthquake, similar to other developing countries, the post-injury survival time in Haiti following an SCI was believed to be 1-2 years.[18] Most patients probably succumbed even sooner, which is in stark contrast to the many months of rehabilitation received by patients in the UK and USA for example who are expected to have a normal life span.[19]

Information gaps

Better information can improve quality of life and indeed save lives. To address the stark gaps in information about SCI, two initiatives were created in March 2010 by existing NGO's (Haiti Hospital Appeal, Team Canada Healing Hands, Healing Hands for Haiti): (a) The Haiti SCI Working Group, consisting of international and local SCI rehabilitation health professionals was set up to increase SCI awareness, education and health care provision; (b) The confidential Haiti SCI database seeks to ascertain the number and locations of people with SCI in Haiti, and to identify their needs, levels of injury and mechanisms of injury as well as referring them to rehabilitation services.[20]

According to data collected by the SCI Working Group, morbidity and mortality rates have decreased since the earthquake, including men and women who have sustained a SCI through gun violence. Many beneficiaries are surviving their injuries for more than two years. One reason for this is because an increasing number of NGOs provide SCI-specific equipment (wheelchairs, cushions, mattresses, urinary intermittent catheters) as well as education such as bladder, bowel, skin care, positioning and physical therapy education for the patients, their families and local health care professionals ("train the trainer" approach). Data related to children with SCI is not available at present. A three year post-earthquake follow up study is planned, and it is hoped this will assist in filling information gaps on SCI more broadly.

While the initiative is encouraging, coordination and information sharing is still limited—the majority of NGOs and civil society focus on providing services and have insufficient time, capacity, or resources to collect information. Privacy concerns also deter some organisations from sharing information and data they do have. International NGO personnel rotate in and out of Haiti, on short—and long-term missions, and knowledge transfer is sometimes poor. In some cases, new staff may not even be aware of the existence of the database. PAHO has been in Haiti for many years and has highlighted the many health care deficits seen in Haiti.[21] The Health Cluster System, an information sharing network, initially concentrated on general health requirements, then coordinated the health needs post-earthquake. However it has had to refocus its attention onto the spread of cholera, which may also affect information dissemination.[22] There was a huge surge in numbers of NGOs providing health care following the earthquake, which contributed to the chaos and disorganisation of the health care system. The Ministry for Public Health has endeavoured to take control stipulating the need for NGO's to register before providing health care. In time, this too should assist in filling essential information gaps.

In conclusion, the UN has highlighted that "the law (on disability) is not yet comprehensive in prohibiting discrimination and promoting equality for persons with disabilities, thus not meeting the principles and standards set forth in the CRPD [Convention on the Rights of Persons with Disabilities]."[23] However a positive policy development occurred in October 2012, when President Martelly and the Government signed the Declaration on Policy for the Disabled, which includes a number of commitments to promote the inclusion of Haitians experiencing disability.[24] Haiti has a Secretary of State for the Integration of Persons with Disabilities, a step ahead of many other nations in this regard, and someone well regarded to make an impact.

Contributors: **Fiona Stephenson**, Registered Nurse (UK), Haiti Spinal Cord Injury (SCI) Database Co-ordinator and member of the Haiti SCI Working Group. Editing was provided by **Cate Buchanan, Mireille Widmer, Emile** LeBrun and **Rebecca Peters.**

Peer reviews were provided by **Yann-Cedric Quero**, independent consultant (Canada); **Aleema Shivji**, independent consultant (UK) and **Kirsten Young**, formerly with the UN Stabilization Mission (Haiti).

References

[1] Child Rights International Network, *Haiti: Child Rights References in the Universal Periodic Review, National Report* (London: CRIN, 2011). Available at: www.crin.org/resources/infoDetail.asp?ID=25843 Accessed 29 November, 2012
[2] Doctors Without Borders, "Treating sexual violence in Haiti: An interview with Olivia Gayraud, MSF Head of Mission in Port-au-Prince," web interview 30 October (2007). Available at: http://web1.doctorswithoutborders.org/news/article.cfm?id=2135 Accessed 26 November 2011. Also see Human Rights Watch, *'Nobody Remembers Us', Failure to Protect Women's and Girls' Right to Health and Security in Post-Earthquake Haiti* (New York: HRW, 2011), p.18.
[3] Interview by Fiona Stephenson with a woman with spinal cord injury due to gunshot who wished to remain anonymous, Cap Haitien, 14 March 2012.
[4] Healing Hands for Haiti Physical Rehabilitation Centre, Port au Prince, Haiti.
[5] Haiti Hospital Appeal, L'Hopital Convention Baptiste D'Haiti, Carrefour La Mort, Cap Haitien, N Haiti.
[6] United Nations Office on Drugs and Crime, *Homicide Statistics 2011* (Vienna: UNODC, 2011), p. 93. Available at: www.unodc.org/documents/data-and-analysis/statistics/Homicide/Globa_study_on_homicide_2011_web.pdf Accessed 25 October 2012.

[7] A. Kolbe and R. Muggah, "Surveying Haiti's post-quake needs: a quantitative approach," *Humanitarian Exchange Magazine*, Issue 48 (London: Overseas Development Institute, 2010); A. Kolbe and R. Muggah, "Securing the State: Haiti before and after the earthquake," *Small Arms Survey 2011: States of security* (Geneva: Small Arms Survey, 2011), p. 240.

[8] United Nations General Assembly, *Children and Armed Conflict: Report of the Secretary-General*, A/65/820-S/2011/250, 23 April (2011), p. 21. Available at: http://reliefweb.int/sites/reliefweb.int/files/resources/Children%20in%20armed%20conflict.pdf Accessed 25 October 2012.

[9] A. Kolbe and R. Muggah (2011), pp. 247-248.

[10] Communications with the Haiti SCI Working Group, January 2012.

[11] United Nations Development Programme, *Human Development Report 2011: Sustainability and equity: A better future for all* (New York: UNDP, 2011).

[12] US Central Intelligence Agency, *CIA World Factbook: Haiti*. Available at: www.cia.gov/library/publications/the-world-factbook/geos/ha.html Accessed 26 November 2012.

[13] Pan American Health Organization and the World Health Organization, *Earthquake in Haiti— One Year Later: PAHO/WHO Report on the Health Situation* (Washington DC: PAHO, 2011), p. 8.

[14] Pan American Health Organization and the World Health Organization (2011), p. 10.

[15] Interviewed by Fiona Stephenson, Port au Prince, 14 February 2012.

[16] Interview with Dr. Fritzgerald Moise, orthopaedic surgeon, traumatologist, and physical medicine and rehabilitation specialist, Port au Prince, 14 February 2012.

[17] Communications with Haiti SCI Working Group and Haiti SCI Referrals, January 2012. Also see, F. Stephenson, "Simple wound care facilitates full healing in post-earthquake Haiti," *Journal of Wound Care* 20/1 (2011), pp. 5-10.

[18] F.A. Rathore, "Spinal Cord Injuries in the Developing World," In J.H. Stone and M. Blouin (Eds), *International Encyclopedia of Rehabilitation* (Buffalo: Center for International Rehabilitation Research Information and Exchange, 2011). Available at: http://cirrie.buffalo.edu/encyclopedia/en/article/141/ Accessed 26 November 2012.

[19] Spinal Injuries Association, *Preserving and Developing the National Spinal Cord Injury Service. Phase 2—Seeking the evidence. Research report* (UK: British Association of Spinal Injury Specialists, 2009), pg. 19.

[20] For further information see Haiti SCI Database www.haitidata.net coordinated by Fiona Stephenson fistephenson@gmail.com

[21] See, for example, Pan American Health Organization and the World Health Organization, *Health: A Right For All—The Challenge of Haiti* (Washington DC: PAHO/WHO, 2006). Available at: www.paho.org/english/d/csu/TheChallengeofHaiti.pdf Accessed 25 November 2012.

[22] Pan American Health Organization and the World Health Organization, *Health Cluster Bulletin: Cholera and Post-Earthquake Response in Haiti*, No. 30 (PAHO/WHO, 2011). Available at: www.who.int/hac/crises/hti/HealthCluster-Bulletin30-21122011-ENG.pdf Accessed 25 November 2012.

[23] UN Office for the Coordination of Humanitarian Affairs, *Bi-Annual Report on Human Rights in Haiti, January—June* (Port au Prince: OCHA, October 2012), p. 9, para 16. Available at: www.ohchr.org/Documents/Countries/HT/MINUSTAH-OHCHRJanuaryJune2012_en.pdf Accessed 10 November, 2012.

[24] "Haiti's Government signs declaration on policy for disabled," *Caribbean Journal* October 4 (2012). Available at: www.caribjournal.com/2012/10/04/haitis-government-signs-declaration-on-policy-for-disabled/ Accessed 27 November 2012.

SPOTLIGHT SECTION
Neville Beling (South Africa)

On the 1 May 1993, gunmen armed with AK-47 rifles, a hand grenade and teargas shot at patrons of the Highgate Hotel in East London, South Africa. Five people were killed and seven injured, three of whom remain permanently disabled. I was shot three times—in my left arm and twice in my back—and today I still have significant hip, pelvis and internal injuries which have left me with a permanent colostomy. The perpetrators have never been found or stepped forward and I am still seeking the truth, closure and justice.[1]

My cousin Roland and I went to the hotel for a few beers. As I was picking up my beer, I heard shuffling and saw a guy run up the stairs wearing a balaclava. Then the firing started. I pushed my cousin off the barstool and by the time I hit the floor I couldn't feel my left arm. I lay on the floor and I thought I can't die now, I didn't say goodbye to my mother. I was 20 years old. My life changed in a split second.

My cousin had passed out when I knocked him off the stool. I thought he was dead but I could not see, because it was pitch dark. The lights had been shot out. I remember seeing yellow powder in the air and then choking on teargas. There was no movement, no screaming, no talking. My left side went numb and I felt no pain.

In hospital
I was in hospital for two years and once had three major operations in a week. On one occasion, as I was being anesthetised, my heart failed. It was to be a double operation and they had already cut open my stomach and left hip. They shocked me 12 times and thought they broke my ribs. As a last option adrenalin was stuck into my heart.

At one stage I had acute septicaemia. I would stand and pus would run out my groin, for weeks. The doctors couldn't figure out where this infection came from as there was so much shattered bone travelling over my body. I gave up and wanted to die. Eventually, they cut further down from my left hip and found rotting bone which was removed.

You lose your dignity in hospital. There are days when you wish for visitors, for family, and when they walk through the door you wish they'd go. There is a lot my family still don't know about what I've gone through.

In hospital, I understood what people might have felt like in concentration camps. I was being tortured, that's how it felt. How much more pain can a human tolerate? I still don't know. If you had a gun you wouldn't think twice just picking it up and blowing your brains out. I wished for it to end—just let me die in theatre.

Now I relive the pain and fear every day. Some days I wake up to the smell of saline. Like the drip is still connected to my body.

Box 1. Zilla Beling: Neville's mother

We got close to the hospital, ambulances were coming in. Traffic cops, police, you name it. We ran in and saw Roland. He was so shocked. We saw Chappy (Neville's nickname) lying on a stretcher and his blood was all over the floor. We couldn't get near him there was so much blood.

The Harrises were looking for their son. Every time they heard an ambulance come in, they would get up to go and check. A minister and doctor walked in and said they would like to speak to them, and told them their son had died. We were all crying.

The longer Chappy was in hospital, the worse he got. I worked during the day and would go there every night to be with him. The nurses would change the sheets and turn him, and he would scream. I used to run out of that hospital. I couldn't stand any more of his screaming.

Do you ever live a normal life again after this? The list is long of the things I no longer do, or dream about. Simple things you probably take for granted: standing at the edge of the sea and feeling the water lap at your feet. Small things are more important than the big things.

Besides the shooting, learning to walk was the worst time of my life. I never knew how important balance was until I did not have it anymore. The physiotherapists would start by getting me to stand alongside the bed, and walk to the basin. It was like telling me to walk 50 kilometres. I was terrified to move.

I still have no idea who did this. I've had 19 long years to be ready for knowing and then I'll be able to then carry on with my life. I need it. I've been through hell and back and I want them to know it.

References

[1] For more detail see C. Ernest (Ed), *Reconciliatory Justice: Amnesties, indemnities and prosecutions in South Africa's transition* (Johannesburg: Centre for the Study of Violence and Reconciliation, 2007), pp. 22-30.

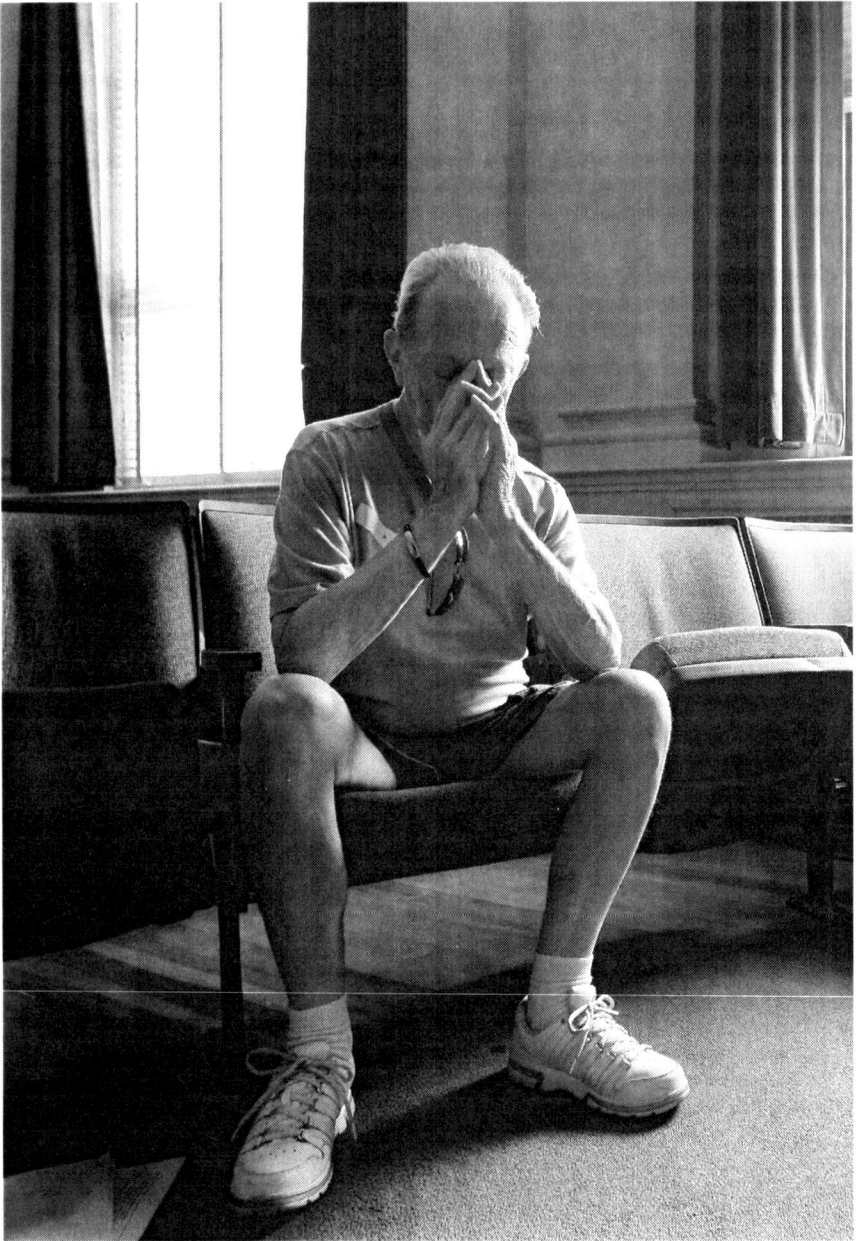

James Meunier, a retired police office on a disability pension listens to news of pension cuts he and others are being asked to accept. Meunier retired in 1979 after being shot in the line of duty in 1978. The Rhode Island (USA) state appointed receiver, running the financially troubled city, asked retired police officers and firefighters to accept significant pension cuts to avoid municipal bankruptcy. (Image: Stephan Savoia/AP, 19 July 2011)

5 Social Protection

Introduction

The cost of health care and disability resulting from gun violence can increase people's risk of falling into poverty, and many gun violence survivors are already impoverished. Where they exist, social protection programmes may cover these individuals for costs associated with their injuries and rehabilitation. After a brief overview of these programmes, this chapter examines whether they are well suited to provide for gun violence victims, or, if the structure of these programmes creates coverage gaps that leave people unprotected. The main conclusion is that many victims—mainly young people working in the informal labour market and their families as well as people who experience short term impairment and disability—are not well covered.

Section 1: Bearing the cost of surviving gun violence

Surviving gun violence can be expensive, the more so if rehabilitation takes a long time. In Burundi, almost 75% of gun violence victims seeking health care need to go into debt or sell their belongings.[1] More than 17% of those seeking treatment did not have access to care, mostly because of finances. In fact, patients can become "imprisoned" in health facilities until their relatives are able to pay their bills.[2] This is exacerbated by the fact that victims of gun violence, if there is a typical victim, are frequently young, poor, and not in the formal labour market.[3] They are therefore less likely than other groups to be provided adequate social protection. Permanent impairments are another aggravating factor. Disability is unequivocally linked to poverty, even without accounting for the extensive extra costs of living with a disability.[4]

Social protection programmes are developed to help individuals and households cope with such external shocks to their livelihoods. They have a long history, going back at least to the "Poor Laws" of Great Britain at the end of the 16th century, which were also punitive in nature, then to Civil War pensions for soldier's widows in the United States in the mid-19th century, and social insurance programmes, such as the first workers' compensation initiatives in Germany in the latter part of that century.

The modern era of social protection programmes began in the first half of the 20th century, with the establishment of social security as a basic human right in the 1948 *Universal Declaration of Human Rights*.

The welfare state in industrialised countries, and the development of new and updated social security schemes, surged in the post-World War II era. The international community sought to define minimum standards through the International Labour Organization's 1952 *Social Security Convention* (No. 102). This was followed by other conventions setting higher standards on particular issues, such as the 1964 *Employment Injury Benefits Convention* (No. 121), the 1967 *Invalidity, Old-Age and Survivors' Benefits Convention* (No. 128) and the 1969 *Medical Care and Sickness Benefits Convention* (No. 130). (For more detail on relevant international standards see Annex 1.)

Many countries have followed the principles outlined in these conventions. They set up detailed legal frameworks covering different aspects of social protection through national laws on occupational incidents and disease insurance, old age pensions, unemployment benefits, family allowances, impairment and injury insurance, compulsory insurance for the self-employed, among others. Worldwide, the most common programmes are targeted at old age, impairment and widowhood, followed by benefits for work injuries and occupational diseases, sickness and maternity care, family allowances and unemployment.[5] Only a few countries (e.g. Albania and Norway) operate with one main social security act or national insurance law covering people across all categories. In a few countries, such as Germany, South Africa and Brazil, social security is a constitutional right.

There has been a quantum leap in the development and adoption of social protection programmes as countries have begun emerging from low and middle-income status.[6] Gaps in coverage still exist, of course, and they can be substantial. For example, in low income countries of sub-Saharan Africa, not more than 5 to 10% of the workforce is covered by mandatory social insurance schemes or national provident funds.[7]

More recent is the notion of disability rights related to such public policy. The United States, Canada, and Spain were among the first countries to enact disability rights legislation in the early 1990s. Since then more than 40 countries have followed suit including the United Kingdom, Uganda, El Salvador, India, and Vietnam.[8] The enforcement of these laws is however highly variable.[9] Disability benefits can weigh quite heavily on state budgets. In the United States, about 12% of all 2008 federal expenditures (USD357 billion) were spent on people of working age with disability.[10] In addition, it is estimated that individual US state expenditures for working-age people with disabilities under federal-state programmes amounted to USD71 billion in fiscal year 2008, for total government spending of about 3% of GDP.[11]

With the agreement of the 2006 UN *Convention on the Rights of Persons with Disabilities* (CRPD) the rights of people living with disability were formalised and also articulated through social and economic development "lenses" (for more detail see Annex 1). Article 28 of the CRPD recognises the right to an adequate standard of living, and in particular the right to "social protection and to the enjoyment of that right without discrimination on the basis of disability." It outlines several measures to safeguard and promote this right, including state assistance for disability-related expenses, adequate training, counselling, financial assistance, housing, and respite care (alternative support for primary caregivers).

Section 2: Typology of social protection programmes
Social protection programmes are government actions intended to mitigate vulnerability, risk and deprivation that are considered socially unacceptable.[12] Today, such programmes are primarily intended to act as safety nets, preventing people from falling into poverty by directly giving them the means to pay for basic goods

and services. However, they are also increasingly designed to develop people's productivity and help them better manage risks, including: poor harvests, loss of employment, death of a spouse, or the onset of an illness or impairment, which can be particularly devastating to low income households.[13] These programmes can do this by providing support such as crop insurance, training programmes, microfinance, or community-driven development programmes aimed at improving infrastructure and livelihood generation in targeted areas with high rates of poverty.

Related but distinct from social protection are compensation schemes for survivors of crime or conflict. These are payments offered as judicial redress for wrongdoings, covering expenses related to the crime, including medical bills, funeral expenses, or loss of income. Box 1 provides examples of such programmes.

Social protection includes cash and in-kind transfer programmes, and programmes such as those providing public employment and community grants to disadvantaged areas. Social insurance is a subset of social protection. It includes contributory programmes, that is, insurance schemes covering participants who pay into the system. Some social insurance programmes are funded by employer contributions rather than by the individuals who would be receiving benefits—for example unemployment insurance as well as workers' compensation programmes that protect against the effects of workplace injuries and illnesses. It also includes other types of insurance (e.g. health insurance, crop insurance) and is sometimes subsidised by the State. This section presents some of the main distinctions used when describing social protection programmes.

Universal vs. categorical

Social protection programmes can be universal or categorical. Universal programmes target the entire population, no matter their characteristics. A good example is national health care, where all citizens (or long-term residents) have access either to a national health system or to government-provided health insurance. Categorical programmes target sub-populations based on particular attributes. Disability benefits are categorical, as are veterans' programmes, or programmes aimed at widows. In a few countries or regions, there are specific funds designed to address gun violence victims. For example, Guatemala has a programme for bus drivers who are disproportionately exposed to gun violence (see the Guatemala chapter for more detail.)

The advantage of categorical programmes is that they can target specific problems and operate at lower costs. In addition, helping particular groups (e.g. veterans) can be more politically popular if they are seen as more deserving. The disadvantage is that people can fall through the cracks, and in some instances—for example, with disability—it can be administratively complex to make eligibility determinations (see Section 3 below).[14]

Sometimes the distinction between universal and categorical is not very clear, for example in the case of benefits for the aging population. They serve a particular group of people, but they are universal in the sense that all people can be eligible at a certain point. Even means-tested programmes, conditional on a certain income threshold, can be considered universal, to the extent that anyone can qualify if their income is low enough.

Cash vs. in-kind

Benefits often come in the form of cash, but sometimes they can be goods or services for example food, fuel, health care, or housing. For people with impairments, this may also include assistive devices, personal assistants, or rehabilitative services. The advantage of cash transfers is that they typically have lower administrative costs and can be used more flexibly by recipients. That is, people can spend the money on their most important needs. Nevertheless, sometimes in-kind benefits are more politically popular because they limit the ability of recipients to 'abuse' benefits by purchasing items not seen as necessities—for example alcohol. In-kind programmes may also be able to make use of surplus goods, often food, or excess capacity, for example bus passes on public transportation.

Contributory vs. non-contributory

Cash benefits are provided through both contributory and non-contributory schemes. In contributory programmes, workers pay an insurance premium, which goes into a fund designed to administer benefits once the workers qualify for the programme—for example, old age and disability pensions. Non-contributory programmes are generally means tested, meaning that only individuals or households below a certain income or asset threshold are eligible. Lower income countries often rely on proxy means tests because actual income or consumption is difficult to determine. These tests often rely on assets.

Non-contributory programmes are often considered universal when eligibility is solely determined by income or consumption levels. They can also be categorical—for example aimed at single mothers or people living with disability. Sometimes eligibility is not based on personal characteristics, but is area-based. This occurs in extremely poor areas where the concentration of poverty is high enough that it is deemed not worth the effort to undertake individual means testing.

Additional conditionality

Another trend is adding conditions on receiving benefits. Conditional cash transfer programmes, which originated in Latin America but have expanded around the world, often make transfer payments conditional on children attending school or visiting health clinics. This is sometimes also called "income management".

Compensation programmes are also subject to strict eligibility criteria, which often raise a delicate distinction between victims and perpetrators. In Canada, for example, families of homicide victims will not benefit from compensation payments if the victim had a criminal record. In India, several assistance programmes exist for survivors of political violence, but assistance is denied if the victim was thought to fight on the side of opposition groups (discussed in the India chapter).

Box 1: Examples of compensation funds for survivors of violence[15]

The United Nations Compensation Commission (UNCC)
The UNCC processes claims for compensation for losses resulting from Iraq's invasion and occupation of Kuwait in 1990-91. The fund was created by UN Security Council Resolutions 687 (1991) and 692 (1991), which established Iraq's legal responsibility for such losses. The resolutions provide that compensation be funded by 5% of Iraqi oil revenues. Since the fund's creation, nearly 100 governments have submitted claims for their citizens, corporations and/or themselves, and more than USD52 billion has been awarded in compensation. Besides claims for the loss of wealth (property, business, etc.) and environmental damage, the Commission received over 6000 claims from individuals who suffered serious personal injury or whose family members died as a result of the invasion and occupation. These individuals sought a total of USD21 million in compensation. Compensation claims were also submitted for mental pain and anguish, but no official compensation figures have been published yet for this category of claims. The UNCC stopped accepting claims in 2005 and is still processing the last set of payments.

Survivors' compensation funds in the United States
The US Department of Justice runs several compensations funds for survivors of terrorist specific violence. The International Terrorism Victim Expense Reimbursement was created as a response to increasing terrorist attacks after the Lockerbie bombing in 1988.[16] For this fund, the Office for Victims of Crime is authorised to set aside some USD50 million annually to support survivors of acts of international terrorism. The fund covers medical expenses (including dental and rehabilitation costs); mental health care costs; loss, repair, or replacement of property; funeral and burial costs; and miscellaneous expenses such as temporary housing, etc.[17] Claims by survivors of the September 11 attacks in 2001 are handled by the US Department of Justice and the specific September 11th Victim Compensation Fund. The Fund operated for two years, giving USD6 billion to victims' families and USD1 billion to those injured. It reopened in 2011 after the Congress had passed the "James Zadroga 9/11 Health and Compensation Act" to provide an additional USD2.8 billion to help those whose claims to the first fund were denied, those who became ill after working at "Ground Zero" (the site of the attack in New York) and those whose illnesses can be linked to the site. Besides this federal Government compensation programme, the New York Community Trust and United Way of New York City operate another fund, which has collected more than USD534 million from two million donors.[18]

Section 3: Closing the gaps in social protection coverage

Social protection programmes often have gaps in coverage. In fact, some form of social security insurance is only available to an estimated 50% of the global population; with 80% not covered adequately.[19] In addition, some programmes only cover certain categories of people or protect against certain types of events. Nearly a third of the world's population has no access to any health facilities or services at all.[20]

How well do social protection programmes cover gun violence survivors? Data that could answer this question are not available, but Table 1 below provides an indication of where the gaps might be. It shows that security personnel (soldiers, police officers etc.) and people in long-term formal employment are the most frequently covered populations. People in informal employment and those not employed (including children) tend to receive less coverage. This section discusses the main gaps in coverage, and presents some positive initiatives to mitigate them.

Including informal workers

The biggest challenge to social protection, and social insurance programmes, in particular, is the coverage of a working age population that is heavily involved in the informal labour market. Workers in these markets are not covered by traditional contributory programmes, and often have irregular work experiences.[21] While the benefit structure is sometimes designed to be progressive, (that is, the expected returns on premiums are higher for lower income people) these programmes often do not reach the poorest of the poor because they are not in formal employment (contributions are typically made through payroll taxes) or because they cannot afford contributions. Many benefits from contributory programmes, therefore, go to the non-poor. That is not to say that all people in the informal sector are poor or even near poor, but they do not have the same level of social protection as their formal sector counterparts.

In some nations, informal workers are permitted to voluntarily contribute to social insurance schemes that are typically financed by payroll taxes. This is widespread in Latin America, and has even been used to establish unemployment insurance for informal sector workers, as in Brazil's Unemployment Insurance Savings Accounts.[22] Another trend is the creation of dual systems that combine contributory programmes with non-contributory social pension programmes, as in Bangladesh and Bolivia.[23] That is, people not covered by a programme through payroll taxes can join it by making voluntary contributions in order to participate in the insurance scheme.

One problem with this dual approach—and also with allowing voluntary opt-ins by informal workers to contributory schemes—is that young and informal workers often have intermittent work experiences, which makes regular contributions difficult. Low levels of voluntary contributions lessen benefits, and if they are low enough can disqualify someone from the programme.

It also is administratively more complex. By fragmenting the population, such schemes can become less efficient. Insurance is most effective when the pool being insured is as large as possible for a few reasons. First, it lowers administrative costs. Second, the larger pools mean more accurate actuarial estimates, which make the fund easier to manage, but maybe most importantly with a large, diverse pool, people with lower risk can subsidise people with higher risks. If sub-populations are split into different programmes then people with higher risks have to start paying more (or receiving less) which can make them less likely to contribute and thus absorb all the risk on themselves.

Another strategy to close gaps in the area of healthcare is to universalise the programme—either with mandatory participation (as in Thailand) or by making buy-in open to all (as in Ghana and Mexico), sometimes with subsidised contributions.

Measuring disability

Some eligibility criteria refer to percentage disabled, which can be difficult to quantify. Even making a reliable assessment of a person's capability to work is difficult. In the US, for example, 53% of applications end up receiving benefits upon applying to the Social Security Disability Insurance programme, but only about 36% of applicants are approved upon their initial application. Some 17% of initial applicants end up receiving benefits after going through a multi-staged appeal process that can involve additional reviews and hearings before an administrative judge.[24] Moreover, disability determination procedures are potentially open to substantial fraud if not done effectively.[25]

Another key issue is which types of impairments are covered. Workers' compensation programmes protect workers against work-related injuries and illnesses, but once again, only within the formal sector. Veterans' programmes only compensate service members for injuries sustained in the line of duty. General health care costs can be covered by national health care systems (e.g., in most countries of the Organisation for Economic Cooperation and Development, also known as the OECD) or through a subsidised health care system for veterans (e.g., in the US). Disability pensions and other long-term disability programmes generally only provide benefits for permanent disabilities that totally preclude work. Partial disabilities are often not covered.

Determining eligibility for benefits covering mental health disorders can be particularly difficult—especially if the effects are episodic, which is not uncommon. Psychological disorders are the least likely to be identified—either by self-identification or government programmes. They have more stigma, are harder to diagnose, and are sometimes intermittent.[26]

Escaping the poverty trap
The cost of disability benefits could be alleviated if beneficiaries were able to return to work. Ironically, the structure of these benefits (e.g. tying benefits to inability for any work) often provides strong disincentives to return to work.[27] Many schemes only cover people who are incapable of working, so disabled people who have limited work capacity must choose between saying they cannot work at all, or working for compensation that could be less than the benefits they will receive. Even if they could work for more compensation than their expected benefits, if their condition worsens and they can no longer work, it can be difficult to prove they should then qualify for benefits given their past work history with the same medical condition. This can make attempting to work a risky decision.

Also, people with short-term impairments—or partial disabilities that would allow continued work, even at a reduced capacity—are less covered. This is true even though a short-term impairment causing a break in employment, or a partial disability that reduces but does not eliminate earning potential, can create a situation that traps a person in poverty. Often poor and near poor people's lives are delicately balanced, and a negative shock—even a temporary one—can have long-term consequences.[28]

Returning to work
The movement towards workfare (that is public employment instead of transfers) poses potential problems for people with disabilities. If workfare jobs are not accessible and accommodations are not made, then disabled people can be excluded.

Some recent efforts are attempting to address that gap. One strategy has been the development of workfare programmes such as Mexico's Programa de Empleo Temporal and India's National Rural Employment Guarantee Scheme. These schemes provide low skilled work in labour-intensive sectors. People with impairments are often targeted for participation in such programmes. In order to be relevant for people living with disability, though, these jobs must come with accommodations, and they usually do not.

The Industrial Rehabilitation Centre in Thailand employs a holistic approach of medical and vocational rehabilitation, personal and family counselling, and job accommodations. It enabled about half of injured workers to return to work after injuries, which would previously have ended their working lives.[29] This centre was funded jointly by the governments of Thailand and Japan, and is open to applicants aged 15 and over who have experienced work-related injuries.

Another positive example from the field of workplace injury is the Return to Work programme of Malaysia's Social Security Organisation, which was launched in 2007 after a pilot in 2005. This programme combined financial support with an array of rehabilitation services. In 2011, 68% of those injured could return to work.[30] The scheme covers: treatment, rehabilitation, orthotics and prosthetics, workplace modifications, vocational retraining and job placement. Certified case managers help in the reintegration process.

In the case of schemes designed to assist workers injured on the job, the costs of disability programmes are often borne by employers. This includes cash benefits and often health benefits, too. This has given rise to disability management practices that mitigate these costs. Where possible, disability management involves both a preventive approach—making workplaces safer—but also a post-injury approach of making job accommodations, improving accessibility, and supporting rehabilitation services. Studies have shown that these practices more than pay for themselves, with reduced worker absenteeism and increased returns to work.[31]

Disability-friendly benefits

Inaccessible transportation and facilities may prevent individuals from applying for or receiving benefits once they qualify. For example, if benefits are distributed at a central location, a disabled person may have no means of getting to that location.[32] If having one's children attend school is a condition of receiving cash transfers, but schools are inaccessible, then some sort of accommodation must be made for families with children with impairments.[33] In India, as of 2005, only 15% of people living with moderate impairments and 21% of those living with severe impairments obtained disability certification.[34] The lack of certification is primarily due to either not knowing about the existence of disability benefits or not having the capacity to access them (e.g., illiteracy, difficulties in accessing or understanding the application process).

Accounting for the full cost of care

Many programmes do not account for the costs of living with disability.[35] These costs can come from extra needs for medical care, personal assistance, assistive devices, transportation and other items—even the extra time it takes to perform various activities.[36] In Vietnam, estimates show that having a disabled family member raises a household's cost of living by about 11.5%.[37] When adjustments were made to the poverty line to account for these costs, the poverty rate among such households rose from about 17% to over 23%. As so many young people are directly affected by gun violence, care costs can be life-long and financially demanding.

Not included in these costs are the care and support that must often be provided by families and friends. In Nicaragua, for example, family members reported providing ten hours of care per day for relatives with impairments.[38] These responsibilities disproportionately fall on women and girls, whose labour is typically unacknowledged and uncompensated.[39] However, examples of good practice exist. In 2008, Uruguay introduced a new family allowance scheme. The scheme provides cash benefits to families with disabled children, which incorporate the economic burden resulting from members of the family no longer being able to work due to caregiving responsibilities.[40] As outlined in the report's introductory chapter, with a disproportionate number of males to females directly affected by gun violence, the caregiving impacts on females stands out as a significantly under-explored dimension of the issue. Women and girls, in this context, become secondary survivors with their own health and wellbeing often compromised by caregiving duties.

In addition, rehabilitation programmes are often not available or are inadequate. In this case, rehabilitation refers not only to medical rehabilitation, but also to vocational rehabilitation, education and training, counselling, the provision of assistive devices, and any other service designed to increase the person's independence. A 2005 global survey revealed that fewer than half of countries had rehabilitation policies and programmes, and only 50% even had legislation in the area (for more details see the Rehabilitation and Recovery chapter).[41]

Publicising benefits
Sometimes individuals fail to claim benefits they would otherwise be entitled to simply because they are not aware of their rights. Low awareness of the availability of benefits can arise from inefficient bureaucracy, communication difficulties (e.g. hearing and vision impairments) or physical isolation.

Table 1. Social protection coverage of gun violence survivors by programme type

	Who is covered	What types of impairments are covered	What is the nature of benefits	Coverage of conflict survivors	Coverage of crime survivors
Social security	Formal sector workers with sustained work experience. In a few instances informal workers able to make independent, sustained contributions.	All types of long-term impairment and resulting disability regardless of cause if they prohibit any employment (or allow only minimal employment).	Cash benefits based on contributions. Medical benefits in countries without national health care, sometimes including medical rehabilitation.	Does not cover soldiers who lack prior work experience. Does not cover civilian victims outside of formal labour market—including children.	Does not cover people without regular formal employment. Does not cover children.
Non-contributory disability benefit programmes	Workers with recognised impairments. Sometimes means tested, so covers poor people.	All types of long-term impairments and resulting disability regardless of cause. Sometimes only severe disabilities, but sometimes a fuller range of disabilities. However, psychological disabilities are often not identified.	Can include things such as cash transfers, rehabilitation services and subsidies for things such as transportation, health, education, and cultural activities.	Potentially all survivors. If means-tested, then only those with low or no income.	Potentially all survivors. If means-tested, those with low levels of consumption.[42]
Workers Compensation	Formal sector workers in employment who are injured on the job.	Work-related disabilities that significantly limit work, whether temporary or permanent, total or partial.	Cash benefits for partial wage replacement—often time-limited. Medical benefits, but for disabling conditions only. Rehabilitation services.	Generally not relevant to this group though this could extend to State security personnel.	Only covers those people in formal employment.

Sector specific, such as veterans' benefits	Military personnel with service-related injuries or illnesses. Programmes for police officers injured in the line of duty	All types of long term impairments and resulting disability—often partial as well as total. However, psychological impairments are often under-identified.	Cash benefits. Sometimes rehabilitative services.	Covers soldiers but not civilians.	Covers soldiers, police officers and other personnel of state security agencies.
Workfare programmes	Working age people.	Only those that do not significantly limit work—rarely are accommodations made to make jobs accessible	Jobs.	Covers working age survivors—but only those who are able to perform the jobs without major accommodations.	Covers working age survivors—but only those who are able to perform the jobs without major accommodations.
National Health Care	Universal coverage.	All types of impairments and resulting disability.	Medical benefits. Sometimes rehabilitative services.	Theoretically universal, but sometimes healthcare facilities are not accessible to people living with disability.	Theoretically universal, but sometimes healthcare facilities are not accessible to people living with disability.

Conclusion

Gun violence survivors are likely to be disproportionately working in the informal labour market in many parts of the world. They are thus insufficiently covered by social insurance schemes designed to provide benefits to people experiencing disability. If their injuries are significant, they may not be able to participate in workfare programmes. If their injuries are temporary, they will probably not qualify for disability benefits even though the short-term shock of job loss and/or medical expenditures could have a lasting impact. These costs are borne not only by the direct victims but also by their families.

At the global level, the 2011 WHO and World Bank *World Report on Disability* shows how people living with disability are often left behind by development, when it comes to education, employment, consumption, and in fact all components of being a full citizen of one's community. The nexus between armed violence, disability and poverty needs to be better understood. There is no mention of disability in the Millennium Development Goals (MDGs). However in the wake of the CRPD, the World Bank is actively considering incorporating disability into its safeguards. UNICEF is currently developing disability indicators across its sectoral programmes, and a number of national development agencies—e.g., AusAID and USAID—have raised the prominence of disability in their activities.[43]

At the national level there are two ways to address this problem. First, social protection schemes could be shored up so that all people experiencing disability, for whatever reason, are better protected. This chapter has pointed at many gaps, as well as some innovative programmes seeking to close them. Second, targeted programmes aimed at survivors of gun violence could be created. How feasible, appropriate and politically tenable such schemes would be is yet to be explored. More universal programmes would better meet all of society's needs, but may be seen as too expensive or difficult to administer. Categorical programmes for gun violence survivors could be less expensive and politically palatable if victims were seen as a particularly deserving group. Funding could come from gun sale taxes, fees from annual gun licence renewals and/or weapons registration, court fines. This is however complicated given that many victims are perceived to be, or are in fact, also perpetrators of gun violence.

Contributors: **Daniel Mont**, Principal Research Associate, University College London and Senior Research Fellow, Leonard Cheshire Disability and Inclusive Development Centre, UK. **Bernd Treichel**, Social Security Expert, International Social Security Association. Editing and additional drafting was undertaken by **Cate Buchanan**, **Rebecca Peters**, **Mireille Widmer** and **Emile LeBrun**.

Peer reviews were provided by **Eva Cox**, policy analyst (Australia); **Peter Hurst** formerly of the International Labour Organization (Switzerland); **Sophie Mitra**, Associate Professor in the Department of Economics at Fordham University (USA); and **Michael Palmer**, Research Fellow, Nossal Institute for Global Health, University of Melbourne (Australia).

References

[1]   Centre for Humanitarian Dialogue, *Assistance to survivors of armed violence in Burundi*, Background paper No. 2 (Geneva: HD Centre, 2006).

[2]   Centre for Humanitarian Dialogue (2006).

[3]   See C. Buchanan, "The health and human rights of survivors of gun violence: Charting a research and policy agenda," *Health and Human Rights* 13/2 (2011), pp.1-14.

[4]   In regards to poverty, S. Mitra, A. Posarac and B. Vick, "Disability and Poverty in Developing Countries: A Snapshot from the World Health Survey," *Social Protection Discussion Paper* No. 1109 (2011); N. Groce, M. Kett, R. Lang, and J. Trani, "Disability and Poverty: The need for a more nuanced understanding of the implications for development policy and practice," *Third World Quarterly* 32/8 (2011), pp.1493-1513; J. Braithwaite and D. Mont, "Disability and Poverty: A Survey of World Bank Poverty Assessments and Implications," *ALTER: European Journal of Disability Research* 3 (2009), pp. 219-232; J. Trani and M. Loeb, "Poverty and disability: A vicious circle? Evidence from Afghanistan and Zambia," *Journal of International Development* 24 Issue Supplement S1 (2012), pp. 19-52; D. Mont and N.V. Cuong, "Disability and Poverty in Vietnam," *World Bank Economic Review* 25/2 (2011), pp. 323-359. For costs, see M. Tibble, "Review of the Existing Research on the Extra Costs of Disability," Working Paper (Leeds: Department for Work and Pensions, 2005).

[5]   Input into this section received from Bernd Triechel, International Social Security Association.

[6]   J.R. Laiglesia, *Coverage Gaps in Social Protection: What Role for Institutional Innovations?* (Paris: OECD Development Centre, 2011).

[7]   International Social Security Association, *Dynamic social security: Securing social stability and economic development* (Geneva: ISSA, 2010), p.11.

[8]   A.S. Kanter, "The Globalization of Disability Rights Law," *Syracuse Journal of International Law and Commerce* 30 (2003), pp. 241-269.

[9]   For example, see the disability rights work of Human Rights Watch www.hrw.org/topic/disability-rights

[10]   G.A. Livermore, D.C. Stapleton and M. O'Toole, "Health Care Costs Are a Key Driver of Growth in Federal and State Assistance to Working-Age People with Disabilities," *Health Affairs* 30/9 (2011), pp. 1664-1672.

[11]   G.A. Livermore et al (2011).

[12]   A. Norton, T. Conway and M. Foster, "Social Protection: Defining the Field of Action ad Policy," *Development Policy Review* 20/5 (2002), pp. 541-567.

[13]   M. Grosh, C. del Ninno, E. Tesliuc and A. Ouerghi, *For Protection and Promotion: The Design and Implementation of Effective Safety Nets* (Washington DC: The World Bank, 2008); A. Banerjee and E. Duflo, *Poor Economics: A Radical Rethinking of the Way to Fight Global Poverty* (Tennessee: Public Affairs, 2011).

[14]   J.D. Stobo, M. McGeary and D.K. Barnes (Eds), *Improving the Social Security Disability Decision Process Committee on Improving the Disability Decision Process: SSA's Listing of Impairments and Agency Access to Medical Expertise*, Institute of Medicine of the National Academies (Washington DC: The National Academies Press, 2007).

[15]   Developed by Bernd Triechel, International Social Security Association.

[16]   On 21 December 1988, a bomb on board of a Pan Am flight from London to New York killed all 259 passengers. The event is also known as Lockerbie bombing as parts of the plane fell into the Scottish town of Lockerbie, killing another 11 people.

[17]   US Department of Justice, Office of Justice Programs, Office for Victims of Crime, *International Terrorism Victim Expense Reimbursement Program, Report to Congress* (Washington DC: DoJ, 2008), p.20.

[18]   The September 11th Fund, *Final Report* (New York: The September 11th Fund, 2004), p.12.

[19]   International Social Security Association, Web page: "About social security," www.issa.int/Topics/About-social-security Accessed 29 November 2012.

[20]   International Social Security Association, *Dynamic Social Security for the Americas: Social Cohesion and Institutional Diversity* (Geneva: ISSA, 2010), p.2.

[21]   International Labour Office, *World Social Security Report 2010/11: Providing coverage in times of crisis and beyond* (Geneva: ILO, 2010), pp.40-43.

[22]   J.R. Laiglesia (2011).

[23] A. Barrientos, "Social pensions in Low Income Countries," In R. Holzmann, D. Dobralino, D. and N. Takayama (Eds), *Closing the coverage gap: The role of social pensions and other retirement income transfers* (Washington DC: The World Bank, 2009), pp. 73-84.

[24] Social Security Advisory Board, *Disability Decision making: Data and Materials* (Baltimore: SSAB, 2006).

[25] T. Hoopengardner, *Disability and Work in Poland*, Social Protection Discussion Paper No. 0101 (Washington DC: The World Bank, 2001); D. Mont, *Disability Employment Policy*, Social Protection Discussion Paper No. 0413 (Washington DC: The World Bank, 2004).

[26] World Health Organization and World Bank, *World Report on Disability* (Geneva: WHO, 2011).

[27] Organisation for Economic Cooperation and Development, *Transforming Disability into Ability: Policies to Promote Work and Income Security for Disabled People* (Paris: OECD, 2003); D. Mont (2004).

[28] A. Banerjee, and E. Duflo, *Poor Economics: A Radical Rethinking of the Way to Fight Global Poverty* (Tennessee: Public Affairs, 2011).

[29] D.A. Perry, *Moving Forward: Toward Decent Work for People with Disabilities: Examples of Good Practices in Vocational Training and Employment from Asia and the Pacific* (Geneva: International Labour Organization, 2003).

[30] International Institute for Social Law and Policy and the Social Security Organisation Malaysia, *SOCSO Return-to-Work Programme in Malaysia: A Handbook 2012* (Clarkson and Kuala Lumpur: IISLP/SOCSO, 2012), p. 61. Available at: www.rtwmalaysia.com/2012/images/stories/9789834230012.pdf Accessed 24 September 2012.

[31] A. H. Hunt, *The Evolution of Disability Management in North American Workers' Compensation Programs* (Kalamazoo, MI: W.E. Upjohn Institute, 2009); J.K. Wendt, S.P. Tsai, F.B. Faiyaz, A. Cameron and L. Derrick, "The Shell Disability Management Program: A Five-Year Evaluation of the Impact on Absenteeism and Return-on-Investment," *Journal of Occupational & Environmental Medicine* 52/5 (2010), pp. 544-550.

[32] A. Marriott and K. Gooding, *Social Assistance and Disability in Developing Countries* (Haywards Heath, UK: Sightsavers' International, 2007).

[33] D. Mont, "Social Protection and Disability," In T. Barron and J.M. Ncube (Eds), *Poverty and Disability* (London: Leonard Cheshire Publications, 2010), pp. 317 -339.

[34] World Bank, *People with Disability in India: From Commitments to Outcomes* (Washington DC: The World Bank, 2009).

[35] A. Marriott and K. Gooding (2007).

[36] M. Tibble, "Review of the Existing Research on the Extra Costs of Disability," Working Paper (Leeds: Department for Work and Pensions, 2005).

[37] D. Mont, and N.V. Cuong (2011).

[38] World Bank, *Social Analysis and Disability: A Guidance Note* (Washington DC: The World Bank, 2008).

[39] E. Esplen, *Gender and care, overview report* BRIDGE, Institute of Development Studies (Brighton: BRIDGE, 2009); J. Brodsky, J. Habib and M. Hirschfield (Eds), *Long-term care in developing countries: ten case studies* (Geneva: World Health Organization, 2003).

[40] International Social Security Association (2010).

[41] World Health Organization and World Bank (2011).

[42] In high income countries means-tests are based on income, but in poor countries where people produce a significant portion of their livelihoods through their own production, engage in significant amounts of bartering, or get paid in informal labour markets where there is no record of their income, it is more common to refer to consumption. Measuring consumption is costly and time consuming, so usually proxy means tests are employed. These rely on assets or living conditions. Studies are undertaken to see the relationship between consumption and assets (e.g., motorcycle, television) and living conditions (e.g., type of house, toilet, etc.) and then a simple means test is devised based on the presence of those assets and living conditions, which can be more easily verified.

[43] For example, see USAID "Disability Initiatives" Web page http://transition.usaid.gov/about_usaid/disability/ Updated 10 January 2012. Accessed 30 November 2012. The Australian Agency for International Development "Disability-inclusive development in Australia's aid program" Web page www.ausaid.gov.au/aidissues/did/Pages/home.aspx Updated 16 April 2012. Accessed 30 November 2012.

SPOTLIGHT SECTION

Paying for Gun-related Impairment in the United States

More than 100,000 Americans suffer gunshot wounds each year: over 31,000 die and over 73,000 are treated in hospital for non-fatal firearm injuries.[1] While national gun violence rates have dropped considerably since the mid-1990s, the United States of America (USA) still has some of the highest rates of homicide and gun homicide of high-income countries worldwide. The majority of homicides (68%) are committed with guns, and most of these victims are male (85% in gun homicides and 90% in gun assaults). Victimisation rates are considerably elevated for minority groups such as African-Americans and Hispanics. Suicide attempts with firearms have a much higher completion rate than suicides attempted by other means, and gun suicides accounted for 61% of gun deaths.

The prevalence of firearms among the US civilian population is also high by international standards. There are almost as many guns (294 million[2]) as people (308 million[3]), though the proportion of households with guns appears to be dropping and ownership varies by region and with urban-rural demographics.[4] Gun laws vary considerably across the 50 states, but in general, civilians are allowed to purchase—and in many cases to carry in public—guns without demonstrating a need or "good cause". Citizens and residents can purchase and use a number of types of military-style weapons that other high-income countries have banned. The secondary (second-hand) market for guns is thought to account for almost 30-40% of all civilian sales.[5]

Surviving gun violence in America

Gun violence is the third-leading cause of spinal cord injury in the US, causing 1,500-2,000 individuals to become impaired each year.[6] These injuries are typically concentrated among populations that face a range of parallel challenges to their health and socio-economic wellbeing. From the initial medical treatment to physical rehabilitation through to long-term recovery and reintegration, many gun violence survivors struggle to find and benefit from services that can meet only a fraction of the demand.

Level 1 trauma centres are hospitals that are equipped to provide the highest level of emergency care to individuals with traumatic injuries. Many patients injured by gun violence are uninsured, indigent, and cannot pay for their care, so taxpayers ultimately cover much of the cost of their hospital treatment. These patients create a heavy financial burden on trauma centres and municipalities.[7] In Chicago in 2011, 670 patients were treated for gun injuries in Cook County hospitals at an average cost of USD52,000 per patient; about 70% had no health insurance.[8] Average health costs in the first year of a traumatic spinal cord injury range from USD311,000 to USD953,000.[9] Hospitals across the country have responded to this fiscal pressure by closing their trauma units. Between 2001 and 2007, more than 69 million citizens lost geographical access to a Level 1 trauma centre; of these, 16 million needed to travel an additional 30 minutes to find a trauma hospital in 2007.[10] This is a serious concern since timely treatment can make the difference between levels of impairment, or between life and death. These closures have mainly affected residents of impoverished urban communities, where much gun violence occurs. In those facilities that have remained open, patients are staying fewer days due to cost-cutting measures.[11] For a perspective from a professional involved in supporting gun violence survivors, see Box 1.

Once a patient's condition has stabilised, he or she may have the opportunity to visit a rehabilitation hospital to work on activities of daily living and occupational therapy. Like acute care stays, the average length of stay at these facilities has reduced—from 98 to 37 days between 1979 and 2005.[12]

Discharge from the hospital brings a new set of challenges. Wheelchair-accessible and affordable housing is scarce, particularly in low income communities. Relocating to a more navigable home is only possible for those who can cover the significant costs. In addition, many survivors are at risk of further violence associated with revenge, especially if the injury was gang-related. The lack of options causes some survivors to live in long-term care facilities such as nursing homes, which are not primarily geared toward serving young disabled men. The *Patient Protection and Affordable Care Act* (the federal health care reform package signed into law in 2010) contains provisions to help young people with disabilities move out of nursing homes to more appropriate housing.[13]

Box 1. Profile: Katie Augustyn[14]

As a social worker at an inner city rehabilitation hospital, I worked in the spinal cord injury unit where most of the patients had been disabled due to gun violence. I remember clearly the attending physician saying, "Those bullets just always find the spinal cord." Many of the people I worked with had become disabled in an instant. The circumstances of many of the shootings followed a pattern: they were secondary to gang involvement, most of the young men arrived at the hospital with little understanding of what happened to them and the consequences of their injury. As these young men began to form a picture of the profound changes that were occurring in their lives, rage was almost always the first feeling. At the beginning of their stay, fellow gang members would visit, and also girlfriends. I would ask: "Who can help care for you?" and frequently got the answer, "Don't worry, my guys got my back." But over the course of the weeks we would see fewer friends, and that's when we could really see the impact of the profound loss.

The clients I worked with typically had a number of outside factors that influenced their health status. These include poverty, environmental barriers, social exclusion, little access to wheelchair-accessible housing, poor education, and a history of drug or alcohol abuse. Many of my clients were oppressed prior to being shot and their injury just made the oppression more glaring. I placed many young, vibrant men in nursing homes with geriatric and mentally ill people because they had no accessible housing. Or they would be denied access to housing due to gang affiliation or a felony record. I worked with young men fearful of applying for disability benefits due to outstanding warrants. Many factors stood in the way of these young men achieving any type of independent life after being shot.

One thing that helped my patients was a peer mentor program. Each patient who had a spinal cord injury would be paired with someone with a similar injury. The majority of the peer mentors had also become disabled due to gun violence. They would explain to the newly injured patient the reality of living with a disability, in a way that a nurse, doctor or social worker couldn't. They talked about how to train your bowels so you don't have to wear a diaper. They told them about how to use a penis pump or Viagra to be able to have sex. They basically showed the newly injured patient that life can go on.

Paying for the effects of victimisation

One of the main challenges of long-term gun-related impairment is the financial burden it puts on victims and their families. The costs range from the purchase of hardware, such as wheelchairs and medical equipment, to professional rehabilitation and recovery services, and in-home caregiving. Many Americans who are shot are not able to cover these costs. The US has a web of assistance programmes to support individuals with disabling injuries, including those injured by firearms, but many gun violence survivors never benefit from them.

Some financial assistance is available to injured and impaired Americans. Medicaid, the national health insurance programme for low income individuals, is often the first stop for survivors. But because the programme is operated by individual states, "there is a great deal of variation today across states in terms of Medicaid coverage, uninsured rate and fiscal capacity."[15] In some states, individuals must choose between holding minimum-wage jobs and Medicaid coverage. Virtually all 50 US states are slashing their Medicaid budgets, which is almost certain to translate into reduced coverage.[16]

Survivors of gun violence may apply for financial assistance through Supplemental Security Income (SSI). SSI is a means-tested programme that provides minimal financial assistance for the elderly, blind, or disabled who have less than USD2,000 in assets for unmarried applicants (or USD3,000 for married applicants). If the injured person has a work history, he or she may also be able to get Social Security Disability Insurance (SSDI), which provides additional resources and is not means-tested. SSI or SSDI benefits are not available to people who have not been employed in jobs that pay into the social security system, nor to undocumented immigrants.

The SSI asset limits present a dilemma for many recovering survivors. If they are able to obtain employment, they soon lose their SSI/SSDI benefits. Most jobs in the US come with health insurance, but not enough to cover rehabilitation costs. Depending on the severity of an individual's impairment, health care will likely be a vital need. Many injured survivors must choose between employment (and being unable to pay for health care) and living in poverty but with SSI/SSDI benefits. Until the *Patient Protection and Affordable Care Act* comes into full effect in 2014, insurance companies can refuse to pay the medical expenses related to pre-existing illnesses, injuries, or impairments.[17]

Aside from these general social assistance programmes, victims of violent crimes (or their survivors in the case of homicides) may be eligible for compensation and assistance from the Crime Victims Fund established by the federal 1984 *Victims of Crime Act* (VOCA). The Fund's income comes from criminal fines and forfeited bonds, assets seized by law enforcement and converted into cash, and contributions from private donors. VOCA funds are disbursed for several types of programmes:

- Grants to state government programmes which reimburse victims for out-of-pocket expenses that result from the crime (e.g. medical expenses, funeral costs, mental health counselling, lost wages).
- Grants to state government programmes which fund support services to victims (e.g. crisis intervention, emergency shelter or transport, criminal justice advocacy, continuing counselling).
- National projects to improve professional standards and services to crime victims.
- Coordinators in the federal agencies and offices around the country to inform victims about their rights, assistance programmes available, and developments in the criminal justice processing of the perpetrators in their cases.
- The Antiterrorism Emergency Reserve, which funds emergency expenses and other services for victims of terrorism or mass violence—including mass shootings.

Survivors apply for assistance from these programmes through state government agencies.

As of August 2010 (latest data), the VOCA fund had reached USD4 billion dollars.[18] The distribution of VOCA funds is at the discretion of Congress, which sets the national cap for disbursement each year. The caps for financial years 2009 and 2010 were USD635 million and USD705 million respectively. The states, in turn, place caps on the amount of support a victim or survivor may receive, for specific categories of assistance and overall. For example, in the state of Georgia a victim may apply for a total of USD25,000 from VOCA funds, including up to USD15,000 for medical and dental expenses.[19]

The cap means that some states run out of VOCA resources and are forced to make tough decisions about who can be compensated. Victim advocate groups argue that the disbursed funds are insufficient to meet the expanding population of crime victims, and that the cap should be raised significantly.[20]

In addition to the cap placed on compensation and services covered, the VOCA fund has an important limitation. Individuals injured during the commission of a crime—and their family members, if the individual was killed—are disqualified from receiving VOCA funds.[21] Since a significant portion of gun crime in the US is associated with drug violence, this disqualification affects an unknown but sizeable portion of victims.

Contributors: Noam Ostrander, Associate Professor and Director of the Masters of Social Work Program, DePaul University, Chicago, USA. **Cate Buchanan**, **Emile LeBrun**, and **Rebecca Peters** also drafted and edited the text.

Peer reviews were provided by **Mary Leigh Blek**, Million Mom March (USA); **Bill Jenkins**, Board member, National Gun Victims Action Council (USA); and **James Mercy**, Acting Director, Division of Violence Prevention, Centers for Disease Control and Prevention (USA). Additional thanks to: **Garen Wintemute**, Director, Violence Prevention Research Program, University of California Davis School of Medicine/ Davis Medical Center (USA); **Jessie Lorenz**, Executive Director, Independent Living Resource Center, San Francisco (USA); **Anne Marks**, Executive Director, Youth ALIVE! (USA); **Rochelle Dicker**, Director, The Wraparound Project, University of California, San Francisco (USA); and **Bob Cantrall**, Office for Victims of Crime, Department of Justice (USA).

References

[1] All figures in this paragraph are from the WISQARS database, National Center for Injury Prevention and Control, US Centers for Disease Control and Prevention, www.cdc.gov/ injury/wisqars/ Accessed 18 November 2012. These statistics (fatal injury data for 2010, non-fatal injury data for 2011) include interpersonal gun violence (homicide and assaults), self-directed gun violence (attempted and completed suicides), and unintentional deaths and non-fatal injuries due to gunshot wounds. In 2010 there were 31,672 gun deaths and 73,505 people treated in hospital for gunshot injuries (not counting airgun injuries, which numbered 13,851). In 2011 the figure for non-fatal gunshot injuries was 73,883, not counting 16,451 airgun injuries.

2   United States Department of Justice Bureau of Alcohol, Tobacco, Firearms and Explosives, *Firearms commerce in the United States 2011* (Washington DC: BATF, 2011).
3   US Census Bureau, *Statistical Abstract of the United States: 2012*. Available at: www.census. gov/compendia/statab/2012/tables/12s0002.pdf Accessed 20 November 2012.
4   A. Brennan, "Analysis: Fewer gun owners own more guns", *CNN*, 1 August (2012). Available at: http://edition.cnn.com/2012/07/31/politics/gun-ownership-declining/index.html Accessed 12 November 2012. The article cites an analysis of General Social Survey data by the National Opinion Research Center (NORC) for the Violence Policy Center.
5   P. Cook and J. Ludwig, *Guns in America* (Washington DC: Police Foundation, 1996). Figures based on surveys from 1995-96.
6   T. Kroll, "Rehabilitative needs of individuals with spinal cord injury resulting from gun violence: The perspective of nursing and rehabilitation professionals," *Applied Nursing Research* 21 (2008), pp. 45-49.
7   P. Cook, B. Lawrence, J. Ludwig and T. Miller, "The medical costs of gunshot injuries in the United States," *Journal of American Medical Association* 282 (1999), pp. 447-54.
8   H. Dardick, "Preckwinkle drops bullet tax, keeps gun tax," *Chicago Tribune* 31 October (2012). Available at: http://articles.chicagotribune.com/2012-10-31/news/chi-preckwinkle-drops-bullet-tax-keeps-gun-tax-20121031_1_bullet-tax-gun-tax-budget-director-andrea-gibson Accessed 19 November 2012.
9   M.J. DeVivo, Y. Chen, S.T. Mennemeyer and A. Deutsch, "Costs of Care Following Spinal Cord Injury," *Topics in Spinal Cord Injury Rehabilitation* 16/4 (2011), pp. 1-9.
10 R. Yuen-Jan Hsia and Yu-Chu Shen, "Rising closures of hospital trauma centers disproportionately burden vulnerable populations," *Health Affairs* 30/10 (2011), pp. 1912-20.
11 T. Kroll (2008).
12 National Spinal Cord Injury Statistical Center, *Spinal cord injury facts and figures at a glance* (Birmingham, Alabama: National Spinal Cord Injury Statistical Center, 2011). Also see T. Kroll (2008).
13 *US Department of Health and Human Services*, Web page, "Affordable Care Act Supports Community Living". Available at: www.healthcare.gov/law/resources/reports/community-living-09112012a.html Updated 12 September 2012. Accessed 19 November 2012.
14 Contributed in March 2012. Katie Augustyn works as a clinical social worker in private practice in Chicago.
15 J. Holahan and I. Headen, *Medicaid coverage and spending in health reform: National and state-by-state results for adults at or below 133% FPL* (Washington DC: Kaiser Commission on Medicaid and the Uninsured, 2010), p. 13.
16 Kaiser Commission on Medicaid and the Uninsured, *Moving Ahead Amid Fiscal Challenges: A Look at Medicaid Spending, Coverage and Policy* (Washington DC: Kaiser Family Foundation, 2011). Available at: www.kff.org/medicaid/upload/8248-ES.pdf Accessed 24 August 2012.
17 The *Patient Protection and Affordable Care Act* was signed into law in 2010 and will be fully implemented in 2014. This Act provides a number of changes to health care in the US. The two most significant changes are: 1) the individual mandate that requires individuals who are not covered under employment-based health care or government-provided health care to purchase health insurance or face a financial penalty; and 2) the Act increases coverage for individuals who have "pre-existing conditions," which health insurance companies had used as justification to deny coverage to individuals.
18 US Department of Justice, Office for Victims of Crime, Web page, "Crime Victims' Fund". Available at: www.ojp.usdoj.gov/ovc/about/victimsfund.html Accessed 26 November 2012.
19 Criminal Justice Coordinating Council of Georgia, Web page, "Victim's Compensation". Available at: http://cjcc.georgia.gov/victims-compensation Accessed 26 November 2012.
20 Campaign for Funding to End Domestic and Sexual Violence, *FY 2012 Appropriations Briefing Book,* National Network to End Domestic Violence (2011), p. 45. Available at: www.nnedv. org/docs/Policy/FY12BriefingBook.pdf
21 Telephone interview by Emile LeBrun with Bill Jenkins, National Gun Victims Action Council and National Coalition of Victims in Action, 24 July 2012.

SPOTLIGHT SECTION
Danilo and the ISRI Rehabilitation Centre
(El Salvador)

I'm 19 years old. I was wounded on 23 August 2011 on the bus, as I arrived at my job as a cook. I was at the back of the bus when three men got on; one stood next to the driver threatening him and the other two began robbing the passengers. One asked me for money but I only had USD10. He threw the money on the floor, and when I reached down for it he shot me three times. The first shot damaged my spine, and then he shot me again while I was lying on the floor of the bus. Another passenger tried to come to help me and they hit him hard with the butt of the gun.

We were only 100m from a police post. The police arrived and took me to the hospital. They didn't accuse me of being a gang member because they knew me, since I worked right there near the police station.

At the hospital I had surgery for damage to my kidney, colon, liver and a lung. I was four days in a coma. Later on I was moved to another hospital where I stayed a month and a week. Then I went home for a few weeks because I was in a plaster cast, and ISRI (Instituto Salvadoreño de Rehabilitación Integral in San Salvador, see Box 1) doesn't take you until you are out of the cast.

I don't know how long I'll be here. ISRI has been excellent, they have helped me a lot. And I have not paid for anything here. When I was in Intensive Care we had to buy medicines, because the hospital ran out.

I have complete paraplegia. Right now I have difficulty using my arms because my bones are broken and the fractures have not healed yet. I have one kidney, my intestines are damaged and part of my lung is gone.

I think I will be able to work again. The main problem is not your body but your mind— If I start thinking I can't do it, then I won't be able to. My boss came to see me in hospital and gave me some money, but I won't be able to get my old job back because the place is too small for a wheelchair to move around. Maybe in another place.

Most of my friends don't see me anymore, except one friend who has been very dedicated—he comes to visit and boosts my morale. I don't know why my other friends have dropped out of my life. My girlfriend has also not changed: she says it doesn't matter to her that I'm disabled. We were together for 6 months before this happened. I don't know if we will get married someday.

At first I had nightmares remembering the attack, but the psychologists at the hospital and here at ISRI have helped me a lot. Their support, and my family and my girlfriend have helped me not to feel depressed and to assimilate what's happened. I feel that my body has changed, but my personality is the same. I've always been a very positive, optimistic person. But it has interrupted my plans for my life. I wanted to keep working, to get a house.

I lived with my mother and my younger sister and brother; my salary was the main income for our family. Now that I'm not working, my mother has gone out to work, but she doesn't earn as much as I did. So it's a big change economically for our family. Since my mother has to work, my aunt is going to be my carer. She has two small children at home and a 16 year old daughter at school. As my aunt will be looking after me, her daughter will have to look after the little ones.

I won't be able to live back home because it's too far to travel, and our street has steps and is very narrow, too difficult for a wheelchair. I'll stay with my aunt who lives near the capital. Her house is not wheelchair accessible, so my uncle will have to carry me in and out of the house.

I didn't want the police to go after the guys who shot me, because I think they might recognise my family members and I want to avoid anything happening to my family. It wouldn't help me if they went to prison in fact it could be worse for me if they are caught, because I would be worried about what might happen next. I don't want to go looking for problems. But I still do worry because my family members ride the bus and you never know what could happen.

I'm friendly with another gunshot survivor here, he's 14 years old and he was involved with a gang and got shot. Although we come from different situations we both ended up here in wheelchairs. When I first arrived and heard he had been a gang member, I was a bit frightened. He actually asked me what gang I was from, and he seemed annoyed when I explained I was not involved with any gang. It's not a real friendship where you can confide in him, but we are friendly.[1]

Box 1: Providing wheelchairs for survivors in El Salvador

Most people who suffer impairment from gunshot injuries in El Salvador are treated at the Instituto Salvadoreño de Rehabilitación Integral (ISRI). In 2011, Rebecca Peters of the Surviving Gun Violence Project visited ISRI and learned of a severe shortage of wheelchairs: some 200 patients of the hospital needed wheelchairs, but had little prospect of receiving them. Rebecca undertook to obtain wheelchairs for ISRI, and subsequently raised USD25,000 through networks of friends and colleagues for that purpose. A US-based NGO, UCP Wheels for Humanity, used the funds to provide 300 chairs and other devices such as walkers, shower chairs, etc. In September 2013 the chairs arrived in El Salvador and a clinic was held at ISRI to fit the chairs precisely to their users (since an ill-fitting wheelchair can lead to pressure sores). Recipients and their families were trained in using the wheelchairs and local staff also received training from two visiting US specialists. Some 60 chairs went to FOPROLYD, an organisation that supports people injured during El Salvador's civil war.[2]

The people receiving the chairs fell mainly into three groups: young men with spinal cord injuries from gunshots; children with cerebral palsy, spina bifida or muscular dystrophy; and frail elderly people. Some of the recipients were already using broken or unsuitable chairs, but many were receiving their first-ever wheelchair.

One recipient was Carlos, age 25, who was shot in the back at age 21 by gang members whom he knew. At the time of his injury, Daniel and his wife Evelyn had a small baby and moved to the other side of the city after the shooting. They have never returned to the neighbourhood where they had lived all their lives. Carlos becoming paraplegic put an economic strain on the family as Evelyn juggles caring for him and for their child, as well as trying to earn money. It also put a strain on their relationship, with Carlos sometimes taking out his anger and frustration on Evelyn. He was given an old wheelchair which wore out further over the past four years, though he attempted to repair the parts as they broke. The UCP wheelchair he received allows him to move around with much less effort, including going over the kerb and turning in a small space—so Evelyn will not have to assist him nearly as much as before.

Two other gunshot survivors with paraplegia who received chairs are Henry (age 17, shot by a police officer) and Dennis (20, shot by gang members in his neighbourhood). Both young men learned to play wheelchair basketball while they were inpatients at ISRI and proved so talented that they are now part of the National Institute for Sport. The Institute provided sports chairs for them to use in training and in competition, but they did not have regular wheelchairs. The sports chairs are designed specifically for basketball—on a smooth, flat surface—and are entirely unsuitable for daily life, especially in a developing country. Henry and Dennis, elite athletes and future champions, have had enormous difficulty in moving around outside the Institute. Now they are looking forward to leading active lives off court as well.

For more details or to donate funds, visit: wheels4survivors.org

References

[1] As told to Rebecca Peters in San Salvador, El Salvador on 15 December 2011.
[2] For information on how people injured during the war were regarded in the peace process see: C. Buchanan and J. Chávez, "Guns and violence in the El Salvador peace negotiations," *Negotiating Disarmament Case Study*, No. 2 (Geneva: Centre for Humanitarian Dialogue, 2008).

A police patrol in the slum area of Soyapango, San Salvador, an area dominated by gangs such as the Mara Salvatrucha and M18 gangs. (Image: Piet den Blanken/Panos, 6 May 2005)

"You never know when you won't get another opportunity to kiss
that little cheek."

Scarlett Lewis, whose son Jesse, aged 6, was murdered at the Sandy Hook
Elementary School on 14 December 2012. Jesse was shot when he ran
towards the perpetrator, trying to save his classmates. In recognition of
his bravery he was given a commander-in-chief's funeral, usually reserved
for heads of state and soldiers who have acted selflessly to save others.

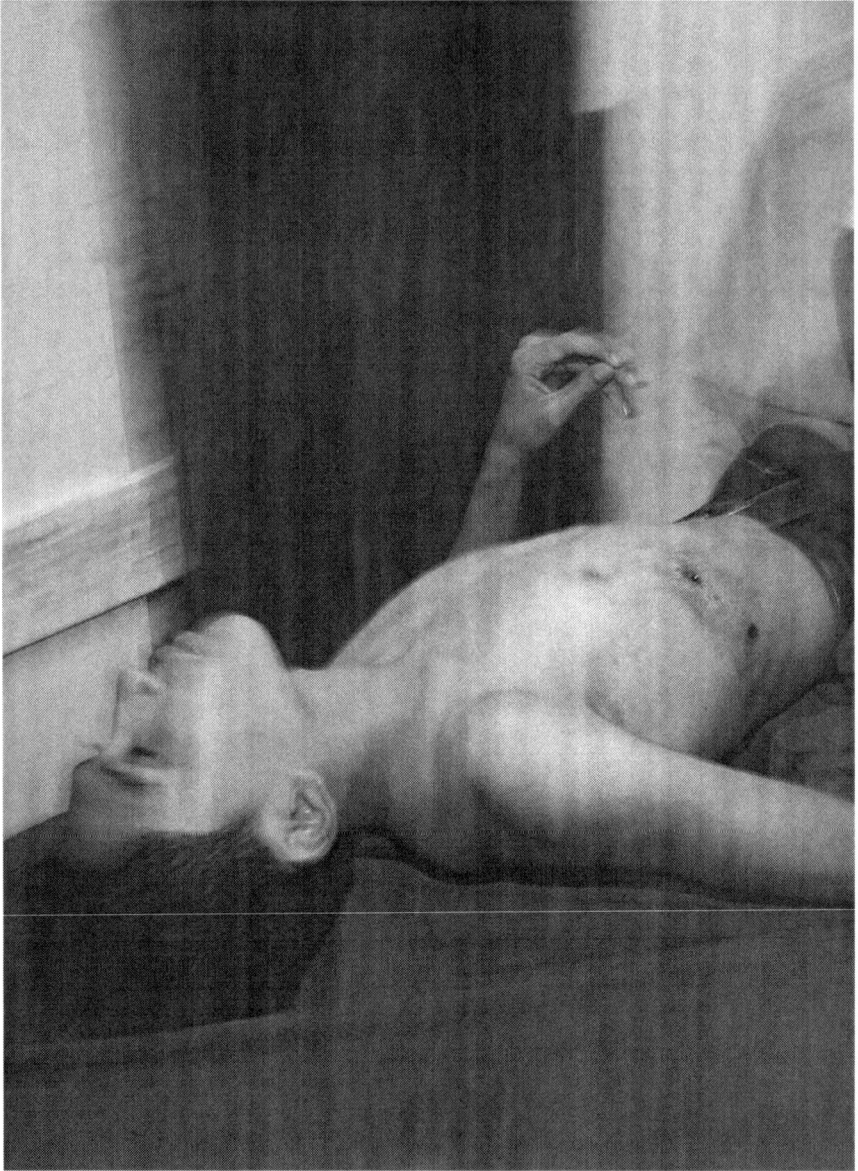

A boy is rushed through an emergency room in Guatemala City with multiple gunshot wounds to the abdomen. (Image: Daniel Leclair/Reuters, 2004)

6 Guatemala

Introduction

This chapter outlines the dimensions of gun violence in Guatemala and the factors contributing to the epidemic. It describes the response of the health system, which succeeds in saving the lives of most gunshot victims but falls far short of providing rehabilitation. Potential sources of economic and psychosocial assistance are identified in the government and non-government sectors. Survivors recount the difficulties they face, especially in earning enough to support their families. Lastly the chapter summarises the relevant national and international norms applying in Guatemala.

Section 1: Violence in Guatemala

Guatemala is the largest country in Central America, which has become the most violent region on earth. As the World Bank has pointed out: "The entire population of Central America is approximately the same as that of Spain, but while Spain registered 336 murders (i.e. fewer than one per day) in 2006, Central America recorded 14,257 murders (i.e. almost 40 per day) in the same year."[1]

The title of world's most violent country tends to rotate between Guatemala, Honduras and El Salvador, which together are known as the Northern Triangle. During the first decade of the century homicide rates in these countries varied from year to year, but were usually in the range of 40-55 per 100,000 people. This compared with average homicide rates around 20/100,000 for Latin America generally, and 2/100,000 for European countries.[2]

The deadliest year in recent Guatemalan history was 2009, with nearly 6,500 homicides, a rate of 46/100,000 population or 18 homicides per day (Table 1). Homicide is the second leading cause of death.[3] The capital, Guatemala City, has 22% of the country's 14 million inhabitants but 40% of the homicides. Among the victims, 89% are male and 71% are aged 35 or younger. Around 83% of homicides are committed with firearms.

Table 1. Homicide in Guatemala, national and capital city

Year	Homicides national			Homicides capital	
	Number	Rate/100,000	Per day	Number	Rate/100,000
2007	5781	43	16	2329	79
2008	6292	46	17	2433	81
2009	6498	46	18	2655	87

2010	5960	41	16	2423	78
2011	5192	35	14	2953	62

Source: Policía Nacional Civil, *Análisis Estadístico Comparativo de la Incidencia Criminal y Acciones Positivas Registradas a Nivel República* (Guatemala: PNC, 2011).

Reliable data on non-fatal firearm injuries are not available, said Dr Sergio Castillo, head of orthopaedics and trauma surgery at one of the two biggest public hospitals: "We don't have statistics—you can only get statistics for the dead. But I would say perhaps four times as many people are wounded as die. We get 15 cases or more in our emergency room in a day. We see wounds nowadays in the city that were previously seen on the battlefield, during the armed conflict. These are not low-velocity projectiles; our patients have been shot with weapons of war. These are large injuries, especially the exit wounds."[4]

Statistics are available on serious criminal assaults reported to the police, and these show non-fatal assaults numbering 10-25% higher than fatal assaults (Table 2). This ratio is much lower than the estimates among health experts like Dr Castillo. It may reflect underreporting due to a lack of confidence in the criminal justice system: according to materials published by the Ministry of Public Prosecutions, "80% of crimes go unreported."[5]

Table 2. Non-fatal criminal injuries and homicides in Guatemala

Year	Injuries	Homicides	Ratio
2007	6238	5781	1.08
2008	6960	6292	1.11
2009	7603	6498	1.17
2010	7542	5960	1.27
2011	5680	5192	1.09

Source: Policía Nacional Civil, *Análisis Estadístico Comparativo de la Incidencia Criminal y Acciones Positivas Registradas a Nivel República* (Guatemala: PNC, 2011).

In terms of age and gender, these assault survivors are broadly similar to homicide victims: overwhelmingly young and male. About 72% of the non-fatal criminal injuries involve guns.

The cost of gun violence

Violence costs Guatemala an estimated 7.7% of its GDP or around USD2.29 billion per year, including health costs, lost productivity, public and private security costs and material losses.[6] About half that amount is health costs. Gun violence is overwhelming the public health system, according to Dr Castillo. He points out that gunshot injuries are generally more expensive than, for example, injuries from a car crash. "That [car crash] patient may have serious injuries but they tend to be more manageable," he said. "A fractured femur, for example, will probably be a closed fracture, so the risk of infection is less and the fracture is much less complicated than with a bullet. A bullet will shatter the femur or the humerus, and these are not ordinary fractures that will heal in 6 weeks—often it takes months to heal, because the bones and tendons are completely destroyed, the vascular and nervous systems are damaged as well, so the patient spends a very long time in hospital. These cases consume a lot of resources in terms of intensive care, medication—also, often we don't have the special material we need for osteosynthesis, to support the healing of the bone. We have a certain amount of that material but not for this huge number of patients. Our budget for materials just runs out. Violence is using up the budgets of the hospitals."[7]

Gun violence: Sources, types and trends
The World Bank asserts that drug trafficking is the single major driver of violence in the Northern Triangle; followed by youth gangs and the proliferation of guns.[8] These three factors reinforce each other, and all are exacerbated by weak and corrupt criminal justice systems.

Drug trafficking produces violence when tensions arise between and within the trafficking organisations. This trade reduces the ability of the criminal justice system to respond and prevent non-drug crime, by absorbing a disproportionate amount of resources and corrupting police and officials. It brings more guns into the region, increasing the likelihood of violence both drug-related and not. The sums of money involved in drug trafficking are so large that human life becomes cheap by comparison.

More than 400 youth gangs (some local and some transnational) are believed to operate in Guatemala, involving about 14,000 gang members.[9] Most are not major participants in the international drug trade, though they may sell drugs locally and provide services such as security to the traffickers. Some of the most terrifying incidents of mass murder have involved gangs, and public perception blames them for 25-67% of violent crime. However, some research suggests that this is an overestimate of the contribution of gangs to overall violent crime in Guatemala.[10]

The proliferation of weapons in Central America was considered a residue of the decades of armed conflict which engulfed the region until the 1990s, but the guns being seized from criminals in Guatemala are of more recent origin.[11] In 2006 Guatemala was the sixth major importer of guns among the 36 countries of Latin America.[12] In 2009 the country had about 400,000 registered guns—92% in private hands and the remainder owned by the state.[13] Estimates on the size of the illegal arsenal range from 500,000 to 1.5 million.[14] The proceeds of taxes on guns go into general revenue rather than being dedicated to any specific purpose such as victim assistance.[15]

The UN Development Programme (UNDP) points to older structural factors underlying the violence in Guatemala, namely extreme inequality and the failure of state institutions.[16] Guatemala is one of the most unequal countries in Latin America, and only Haiti is poorer (ranking lower on the Human Development Index). With high unemployment and no social safety net, crime becomes a livelihood for many people.

The severe institutional weakness of the state creates conditions that enable small and large-scale crime to flourish. Local police are ineffectual, due to corruption or intimidation by better-armed and better-funded criminals. The problem of impunity is so severe in Guatemala that a special agency was created in 2008 to address it: CICIG (Comisión Internacional Contra la Impunidad en Guatemala or the International Commission Against Impunity in Guatemala).[17] The indicator most often cited is the low rate of homicide investigation and conviction: in 2012, only 28% of homicides resulted in prosecution, leaving 72% unsolved.[18] This was at least an improvement over previous years, when CICIG said 98% of homicides in Guatemala were unsolved.[19]

Inequality, impunity and the weakness of the state are part of the legacy of the armed conflict that engulfed Guatemala for 36 years until 1996. The 2011 report of the Human Rights Prosecutor stated: "Guatemala remains a society traumatised by violence and impunity, generating multiple forms of injustice and social inequality including discrimination, racism, exclusion and extreme poverty. These characteristics of the post-conflict reality constitute a constant source of aggression against large segments of society who suffer the effects of being overlooked because of corruption, lack of government control and ineffectiveness of the state."[20]

César Dávila, Director of the National Restitution Programme, takes a similar view of the relationship between the past conflict and the present crime wave: "Many people lost hope. People who once grew crops to feed their families were displaced to urban areas where they had to find a way to survive. Unresolved trauma and sorrow, the experience of being abused and powerless and of nothing being done to the perpetrators, combined with the structural inequality in our society which was intensified by the conflict—all these factors create a breeding ground for violence. You hear people say 'If they hadn't murdered my father I might not have taken this direction'..."[21]

UNDP says the clandestine groups which have a grip on the modern Guatemalan state, enriching individuals through illegal activity, have their origins in the political economy of violence created during the war.[22] The tradition of violence as a means of doing business persists, even as the country tries to move toward a modern democratic state.

Section 2: Surviving being shot
Guatemalans who are shot and do not die immediately are usually taken to a local hospital for emergency treatment. Some survivors reported that upon arriving at the emergency room they were approached by police, who automatically suspect gunshot victims of being gang members.

Subsequent treatment is provided in a public, social security funded or private hospital, depending on the patient's insurance status. Very few people have private insurance, and only 20-30% of the population is in the social security system.[23] As noted earlier, public hospitals do not always have the resources needed to care for gunshot patients. If the hospital runs out of medicines or materials, the patient may have to wait a long time for treatment, which can affect the extent of longer term impairment. Dr Sergio Castillo expressed frustration: "We are able to save their lives, but we don't necessarily have the capacity to provide the treatment that would produce optimum healing. But there's not much point in saying 'we've saved your life' and nothing else. The patient should be able to function as a productive member of society."[24]

The experience of spending weeks or months in hospital varies. Social security hospitals are better funded than public hospitals and do not suffer from the same shortages. However, relatives of public hospital patients may be asked to buy medicines, bandages or other supplies at a pharmacy and bring them in. In addition, some survivors interviewed complained about rough treatment, unclean facilities and a lack of information in hospital.

Once the initial wounds are repaired, rehabilitation presents new challenges, and the difference between the social security and the public hospitals becomes apparent. Social security hospitals give their patients wheelchairs, prostheses, and crutches, whereas public patients must buy their own. Social security patients are discharged to the residential programme at the hospital run by IGSS (Instituto Guatemalteco de Seguridad Social or Guatemalan Social Security Institute) where they may spend several months in rehabilitation. The major public hospitals also have rehabilitation facilities, but their patient numbers are so large that no one receives appropriate or intensive treatment. Instead the patients are sent home and given appointments to return to the hospital for rehabilitation sessions.

Suzy, 27, was hit in the spinal column by a stray bullet in her neighborhood, Paraíso II in Guatemala City. (Image: Heidi Schumann, 2006)

Dr Castillo lamented: "Many patients live in remote places where it may be a four—or five-hour walk to the road where the bus comes. Those patients can't travel to the hospital, so they end up just staying at home. Even those who live in the capital may have no transport to get to the hospital. Someone who is paralysed can't come on the bus, and there is no one to drive them, but the taxi fare to the hospital can be more than a family earns in a day. So they end up staying home, then they get pressure sores and infections, and end up coming back to the hospital in an ambulance, and being admitted for perhaps a month."

Pressure sores and urinary tract infections are common causes of premature death in Guatemalans with spinal cord injuries. Most of the paralysed survivors interviewed said they had suffered very badly from these two conditions, and had not been taught in hospital about how to avoid them.

Psychological services are especially underdeveloped, said Dr Castillo. "A 21-year-old who was healthy and who suddenly faces life in a wheelchair needs a great deal of psychological help. But our mental health departments are overloaded, and we don't have enough trained staff."

Forms of government assistance

Social protection
The only type of social protection in Guatemala (as in most of Latin America) is a contributory social security system, providing benefits only to people who have contributed through their employment in the formal sector. However, 70-80% of Guatemalans are either unemployed or working informally, and thus are ineligible for social security.[25]

People who do qualify for a disability pension receive about half their average pre-impairment salary, plus 10% for a spouse and for each child under 18.[26] One survivor was receiving the pension; nevertheless, his household was suffering financial strain: "What I never wanted to see happen has happened: that my children don't have what they need. I can't give my children what I used to be able to—we can't give them milk any more, or new shoes. My wife never had a job before, but she has begun cleaning houses to help with the costs. She earns 500 quetzals [USD64] a month but I was earning 4000 quetzals [USD510] before, so it is a huge difference."[27]

National Restitution Programme
The National Restitution Programme (Programa Nacional de Resarcimiento or PNR) provides compensation and assistance to civilians who suffered human rights violations during Guatemala's 36-year internal armed conflict. The Programme was created in 2004 on the recommendation of the Historical Clarification Commission (Comisión para el Esclarecimiento Histórico), the national truth and reconciliation commission.

An estimated 200,000 people were murdered during the conflict, and many thousands more were tortured, injured, kidnapped, raped, traumatised or displaced.[28] The fate of tens of thousands of people is still unknown. The impact was worse in rural areas, where a large proportion of the population is indigenous. So far the PNR has processed about 30,000 claims for restitution, with about 20,000 to go. These 50,000 cases involve some 70,000 individual and community claimants.

The PNR has five pillars:

- Restoring dignity to victims—commemorating the dead and disappeared; listening to and compiling the survivors' stories; searching for, exhuming and identifying the remains of citizens murdered by state forces; and funding funeral services and gravestones.
- Cultural restitution—aimed at restoring the social fabric of indigenous communities displaced or destroyed by the conflict. It includes writing community histories based on the memories of elders, supporting the learning of indigenous languages, encouraging traditional artistic and cultural activities, and recognising or restoring indigenous names for people forced to adopt Spanish names.
- Material restitution—building houses and/or providing land to people who lost or were forced to leave their homes. Some 3500 houses have been built so far.
- Monetary restitution—cash payments to families of 24,000 quetzals (USD3,100) for each person murdered or disappeared, and 20,000 quetzals (USD2,600) to survivors of torture, rape or other serious human rights violations.
- Psychosocial support and physical rehabilitation—for civilians who are physically or mentally impaired as a result of the conflict. PNR has psychologists and counsellors, and the Ministry of Health provides physical rehabilitation, prostheses or medical procedures. This category of assistance also includes scholarships for people whose education was discontinued because of the conflict or because of the impairment they suffered.

With an emphasis on repairing the social fabric, PNR takes a collective approach in much of its work. Incidents of violence during the conflict often affected entire communities, so psychosocial support includes family, group, and community therapy and self-help groups. As of early 2012, 136 community mental health studies had been conducted, enabling an understanding of the collective local impact of the violence. Psychosocial support is integrated as far as possible with the other four types of PNR restitution.

Another way of helping individuals and communities affected by violence is to address the problem of impunity. PNR Director César Dávila said the agency has referred about 14,000 cases to the Justice Ministry, requesting prosecutions for crimes committed during the conflict. The armed conflict ended in 1996, so people injured by more recent gun violence are not eligible for assistance from PNR. Is the programme an example that could be adapted to help the thousands who become new gun violence survivors each year? Since the family and the local community are still important units of social organisation in Guatemala—and given the close relationship between conflict and crime—Dávila believes the collective approach could be applied to survivors of criminal as well as conflict related violence.

Justice system

The Ministry of the Public Prosecutor (Ministerio Público) is a potential source of psychosocial support for survivors. The Ministry is implementing the 1985 UN *Declaration of Basic Principles of Justice for Victims of Crime and Abuse of Power* through three structures: the Department for Coordination of Victims' Care, a Victims' Care Office in each of the 22 provinces, and the National Victims' Care Network, which has local counterparts in each province. These networks are made up of government agencies, NGOs, and individuals with relevant skills. Their main function is public awareness to strengthen victim support generally, but they may also assist individual survivors.

A primary or secondary survivor of crime can receive psychological, social work, and medical support from the local Victims' Care Office. The Office also advises and supports the victim during the trial of the perpetrator, in order to prevent further suffering due to the criminal justice process. IEPADES, a local NGO, has worked with the Ministry to develop a victim assistance manual for use by police and criminal justice officials.[29] The manual provides detailed recommendations about how to interview and provide "emotional first aid" to a distressed, shocked or frightened crime victim. It also sets out the rights of victims in the criminal justice system.

At present, this system has three main limitations in terms of its usefulness to survivors of gun violence. Firstly, the system privileges certain crimes over others. Thus, the survivors of partner and family violence, sexual assault, child abuse and human trafficking can receive timely and specialised assistance, and they have rights enumerated in laws dedicated to those specific offences.[30] However, much less is available for victims of robbery or common assault, or for people whose family members are murdered in circumstances other than the priority crimes.

A second limitation: since the victims' care system is part of the criminal justice process, it only assists victims who have made a formal complaint to police. However, many gun violence survivors have little contact with the police or the larger criminal justice system. The victim assistance manual notes that in 80% of crimes no complaint is lodged—because the victim is too distressed to speak to the police, frightened of reprisals, or lacking confidence in the justice system; or due to discrimination or a lack of knowledge of victims' rights.[31]

Most of the gun violence survivors interviewed in Guatemala had little or no contact with the criminal justice system, despite the gravity of the crimes which had left them severely and permanently impaired. The only one who had received support from the Ministry's victim care mechanisms was Adelma Cifuentes, a woman shot by a contract killer hired by her husband. Since this crime was categorised as partner and family violence, she received assistance from a range of government and non-government agencies which helped her to lodge a complaint, obtain a restraining order, get medical and psychological assistance, find a support group and even deal with the media once her husband was convicted and sent to prison. This was a rare example of holistic assistance. None of the other interviewees had been offered any assistance by the Victims' Care Network.

The third shortcoming also arises from the link between care of victims and criminal prosecution. The focus is entirely on the immediate aftermath of the crime and (if an offender is arrested) the duration of the trial. Once the criminal process finishes, so does the victim support. For survivors of gun violence, the greatest need for support may arise some time later, once their financial savings are exhausted and the burden on carers begins to weigh heavily. At that point little or no assistance is available from any state agency.

Civil society assistance to survivors

Civil society organisations provide some assistance to survivors of gun violence in Guatemala, though none is specifically dedicated to that constituency. Due to years of advocacy by NGOs and UN agencies, stopping violence against women is now a high priority and many local organisations are working on the topic. The best known of these is Fundación Sobrevivientes (Survivors Foundation). Created in 1999 to help survivors of sexual abuse, the group now has a high media profile for its campaigns against partner and family violence, child sexual abuse, sexual harassment and sexual assault, human trafficking, illegal adoptions, and impunity for violent offenders.[32] Sobrevivientes also provides primary and secondary survivors of gender-based violence with legal assistance, counselling, referrals, and crisis support. It operates one of Guatemala's four women's refuges, and helps women to sue delinquent ex-husbands for child support. Sobrevivientes supported Adelma Cifuentes and encouraged her to push for the prosecution of her husband.

Another group working primarily with women is the Association of Widows of Urban Bus Drivers (see Box 1).

Box 1: The bus drivers' widows[33]

One of the most dangerous occupations in Guatemala is driving a bus: 780 drivers and 255 drivers' assistants were murdered in the six-year period 2006-11.[34] This violence is attributed to organised crime groups which systematically target bus owners and drivers for extortion. Some drivers refuse to or cannot pay, but many are killed despite paying the "quota".

People murdered on buses, Guatemala

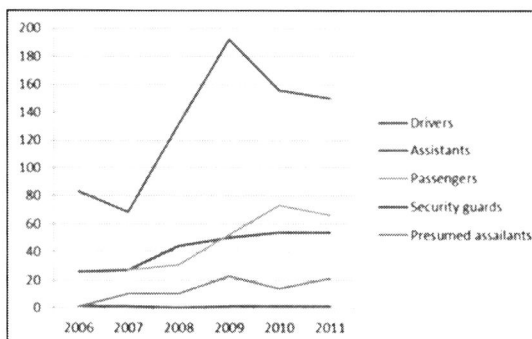

The Association of Widows of Urban Bus Drivers (Asociación de Viudas de Pilotos Urbanos) was formed in 2009 to seek financial, psychological and social support for the families left destitute by these murders. They are not covered by social security, since drivers are employed informally by private bus owners.

Most of the widows have young children and were completely dependent on their husbands' income. Most have only a primary school education; some are illiterate. They look for work cleaning houses, washing clothes, begging or guarding parked cars. Ingrid Escobar, whose husband was murdered in 2007, earns 2 quetzals (USD0.26) per pair of trousers washed and 1 quetzal per shirt—not enough to support her two children.

Unable to pay rent, many widows are obliged to move in with relatives. Their children may drop out of school in order to earn extra money—ironically, one common form of employment is helping at the bus depot or on the buses. Babies are left with neighbours or relatives during the day. "My husband and I always tried to spend a lot of time with our children, to communicate closely with them, so they wouldn't go down the wrong path," said Olga Larios.[35] His death in 2009 left her no choice but to leave them alone while she looked for work.

In some cases the violence involves more than one member of the family. Driver Cristián Herrarte was followed home from the depot by assassins in September 2011; he survived the attack but his wife Alma Hernandez was killed. Some drivers take their children with them on the buses on weekends, so children have witnessed their fathers' murders. Sometimes husbands and wives work together on the buses as driver and assistant; four siblings (aged 3 to 14) lost both parents in the same shooting in October 2010. They went to live with an aunt who already supports her own four children by washing clothes.

The Association has campaigned for government assistance for the widows, with only partial success. The Ministry of Social Welfare now pays 300 quetzals (USD39) per month for each child under 16, for two years from the parent's murder. However, this is only paid to families of drivers on the major city routes, so the families of drivers' assistants, and those in smaller cities, miss out.

No benefit is paid to the families of drivers who survive their attacks. Jorge Choy was left paraplegic when attackers shot him as he sat behind the steering wheel in 2008 (see image). Today he sells trinkets from his wheelchair, while his wife Jessica Choy does washing and ironing. "The worst thing," she said, "is to have no food in the house and hear your children say 'I'm hungry, I want something to eat'."[36]

The National Institute for Technical Training (Intecap) has begun free training courses in bookkeeping, cooking and computing for the widows, giving them hope of finding better paid work. The Association runs a Saturday clinic staffed by university psychology students. The mental health problems suffered by the survivors include speech and behavioural disturbances, sleeplessness, anxiety and depression.

In January 2012 the Government announced a task force to combat crime on the buses and weed out extortion gangs which may have infiltrated the bus companies. The Association welcomed the announcement but continues campaigning for increased security on the buses, and calling for the murderers to be prosecuted. Despite busloads of passengers witnessing most of the murders, Ingrid Escobar said, "I don't know a single widow who has had justice."[37]

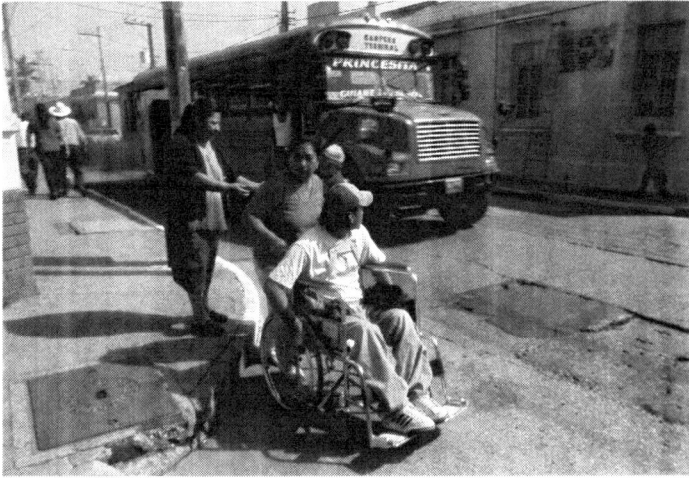

Jorge Choy, 23, a former driver who was wounded in 2008 during an attack on his bus. He is going to the Human Rights Ombudsman's office in Guatemala City. About 150 widows of murdered bus drivers met there asking for improved security and financial help in the form of a monthly payment. On average one driver is killed every other day. (Image: Daniel LeClair/Reuters, 27 October 2009)

Transitions Foundation

An innovative (and perhaps unique) organisation is Transitions Foundation (Fundación Transiciones), a self-help and service organisation led by a gun violence survivor. Executive Director Alex Gálvez was a 14 year old buying a soft drink in a shop in 1992 when he was shot. He survived with paraplegia, and spent the next three years in hospitals battling secondary infections. He had the extraordinary good luck to receive treatment in the USA, which saved his life. At age 17 Gálvez returned home and, together with three other young people with mobility impairments, established Transitions in La Antigua, the old capital of Guatemala.

Today Transitions has 28 members/employees who are leading healthy, active, and productive lives. Most are young men who use wheelchairs, and around half are survivors of gunshot injuries. They work in a wheelchair fabrication and repair workshop, prosthetics clinic, print shop, and classroom for local children with disabilities. They also constitute the national wheelchair basketball team, and won the Central American and Caribbean championship in 2010. In 2010 they made 96 personalised wheelchairs suitable for Guatemala's dirt roads and rough terrain, helped more than 100 other clients with wheelchair repairs or modifications, assisted 49 patients with prosthetic devices, taught 12 children with special needs and served 49 customers in the print shop. A constant cycle of teaching and learning goes on, as members who have had outside training in welding, prostheses fabrication and computers pass their knowledge on to colleagues. All the members learn English, practising during conversation classes with foreign volunteers. These activities do not generate enough income to cover costs, so the organisation relies on donations and grants from foreign donors to survive.

157

The jovial atmosphere in the rambling house belies the fragile physical and mental state in which many members arrived at Transitions. For most, the first months are dedicated to an intense effort to bring infections under control, and learning preventive self-care. In a supportive environment, encouraged by others who have suffered similar injuries and impairments, frightened and depressed young people are transformed (see Box 2).

Box 2. Profile: Juan Miguel[38]

Juan Miguel is a slight, bright-eyed boy who looks much younger than his 17 years. He became paraplegic at age 16, shot by members of his own gang for refusing an assignment to kill someone. Having left school at age 10, he had been working as a drug runner in Guatemala City. The assailants left him for dead, but passers-by called an ambulance and his life was saved. Hospitalised for five months, he did not realise he would never walk again until he overheard a conversation among medical staff about his condition.

He was discharged to his grandparents' house where his 15 year old sister became his caregiver. The wheelchair the hospital sold him was too heavy to operate himself, and he could not get in or out of the chair unassisted. His relationship with his grandparents was strained since Juan Miguel was no longer able to contribute financially. In a welcome surprise, his father (who had left when Juan Miguel was a baby) reappeared, having heard from a neighbour about his son's misfortune. His father occasionally helped pay for food, medicine and catheters. However, the burden of care fell on Juan Miguel's sister, who did the shopping and cooking, changed his clothes, took him to church and rubbed his limbs when he experienced pain.

His father brought him to Antigua after hearing about Transitions on TV. In the six months between leaving hospital and arriving at Transitions, Juan Miguel received no physical or psychosocial therapy, no training and no advice about his future. Since joining Transitions he has received counselling and support, learned how to avoid pressure sores and kidney infections, acquired a custom-built wheelchair and begun working in the print shop. This is his first-ever employment opportunity outside of crime. He hopes to learn to use computers and drive a car. "I consider myself a normal person now, not useless—even though I can't do the things I did before, I can do some new things now." He lives at Transitions and says, "Thank God I found this new family."

Juan Miguel received some counselling in hospital, which he found very helpful. He noted that some of his fellow patients, also paralysed by gunshots, refused counselling because they were too distressed to talk about what had happened to them. One counsellor in particular made an effort to connect with him, dropping by to visit when she had time, and this helped him to feel less alone.

Juan Miguel knows the person who shot him but has not informed the police, fearing that the gang will come to complete the task of killing him. When he visits the capital he avoids the gang's neighbourhood. He has become a Christian and asks for peace and wisdom, not hatred. "I ask God to forgive them even though they have put me in a wheelchair. I have forgiven them, so I feel at peace; it would torment me if I still hated them."

Dr Sergio Castillo says the role of other survivors in helping rehabilitation is very important: "I've seen the boys from Transitions speak to patients in hospitals, and it changes the patients' outlook: patients react to them in a completely different way, compared with a doctor like me talking to them. People who have acquired such a serious impairment need to feel that they can be useful members of society. If you have an impairment and you see someone with the same impairment who is succeeding, it gives you hope. I wish Transitions could be funded to work with our patients, and with health professionals. Even the wheelchairs they make are much better than the ones you buy commercially, because the Transitions guys know exactly what the patient will be experiencing." [39]

Transitions are active participants in the International Action Network on Small Arms, the international movement to prevent gun violence. However, the organisation has been primarily focussed on service rather than advocacy. Nonetheless, given the sheer number of survivors in Guatemala and elsewhere in the Northern Triangle, Gálvez believes the time has come to establish a national or regional survivors' movement.

Section 3: Standards and normative frameworks
Guatemala's Constitution recognises a right to possess and carry guns for personal use.[40] The right is not absolute, but subject to regulation. The necessity of regulating guns was emphasised in the peace agreements which brought an end to the armed conflict.[41] In this regard the peace agreements were implicitly criticising the permissive 1989 gun law.[42] Despite these commitments, it took years of lobbying by civil society groups for Guatemala to pass a new gun law in 2009.[43] The new law incorporates international commitments including the UN Programme of Action on small arms,[44] UN Firearms Protocol,[45] International Tracing Instrument,[46] Organisation of American States' Firearms Convention,[47] Central American Code of Conduct[48] and *Framework Treaty on Democratic Security in Central America*.[49] It contains some major improvements over previous legislation, including tougher licensing requirements for gun carrying as well as regulation of guns owned by government agencies and private security companies. The law does not mention victims or survivors.

Guatemala is a focus country for the *Geneva Declaration on Armed Violence and Development*, and one of the few countries that has reported on its implementation of the Declaration. The new gun law is considered to be the Government's most significant achievement in relation to preventing armed violence, and IEPADES has taken the lead on violence prevention activities with children and young people.[50]

The country has a substantial legal framework recognising the rights of people with disabilities. When Guatemala ratified the 2006 UN *Convention on the Rights of Persons with Disabilities* (CRPD) in 2009, legislation on the topic had already been in place for over a decade. The *Law on Support for People with Disabilities* was passed in 1996;[51] a national policy on disability was released in 2006 and formally approved by the government in 2008.[52] Guatemala has ratified the International Labour Organization's 1983 *Convention on Vocational Rehabilitation and Employment (Disabled Persons)* (No. 159) and the associated Recommendation (No. 168), as well as worked to implement the 1993 UN *Standard Rules on the Equalization of Opportunities for Persons with Disabilities*. Guatemala hosted the 1999 meeting of the Organization of American States, which adopted the Inter-American *Convention on the Elimination of All Forms of Discrimination Against Persons With Disabilities*. The Constitution explicitly recognises the rights to rehabilitation and employment for people living disability.[53]

Despite these legal commitments, the national disability policy admits that: "People with disabilities have few opportunities to integrate and participate in Guatemalan society."[54] As the Government noted in a Geneva Declaration meeting, "We have a tendency to pass laws without putting in place the supporting regulations or a budget, and without identifying the institutions to implement them."[55]

Responding to a campaign by civil society, the 1996 disability law also created a peak body called CONADI (Consejo Nacional para la Atención de las Personas con Discapacidad or National Council on Support for People with Disabilities). CONADI is a hybrid body made up of government ministries (human rights, education, health, labour, and social welfare) and NGOs representing people living with different types of disabilities. This body is responsible for coordinating the implementation of the national disability policy and the CRPD. It is currently drafting the country's first report on implementation of the CRPD.

More than 50 disability rights groups are affiliated with CONADI, and many of these provide advice, assistance and advocacy which could benefit survivors of gun violence. For example, the Independent Life Collective (Colectivo Vida Independiente) campaigns for public transport to be made wheelchair accessible.[56]

Since the primary concern for people with disabilities is employment, CONADI is working with chambers of commerce and INTECAP, the National Training Institute, to create opportunities such as a training programme for micro entrepreneurs. CONADI works with a range of other government agencies, including the National Literacy Committee. The new national identification card system will record information on disability, making it possible to target services where they are most needed.

People with visible disabilities are rare in Guatemalan public life. One exception is Silvia Quan, the country's Ombudsman for disability rights. Quan's background is in civil society organisations advocating for disability rights, and she is a member of the UN CRPD Committee. She says Guatemala's disability policy and legislation need to be updated to comply with the CRPD—for example, disability should be characterised less as a medical problem and more as a matter of human rights. "Discussions on disability tend to be very dominated by health professionals," she remarked. "But for disabled people, health is only one aspect of our lives. We get sick just like anyone else, and sometimes our impairment results from an illness or injury, but our disability is not a matter of health—it's a matter of how society treats us."[57]

Quan said the phrase "human rights" is often met with suspicion in Guatemala (as in other countries of the region), because of its perceived association with the defence of criminals. Public awareness campaigns by disability groups tend to emphasise acceptance or compassion rather than rights. A great deal of human rights education remains to be done—for people with disabilities, the professionals who work with them, and the general public.

In terms of assistance to survivors of gun violence, Guatemala has focussed almost entirely on physical health, said Quan. Topics like mental health, sexuality and employment receive very little attention. The Government has no policy on the employment of people living with disability, unlike for example El Salvador, where the public sector has a quota of 2% for employing people with impairments. As mentioned earlier, little support is available from the welfare system, and most Guatemalans have no financial safety net if they become injured and can no longer work. In a family that is already struggling financially, the additional strain caused by loss of an income and the burden of caring for a disabled relative may prove too much, leading to the collapse of the household and the disabled person being left to beg on the street. Quan noted that the largest category of complaints received by her office relates to people living with disabilities being abandoned by their families—an indicator of the crisis in disability care.

Conclusion

Guatemala is still seeking to repair the damage done during its period of armed conflict, but rates of gun violence are at warzone levels. With many thousands of people surviving gun violence each year, the country needs to develop and implement stronger policies for prevention, but also to respond to the needs of this rapidly growing population. Though resources are in short supply, there are examples of local programmes that could be adapted or expanded to assist survivors. Equally important, there is recognition and willingness by government and non-government representatives of the urgent need for action.

Contributors: Rebecca Peters, independent consultant; Senior Associate, Surviving Gun Violence Project.

Peer reviews were provided by **Carmen Rosa de León**, Director, IEPADES (Guatemala); **Silvia Quan**, Disability Ombudsman for Guatemala (Guatemala); **Alex Gálvez**, Director, Transitions Foundation (Guatemala); and **Chris Stevenson**, independent consultant (USA).

References

[1] World Bank, *Crime and Violence in Central America: A development challenge* (Washington DC: World Bank, 2011), p. 1. Available at: http://siteresources.worldbank.org/INTLAC/Resources/FINAL_VOLUME_I_ENGLISH_CrimeAndViolence.pdf Accessed 15 October 2012.

[2] United Nations Office on Drugs and Crime, *2011 Global Study on Homicide: Trends, Contexts, Data* (Vienna: UNODC, 2011). In 2010, the UNODC reported that Honduras was the most violent country, with a homicide rate of 82/100,000 (p. 93). Available at: www.unodc.org/unodc/en/data-and-analysis/statistics/crime/global-study-on-homicide-2011.html Accessed 15 October 2012.

[3] C. Mendoza, "La Muerte Prematura de los Jovenes Guatemaltecos," *The Black Box blog*, 30 October (2011). Available at: http://ca-bi.com/blackbox/?p=5807 Accessed 18 October 2012. The leading cause of death is respiratory illness.

[4] Interview by Rebecca Peters with Dr Sergio Castillo, head of orthopaedics and trauma surgery at Roosevelt Hospital, Guatemala City, 8 December 2011.

[5] Departamento de Coordinación de Atención a las Víctimas and IEPADES, *Manual de Atención a la Víctima*, Tomo 1 (Guatemala: Ministerio Público, 2010), p. 36.

[6] C. Acevedo, *Los costos económicos de la violencia en Centroamérica* (San Salvador: Consejo Nacional de Seguridad, 2008), p. 14. Available at: www.votb.org/elsalvador/Reports/costofviolence.pdf Accessed 15 October 2012.

[7] Interview with Dr Sergio Castillo, 8 December 2011.

[8] World Bank (2011), p. 1.

[9] World Bank (2011), p. 15. Estimates vary: UNDP's Human Development Report cites government estimates of 8000-10,000 gang members in the country. UNDP, *Guatemala: ¿Un país de oportunidades para la juventud? Informe Nacional de Desarrollo Humano 2011/2012* (Guatemala: UNDP 2012), p.178.

[10] D. Rodgers, R. Muggah and C. Stevenson, *Gangs of Central America: Causes, Costs, and Interventions*, (Geneva: Small Arms Survey, 2009) Available at: www.smallarmssurvey.org/fileadmin/docs/B-Occasional-papers/SAS-OP23-Gangs-Central-America.pdf Accessed 15 October 2012.

[11] C.R. de León-Escribano, "Tráfico ilícito de armas y municiones: Guatemala y la región centroamericana," *Urvio* 10 (Quito: FLACSO, November 2011), pp. 77-92. Available at: www.flacsoandes.org/urvio/img/RFLACSO-05-U10-Leon.pdf Accessed 28 November 2012.

[12] J.C. Purcena, "El balance de la balanza: exportaciones e importaciones de armas pequeñas y ligeras (APL), sus partes y munición en América Latina y el Caribe 2000-2006," *En la Mira: Observador Latinoamericano de Armas de Fuego* 23/3 August (2008). Available at: www.comunidadesegura.org.br/files/active/o/balanza.pdf Accessed 15 October 2012.

[13] Comisión Internacional Contra la Impunidad en Guatemala, *Armas de Fuego y Municiones en Guatemala—Mercado legal y tráfico ilícito* (Guatemala: CICIG, 2009), p. 61. Available at: http://cicig.org/uploads/documents/informes/INFOR-TEMA_DOC01_20091201_ES.pdf Accessed 15 October 2012.

[14] J. Restrepo and A. Tobón García (Eds), *Guatemala en la Encrucijada: Panorama de una Violencia Transformada* (Geneva: Geneva Declaration Secretariat, 2011), p. 65. Available at: www.genevadeclaration.org/fileadmin/docs/Guatemala_book/GD-Guatemala.pdf Accessed 15 October 2012.

[15] Superintendencia de Administración Tributaria, *Arancel Centroamericano de Importación 2013* (Guatemala: SAT, 2013), pp. 690-692.

[16] UNDP/PNUD Programa de Seguridad Ciudadana y Prevención de la Violencia, *El costo económico de la violencia en Guatemala* (Guatemala: PNUD, 2006), p. 67. Available at: http://pdba.georgetown.edu/Security/citizensecurity/guatemala/presupuestos/EstudioCostodeViolencia.pdf Accessed 15 October 2012.

[17] In its first two years CICIG contributed to the expulsion of 1,700 people from the police service for corruption, including 50 senior officials and the deputy director of the national police. Ten prosecutors were also dismissed and the Attorney General was replaced. World Bank (2011), p. 33.

[18] C. Paz y Paz, *Ministerio Público—Presentación de Resultados 2012* (Guatemala: Ministerio Público, 2013), p. 25. Available at: http://cicig.org/uploads/documents/2012/0046-20121213-DOC01-ES.pdf Accessed 6 March 1013.

[19] Impunity Watch, Centro Internacional para la Justicia Transicional and Plataforma Holandesa contra la Impunidad, *Cambiar la cultura de la violencia por la cultura de la vida: Los primeros dos años de la Comisión Internacional contra la Impunidad en Guatemala* (Guatemala: Impunity Watch, 2010), p. 15. Available at: www.impunitywatch.org/upload/UserFiles/file/CICIG%20Report%20(IW,%20ICTJ,%20Dutch%20Platform).pdf Accessed 15 October 2012.

[20] S. Morales Alvarado, *Informe Anual Circunstanciado, Tomo II, Memoria de labores 2011* (Guatemala: Procurador de los Derechos Humanos, 2012), p. 33. Available at: www.pdh.org.gt/index.php/documentos/informes.html Accessed 15 October 2012.

[21] Interview by Rebecca Peters with César Dávila, Director of the National Restitution Program, Guatemala City, 9 December 2011.

[22] UNDP/PNUD Programa de Seguridad Ciudadana y Prevención de la Violencia, *Informe estadístico de la violencia en Guatemala* (Guatemala: UNDP, 2007), pp. 10-11. Available at: www.who.int/violence_injury_prevention/violence/national_activities/informe_estadistico_violencia_guatemala.pdf Accessed 15 October 2012.

[23] F. Carrea, M. Castro, and A. Sojo, *La cobertura del sistema de pensiones en Guatemala, Nicaragua y Honduras: sendas asignaturas pendientes*, Consultants' paper for CEPAL (Lima: Economic Commission for Latin America, 2009), p. 3. Available at: www.eclac.cl/dds/noticias/paginas/4/38224/MariaCastro-foro2-Guatemala.pdf Accessed 18 October 2012.

[24] Interview with Dr Sergio Castillo, 8 December 2011.

[25] F. Carrea et al (2009), p. 3.

[26] International Social Security Association, *Country profile: Guatemala*. Available at: www.issa.int/Observatory/Country-Profiles/Regions/Americas/Guatemala/Scheme-Description/(id)/105619 Page updated 1 July 2011. Accessed 29 March 2012.

27 Interview by Rebecca Peters with Jorge, patient with paraplegia at IGSS Rehabilitation Hospital, Guatemala City, 9 December 2011.

28 Comisión para el Esclarecimiento Histórico, *Guatemala, Memoria del Silencio, Conclusiones y Recomendaciones* (Guatemala: UNOPS, 1999), p. 21. Available at: http://shr.aaas.org/ guatemala/ceh/gmds_pdf/cap4.pdf Accessed 18 October 2012.

29 Departamento de Coordinación de Atención a las Víctimas and IEPADES, *Manual de Atención a la Víctima*, Tomos 1-3 (Guatemala: Ministerio Público, 2010).

30 For example, the *Law against Femicide and other forms of Violence against Women; the Law to Prevent, Punish and Eradicate Family Violence*; the *Law for the Protection of Children and Adolescents; the Law against Sexual Violence, Exploitation and Trafficking in Persons*. The intake form used to collect data on crime victims illustrates the priorities of the system: the options under "Reason for receiving assistance" are: "Sexual offences, Psychological damage, Family and partner violence, AIDS, Substance dependency, Sexually transmitted diseases, Social problems (eg prostitution, youth gangs, etc.) and Other." Departamento de Coordinación de Atención a las Víctimas and IEPADES (Tomo 1) (2010), p. 21.

31 Departamento de Coordinación de Atención a las Víctimas and IEPADES (Tomo 1) (2010), p. 36.

32 See www.sobrevivientes.org

33 This box was compiled from material appearing between 2009 and 2012 in the Guatemalan press, including the newspapers *Milenio, El Periódico, Noticias de Guatemala, Prensa Libre* and Periodismohumano.com.

34 S. Morales Alvarado, *Informe Anual Circunstanciado, Tomo I, Situación de los Derechos Humanos en Guatemala 2011* (Guatemala: Procuraduría de Derechos Humanos, 2012), p. 102. Available via: www.pdh.org.gt/index.php/documentos/informes.html Accessed 15 October 2012.

35 M. Sandoval, "Las viudas de pilotos de buses se capacitan," *El Periódico*, 14 December (2009). Available at: www.elperiodico.com.gt/es/20091214/pais/128598 Accessed 2 April 2013.

36 "En Guatemala se niegan a pagar 'protección'", *Milenio* 7 September (2011). Available at: www.milenio.com/cdb/doc/noticias2011/f1fc54f42577319b06ab52e8eea2b8ce Accessed 2 April 2013.

37 A. Martínez, "Con el alma partido", Periodismohumano.com, 17 May (2010). Available at: http://periodismohumano.com/mujer/con-el-alma-partida.html Accessed 2 April 2013.

38 Interviewed by Rebecca Peters in Antigua, Guatemala, on 5 December 2011.

39 Interview with Dr Sergio Castillo, 8 December 2011.

40 1985 *Constitución Política de la República de Guatemala*, Article 38.

41 1994 *Acuerdo Global de Derechos Humanos*, Article IV(2); 1996 *Acuerdo sobre fortalecimiento del poder civil y función del Ejército en una sociedad democrática*, Articles 26(d), 33, 34, 42.

42 Decreto 39-89, *Ley de Armas y Municiones.*

43 Decreto 15-2009, *Ley de Armas y Municiones*. Published as IEPADES, *Ley de Armas y Municiones anotada y su reglamento* (Guatemala: IEPADES, 2011).

44 2001 UN *Programme of Action to Prevent, Combat and Eradicate the Illicit Trade in Small Arms and Light Weapons in all Its Aspects.*

45 2001 *Protocol against the Illicit Manufacturing of and Trafficking in Firearms, their Parts and Components and Ammunition* (supplementing the United Nations *Convention against Transnational Organized Crime*, 2000), ratified by Guatemala in 2003.

46 2005 *International Instrument to Enable States to Identify and Trace, in a Timely and Reliable Manner, Illicit Small Arms and Light Weapons.*

47 1997 *Inter-American Convention against the Illicit Manufacturing of and Trafficking in Firearms, Ammunition, Explosives, and Other Related Materials* (CIFTA). Ratified by Guatemala in 2002.

48 2005 *Code of Conduct of Central American States on the Transfer of Arms, Ammunition, Explosives and Other Related Material.*

49 1995 *Tratado Marco de Seguridad Democrática en Centroamérica*, ratified by Guatemala in 1997.

50 Secretaria Técnica del Consejo Nacional de Seguridad, *Informe Nacional sobre el progreso en la implementación de la Declaración de Ginebra sobre la Violencia Armada y el Desarrollo* (Guatemala: Comisión para la Reducción y Prevención de la Violencia Armada, 2011).

51 *Ley de Atención a las Personas con Discapacidad y su Reglamento*, Decreto No 135-96.

52 Consejo Nacional para la Atención de las Personas con Discapacidad, *Política Nacional en Discapacidad* (Guatemala: CONADI, 2006). Available at: www.conadi.gob.gt

53 1985 *Constitución Política de la República de Guatemala*, Articles 53 (rehabilitation) and 102 (employment).

54 Consejo Nacional para la Atención de las Personas con Discapacidad (2006), p. 44.

55 D. Zavala, *Informe sobre las Prácticas Prometedoras para la Reducción y Prevención de la Violencia Armada* (Geneva Declaration and UNDP, 2011), p. 32. Available at: www.genevadeclaration.org/fileadmin/docs/regional_seminars/Guatemala_AVRP_Seminar_2010_DZevala_ESP.pdf.

56 See http://colectivovidaindependiente.org/.

57 Interview by Rebecca Peters with Silvia Quan, Disability Ombudsman, Guatemala City, 3 December 2011.

"The new ExtremeShock™ Explosive Entry
tactical defense rounds represent the ultimate
refinement in lethal bullet technology.
The compressed Tungsten-NyTrilium™ Composite
fragments upon impact, leaving a wound
channel of catastrophic proportions."

Advertisement for a bullet at
www.extremeshock.usa.com

SPOTLIGHT SECTION
Gun violence and Masculinity

"Martin", a 23 year old black man, was shot in the lower back and right leg in December 2011, during a fight with another young man while playing *ama-dice* (a popular gambling game using two dice) in Alexandra township, Johannesburg.[1] Young men often gamble with money and valuable items such as cell phones, watches and clothes—and fights over these items are common. Because the perpetrator did not come to his house and apologise, Martin feels angry and seeks revenge once he recovers. This reflects research findings that victims of violence are at increased risk for becoming perpetrators themselves.[2] Martin's desire for revenge is emblematic of dominant cultural norms in many places that legitimise the use violence and aggression to restore "being a man."[3] Martin declares, "I'm not just going to shoot him when I pay revenge. I'm going to kill him."[4] Martin appears emasculated; the incident has deeply affected him both psychologically and physically, and he now uses a wheelchair. He talks about feeling lonely, depressed and alienated from friends due to his inability to walk: "You feel like you are nothing. Now your mother does everything for you, including bathing you. You really feel like you lost your being and your manhood as a man."[5]

This piece explores the relationship between violent expressions of masculinity, gun violence and gender-based violence, based on interviews in 2009 to 2011 with black men aged 16-25 years in Alexandra township, a working-class community in Johannesburg that experiences high levels of violence.[6]

Young men between the ages of 17 and 25 years are responsible for most acts of gun violence in South Africa, indeed worldwide.[7] Several studies have explored the relationship between masculinity and gun violence, and in particular the prevailing cultural stereotypes of what it means to be a man or a boy.[8] Among the findings, the research indicates that involvement in gun violence is seen as one way of asserting one's manhood.[9] As "Thato", a 19 year old man from Alexandra states: "To show that you are a real gangster you must have a gun. You see, if you have a gun you have everything. The world is yours and no one can touch [you]."[10] Several years later, he boasted about being involved in a shooting with a rival gang: "Yeah, it was war [laughing] but I survived. I didn't get hurt, you see [laughing]."[11] Shooting someone proves bravery and legitimises claims to manhood—particularly if the victim is another male.[12] Gun violence can be used to assert power and control, in the process, the man who is wounded or killed becomes emasculated.

Masculinity in crisis and women as victims of gun violence
High levels of gun violence against women are indicative of a crisis of masculinity in post-apartheid South Africa.[13] Due to high rates of unemployment, many black men have difficulty asserting their masculinity by securing jobs, marrying, fathering

children or establishing their own households; meanwhile women are seen to be usurping roles previously held by men.[14] Some men have lashed out violently in response to these dynamics, including by using guns to threaten or intimidate women.[15] By using violence, young men fall back on their power to humiliate and punish economically successful women to maintain a sense of domination.

Alternative notions of masculinity

Stereotypes of race and class tend to associate young black men with gangs, crime and violence.[16] Nevertheless, some young men in Alexandra are able to reject notions of violence associated with masculinity (e.g. by not joining gangs, supporting campaigns against gun violence and violent crime). As "Themba" reflected: "You know, people always think boys in Alex are violent or steal. Not all of us steal or are involved in crime or carry guns."[17] However, these young men feel marginalised because their non-violent voices are not as popular or celebrated as those of young men who carry weapons and belong to gangs. As a result, they often feel ambivalent about their version of masculinity. Initiatives to support young men (in South Africa and elsewhere) to develop and embrace alternative versions of masculinity therefore ought to be key components of violence reduction strategies, ensuring a focus is also included on young men who are already injured and disabled from gun violence to circumvent revenge and retribution.

Contributors: Malose Langa, lecturer in the School of Community and Human Development, University of Witwatersrand, South Africa; Community-Counselling Psychologist; and researcher at the Centre for the Study of Violence and Reconciliation. **Cate Buchanan** and **Rebecca Peters** provided further drafting, fact checking and editing.

Peer review was provided by **Noam Ostrander**, Associate Professor and Director of the Masters of Social Work Program, DePaul University, Chicago (USA).

References

[1]   This is a pseudonym to protect his identity.
[2]   K. Ratele, "Watch your man: Young black males at risk of homicidal violence," *South African Crime Quarterly* 33 (2010), pp. 19-24.
[3]   See for example, R. Ostrander, "Meditations on a bullet: Violently injured young men discuss masculinity, disability and blame," *Child and Adolescent Social Work Journal* 25 (2008), pp. 71-84.
[4]   Interview by Malose Langa with "Martin" in Alexandra, South Africa, 22 January 2012.
[5]   Interviewed in Alexandra on 22 January 2012.
[6]   For more on the history of Alexandra see P. Bonner and N. Nieftagodien, *Alexandra: A history* (Johannesburg: Wits Press, 2008).
[7]   World Health Organization, *World report on violence and health: Summary* (Geneva: WHO, 2002), p. 1.
[8]   R. Ostrander (2008); C. Buchanan, "The health and human rights of survivors of gun violence: charting a research and policy agenda," *Health and Human Rights* 13/2 (2011), pp. 1-14; K. Ratele (2010); R. Morrell, *Changing men in Southern Africa* (Pietermaritzburg: University of Natal, 2001); G. Barker, *Dying to be men: youth, masculinity and social exclusion* (London: Routledge, 2005).

9   R. Connell, *Masculinities* (Polity Press, Cambridge, 1995).
10 Interview by Malose Langa with 'Thato', Alexandra, 12 September 2009.
11 Interviewed 13 December 2011.
12 A. Whitehead, "Man to man violence: How masculinity may work as a dynamic risk factor," *The Howard Journal* 44/4 (2005), pp. 411-420.
13 R. Jewkes, Y. Sikweyiya, R. Morrell and K. Dunkell, "Understanding men's health and use of violence: interface of rape and HIV in South Africa," *Medical Research Council Policy Brief* (Pretoria: MRC, 2009); R. Jewkes, L. Penn-Kekana and J. Levin, "Risk factors for domestic violence: Findings from a South African cross-sectional study," *Social Science and Medicine* (2002), pp. 1603-1618.
14 M. Hunter, "Cultural politics and masculinities: Multiple-partners in historical perspective in Kwa-Zulu Natal," In G. Reid and L. Walker (Eds), *Men behaving differently* (Cape Town: Double Storey, 2005), pp. 139-160.
15 R. Morrell, (2001).
16 S. Jensen, *Gangs, politics and dignity in Cape Town* (Johannesburg: Wits Press, 2008).
17 Interview by Malose Langa with "Themba", Alexandra, South Africa, 16 September 2011.

"[One] night, at 7 o'clock, armed bandits attacked my house... they fired at me. I have an open wound and fractured my femur (thigh bone). In the morning, the people from the church came and took me to the hospital in Gitega where I spent several months. The nurses finally asked me to pay a sum of money, although I had none. From that day, the nurses stopped treating me properly. My wound and fracture became infected. Nobody came to change the dressing. The nurses isolated me in a room so as to distance me from the other patients because my wound was purulent. The nurse only came to cover the wound. I was expecting to die."

Déo, 47 years old, Burundi

Médecins Sans Frontières, *Access to healthcare in Burundi: Results of three epidemiological surveys* (Brussels: MSF, 2004).

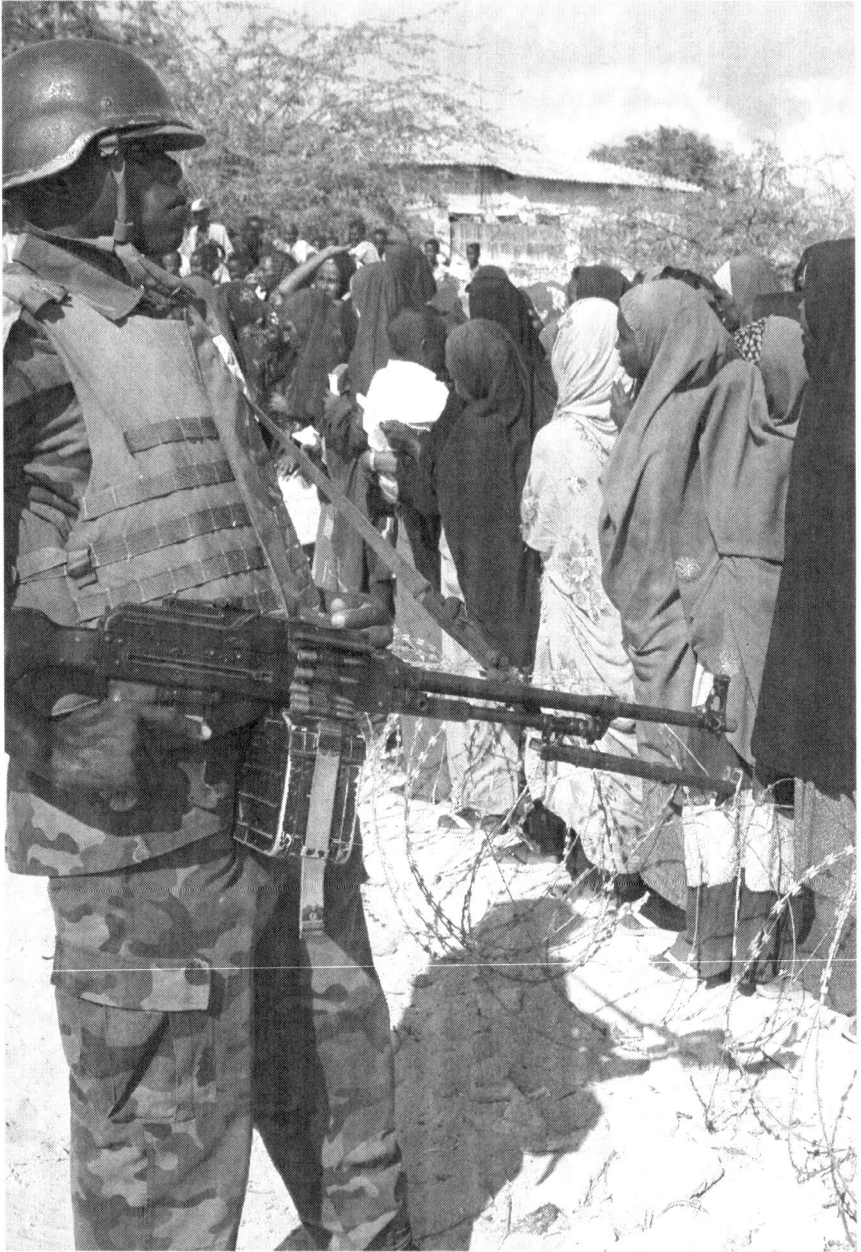

A soldier from the African Union (AU) peacekeeping force stands guard by people awaiting treatment at an Outreach Therapeutic Centre Programme on the edge of the AU military base in Mogadishu, Somalia. (Image: Siegfried Modala, April 2010)

7 Somalia

Introduction
Almost everyone in Somalia and Somaliland has been marked by the country's decades-long experience of political or tribal wars. In some areas, conflict-related violence persists to this day.[1] In others, it has been supplanted by crime associated with youth gangs, gunrunners, or pirate networks. Many young people in the capital, Mogadishu, one of the worst hit areas, have no sense of the meaning of "peace" and little faith in the future. Asked to define the term "safety", an inhabitant of Hodan district in Mogadishu—from 2008 to 2011 a frontline between troops of the Transitional Federal Government and al-Shabaab militias—replied, "safety is when someone has been attacked but survived."[2]

This chapter highlights the experiences of Somalis whose lives have been affected by gun violence. It outlines how patterns of violence have evolved and diverged across the country in the past 20 years, and describes contemporary forms of violence and crime. It then explores obstacles facing survivors where medical and psychological services are poor or non-existent, trust in the fledgling justice and security sectors is low, and where traditional elders or religious leaders may be powerless in the face of new forms of violence. The chapter also describes nascent institutions attempting to provide help. It concludes with recommendations for international assistance, emphasising the need to consider health systems as a whole, rather than targeting particular conditions for support, and highlighting the role of private or informal service providers in the fields of health and justice, as they are often the first port of call for survivors of gun violence in such contexts.

Section 1: Evolving patterns of violence in the Somali region
Somalia gained independence in 1960, combining territories previously colonised by Britain and Italy. Following a bloodless coup in 1969, the country fell under a military regime led by General Muhammad Siad Barre. These were the "golden years" of Mogadishu, then a thriving, cosmopolitan capital. Throughout the country, clan identities were muted, and individuals and families freely moved around. Barre had robust policies for gender equality, and women could be seen strolling down the Mogadishu beachfront with uncovered hair and wearing Western clothes. But Barre's policies became increasingly repressive and unpopular. His failed military intervention in Ogaden (Ethiopia) in 1977-78 caused some 14,000 battle deaths, and left many thousands of veterans with injuries and trauma (see Box 1 on survivors of the Ogaden campaign).[3]

Figure 1. Map of Somalia and Somaliland

Map: Source: United Nations, Department of Field Support, Cartographic Section, Map No. 3690 Rev. 10, December (2011).

In the 1980s, Somalia descended into civil war. Opposition to Barre's regime gradually coalesced into a number of armed movements, increasingly organised along clan lines. In Mogadishu, businesses closed and entire families fled. The rebellion in 1991 eventually pushed Barre out of Mogadishu into exile in Nigeria. In the aftermath, Somalia became more divided than ever.

Box 1: Survivors from the Ogaden campaign[4]

Following Somalia's humiliating defeat, soldiers returning from the Ogaden campaign in 1978 encountered anything but a hero's welcome. About 100 soldiers and officers who suffered physical injuries were admitted to the De Martino hospital in Mogadishu for treatment. More than 30 years later, some of them are still there. Some 97 male war veterans view the old colonial hospital as their home (in mid-2011). They are aged between 45 and 60 years and generally have physical impairments.[5] An additional 156 veterans with impairments linger around the hospital, often visiting it on Saturdays in the hope of finding some support.[6] They were infantry soldiers, commanding officers, medical assistants, technicians, mechanics, drivers, and trainers. Today, they live in squalor. Aging, with evident physical weaknesses due to poor health conditions, malnutrition, and destitution, they sit idle and dispirited in the shade of the trees. Some need medical assistance, but even basic surgery requires money they do not have. One said: "If I had income I would have the bullet in my body removed."[7] Others require wheelchairs for mobility. One wheelchair-bound man has to somehow feed eight people in addition to himself—his wife, six children, and an aged mother.[8] Even the able-bodied veterans find it difficult to make a living for themselves and their relatives. Only one man has no dependents: he was injured at the age of 20 and was never able to have a family.[9] Some veterans are too weak to work and depend on charity to survive.

Survivors at the De Martino hospital organised themselves and nominated a chairperson. They also have a spokesperson who handles relationships with the community, elders, and local administration. The government does what it can in support, generally on the private initiative of its officials. In March 2011, it gave the veterans a one-off payment of USD100 each. In 2007 they had each received USD100 from the then Prime Minister.

With support from the Government of Germany, the local NGO Daryeel Bulsho Guud launched an encouraging initiative in 2007. The project trained veterans with adequate vision and physical fitness to use sewing machines to produce mosquito nets. The nets were sold for profit on the local market, and a share of the income was reinvested into new raw material for the production of nets. Sadly the programme closed after a few months when income was spent instead on immediate living expenses and raw material was no longer available. The idle sewing machines are still in storage at the De Martino hospital.

Mogadishu

In 1991-92, Mogadishu became the epicentre of the confrontation. This began some of the worst years of fighting in Mogadishu. Militia members wielded near absolute power; sexual violence by gangs, harassment, and killings of opposition, minorities, and displaced persons were routine. The city fragmented into zones controlled by opposing clan-based factions, and Mogadishu lost its cosmopolitan atmosphere.

Several unsuccessful attempts to restore the peace in Mogadishu took place in 1992 and 1993, led by local elders or peacekeeping missions.[10] The last Western troops deserted Mogadishu in 1995, leaving a political vacuum, many weapons, and a new generation of warlords fighting over the spoils of the state. Years of diplomatic efforts to end the bloodshed led to the establishment in April 2005 of a government-in-exile, the Transitional Federal Government (TFG), which relocated to Somali soil a few months later.

In 2006, in opposition to the TFG, the Islamic Courts Union (ICU) took control of Mogadishu and subsequently expanded its control over South Central Somalia, introducing a period of relative stability. Through the powerful presence of the

Islamic courts, anyone who committed a crime was prosecuted, regardless of clan affiliation. For the first time in 15 years, basic services such as rubbish collection were provided, and people could freely walk on the streets, even at night.

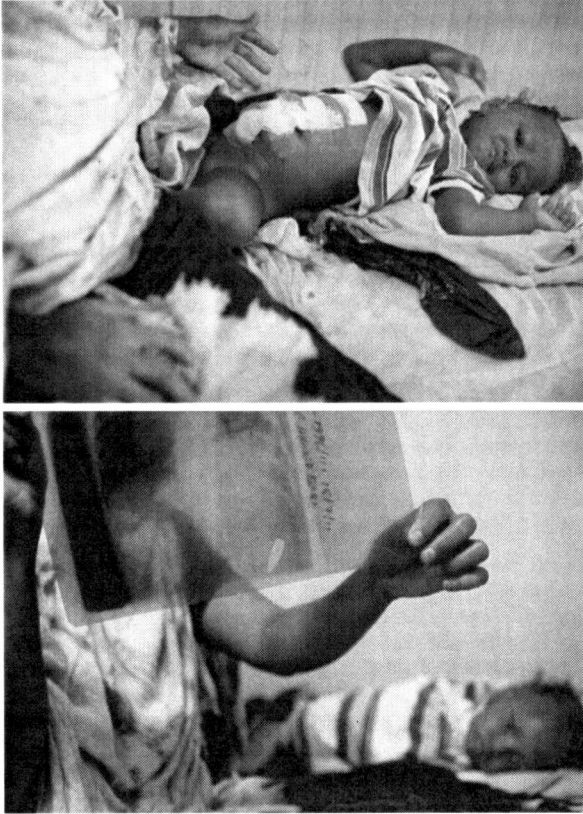

Falso Mohammed Mohammed watches over her child Fara, who received a gunshot wound to her stomach, where the bullet remains, in the outpatient department on the African Union peacekeeping base in Mogadishu, Somalia. (Images: Kate Holt, 30 July 2011)

The respite did not last long. In January 2007, Ethiopian troops invaded the country, and remained until January 2009. The African Union deployed a new peacekeeping force in Mogadishu, the African Union Mission in Somalia (AMISOM). The ICU disbanded and fled, but many of its hardline members regrouped as new Islamic armed opposition groups, including Hizbul Islam and al-Shabaab.[11] Violence took an ideological dimension, chiefly marked by confrontation between the TFG and Islamists. The TFG barely controlled a few Mogadishu districts with AMISOM support. In areas controlled by al-Shabaab, including the rest of South Central Somalia, Shari'ah law was strictly enforced. The TFG only extended its control over the whole of Mogadishu in July 2011. In September 2012, after the mandate of the TFG ended, a President was elected indirectly—the first time since 1991 a new leader was chosen inside the country.

Statebuilding processes in the north

While south central Somalia never managed to extricate itself from conflict, other parts of Somalia followed a different trajectory after 1991. In the northwest region of Somaliland, an inclusive clan alliance declared independence in May 1991, but the statebuilding process would last several years.[12] Clan wars broke out periodically from 1992 to 1997, triggering a series of peace conferences; these eventually led to the adoption of a constitution and the recognition of the Somaliland authorities by most clans. Since then, Somaliland has been remarkably stable, as demonstrated by the peaceful transition of power in July 2010 following presidential elections.

Puntland, in the northeast tip of the country, has embarked on a similar state-building process.[13]

Following the fall of Barre's regime, Puntland's population increased, as scattered members of local clan groups fled from the south and northwest back to their homeland. Puntland had not succumbed to the same intensity of violence and destruction as the rest of Somalia, and much of its infrastructure and public buildings remained. Sporadic hostilities between rival political and clan groups eventually led to a 1998 power-sharing agreement and the formation of the Puntland administration. Puntland declared its autonomy, never breaking entirely with Somalia's central government, even though warfare between rival politicians erupted again in 2001-03.

Gun violence: Sources, types and trends

Insecurity in the Somali region is very different today from what it was in the early 1990s. A 2010 crime and victimisation survey by the Observatory of Conflict and Violence Prevention (OCVP) highlighted stark differences between districts.[14]

Some areas have succeeded in eradicating the most overt forms of violence. For example, the district of Burao (Somaliland) rarely experiences gun crime. However, clan conflicts still erupt in Somaliland and Puntland districts, often over grazing pastures and access to water points.[15] Criminals and Islamist ideological combatants have replaced warlords; conflict has given way to new forms of violence, including organised crime and youth gangs. Pirate groups openly challenge the state apparatus in Puntland. In the coastal town of Bossaso, the people's primary concerns are "unknown killings"; as distinct from revenge killings, which are culturally sanctioned, and understood.[16] Unknown killings are assassinations based on political or ideological motives, targeting prosecutors, judges, religious leaders, elders, or any intellectual or activist speaking up against violence and extremism. Clans and the Puntland Government have so far been unable to counter this kind of violence.

Criminal victimisation rates remain high. Between 5.4% and 12.3% of households experienced at least one assault over a 12-month period, depending on the district.[17] While just one homicide was captured by the survey in Burao (Somaliland) and Bossaso (Puntland), 3.7% of households in Mogadishu (South Central Somalia) and 7.6% in North Galkayo (Puntland) experienced one or more incidents over the same period.

Guns remain ubiquitous—most commonly assault weapons.[18] The OCVP survey found self-reported firearm ownership ranging from 4.7% to 17.8% of all households, but actual rates are probably significantly higher.[19] In a 2009 survey in Somaliland, 73.6% of respondents admitted owning at least one firearm. Based on this, the researchers estimated that there were 550,000 personal firearms in Somaliland alone. Guns are however rarely carried in public places.[20]

In contrast, open carrying of guns is common elsewhere in the Somali region. In Mogadishu and Galkayo, guns are highly visible and frequently used. In Mogadishu, the OCVP survey revealed that almost three-quarters of assaults were carried out with a firearm; in addition, 10% involved explosives (Figure 2). Even hand grenades and improvised explosive devices are used in interpersonal violence.[21]

Figure 2. Weapon used in assault cases, Mogadishu, 2009-10

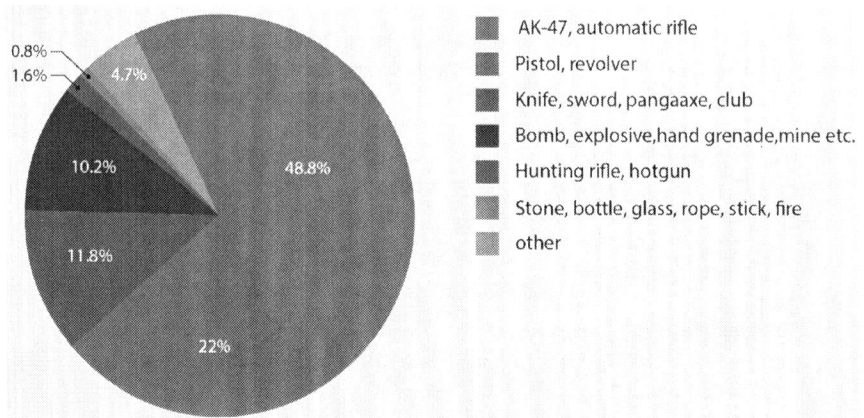

- AK-47, automatic rifle
- Pistol, revolver
- Knife, sword, pangaaxe, club
- Bomb, explosive,hand grenade,mine etc.
- Hunting rifle, hotgun
- Stone, bottle, glass, rope, stick, fire
- other

Source: Graphic generated from OCVP survey data.

Standards and normative frameworks

Somalia's ability to sign international treaties was largely a fiction as long as the government's control of the country did not extend beyond Mogadishu, and appeared shaky even there. The situation could be changing now. The Federal Government of Somalia is not yet a party to the 2006 *Convention on the Rights of Persons with Disabilities*. It is however a party to the 1966 *International Covenant on Civil and Political Rights* and *International Covenant on Economic, Social and Cultural Rights*, as well as the 1989 *Convention on the Rights of the Child*.

At the national level, in theory, the 1963 *Somali Public Order Law* regulates possession and use of guns in Puntland and South Central Somalia. Under this law, traders in firearms must be registered; private owners require authorisation by the Governor, and only "non-automatic" weapons can be authorised for private use.[22] Puntland replaced it in 2000 with a *General Security Law*,[23] but the Ministry of Security recognises the law is inadequate and it has not been implemented.[24]

Somaliland does not recognise the authority of the Federal Government, but lacks the international recognition that would enable formal ratification of international norms. It passed new firearms legislation in 2010, stipulating that a permit valid for four years can be issued for one gun and one magazine of ammunition.[25] The law falls short of internationally accepted practice in a number of ways—for example, some firearm permits can be inherited. Action plans for small arms control were developed in 2009 in both Somaliland and Puntland, but resources have not been set aside for their implementation and the plans now seem largely forgotten.

Guns continue to find their way into Somalia, despite the UN arms embargo instituted in 1992.[26] According to the UN Monitoring Group on Somalia and Eritrea, weapons entering the country in 2011 mainly came by sea from Yemen, principally through the Puntland port of Bossaso.[27] Some 80% of these weapons were destined for Mogadishu and South Central Somalia; the remaining 20% were for piracy operations and inter-communal disputes in different locations. In addition to the illicit trade, up to half the ammunition legally destined for the TFG were thought to be diverted to non-state actors.[28]

Section 2: Victims and survivors

According to the OCVP survey, males aged 15 to 29 are the most frequent victims of assault. But in Bossaso, almost as many cases of assault against women were recorded as against men.[29] Victims of homicides are primarily males aged 15 to 39. Victims of sexual violence are overwhelmingly females aged 15 to 19.

In assault cases, there appears to be a correlation between type of perpetrator and severity of the resulting injuries. In Mogadishu, where most perpetrators were identified as individual criminals or members of organised armed groups, assaults often resulted in hospitalisation. In contrast, in Las Anod, where most perpetrators were identified as acquaintances or neighbours, injuries tended to be light (Figure 3). Organised armed groups were more likely to use heavy weaponry. The survey did not inquire about long-term impacts, impairment, disability, or trauma resulting from the assaults.

Figure 3. Severity of injury resulting from assault, Las Anod and Mogadishu, 2009-10

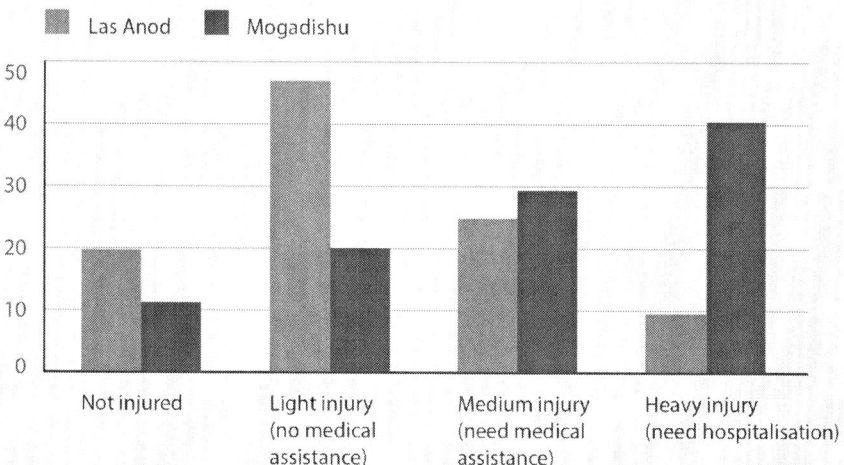

Source: Graphic generated from OCVP survey data.

Health systems

In districts of Mogadishu under control of the TFG at the beginning of 2010, there were five hospitals, several maternal and child health (MCH) clinics, a mental health hospital, and health posts.[30] These overcrowded facilities were often unable to meet the demands of the host community and internally displaced people. IDPs have overtaken some facilities to use as housing. Without the support of international agencies, even minimal services could not be sustained.

In 2011, two studies assessed the functional capacity of the health sector in Somaliland and Puntland.[31] These identified 15 hospitals, 87 MCH centres, and 165 health posts in Somaliland; and 4 hospitals, 69 MCH clinics, and 119 health posts in Puntland.[32] Somaliland had 100 qualified active physicians, both public and private, while Puntland had 74, of whom 42 were private practitioners.[33]

Both studies found that the health sector is severely under funded.[34] Donor coordination and transparency are major challenges. Service provision is inadequate and (in the absence of state action) relies heavily on NGOs and the private sector—particularly pharmacies, which are often the first port of call, but also traditional healers and clinics. The services available are often determined by the priorities of financing organisations and NGOs, rather than by the needs of the population.[35] In Somaliland, for example, so much support is geared towards maternal and child care that "it is nearly impossible for an adult male to get secondary care in the public sector."[36] In Puntland, the Minister of Health opined: "...there is no public healthcare system."[37]

In Somaliland the law only allows patients to be charged for certain tertiary services; however, shortages of equipment, consumable supplies, and drugs inflate the out-of-pocket costs to patients.[38] Distance, lack of staff, and lack of training are also obstacles. Gaps in staffing mean some clinics stand empty, while others are overcrowded. In Puntland, large areas of nomadic lands are not covered by any public or NGO-run health facilities.[39] Where facilities exist, costs are often based on a patient's estimated ability to pay.[40] Public health workers are underpaid and often rely on a second occupation, leading to absenteeism and undermining the credibility of the system.[41] For all these reasons, it is estimated that less than 15% of rural people in Somaliland use the public system for regular complaints, with similar trends identified in Puntland's Karkar region.[42]

Planning for development of the health sector is underway at three levels: a national development plan, a sectoral health policy or strategy, and an implementation plan. The latter is the donor-supported Essential Package of Health Services (EPHS) being rolled out in Somaliland and Puntland.[43] It advocates ten health programmes, of which three are particularly relevant for survivors of gun violence: first aid and care of the critically ill and injured, including lifesaving support and wound management; management of chronic and other diseases, including neurological illnesses (care of paralysed people); and mental health. The overall aim is to raise the quality of services provided in existing facilities rather than increasing the number of facilities.[44]

Somaliland has a Draft National Health Policy,[45] and in 2011 launched a National Development Plan (2012-16), which contains an analysis of the health sector.[46] It casts doubt on the Essential Package of Health Services, deeming it "not feasible yet".[47]

In Puntland, a National Development Plan and a Draft Health Strategic Framework (2011-15) are also in development.[48] This could be an opportunity to guide policy for health and justice system responsiveness to the needs of survivors of armed violence.

Notions of justice

Survivors are rarely able to seek legal redress through the police or formal justice system. The OCVP survey revealed that only 5.4% of cases of assault are reported to the police. Asked about reasons for not reporting assaults, almost half of Mogadishu residents said: "There is no one to report crime to." In cases of sexual violence, 42% of Mogadishu victims said they were too embarrassed to report the crimes.[49]

Respondents generally expressed low trust in police and especially in statutory courts, but informal actors fared better. In Somalia it is often up to elders and religious leaders to intervene in crime and conflict (the former having the potential to degenerate into the latter), using a mixture of Shari'ah and traditional *Xeer* law. In all the locations surveyed, assaults and sexual violence were first reported to clan elders, far ahead of the police and religious leaders.

In pastoral communities revenge is often sought before or instead of embarking on processes of justice, compensation, or reconciliation.[50] (See Box 2 for an example of clan revenge and resulting conflict). Clan elders play a prominent role in justice and security because they are the cornerstones of the traditional Somali justice and conflict resolution mechanism, known as *Xeer*.[51] This system rests on the clan structure of Somali society, in which a community is composed of a hierarchy of units. The smallest of these units is the *diya* group, an extended family group collectively liable for the payment of compensation monies in case of death or injury, whether intentional or accidental.

Xeer considers both the perpetrator and the victim of any crime or accident to be under the custody of their community or clan group.[52] The perpetrator's group must accept responsibility and apologise to the victim's group by offering, if appropriate, an "initial medication kit" (*dhiig joojin* in Somali)—in actual fact a sum of money. The victim's group must accept the apology and give the money to the individual so that treatment can begin. A process of rating and evaluation of the crime (fact finding) also starts.

Xeer provides indicative levels of compensation, expressed in numbers of camels to be collected and paid by the offender's *diya* group. Traditionally, 100 camels are paid if a man has been killed intentionally, or 50 if the victim is a woman.[53] Unintentional killings are compensated by 60 to 70 camels for a man, or 30 to 35 camels for a woman. For impairments, 50 camels are paid for the loss of an eye, or 10 for the loss of a thumb. These figures are only indicative, however, and actual compensation is decided by clan elders in negotiations that can take weeks or months. Compensation is shared among the victim's *diya* group depending on who was affected by the crime or accident and how the victim will get a share, though not the entire amount. Today compensation is often paid in cash rather than camels.

Box 2. Profile: Adam's story[54]

My name is Adam, I am 26 years old. I am from Qoryoley, about 120km from Mogadishu. The incident happened in 2008. My family and I were farming. It was harvest time and we produced raw oil from sesame seeds. A gang appeared and wanted to take all the produce from us. They fired four bullets at me and one of them hit my knee. I just fell on the ground. They came close to me and wanted to kill me. But I had my *toorey* [traditional Somali sword] and I defended myself and managed to injure one of the gang members. They fled.

After hours my sister found me on the ground. She called my brothers and they picked me up and took me home. There was no hospital nearby and we feared that the gang might come back. Al-Shabaab was all around us. My parents were extremely upset and thought I would die. They went to report to the elders of my clan.

The next morning fighting broke out between my clan and the gang's clan. My two brothers decided to participate in the revenge. They had guns, because earlier they had been in the government army. The elders encouraged the revenge and mobilised the clan youth. The fighting went on for two full months. Many people on both sides died or were injured. I was slowly recovering but we had no medicine or hospital.

After two months the elders saw that the situation was not progressing and invited a third clan to mediate. The opposing clan first denied that they had shot me and wanted to steal our produce. Finally they admitted it, but tension remained high. The discussion of compensation dragged on for years. They finally paid 10,000,000 Somali shillings (USD500) as *diya*,[55] but the money went to the elders and not to me. I left the area and came to Bossaso.

Note: When he was interviewed in February 2012, Adam still walked with a limp and experienced pain.

In case of large scale inter-clan fighting, the compensation agreement is generally included in a local peace agreement (see Box 3 for an example of such an agreement). The *Xeer* process contains elements of reconciliation and restorative justice, through the recognition by the offender's group that a wrong has been committed. Delays in payment can lead to retaliatory killings or the resumption of armed hostilities between the groups.

Box 3: Peace agreement between the Ali Saleban and Ali Jibrahil clans (Bari region, Puntland) signed on 7 November 2010 (summary translation)

I. Implementation of the agreement

- Ceasefire from 2 November 2010;
- Anyone violating the ceasefire will be judged according to Shari'ah law;
- Commitment to strengthen the security of Puntland in general, and between the two clans in particular.

II. Compensation for the casualties

- Ali Saleban clan to pay diya for 26 dead among the Ali Jibrahil;
- Ali Jibrahil clan to pay diya for 11 dead among the Ali Saleban;
- Diya for each person is that of the Garowe conference, namely USD26,300.

III. Timing of the diya payments

- One third of the payment to be paid on 30 November 2010;
- The rest has to be paid by 31 March 2011;
- All parties should pay their payment directly in cash without deducting the other side's payment. (…)

V. Judgment of the case of injured and wounded people

- All the cases of injured people will be evaluated according to Islamic Shari'ah;
- The list of injured people will be submitted by the two clans within 10 days of the signature of this agreement;
- The committee to review the injuries are (list of names removed)
- All remaining and unsolved issues should be discussed in the upcoming conference of the two clans on 30 November 2010, God willing.

Xeer is therefore like a proto-social security scheme through which survivors of violence can obtain compensation, at least as a one-off payment to the larger family group. The *Xeer* tradition has shaped expectations of survivors of violence in the Somali region, specifically for fact-finding and some form of monetary or material compensation to their group, whether the harm done was intentional or accidental.

Xeer has its limitations. First, it has little relevance for some forms of modern violence, such as 'unknown killings', or violence perpetrated by freelance militia or youth, who have no respect for elders and therefore escape the reach of traditional social control mechanisms. In a city like Mogadishu, for example, elders have seen much of their legitimacy eroded. Second, victims of violence from minority clans, or those who have been displaced by hardship and violence, are unlikely to be adequately represented even if they have elders able to confront the perpetrator's group. Third, the collective approach of *Xeer* dilutes both the responsibility of the perpetrators and the ability of victims to obtain compensation. Finally, the sheer scale of violence in some areas exceeds the financial capacity of *diya*-paying groups.

Violence against women is also inadequately addressed with traditional mechanisms. It is generally only reported to elders when it threatens the clan balance, for example if a woman is physically injured by her husband from another clan, in which case the wife's clan might demand compensation. In cases of sexual violence, clan elders occasionally still enforce the traditional Somali practice of marrying victims to their perpetrators.[56] Some focus group participants justified this tradition by arguing that the stigma attached to rape would prevent the victims from marrying otherwise. But some criticised the practice because (a) such marriages are likely to break down, leaving divorced women and their children vulnerable, and (b) the practice could be an incentive to rape. Indeed, in a society where a man is expected to pay a dowry to marry, poor young men allegedly commit rape to be able to marry for free.[57] Interestingly, the OCVP survey indicated that sexual violence is reported more often to the police than to elders, but the number of cases captured in the survey was too low to draw definitive conclusions.

Section 2: New approaches
With social customs unable to address the needs of many victims of gun violence, and weak health and justice systems, new initiatives are required to address gaps. This section presents two promising initiatives.

Youth for Change programme: Rehabilitating young perpetrators
In the Somali region, it is well understood that youth who become involved in gangs, militias, or criminal groups are often victims of poverty, unstable family backgrounds, or previous exposure to violence (see Box 4). Acknowledging this, a number of municipalities in Somaliland, Puntland, and Mogadishu teamed up with civil society and United Nations agencies at the end of 2010 to implement an innovative rehabilitation programme for youth involved in armed violence.[58]

The Youth for Change programme is innovative on a number of fronts. Participants are selected by the regional governor, the mayor, and the police commander, working with civil society representatives. This partnership enables the identification of suitable candidates, including known repeat offenders, petty criminals, gang or militia members, and drug users. In time, the programme is intended to develop into a probation or parole programme offering a much-needed alternative to incarceration.

Box 4. Profile: Ahmed[59]

My name is Ahmed and I am 11 years old. I live on the streets in Bossaso because my mother has passed away and my father is in Galkayo. I have nobody to take care of me. But I do not need anyone—anyway there is an old mama who brought me to this centre [where the Youth for Change programme is being implemented]. I have my gang, we are three and I am the leader. We always hang out together and we have our tactics to get money from people. They arrested me a couple of times but then I always get out. Although I like being in the jail: at least I get food.

There is a black market where I used to sell stolen mobile phones. Then we had a lot of food. We are very strong. When other gangs attack us we fight back. Last time we stoned another kid to death because his gang tried to rob us. Our main area of operation is the port. There is always a lot going on. We clean the sailors' shoes and the deck. The sailors are from India and Pakistan. They pay us in fuel. We used to get five to ten litres of fuel that we sell on the market. Then we eat well. Sometimes they are very bad, they try to touch our private parts and ask for services. But now I carry a knife and protect myself and my team.

Another innovation is the programme content.[60] Traditionally, the focus is placed on vocational skills training, in the expectation that a job will help prevent a relapse into violence. But vocational training cannot guarantee jobs in economically depressed contexts.[61] The programme emphasises social transformation, with classes and practical activities covering social skills, the rule of law, governance, and peacebuilding—including a discussion of the role of firearms. It assumes that a change of mindset coupled with the reactivation of social ties can trigger behavioural changes and therefore reduce armed violence.

Participants must sign a social contract, including a code of conduct regulating behaviour during an informal probation period. The code includes enforcement mechanisms ranging from soft mentorship to a disciplinary committee based on the principles of restorative justice.

There were 2,000 youth enrolled in the programme in early 2012, including 700 children under 18. In Burao, the District Council asserted that the programme had led to a marked reduction in crime.[62] Beyond anecdotes, a specialised tool has been developed to gauge the attitudes of youth beneficiaries at the beginning and end of the six-month programme, enabling a form of evaluation. Lessons have yet to be drawn from this initial phase, but strong support from local and national authorities makes it likely that the exercise will continue into the future.

Mogadishu: Civil society assisting survivors of sexual violence
A comprehensive picture of the scale of sexual violence is difficult to obtain in many countries due to under-reporting. Somalia is no exception. The OCVP survey recorded 46 cases of sexual violence in Mogadishu in the 12 months preceding the survey, two of them against men and boys. This is just the tip of the iceberg. One crisis centre run by the Somali Women's Development Centre (SWDC) in Mogadishu records up to 30 cases per month.[63]

Perpetrators of sexual violence are often identified as "men in uniform", and thus likely to be armed with guns.[64] SWDC recorded 158 cases of violence against women, half of which were rapes, in its Mogadishu centre from August 2011 to February 2012. In 25% of cases, the perpetrator was thought to be a militia member; in another 25% he was thought to be a member of the TFG army.[65] Ms Nur, an 18 year old victim, spoke of "being raped by two Shabab fighters at a displaced-persons camp in October. She said the men did not bother saying much when they entered her hut. They just pointed their guns at her chest and uttered two words: 'stay silent'."[66]

SWDC's crisis intervention centre, established in 2000, is a support service catering for people who have suffered physical, sexual, or psychological violence and human rights abuses. SWDC's community mobilisers, often in IDP camps, identify cases. The centre provides psychosocial support, counselling, and advice on where to receive medical care and legal aid. People requiring immediate medical support are referred to the hospital. The lack of safe shelters for survivors who decide to take legal action is a major problem: survivors sometimes move to reportedly safer IDP camps, but their safety is by no means guaranteed.

Similar community-based crisis centres have sprung up elsewhere. Poor government oversight, and competition for funding, means that they tend to compete rather than cooperate.

Conclusion
Providing assistance to survivors of gun violence in the Somali region is a daunting task compounded by the challenges arising from a failed state. But understanding the nature of violence and of its perpetrators and victims reveals opportunities for action and support. Assistance to survivors should be a key programmatic component of stabilisation efforts in conflict and post-war situations like Somalia.

Well-conceived assistance to survivors can contribute to stabilisation by affirming the role of the state in the visible delivery of basic services, and by supporting society's more vulnerable members.

Firstly, survivors require medical care to minimise the extent of impairment and subsequent disability. The Somali context highlights the difficulty of prioritising needs when resources are desperately scarce. Bypassing the state to deliver health services to the population is a risky strategy that can undermine the growth and strengthening of the public health sector. Vertical support to specific diseases or conditions—for example, in favour of survivors of gun violence—must be balanced with horizontal support to the health system as a whole. In Somaliland and Puntland, the Essential Package of Health Services is a good starting point to channel such support.

Donor trust funds to the health sector can help "defragment and de-projectise" the system.[67] However, the disproportionate leverage of donors on policies and priorities in Somalia and Somaliland (as in other aid-reliant countries) confers on them a delicate responsibility when it comes to assessing the needs of the population. Adequate data collection to improve service provision is essential, and constitutes an area of useful international support. The transparency and accountability of donors would be improved if recipient governments were supported to maintain a budget for the system as a whole, as well as one for funds channelled directly to specific facilities or local institutions. Together, such measures can ensure that funds are allocated according to actual needs.

Private service providers like pharmacies and traditional healers play important roles in the Somali healthcare picture. Such "first responders" could be included in a referral system. In situations where State capacity is particularly poor, as in Mogadishu, civil society initiatives fill an important gap.

However, even if the role of private and informal actors is acknowledged, it is important to concurrently strengthen the State's regulatory and coordination functions, to support the statebuilding process. Another reason why donors should not focus only on private initiatives is that receiving substantial international funding can undermine the local ownership and legitimacy of such initiatives and induce donor dependency. Involving local governments in decision-making is essential.

A similar balancing act is called for in the fields of justice and security. Support to the formal institutions of police and judiciary is warranted, but informal justice and security systems should not be neglected, particularly where these are more culturally relevant. The difficulty here is for the international community to gauge whether they can help strengthen local coping mechanisms without replacing or undermining them.

Finally, prevention of violence and victimisation remains an integral part of assistance to survivors. During the state building process in Somaliland, the local community succeeded in significantly changing norms on the carrying and use of firearms. Working with perpetrators of violence—themselves often survivors of violence—can also be productive in conflict and post-war situations. These are just some options for civil society, governments, donor and aid agencies to consider when working in fragile states.

Contributors: Mireille Widmer, independent consultant; Senior Associate, Surviving Gun Violence Project; formerly with the United Nations Development Programme in Somalia. Statistical analysis for the chapter was conducted by **Yann-Cédric Quero,** consultant criminologist. Interviews were conducted by **Lilla Schumicky, Shu'aib H. Ibrahim** and **Abdikarim Nor.**

Peer reviews were provided by **Alejandro Bendaña,** Programme Manager, Rule of Law and Security, UNDP Somalia (Kenya); **Nicolas Florquin,** Senior Researcher, Small Arms Survey (Switzerland); **Mohamed Ahmed Jama,** Director, Somali Organisation for Community Development Activities (Somalia); **Karina Lynge,** Head of Programme Development, Armed Violence Reduction, Danish Demining Group (Kenya); and **Abdullahi Mohammed Odowa,** Director, Observatory of Conflict and Violence Prevention (Somaliland).

References

1   The Somali Republic is generally considered a failed state, as its national government lacks control over large parts of the territory. However, two entities are informally recognised. Somaliland, in the northwest, declared independence in 1991. While not officially recognised, it increasingly enjoys bilateral relations with Western states. Puntland, in the northeast, declared its autonomy in 1998 but still considers itself part of the state of Somalia. The rest of the territory is referred to as South Central Somalia. For the purpose of this chapter, the terminology "Somalia and Somaliland" refers to the entire territory of the Somali Republic. Note that most of this chapter was written before the election of a new Somali President in September 2012.
2   Focus group discussions with a total of 80 residents, 20 each from four Mogadishu districts, October 2010, conducted by the Somali Youth Development Network (SOYDEN).
3   L. Bethany and N.P. Gleditsch, "Monitoring trends in global combat: A new dataset of battle deaths," *European Journal of Population* 21/2-3 (2005), pp. 145-166. Draws on PRIO Battle Deaths Dataset, Version 3.0.
4   Ten interviews with male veterans were conducted at De Martino hospital on 23 August 2011 by the Somali Organisation for Community Development Activities (SOCDA). All testimonies are on file with SOCDA.
5   Testimonies collected refer to various physical impairments, including missing limbs (one or two legs or hands) and facial injuries (missing teeth, cheeks or eyes).
6   Possibly some survivors from this larger group were injured in the civil war that took place in Somalia since 1991, rather than in the earlier Ogaden campaign.
7   Interview with 56-year-old male suffering from bullets or bullet fragments in his leg, hand and head. He has a dependent wife and three children.
8   Interview with 55-year-old male injured in both legs.
9   Interview with 50-year-old male injured in the stomach. "The bullet is still in the bladder," he said.
10 These were: the United Nations Operation in Somalia I (UNOSOM I, April-December 1992), the Unified Task Force (UNITAF, December 1992-May 1993), and the United Nations Operation in Somalia II (UNOSOM II, March 1993-March 1995).
11 These two groups joined forced in December 2010.
12 Much of the information that follows is drawn from M. Walls (Ed), *Peace in Somaliland: An Indigenous Approach to State-Building* (Hargeisa: Academy for Peace and Development and Interpeace, 2008).

[13] P. Johnson (Ed), *The Search for Peace: The Puntland Experience: A Bottom-up Approach to Peace and State Building* (Garowe: Puntland Development Research Centre and Interpeace, 2007), p. 22.

[14] The crime and victimisation survey was carried out in ten Somali districts (Burao, Las Anod, Bossaso, Galkayo, and six districts in the capital, Mogadishu) between December 2009 and July 2010. It was supported by the United Nations Development Programme, Somalia office. All locations chosen are also regional capitals, and together account for a substantial share of the Somali population. A total of 4,700 questionnaires were collected through a random sampling methodology. Rural areas were included within district boundaries, but are likely underrepresented overall. Data was collected at district level and does not permit extrapolation of trends for Somaliland, Puntland and South Central Somalia. However, focus group discussions also captured more general comments: 30 focus group discussions were held in the five survey locations between June and October 2010. Discussions were held with groups of women, youth, local authorities, elders, and religious leaders, internally displaced persons, and individuals from rural areas. In total an estimated 450 individuals were consulted, of which about one-quarter were women and girls. Results were published in 2011 in the form of Safety and Security District Baseline Reports, which were validated by local communities and authorities prior to publication. Additional statistical analysis of the dataset was conducted for this chapter by Yann-Cédric Quéro, criminologist, University of Montreal. Data is referred to in this chapter as "OCVP survey".

[15] The frequency of clan and community disputes was reviewed in the five *Safety and Security Baseline Reports* published by the OCVP. Available at: www.ocvp.org. Accessed 26 November 2012.

[16] Focus group discussions conducted by SORSO, Bossaso, July 2010. Unknown killings are mentioned as the primary concern by all focus groups except internally displaced persons, who rank it second, after violence against women.

[17] Source: OCVP survey. The lowest figure was recorded in Bossaso (Puntland), the highest in Las Anod (Sool region, disputed area between Somaliland and Puntland).

[18] Between half and three quarters of the weapons owned by survey respondents were declared to be Kalashnikov-type assault weapons.

[19] The lowest figure was recorded in Bossaso (Puntland), the highest in Las Anod (disputed Sool region). These are the same extremes as for victimisation rates.

[20] Danish Demining Group and Small Arms Survey, *Community Safety and Small Arms in Somaliland* (Copenhagen: DDG and SAS, 2009), p. 53 and p. 60.

[21] UN Monitoring Group on Somalia and Eritrea, *Report pursuant to Security Council resolution 1916* (2010), United Nations Security Council 2011, p. 44. Available at: www.un.org/ga/search/view_doc.asp?symbol=S/2011/433. Accessed 10 November 2012.

[22] *Public Order Law* No. 21 of 26 August 1963, particularly articles 21-34. English translation available at: www.somalilandlaw.com/Public_Order_Law_1963_full_copy.pdf Accessed 24 November 2012.

[23] *General Security Law* No. 1 of 23 January 2000, particularly articles 11-15, cited in Puntland Ministry of Security and DDR and United Nations Development Programme, *Small arms control needs assessment in Puntland,* Unpublished report (2009).

[24] Puntland Ministry of Security and DDR and United Nations Development Programme (2009).

[25] Law No. 39/2010 on the control of firearms. Somali version available at: www.somalilandlaw.com/Xeerka_Xakamaynta_Hubka_Fudud_Final_Nov_2010.pdf. Accessed 26 November 2012.

[26] UN Security Council Resolution 733, 23 January 1992.

[27] UN Monitoring Group on Somalia and Eritrea (2011), p. 41. Other sources of weapons mentioned include Ethiopia and Eritrea.

[28] UN Monitoring Group on Somalia and Eritrea (2011), p. 44.

[29] Y.C. Quéro, M. Widmer, K. Aitken and L. Peterson, *Safety and Security District Baseline Report: Bossaso* (Hargeisa: OCVP, 2011), p. 22. Available at: www.ocvp.org/resources/doc_download/22-bossaso-district-safety-and-security-baseline-report. Accessed 20 November 2012.

[30] Y.C. Quéro, M. Widmer and L. Peterson, *Safety and Security Baseline Report: Mogadishu* (Hargeisa: OCVP, 2011), p. 17. Available at: www.ocvp.org/resources/publication. Accessed 15 December 2012.

[31] Geopolicity, *Study on Sector Functional Assessments within Education, Health and WASH Sectors in Puntland*, Final Draft Report, unpublished, November (2011); and Geopolicity, *Study on Sector Functional Assessments within Education, Health and WASH Sectors in Somaliland*, Final Draft, unpublished, January (2012). Hereafter referred to as "Somaliland study" and "Puntland study" respectively.

[32] Somaliland study, p. 85; Puntland study, p. 58.

[33] Somaliland study, p. 85; Puntland study, p. 60.

[34] Somaliland study, pp. 83, 95 and 105; Puntland study, pp. 55 and 71. In both regions the sector is severely underfunded. In Puntland, the health budget was around USD400,000 in 2011, corresponding to a mere 1.38% of government resources; its share has been decreasing since 2009. In Somaliland, although the government doubled its allocation to the health sector in 2011, it still barely reaches 3% of total government spending, or approximately USD1.5 million.

[35] Somaliland study, p. 93 and 96; Puntland study, p. 55 and 57.

[36] Somaliland study, p. 93. Secondary health care refers to health specialists to whom patients may be referred, whether they work in a hospital or not. Primary health care refers to professionals who act as first point of consultation for patients at the local level. They can be general practitioners or nurses, but more often in the Somali context will be a community health worker or pharmacist. Tertiary health care refers to specialised consultative care for inpatients in a hospital setting, including surgical interventions.

[37] Puntland Minister of Health Dr. Abdullah Warsame, quoted in Puntland study, p. 55.

[38] Somaliland study, p. 82.

[39] Puntland study, p. 57.

[40] Puntland study, p. 57 and 71.

[41] See for example Puntland study, p. 59.

[42] Somaliland study, p. 93; Puntland study, p. 66.

[43] N. Pearson and J. Muschell, *Essential Package of Health Services, Somalia 2009* (UNICEF and European Commission, 2009). Available at: http://eeas.europa.eu/delegations/somalia/documents/more_info/essential_package_for_health_services_in_somalia_2009_en.pdf. Accessed 14 November 2012.

[44] For example, no assistive devices are on the EPHS lists of essential drugs, supplies and equipment, and violently acquired impairments is not included in proposed list of indicators. N. Pearson and J. Muschell (2009), Annex 8 and 9, pp. 81-100.

[45] Somaliland study, pp. 82 and 103.

[46] Republic of Somaliland, *National Development Plan (2012-2016)* (Hargeisa: Ministry of National Planning and Development, 2011). Available at: http://slministryofplanning.org/index.php/component/content/article/75-somaliland-national-development-plan.html. Accessed 14 November 2012.

[47] Republic of Somaliland (2011), p. 222.

[48] Puntland study, pp. 60 and 80.

[49] Y.C. Quero, M. Widmer and L. Peterson (2011), pp. 31-32. Though not necessarily representative of other survey locations, Mogadishu was the only location where the number of respondents was sufficient to allow further analysis of responses.

[50] As told to Lilla Schumicky in Bossaso, 29 February 2012.

[51] Compensation (or blood) money.

[52] Sedentary farming or fishing communities are more likely to resort immediately to clan reconciliation and justice mechanisms. Email conversation between Mireille Widmer and Mohamed Jama, Director, Somali Organisation for Community Development Activities, 24 August 2012.

[53] A good description of this system can be found in N. Grubeck, *Civilian harm in Somalia: Creating an appropriate response* (Washington DC: CIVIC, 2011), pp. 25-31. See also Watershed Legal Services, *Analysis of the three legal systems of the Somali areas* (Hargeisa: Danish Refugee Council, 2011).

[54] The information in this paragraph was shared by Mohamed Jama in an email conversation with Mireille Widmer, 24 August 2012.

[55] Figures presented in M. Van Notten, *The Law of the Somalis: A stable foundation for economic development in the Horn of Africa*, S. H. MacCallum (Ed) (Trenton, NJ: Red Sea Press, 2005), pp. 70-71, cited in N. Grubeck (2011), p. 29.

[56] Elders agreed to leave cases of rape to be handled by secular (statutory) courts in national declarations adopted in 2006 in Somaliland and in 2009 in Puntland (the latter was reiterated and strengthened in 2010). However, implementation of the declarations is still lacking. See *National declaration of Somaliland traditional leaders* (Hargeisa, December 2006) and *Declaration from the Puntland traditional leaders conference* (Garowe, February 2009). Unpublished, on file with the author.

[57] This perverse effect was mentioned in focus groups discussions in Burao and Las Anod.

[58] Target districts include Burao in Somaliland, Bossaso and Galkayo in Puntland, and eight Mogadishu districts that fell under the control of the Transitional Federal Government at the end of 2010. The UN agencies that supported the programme in 2011 were the UNDP, UNICEF and the International Labor Organization.

[59] Testimony of a Youth for Change programme beneficiary collected by Lilla Schumicky in Bossaso, 22 October 2011.

[60] This section applies to beneficiaries above 18 years of age. Underage beneficiaries participate only in educational activities covering literacy, numeracy, health, and basic sciences.

[61] In addition, job creation has yet to be demonstrated to reduce armed violence. For more on this issue see: O. Walton, *Youth, armed violence and job creation programmes: a rapid mapping study* (Norwegian Peacebuilding Centre and Governance and Social Development Resource Centre, 2010). Available at: www.gsdrc.org/docs/open/EIRS11.pdf. Accessed 20 November 2012. See also, Mercy Corps, *Examining the links between youth economic opportunity, civic engagement, and conflict: Evidence from Mercy Corps's Somali Youth Leaders Initiative* (Hargeisa: Mercy Corps, 2013).

[62] Comment by Abdirizak Moxamed Jamal, Burao District Counsellor, member of the District Safety Committee, Hargeisa, 1 February 2012.

[63] Email correspondence between Mireille Widmer and the Somali Women's Development Centre, 5 February 2012.

[64] Conversation between Mireille Widmer and Mama Zahra of the Somali Women's Development Centre, Mogadishu, 19 December 2011.

[65] SWDC, Gender-based violence trend analysis (August 2011-February 2012), received by email on 18 March 2012.

[66] J. Gettleman, "For Somali women, pain of being a spoil of war," *New York Times* 27 December (2011). Available at: www.nytimes.com/2011/12/28/world/africa/somalia-faces-alarming-rise-in-rapes-of-women-and-girls.html?pagewanted=all&_r=0. Accessed 22 November 2012.

[67] Somaliland study, p. 116.

SPOTLIGHT SECTION
Lomeruka Kristen (Uganda)

Lomeruka Kristen is a widowed mother of six, aged around 50. She is a woman of the Tepeth tribe, a nomadic pastoral group from Karamoja in northeastern Uganda.

Thirteen years ago Kristen was working with others in the garden when a group of cattle raiders from the neighbouring village of Loputuk attacked her village. Shot in the arm with an AK-47, Kristen was brought to hospital; her injury became infected and eventually her arm had to be amputated. Responsible for most of the work of the household, Kristen wondered how she would provide for her family. She felt like taking her life. The nurses at the hospital tried to comfort her, telling her it was not the end of her life—to date, that is the only counselling she has received. Kristen's difficulties were compounded by the death of her husband due to illness shortly after her release from hospital.

Kristen described how her impairment has severely constrained her ability to earn a living. Previously the family breadwinner, she was supporting herself and her children through cash labour, local brewing, and collecting and selling firewood and charcoal. Kristen is now unable to meet the needs of her family, and all but one of her children have left the village to seek work elsewhere. In order to eat one meal a day, Kristen relies on the help of her remaining daughter who works more than 12 hours a day, and on small tokens of charity from the community.

Kristen has witnessed both the humanity and inhumanity of her situation. Some people are sympathetic and give her what they can, while others abuse her and tell her she is worthless. As a result of experiencing abuse within and outside of her community, Kristen isolates herself and feels weak.

Kristen's resilience is no thanks to the government or the NGOs operating in Karamoja. Kristen said she was mentally unstable for a long time and received no psychosocial or financial support. Though the World Food Programme operates in her community, she is unable to participate because it requires physical work in exchange for food or cash. This has made her dependent on the good will of community members, which has decreased over time.

When asked how she maintains positivity, Kristen explained that she has accepted herself as she is; when she is emotionally abused, she heals herself through crying and her faith in God. Her biggest source of strength comes from daily prayer. Despite her hardships, she thanks God that she survived the attack. Since her injury, this is the first time someone has come to speak to her about her situation; she feels hopeful.[1]

Lomeruka Kristen. (Image: Courtesy of Sara Hylton, 2012)

Contributors: Sara Hylton, former Armed Violence Reduction Project Officer, Danish Demining Group in Karamoja, Uganda. **Lilu Thapa,** Head of Programs and Armed Violence Reduction, Danish Refugee Council and Danish Demining Group in Uganda.

References

[1]   Told to Sara Hylton and Lilu Thapa in Karamoja in February 2012

SPOTLIGHT SECTION
Quality Rehabilitation and Links
to Violence Reduction

Homicide remains one of the leading causes of death among youth and young adults aged 15 to 34 years in the United States (USA), despite reductions in youth deaths in recent years. Homicide disproportionally impacts males, and urban youth of colour. It is the leading cause of death among African Americans aged 15-34, and second among Hispanics of this age group, but only fifth among non-Hispanic whites in this age group.[1]

What is more, those who survive a gunshot are likely to be injured again. In the 1990s, recurrent violence-related trauma accounted for up to 45% of all hospital trauma admissions.[2] A 1989 retrospective study of victims of violence in Detroit found that 44% of patients were re-injured over a five-year period.[3] At the five-year follow-up point, 20% of the individuals had died; and rates of unemployment and substance misuse were 67%. Risk of injury acquired in a retaliatory act amongst young people who were already victims of violence is 88 times higher than among those who were never exposed to violence.[4]

Another key conclusion, echoed in other studies, was that being the victim of violence also significantly increases the likelihood of becoming a perpetrator of violence: exposure to gun violence approximately doubles the probability that an adolescent will perpetrate serious violence over the two subsequent years.[5] The World Health Organization has also cautioned that victims of violence are themselves at increased risk of committing violence against others; this provides a powerful rationale for directing more attention and resources to their care.[6]

Risk factors for acquaintance and street violence recurrence remain poorly understood, but may include gang involvement, poor academic achievement, poverty, psychiatric disturbances, and alcohol or other substance abuse.[7] These risk factors likely also adversely affect the rehabilitation process. Hospitalised survivors of gunshot injuries—compared to survivors of other types of injuries— report significant declines in physical and/or mental health at eight months post-discharge, with more than 80% reporting moderate or severe post-traumatic stress. Many of those interviewed noted not receiving a single consultation for mental health services.[8]

Rehabilitation can be further hampered by dismissive attitudes, prevalent in the trauma and rehabilitation field, which consider patients injured as a result of violence as less responsive to rehabilitation than those injured by other means. There is also a tendency by some professionals to view survivors of violence as more culpable for their injury and less deserving of the benefits of rehabilitation (see the Rehabilitation and Recovery chapter for more detail).[9]

Young people reflecting on their experiences confirm this attitude from some professionals: "many people—including some health care providers—think that adolescent victims of violence are uniformly bad kids who probably deserved what they got."[10] Admitted to a local trauma centre for a gunshot injury, Ronnie, aged 20 at time of injury, reflected on his experience and that of others: "They just wasn't taking care of people like they was supposed to. I didn't want my mom seeing me all bloody and coming out of the hospital. And I didn't have a belt on, 'cause they took my belt. And this lady say, 'He ain't nothing but another gang banger.'"[11]

Quality services for young gunshot victims can effectively treat the effects of injury and trauma, address risk factors for re-injury and facilitate pathways out of violence for young patients. Studies of acute stress reported by violently injured youth in emergency departments suggest that early detection of high-risk youth in the immediate post-injury period offers an opportunity to prevent long-term psychological harm.[12] Other studies demonstrate that victims of violence aged 10-24 can change their lifestyles to avoid becoming repeat "clients" to emergency departments for treatment of gunshot wounds and stabbings, and that change can be initiated by health professionals who choose to do more than "treat them and street them".[13]

Young people often describe being shot or stabbed, or witnessing violent injury to others, as an "awakening," a "wake up call," akin to being "slammed against a wall", prompting them to re-examine their lives. These are "teachable moments" for guidance and redirection by caring and competent health professionals, peers, and other role models, to assist those who have become enmeshed in violence to extricate themselves, break the cycle of violence, and support positive youth development. The "teachable moment" may be useful in assisting the survivor and their family to become engaged in future violence prevention activities.

"When I woke up from being shot, I couldn't talk, I couldn't move, I couldn't eat, and I couldn't breathe without the help of a machine. In fact, for the first six months, I couldn't communicate with anyone at all. All I could do was lie there and think. You hear gang members say all the time, "I'm not afraid to die." But let me tell you, when you are lying there gasping for air, bleeding, going into shock, rushing toward death, that hard core is gone and all that's left is fear. As for me, I had to learn to forgive. I had to let go of my anger toward the person who shot me, or it would have soured my life. Once I got over that boulder, I felt there was so much more that I could accomplish in rehabilitation, spiritually, mentally, and socially in my life." (José, age 20, shot at age 17, Boston.)[14]

For many young violence victims, however, these critical opportunities are missed. Violent injury becomes another episode of routine violence of little consequence in their lives—reinforcing a delinquent identity and propelling the young person further into active violence perpetration and crime.

Albert was shot on three separate occasions—at age 14, 15, and 17—in Los Angeles. In the first two incidents, he was the intended target. The third time, he was shot accidentally by one of his friends. Albert describes the times he was shot; the first was a drive-by shooting: "We were just walking to the store and somebody just started letting off on us. A car pulled up, and they just started blasting on us. The second time I got shot, I was involved in a shoot-out with somebody, and I ended up catching a bullet. The last one that confined me to a wheelchair was actually an accidental shooting; it was an accidental shooting where I was just messing with guns and the gun went off and hit me in my stomach. I was shot at age 17. The bullet lodged, it struck me through the front of my stomach, and it lodged in my spine, which confined me to a wheelchair for the rest of my life."[15]

Only a very few large urban paediatric, trauma, and acute rehabilitation centres take advantage of the opportunity that a violence-induced injury presents. For example, one study of 56 spinal cord injury rehabilitation inpatients admitted for gunshot related injuries (most of whom had pre-injury involvement in the criminal justice system and/or previous violent injury) identified a total of 55 missed opportunities for social service interventions. In only one case was a relevant intervention initiated to deter future injury.[16] This study concluded that more aggressive efforts at service (health, social, justice) intervention could deter future impairment and violent perpetration and victimisation.

For most injured youth, discharge planning is partial. Good practice ought to include at least four key components for successful transition from an institution or hospital to the community for youth at high risk of future violence perpetration or victimisation:

- Assessment of the psychosocial needs of the individual and risks posed to themselves and broader public health and safety;
- Planning for the treatment and services required to address these needs;
- Identifying required programmes responsible for post-discharge services; and
- Coordinating the aftercare plan to ensure appropriate service delivery and mitigate gaps in care.[17]

Exceptions exist, however. One example is Carl, shot at 14 years old in Boston, and suffers from spinal cord injury. Due to the severity of his impairments, he was referred to a hospital school, where his adolescent development needs (schooling, recreation, and vocational) were met through an intensive residential rehabilitation programme.[18] "When I came here and got exposed to what I can do, what I haven't seen, it was a whole new ballgame. Let's pull out the rug, and let's get ready for this new life. I was exposed to caring for myself in the position I'm in now. Caring for myself on an everyday living basis. As far as coming here, it gave me back inclusion, where playing sports is what I always looked for in a high school. Not necessarily academics, but it's definitely keeping me where I'm supposed to be. Graduated. Just the whole support here is like one big family."[19]

Hospitals typically discharge violently injured patients without an assessment of young patients' risk of retaliation or organising the necessary community support. In a more advanced form, discharge planning involves the creation of an individualised aftercare plan or case management.[20]

Where programmes exist, their effectiveness varies. One 18 year old man, Martin, benefitted from a violence prevention intervention in hospital, but without follow-up services and support in his community once he was discharged, the programme fell short. Martin reflected that the programme was insufficient to keep him safe once he returned to his community, where his old rivals were waiting for him: "But it [the hospital violence intervention] really didn't do nothin' when I was, like, out and at home, goin' out to the bus stop. That's when it really hits home, when you gotta walk down the street, when you gotta go to the bus stop, when you gotta go to the store. That's when it's really different than bein' at those meetings. What do you do in real life when these guys are ready to whoop you?"[21]

Martin received little follow-up post-hospital other than a weekly support meeting; he was released back into the community and into the same life situation. His search for protection from further injury, due to an unresolved set of issues he faced on the street led him to illegally purchase a gun, eventually leading to gun possession charges: "First, when I first went around the way, I was kinda like scary. But after like a few days, I was back outside, and that's when I started gettin', I said now I need to get me somethin' to hold on to, and then I... that's when we started... that's when we got that piece to hold on to, and then the next year is when I had got into that trouble with the gun situation."[22]

Well-structured programmes do make a difference. A care management study of hospital-based interventions found that they reduce the risk of violent injury recidivism fourfold. For start-up and maintenance of a violence intervention programme, it is essential to know where to focus collaborative efforts in communities to target the limited resources for risk reduction activities. Securing mental health care and employment for clients appears to be predictive of success. The value of early "high-dose" intensive case management is also essential for reducing recidivism.[23]

Peer support and transformative role models cannot be underestimated in this process. George reflected at the age of 24, after an injury from gun violence, on one of his role models, a peer who had left behind a life of violence: "Felipe, who was in a wheelchair; he worked with a project called U-Turn, and one day I seen him in a magazine article which was called Barrio Warrior. And I seen him in there, he was getting a diploma, and in the chair. And one day he came to the church, and he spoke and his testimony, how he overcame, it impressed me, you know. I liked what he was doing."[24]

Building on emerging practice first established in the 1990s to provide community-based case management and targeted services to high-risk populations to reduce risk factors for re-injury and retaliation; hospitals in several major US cities have now come together under the National Network of Hospital-based Violence Intervention Programmes (NNHVIPs).[25] Strategies combine nonviolent problem-solving skills such as mediation and negotiation that challenge the beliefs that rely on violence, referrals to other parts of health care systems and social services and case-management. Rigorous evaluations have demonstrated promising results in preventing violent re-injury, violent crime, and substance misuse (see Box 1).

Box 1: Evaluating hospital-based violence intervention programmes and cost savings[26]

Studies suggest hospital-based violence intervention programmes are effective across a range of outcomes, translating into substantial cost savings. Among the findings:

- A Baltimore programme found significant reductions in misdemeanour offenses, feelings of aggression, and improved self-efficacy.[27]
- Evaluation of the R. Adams Cowley Shock Trauma Center in Baltimore, Maryland, found that the intervention group was half as likely to be convicted of any crime and four times less likely to be convicted of a violent crime, translating into approximately USD1.25 million in incarceration cost savings. This group also had lower hospital recidivism rate (5% vs. 26%), saving an estimated USD598,000 in health care costs.[28]
- A Chicago programme found that participants were significantly less likely to report re-injury.[29]
- An evaluation of a Richmond (Virginia) programme concluded that the intervention group had higher rates of use of social and welfare support services and lower rates of substance misuse.[30]
- A retrospective cohort study of Oakland's Highland Hospital programme found participants had significantly reduced involvement with the criminal justice system.[31]
- The Wraparound Project at San Francisco General Hospital found that the six-year violent re-injury rate among clients was 4.5%, compared with 16% for a control group.[32]
- At Wishard Hospital in Indianapolis, the one-year re-injury rate for programme participants was 3%, compared with 8% for a control group.[33]

In 2013, there are promising policy developments to prevent firearm violence along with a renewal of federal Government commitment to firearm injury research and prevention after a 17-year hiatus.[34] Further, the 2012 US Department of Justice Defending Childhood Initiative calls for the launch of a national initiative to promote professional education, training, and standards among those working with children exposed to violence, underscoring their responsibility to provide trauma-informed services and trauma-specific evidence-based treatment.[35] This could bode well for the incorporation of hospital-based initiatives to address violence as part of the spectrum of multi-disciplinary responses to prevent and reduce violence and crime, provide quality rehabilitation to young people, and improve the life chances, support families and caregivers of survivors and communities impacted by gun violence.

Contributor: Joan Serra Hoffman, violence prevention specialist, Social Development Unit, Sustainable Development Department, World Bank. The piece was written in a personal capacity and does not necessarily reflect the views of the World Bank Group.

References

1   Centers for Disease Control and Prevention, Webpage, "Injury Prevention & Control: Data & Statistics (WISQARS), Leading Causes of Death". Available at: www.cdc.gov/injury/wisqars/leading_causes_death.html Accessed 28 May 2013.

[2] W.A. Goins, J. Thompson and C. Simpkins, "Recurrent intentional injury," *Journal of the National Medical Association* 84/5 (1992), pp.431-435.

[3] W.A. Goins, J. Thompson and C. Simpkins (1992).

[4] M.D. Dowd, "Consequences of violence. Premature death, violence recidivism, and violent criminality," *Pediatric Clinics of North America* 45/2 (1998), pp. 333-340; R.M. Cunningham, L. Knox, J. Fein, S. Harrison, K. Frisch, M. Walton, R. Dicker, D. Calhoun, M. Becker and S. W. Hargarten, "Before and after the trauma bay: the prevention of violent injury among youth," *Annals of Emergency Medicine* 53 (2009), pp. 490-500.

[5] J.B. Bingenheimer, R.T. Brennan and F.J. Earls, "Firearm exposure and serious violent behaviour," *Science* 308 (2005), pp. 323-326. See also: R.M. Cunningham et al (2009); W.A. Goins et al (1992).

[6] A. Butchart, A. Phinney, P. Check and A. Villaveces, *Preventing Violence: A Guide to Implementing the Recommendations of the World Report on Violence and Health* (Geneva: World Health Organization, 2004), p. 61. See also R. M. Cunningham et al (2009).

[7] P. Devlieger and F. Balcazar, "Bringing them back on the right track: Perceptions of medical staff on the rehabilitation of individuals with violently acquired spinal cord injuries," *Disability and Rehabilitation* 32/6 (2010), pp. 444-451; T. Kroll, "Rehabilitative needs of individuals with spinal cord injury resulting from gun violence: The perspective of nursing and rehabilitation professionals," *Applied Nursing Research* 21 (2008), pp. 45-49.

[8] A.L. Greenspan and A.L. Kellermann, "Physical and Psychological Outcomes 8 Months after Serious Gunshot Injury," *Journal of Trauma-Injury Infection and Critical Care* 53 (2002), pp. 709-716.

[9] T. Kroll (2008); P. Devlieger and F. Balcazar (2010). Also see, R. L. Waters, J. Cressy and R.H. Adkins, "Spinal cord injuries due to violence," *American Rehabilitation* (1996), pp.10-15.

[10] American Academy of Pediatrics, Task Force on Adolescent Assault Victim Needs, "Assault victim needs: A review of issues and model protocol," *Pediatrics* 98/5 (1996), pp. 991-1001; American Academy of Pediatrics, Committee on Adolescence, "Firearms and adolescents," *Pediatrics* 98 (1998), pp. 784-787.

[11] J.S. Hoffman, *Youth Violence, Resilience and Rehabilitation* (New York: LFB Scholarly, 2004), pp.81-82.

[12] J.A. Fein, K.R. Ginsburg, M.E. McGrath, F.S. Shofer, J.C. Flamma and E.M. Datner, "Violence prevention in the emergency department: Clinician attitudes and limitations," *Archives of Pediatrics and Adolescent Medicine* 154 (2000), pp. 495-498. See also: H.J. Lim, M. McCart, W.H. Davies, A. Calhoun and M.D. Melzer-Lange, "Risk for repeated emergency department visits for violent injuries in youth firearm victims," *Clinical Medicine Insights: Trauma and Intensive Medicine* 2/1 (2009), pp.1-7; and C. Snider and J. Lee, "Youth violence secondary prevention initiatives in emergency departments: a systemic review," *Canadian Journal of Emergency Medicine* 11 (2009), pp. 161-168.

[13] L.S. Zunz and J.M. Rosen, "Psychosocial needs of young persons who are victims of interpersonal violence," *Pediatric Emergency Care* 191 (2003), pp.15-19.

[14] J.S. Hoffman (2004), p. 4.

[15] J.S. Hoffman (2004), pp. 61-62.

[16] Study conducted between 1990 and 1998. M.V. Ragucci, M. M. Gittler, K. Balfanz-Vertiz and A. Hunter, "Societal risk factors associated with spinal cord injury secondary to gunshot wound," *Archives of Physical Medicine and Rehabilitation* 82 (2001), pp. 1720-1723.

[17] R. Cunningham and L. Knox, *Reinjury Prevention for Youth Presenting with Violence-Related Injuries: A Training Curriculum for Trauma Centers*, Southern California Center of Academic Excellence on Youth Violence Prevention in Collaboration with the University of Michigan Department of Emergency Medicine Injury Center (2008), p.49.

[18] J.S. Hoffman (2004), p. 85.

[19] J.S. Hoffman (2004), p. 85.

[20] J.S. Hoffman (2004), p. 88; R. Cunningham and L. Knox (2008), p. 49.

[21] J.S. Hoffman (2004), p. 88.

[22] J.S. Hoffman (2004), p. 87.

[23] R. Smith, S. Dobbins, A. Evans, K. Balhorta and R.A. Dicker, "Hospital-based violence intervention: risk reduction resources that are essential for success," *Journal of Trauma and Acute Care Surgery* 74/4 (2013), pp. 976-980.

[24] J.S. Hoffman (2004), p.132.

[25] See http://nnhvip.org/

[26] Drawn from: J. Purtle, R. Dicker, C. Cooper, T. Corbin, M. Greene, A. Marks, D. Creaser, D. Topp and D. Moreland, "Hospital-based violence intervention programs save lives and money," *Journal of Trauma and Acute Care Surgery* 74 (2013), pp. 976-982.

[27] T.L. Cheng, D. Haynie, R. Brenner, J.L. Wright, S.E. Chung and B. Simons-Morton, "Effectiveness of a mentor-implemented, violence prevention intervention for assault-injured youths presenting to the emergency department: results of a randomized trial," *Pediatrics* 122 (2008), pp. 938-946.

[28] C. Cooper, D.M. Eslinger and P.D. Stolley, "Hospital-based violence intervention programs work," *Journal of Trauma Injury, Infection, and Critical Care* 61 (2006), pp. 534-540.

[29] L.S. Zun, L. Downey and J. Rosen, "The effectiveness of an ED-based violence prevention program," *American Journal of Emergency Medicine* 24 (2006), pp. 8-13.

[30] M.B. Aboutanos, A. Jordan, R. Cohen, R.L. Foster, K. Goodman, R.W. Halfond, R. Poindexter, R. Charles, S.C. Smith, L.G. Wolfe, B. Hogue and R.R. Ivatury, "Brief interventions with community case management services are effective for high-risk trauma patients," *Journal of Trauma Injury, Infection, and Critical Care* 71 (2011), pp. 228-237.

[31] D. Shibru, E. Zahnd, M. Becker, N. Bekaert, D. Calhoun and G.P. Victorino, "Benefits of a hospital-based peer intervention program for violently injured youth," *Journal of the American College of Surgery* 205 (2007) pp. 684-689.

[32] R. Smith, S. Dobbins, A. Evans, K. Balhorta and R.A. Dicker (2013).

[33] G. Gomez, C. Simons, W. St John, D. Creasser, J. Hackworth, P. Gupta, T. Joy and H. Kemp, "Project Prescription for Hope (RxH): trauma surgeons and community aligned to reduce injury recidivism caused by violence," *The American Surgeon* 78/9 (2012), pp.1000-1004.

[34] The Centers for Disease Control and Prevention is the US Government's highest public health research agency. In January 2013, the Obama Administration lifted a 17-year ban on working on gun violence. See White House, *Now is the time* (Washington DC: White House, 2013). Available at: www.whitehouse.gov/sites/default/files/docs/wh_now_is_the_time_full.pdf Accessed 3 June 2013.

[35] Department of Justice, *Defending Childhood Taskforce, Final Report* (Washington DC: DoJ, 2012). Available at: www.justice.gov/defendingchildhood/cev-rpt-full.pdf Accessed 10 May 2013.

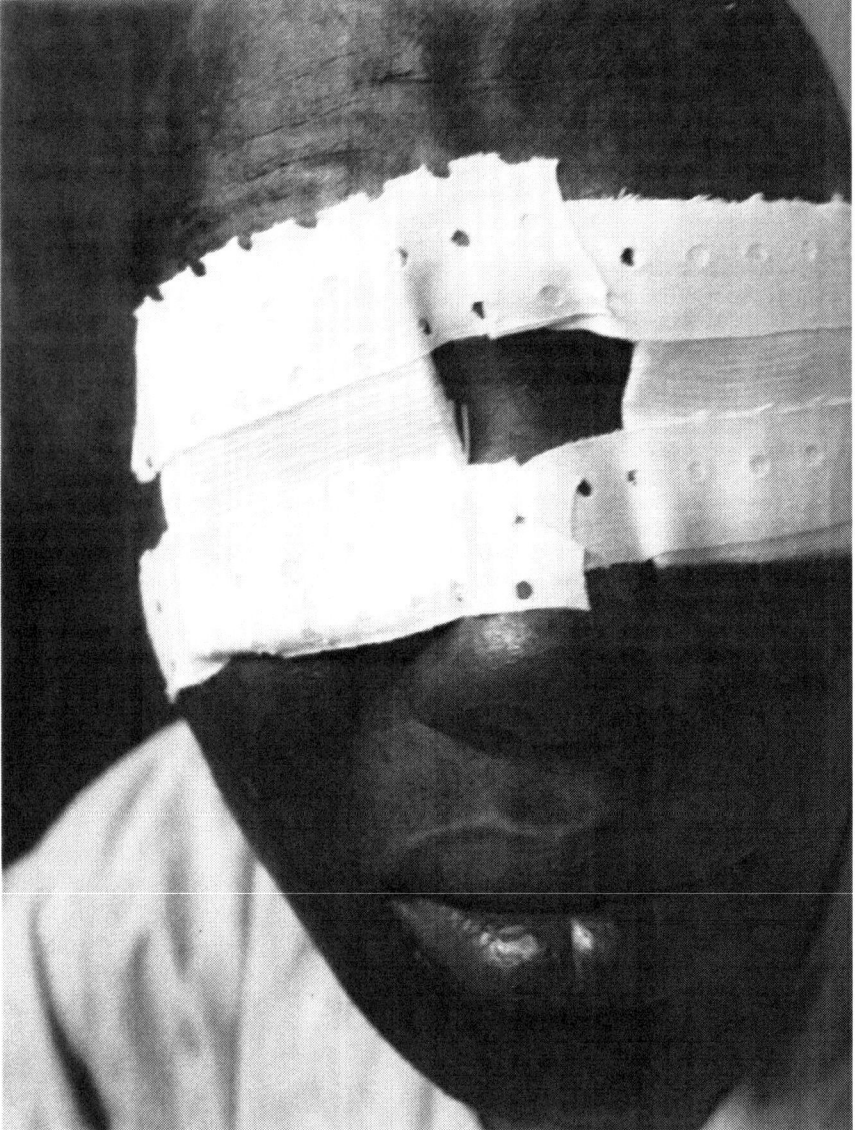

Siaka Kone, 25, his face wounded by a gunshot during riots, recovers at Donka hospital in Conakry, Guinea. (Image: Luc Gnago/Reuters, 17 February 2007)

"The gun lobby finds waiting periods inconvenient. You have only to ask my husband how inconvenient he finds his wheelchair from time to time."

Sarah Brady, whose husband James Brady was among four people shot during an assassination attempt on US President Ronald Reagan on 30 March 1981. James and Sarah Brady gave their name to the Brady Campaign to Prevent Gun Violence. In 1994, in his honour, the *Brady Handgun Violence Prevention Act* came into effect.

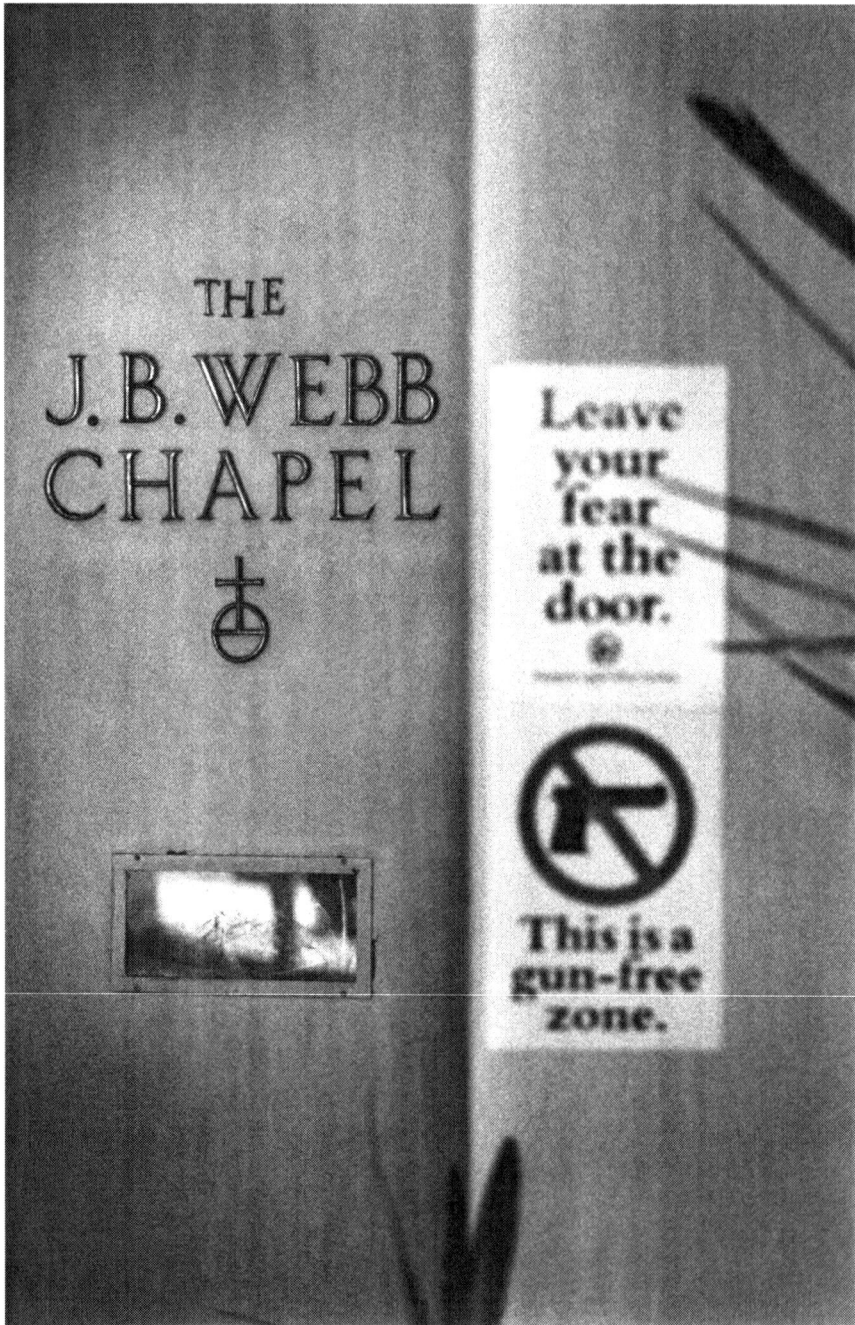

A sign asks visitors to the J.B. Webb Chapel Central Methodist Mission, Johannesburg, to leave their weapons outside. (Image: Dieter Telemans/ Panos, December 2000)

8 South Africa

Introduction
With violence rates much higher than the global average, gun injuries still present a significant burden to health, justice and social welfare systems in South Africa. The national Government has taken important steps in recent years on two fronts: establishing policies to reduce gun violence; and raising standards for victim services and rights. But a lot of work is still necessary to ensure that policy initiatives are fully implemented. The force of law does not back up many promising policies and the nation's underfunded and poorly coordinated public sector institutions have not been able to implement them.

This chapter explores the gap between national laws and policies and practice in a country that continues to experience high levels of gun violence, despite significant reductions over the last ten years. It sketches the post-1994 policy environment, highlighting innovative policies such as the 1996 National Crime Prevention Strategy (NCPS) and the Victim Empowerment Programme (VEP), examining whether such guidelines and policies are improving the lives of people impaired by gun violence.

Section 1: Violence in South Africa
Violence and unintentional injuries are the second leading cause of deaths and injury in South Africa after HIV and AIDS.[1] In 2000 there were almost 60,000 deaths due to injury, including accidents, inter-personal violence, or self-directed violence. This is higher than the average for the African continent, and nearly twice the global average.[2] Interpersonal violence is a leading risk factor, responsible for nearly half the nation's injury deaths.[3]

During the transition from apartheid to democracy (1990-94), there was a dramatic surge in violent crime, with homicides peaking in 1995 at 67 per 100,000.[4] Since 2000, there has been a steady drop in several violent crime categories, with murder showing the most significant decrease.[5] The 2010-11 murder rate represents a 50% reduction in homicide over the 17-year period following democratic elections in 1994.[6] However, homicide remains one of the leading causes of non-natural death.

Young men are disproportionately engaged in violence both as perpetrators and victims, with the highest homicide rates found in men aged 15-29 years (184 per 100,000 population).[7] Apart from homicide, South Africa also suffers significant rates of attempted murder (31.1 per 100,000), common assault (371.8 per 100,000), assault with the intent to inflict grievous bodily harm (397.3 per 100,000) and rape and sexual assault (132.4 per 100,000).[8]

The majority (75%) of the total trauma caseload comprises men.[9] Many are the result of direct or indirect involvement in criminal or gang activities, or being caught in the crossfire, or due to mistaken identity.[10] The blurring of lines between victims and perpetrators has consequences for service provision. Some young men with gunshot wounds are regarded with prejudice by hospital and clinic staff, which may compromise their treatment.[11] Thembani and Mark, interviewed for this chapter, felt that they experienced animosity or indifference from the emergency workers who were first on the scene when they were shot (see Box 1).[12] In their opinion, this translated into delays in police arriving, or in getting emergency medical treatment such as pain medication.

Apart from the presence of firearms, the high levels of violence are compounded by factors such as socio-economic inequality; social norms that support and legitimise the use of violence, in particular male-on-male violence; weak law enforcement; and wide exposure of children to violence, giving rise to the intergenerational recycling of violence.[13] Inequality is South Africa's most damaging social problem; the country is ranked as one of the most unequal societies in the world. A global study on homicide suggests that there is an association "between crime, development and income distribution", and that countries with high levels of income inequality are "afflicted with homicide rates almost four times higher than more equal societies."[14]

Gun violence: Sources, types and trends

In the colonial period, gun ownership was generally limited to European settler communities. During the apartheid era, guns were further concentrated in the hands of the white population—including the military and security services and among civilians.[15] It was only with the rise of liberation movements that young black men and women were armed in so called self-defence and self-protection units.[16] For many people the AK-47 became the symbol of liberation.[17] As in other societies, gun ownership and use is strongly gendered.[18]

Publicly available data on the impacts of guns is inadequate to assess the full scope of injury and disability. The national police release a single, aggregate figure for homicides, which combines gun and non-gun killings, and there is concern that the figure is subject to manipulation. Other than periodic health reports from a limited number of urban areas, the number of non-fatal firearm injuries sustained each year, and the circumstances around them, are unknown. Despite data challenges, it is clear that survivors of violence constitute a significant population.

The passage of the 2000 *Firearms Control Act* (FCA) likely played a role in the decline of gun violence.[19] The FCA established a national arms control and management system to regulate the supply, possession, safe storage, transfer and use of firearms, and to prevent the criminal or negligent use of weapons.[20] The FCA significantly strengthened regulation over the possession and use of firearms.[21] It introduced a two tier licencing system: a would-be owner first applies to be declared fit to obtain a firearm licence and issued with a competency certificate, then applies for a firearm licence which licences the person and registers the gun. The system allows the process to be slowed down for further investigation, or halted completely if issues such as acute mental illness or history of violence emerge. The FCA also allows police search and seizure powers without warrants and raises the maximum prison sentence for illegal possession of a firearm to 25 years. A further influence on the normative framework is the 2001 Southern African Development Community Firearms Protocol, ratified in 2003.[22]

The number of registered firearms and gun owners decreased from 3.5 million guns among 2.4 million owners in 1994[23] to approximately 2.9 million guns among 1.5 million owners by August 2011.[24] The reduction in gun ownership levels has been reflected in a massive reduction in the number of gun dealers: a 90% reduction from 2000 to 2006.[25]

Unlike the levy placed on motor vehicle fuel, which goes directly to the Road Accident Fund (RAF), the 14% sales tax on firearms is not earmarked for health and justice costs generated by gun violence. Instead, firearm sales tax goes into general revenue. The RAF has been beset by a number of problems including delays in compensation to claimants. Nevertheless the idea of an analogous tax earmarking system in relation to alcohol is supported by a growing number of policymakers, researchers and advocates, as a way of offsetting the substantial costs of alcohol-related injuries.[26] The National Treasury is generally opposed to earmarking of state revenue, as it believes it skews the allocation of funds across the various departments.[27] These concerns noted, there is potential for targeted use of the tax proceeds of gun sales. El Salvador was the first country to establish a firearm tax that directly contributes to health programmes (see Spotlight section, El Salvador Gun Tax and Victims' Services).

Section 2: Assistance for survivors
This section reviews the main areas of support available to survivors of injury and violence in South Africa, including trauma care and rehabilitation and the system of social protection. It also looks at the division of responsibility for service provision, oversight and coordination at governmental level(s).

Trauma care and rehabilitation services
A trauma patient's ability to access emergency management services (EMS) is largely dependent on their financial and geographic circumstances.[28] The six provincial public hospitals with Level 1 trauma units are clustered in four provinces—five other provinces have no public hospitals with Level 1 trauma units.[29] While some private hospitals have emergency trauma units, most of them are not equipped with the specialist skills or equipment required for a Level I trauma service.[30] Rural areas are mostly serviced by mobile clinics, primary health care facilities, or district hospitals. The average response time of the EMS for Level I trauma unit hospitals is 12-15 minutes.[31] However, in a province like KwaZulu-Natal with substantial rural areas, it can take up to 18 hours for an inter-hospital transfer.[32]

The history of apartheid still shapes the allocation of health services and resources, contributing to stark racial, socio-economic, rural-urban differentials in health outcomes as well as between the private and public health sector.[33] For example, in 2005, spending per private medical insurance member was nine times higher than public sector expenditure, with a specialist doctor serving almost 11,000 patients.[34]

Socio-economic status and access to resources are even more decisive in access to post-operative rehabilitation and recovery care, particularly when the injuries result in lasting impairments. Patients with private medical insurance can receive treatment such as regular physical therapy, but may still require significant investment on the part of family and friends. This creates a significant financial burden on a survivor's support system, and a sense of powerless and dependency for the injured. Carol Bell became paralysed on her right side in 1988 when her husband shot her. While grateful for her family's support, she also found being dependent on them difficult: "At the age of 35 I had to go onto my father's medical insurance. He had just retired but took me to my physio three times a week for three years."[35]

There is no data on the number of survivors of gun violence left with permanent impairments every year. According to the 2010 General Household Survey, 6% of South Africans aged five years and older were classified as disabled.[36] The 2001 Census further revealed that 30% of people identifying as living with disability reported a physical impairment.[37] In common with other countries, data suggests that people living with disability are disproportionately represented among the poor, with prevalence rates for disability being highest in the three provinces with the highest concentration of poverty (Eastern Cape, KwaZulu-Natal and Limpopo). The distribution of disability is also racially disproportionate, with black Africans likely to have higher prevalence rates.[38]

Rehabilitation facilities are generally inadequate to meet demand, especially for specialised care as in the case of spinal cord injuries or traumatic brain injury. To illustrate this pressure, in 2009 Groote Schuur Hospital had 654 patients with moderate to serious head injury (out of over 10,000 trauma cases).[39] Only 16 of these individuals were "allocated a place at a rehabilitation centre with 70% (n=457) being sent directly home to an underprepared family. The rest were sent to a step down care facility with no rehabilitation mandate."[40] Trauma surgeon Dr Tim Hardcastle notes that most patients are "sent home to lie in bed and die."[41] Because many patients have so little access to professional rehabilitation, family members play an essential role in recovery, as do a survivor's own individual capacities and agency. Follow up appears to be limited—none of the survivors interviewed for this chapter had home visits by any health professional once discharged.

Box 1. Profile: Mark Roberts

When I was 16 I dropped out of school and spent my days hanging out on street corners with the "bad boys", smoking, drinking, and getting up to no good. One Saturday in 2007 there was a gang shooting in Hanover Park.[42] That evening, after visiting my girlfriend, I was walking back home when suddenly there were two guys in front of me—they wore balaclavas and had machine guns. I was scared and did not know what to do, so just turned and ran in the opposite direction. They started shooting at me. I felt the bullet go into my back, I fell, I couldn't stand up, I saw the blood all around me and I thought: "God, I'm not ready to go yet." People came out of their houses and someone picked me up, put me in their car and took me to the day hospital. I was in extreme pain but was not given any painkillers and just had to wait. I didn't cry. The nurses ignored me. I waited for 30 minutes for the ambulance to take me to Groote Schuur Hospital.[43] The bullet entered my left buttock, passed through my bladder and came out in the front of my right leg. I was in hospital for eight months, and got physiotherapy almost every day. I spent another year in bed at home. I got constant bladder infections and had difficulty managing my catheter.

My family were my main support—my sister visited me every day while I was in hospital and my mother spoke to me about this incident "pulling me right", meaning that it was an opportunity to turn over a new leaf.

When I got home I used to have a lot of nightmares—I kept on seeing the two guys with their balaclavas and I thought they were coming to get me. I did not see a social worker nor get any counselling, either while I was in hospital or at home. The hospital gave me crutches—my right leg was weak and I limped. I used them for about three weeks and then returned them to the hospital.

Although I have serious scars I have no problems, except sometimes when I run I feel that my right leg is going to give in. When I was 19 I went back to school. I am now in my final year and a prefect at Mountview High School. Some people know what happened to me but not everyone. A lot of the guys in the township think that I am cool because I have scars on my body and survived being shot.

Health insurance and social protection
Financial support for survivors of gun violence mainly comes in two forms: health insurance, to cover actual medical expenses and social security benefits to support livelihoods.

In nearly a quarter of all households (24%) at least one member has private medical insurance.[44] Those who do not have any medical insurance are entitled to receive health care at a public health facility, with the fee structure based on a sliding scale relative to total household income. However, one study found that a "considerable portion of the groups exempted from user fees still pay for services."[45] This illustrates the "'discretionary power' of providers and bureaucrats who determine who qualifies for exemptions."[46] In practice it means that many health clinics are demanding fees regardless of a person's means, knowing that demand outstrips supply and some are engaged in bribery to move people up queues. In addition one of the key barriers to accessing health care services was transportation costs and travel distance, especially for black Africans, poor, and rural residents.[47]

Social protection is designed to provide income security for individuals through social insurance and social assistance.[48] Social grants are regulated under the 1992 *Social Assistance Act* and implemented by the South African Social Security Association (SASSA).[49] Section 27 (1c) of the Constitution states: "everyone has the right to have access to social security including, if they are unable to support themselves and their dependents, appropriate social assistance."[50] Five types of benefits may be applicable to those with impairments caused by gun violence: disability grants, child support grants, grants in aid, care dependency grants, and social relief and distress grants.[51]

In February 2011 (latest data), approximately 15 million people were receiving social security payments, compared with just over two million in 1998. The largest group of beneficiaries are roughly 11 million Child Support Grants (CSG), with just over one million others receiving Disability Grants. The Government's 1998 decision to raise the cut-off age for CSGs from seven to 18 years increased the uptake markedly.[52] Despite this increase it is estimated that a further 10% of children eligible for the grants are not receiving them.[53]

Although the social grant system is regarded as having had a major impact on poverty relief over the last decade, there are numerous challenges both in its mandate and application. Unemployed people between 18 and 59 are excluded from any form of social protection, as are people with chronic illnesses such as HIV/AIDS. The Disability Grant can be awarded on either a temporary or permanent basis; many people are able to access a temporary grant for 12 months, after which they have to reapply.[54] The absence of a uniform tool to assess impairment and other potentially overlapping conditions such as chronic illness, as well as over-reliance on a medical lens in assessments, appears to create confusion and potential for abuse of the system; and can result in sudden termination of grants.[55] Other challenges include the delays in grant awards (up to a year), restrictive or limited criteria and, no form of assistance for children under the age of 18, unless they have a permanent impairment.[56] Ratula Beukman of the Black Sash Trust remarked that, given these exclusions, "care-givers are essentially providing assistance to the state."[57]

Service coordination and oversight

Services to survivors are concentrated within three key national departments: health, education, and social development.[58] These are oriented towards services to assist individuals in achieving self-care and positive social interactions, and entering the work force. Services include physical rehabilitation, psychosocial support, education needs, and access to the social security grant system.[59] Several other departments play an important role in creating a barrier-free environment, including provisions for accessing voting booths, sign language in courts and entering the labour market without prejudice.

The overarching government agency responsible for monitoring the provision of services to persons living with disability is the Department for Women, Children, and People with Disabilities (DWCPD). It collates and integrates information across various government departments through focal points, evaluating progress on mainstreaming disability rights and standards. However, it does not provide any direct services.

The inter-sectoral approach, which characterises much of the policy and legislative frameworks, is not as effective as hoped. The head of the National Planning Commission, Minister Trevor Manuel, acknowledges that poor institutional framework, as well as the low skills base and weak coordination, has given rise to "uneven and poor performance" of the public service and local government in particular.[60] The Commission suggests that a more proactive and pragmatic approach is needed to managing the intergovernmental system to "ensure a better fit between responsibility and capacity."[61]

The Department of Social Development (DSD) has been responsive to suggestions for improvement and together with SASSA is in the process of developing a national standardised and uniform assessment tool to address some of these challenges.[62] The South African Human Rights Commission also features a complaints mechanism relevant for people living with disability and will assist a complainant in seeking redress if their rights have been violated.

Section 3: The criminal justice system

In recent years the national Government has developed policies and plans designed to improve access to the criminal justice system for victims of crime. But implementation of these policies has lagged. This section describes some of the most important strategies and their current level of implementation.

National Crime Prevention Strategy

In 1995 the Government regarded the prevention of crime as a national priority and recognised the need to develop an integrated response to crime and violence and enable a greater role for civil society and communities in crime prevention.[63] In 1996, the Department of Safety and Security (now called the Department of Police) developed the National Crime Prevention Strategy (NCPS), which was adopted as national policy. Gun crime was identified as a priority, including the review of national firearms legislation.

The NCPS aimed to reduce injury and interrupt the cycle of violence by intervening before the event. The strategy stated that addressing the needs of survivors was a "vital dimension of effective crime prevention."[64]

The NCPS remains an innovative policy framework, but with the exception of the Victim Empowerment Programme (VEP) component, it is not being implemented.[65] Effective implementation would require a level of integration and interaction across government departments yet to occur.[66] At the same time, the government's approach to crime has gradually moved away from crime prevention towards suppression.

Victim Empowerment Programme

Established in 1998, the VEP promotes "a victim centred approach" to crime prevention.[67] It is a multi-faceted programme calling, for example, for a national network of service providers; victimisation surveys; and adequate rehabilitation services.[68] It also proposes an effective witness protection programme and a victim's compensation fund. The VEP allocates responsibilities across six government agencies, with the DSD responsible for ensuring that the partnership provides "easier access to a continuum of services by victims", with a targeted focus on women and children.[69]

The DSD is also responsible for managing the national and provincial VEP forums, which "plan, monitor and evaluate the delivery of services to victims by the different spheres of government."[70] The inter-sectoral collaboration of the VEP extends to the NGO sector, which is involved both in the provincial forums and in service delivery, especially in the area of psychosocial support. This partnership with civil society is not always easy. Nomfundo Mogapi, who represented the trauma sector at the Gauteng Provincial VEP Forum, is of the view that rather than just providing complementary services, "NGOs are actually doing the work of government."[71]

Under the VEP, each police station across the country should have a VEP officer who is a member of the Community Police Forum.[72] Police officers are required to inform victims of their rights, refer people to victim support services, and give feedback on the status of the case, including the outcome of bail hearings, court referrals, and protection from offenders.[73] The VEP has a particular focus on the needs of women survivors of partner and family violence.

Amanda Nkosi, a single mother of two, was shot in the leg by police during a protest against poor learning conditions at the local school. As a result of being shot Amanda was in hospital for nearly six months and lost her job. Unemployed and permanently impaired, she made a claim against the police but no progress had been made at the time the photo was taken. (Image: Nikki Roxon/Panos, June 2010)

Although substantial effort has gone into training VEP officers, especially over the first ten years of the programme, they are not present in all police stations and their quality of service is uneven.[74] Many police are failing to maintain the Domestic Violence Register. This has serious implications for moving a case through the criminal justice system and can result in women and girls dropping out of justice processes.

Significant developments under the VEP since 2000 include the implementation of regular victimisation surveys and the establishment of a national network of service providers.[75] Its practical impacts, in terms of addressing the needs of survivors, are harder to ascertain.

Survivor perspectives
Most of the survivors interviewed for this chapter gave very negative accounts of their dealings with the police and courts. Many experienced secondary victimisation. Little or no information on the investigations was forthcoming; survivors usually had to initiate contact with the police and in some instances pursue their own course of justice by hiring private investigators or directly approaching the Central Firearms Registry to investigate the case. "If we had not gone out and pursued a consequence for the death of our child then nothing would have happened to the man who acted negligently with his firearm," one mother reflected.[76] Other problems experienced by survivors include insensitive court officials (clerks, prosecutors, and magistrates),

especially in intimate partner and family violence cases, and lengthy delays in court cases, which can act as an impediment to protecting victims.[77]

Survivors often struggle to track their case through the criminal justice system, in part because they are assigned a different case number by each part of the system (police station, medical facility, court and parole office), and because officials often change during the course of the case.[78] Case tracking is so inefficient that even criminal justice system staff have difficulties keeping abreast of cases (see Box 2).[79]

Box 2. Profile: Christine Buchanan

I awoke in the early hours of 29 December 2007 and saw intruders in our bedroom. I turned to alert my husband Charles. I expected Charles to tell me to do as I was told (I am the feisty one, he is the calm one) but to my utter surprise he jumped on the intruder closest to him and started screaming, hitting and punching him. I started hitting another intruder. I have no idea how much time passed; it seemed to take forever, yet was over in an instant. Suddenly I saw a flash of light, felt a stinging sensation at the base of my neck and fell down as I heard the gunshot. I heard a second shot and then they were gone.

Charles had been pistol-whipped on the head and with blood pouring into his eyes he couldn't see. I stayed calm and told him to wipe his face and tried to staunch the bleeding in my neck. I tried to call the emergency services twice but the line went dead. I finally called Sandton Emergency Clinic. Charles went out to open the security gate and I heard him bellowing for help, then silence. I had no way of knowing if he was alive or dead.

The paramedics, accompanied by a neighbour, arrived within a seemingly short time. I was lying flat on my back, afraid to sit up in case I lost consciousness or sustained brain damage. We were taken to Sandton Clinic, where I saw my darling husband on the next bed giving me a smile and a thumbs-up. I had sustained a gunshot to the right shoulder, through the brachial plexus, the right lung, the right clavicle and a few ribs. He had mild concussion and a ricochet through the back of his thigh exiting through the groin.

The police came to interview us in the hospital, but because our accounts differed, they told us to get our story straight and then left. Our children arrived within hours, also traumatised. I couldn't sleep—every time I closed my eyes I saw the shapes in the room all over again.

After seven days I was discharged. I couldn't face going back to the house so we moved into my son's apartment. I was very weak, felt vulnerable and was utterly dependent, which I hated—my daughter washed my hair, buttered my toast and helped me get dressed. It was painful watching my husband needing help, being unable to drive, being so tired, so childlike at times. We finally returned to our house after six weeks, after our home security system had been beefed up. One big frustration has been the lack of action on the part of the police. They were mostly unresponsive, made only two follow up visits, and almost five years later the case remains on some police officers' desk, unsolved. I feel the police assigned to our case were ineffectual and I have little time for them.

The slow process of recovery continues. A lot has changed—my body image changed—it is not just about my paralysed right arm. This is a new Christine: I have learned to ask for help; I am much more focused on what I want from life. My cognitive functioning has been impaired thanks to the drugs I need to control the pain. I could have died. I didn't. I got on with life.

Ways forward

Attempts have been made to improve the VEP. In 2009 the National Policy Guidelines for Victim Empowerment were adopted, reiterating several key recommendations of the NCPS (promoting a victim-centred approach to criminal justice; developing effective inter-departmental and intersectoral collaboration; and guiding the process of monitoring, evaluating and reporting by implementing structures).[80] In particular, the Guidelines recognised the need to identify and clarify sector-specific roles and responsibilities.[81] They also recognised the ongoing lack of funding and vision among political leaders and some of the key government departments.

Another weakness of the VEP is that it is not backed by the force of law. Between 2000 and 2011 the Law Reform Commission examined the possibility of establishing a compensation fund for victims of crime.[82] One report concluded that it was not a "viable option" because of the estimated cost of R4.7 billion/USD587 million.[83] But in its recommendations, the Commission admitted that the VEP "still lacks the ability to deal effectively with all the issues relating to victims of crime."[84] The Commission's main recommendation was to develop legislation (based on the NCPS policy) to provide standards for the treatment of victims.

In reviewing the feasibility of a legislative framework for the VEP, the Rape Crisis Cape Town Trust suggested that a Road to Justice Card be created to ensure that victims and the state are able to track information about a case. Allocated a unique number, the Card would allow the survivor to have access to the names of those responsible for the case, to have a record of each different case number used by the various parts of the system, and to have a visible record of the progress being made.[85]

Section 4: Standards and normative frameworks

The official approach to survivor assistance is not contained in a single policy document, but rather "a complex assortment of legislation, policy documents, and government programmes" that continue to evolve.[86] This section describes these norms and their relation to established and emerging international standards.

Crime victims' rights

Relevant legislation includes the 1998 *Domestic Violence Act*, the 1983 *Child Care Act*, the 2008 *Child Justice Act*, and the 2012 *Sexual Offences Amendment Act*.[87] One law that should contain a survivor focus is the FCA which recognises the right to "security of the person" and the right to "be free from all forms of violence", but is silent on the needs of those who survive a gunshot.[88] There may be an opportunity in the coming years when it is expected that legislators will review the FCA to include the rights of survivors, and possibly consider the establishment of a Violence Survivors' Compensation Fund to cover costs related to medical care, counselling, rehabilitation, lost wages and home modification.

In parallel, two central policy initiatives aimed specifically at addressing the needs of survivors are the VEP, already mentioned above, and the Victims' Charter.

Adopted in 2004, the Service Charter for Victims' of Crime (known as the Victims' Charter) became the first official policy relating to crime victims, and was "intended to confer a set of rights upon crime victims."[89] These include the right to offer and receive information, to receive compensation and assistance, the latter including the right to have "access to available social, health and counselling services, as well as legal assistance."[90] One analyst has noted that although the Charter is a worthy statement of intent, it "confers nothing new and gives no more rights than what already exists in law (i.e. Criminal Procedure Act (1977)... [and] it implies obligations and duties on the state but there is no statutory obligation for example, to provide assistance such as shelter for women survivors."[91]

Disability rights

A well-developed body of policies and legislation exist to address disability discrimination and increase services. Many of the policy innovations were developed during the political transition and articulate a "transformation agenda" to full and equal rights for all South Africans. For the disability rights movement this laid the basis for "the recognition of disability as a human rights and development issue; and the creation of equal opportunities for disabled people."[92] The Constitution promotes and protects the human rights of people living with disability, guarding against any form of discrimination on the basis of disability.[93] In this post-1994 democratic environment, several new laws were enacted to specifically address the issue of disability discrimination, notably the 1998 *Employment Equity Act* and the 2000 *Promotion of Equality and Prevention of Unfair Discrimination Act*.[94] A significant aspect of the latter *Act* is that it requires both the public and private sectors to take responsibility for the promotion of equality. It also aligns with the rights articulated in the 2006 UN *Convention on the Rights of Persons with Disabilities* (CRPD, for more detail see Annex 1).

Disabled People South Africa (DPSA), the most organised voice of the disability rights movement at the time, played a critical role in policy formulation, most notably ensuring the inclusion of specific clauses in the Constitution.[95] In the early 1990s the DPSA also spearheaded the idea of a *Disability Rights Charter*, which expressed the demands of people living with disabilities regarding their rights, and in particular highlighted how people experience discrimination in different ways. This Charter played a significant role in emphasising the importance of a comprehensive and integrated approach to addressing disability nationally, which subsequently influenced the approach adopted by the Integrated National Disability Strategy (INDS) in 1997. The disability rights movement also lobbied for the principle of self-representation across all spheres of government as well as on all relevant public bodies.[96]

Many of the general principles found in the CRPD, such as full and effective participation and inclusion in society, equality of opportunity and equality between women and men, have been central to how both government and the disability movement have articulated disability rights.[97] This was seen for example in the mandate of the Office on the Status of Disabled Persons (OSDP) to mainstream disability issues into all sectors of society, and carried through in the development of the INDS, which provided the "framework for integrating disability into all aspects of government functioning."[98] One of the key objectives of the INDS is the "attainment of a good and equitable quality of life for disabled persons in the country."[99] The strategy requires the integration of disability concerns into all policies, plans, and programmes, as well as a whole of government approach to programme design and implementation.

Despite the adoption of these goals in 1997, it took the national Government more than ten years to develop an integrated approach. Currently it is unclear to what extent this is being carried out, especially given the tendency to adopt new policies whenever a new structure or agency is created to address new challenges or perceived gaps.

South Africa was one of the first countries to sign and ratify both the CRPD and the *Optional Protocol* in 2007. It submitted its first implementation report in early 2013.[100] Since 2009, the mandate of the OSDP (now disbanded) rests with the DWCPD.[101] It is responsible for integrating the CRPD into national law and has developed a draft disability policy. It also coordinates the training of all designated focal points on disability across all government departments to effect mainstreaming and has prioritised the development of a monitoring and evaluation framework to track progress on the implementation of the CRPD. [102]

As noted above, a key challenge for ensuring that an inter-governmental approach works is whether the various government departments understand their specific roles and responsibilities in relation to mainstreaming disability, and how they intersect with each other for maximum impact. Another challenge is the diminished sphere of influence and reduced capacity of the disability rights movement, which is fragmented and lacks a strategic focus, especially in relation to the CRPD.[103]

Conclusion

Within a complex policy environment, South Africa has put in place important measures to address both the injustices of the past and the ongoing challenges of poverty, inequality, and violence, as well as to ensure more equitable access to services such as universal health care. In particular it has instituted an extensive and successful set of social protection measures through the social grant system, which has had a significant impact on bolstering incomes of impoverished households. Though the evidence base is weak, it also appears that the FCA is reducing civilian access to firearms, contributing to a significant reduction in overall homicides and femicides.

Despite laudable policy developments, service delivery remains poor. One important reason is the lack of a firm legal obligation to implement the policies. An ineffective and inefficient public sector is another. According to the 20-year national development plan released in 2012, substantial institutional reforms are needed before the public sector can meet its responsibilities to those in need. The plan singles out weak coordination and capacity for improvement, and a more integrated approach to service delivery.[104]

Finally, the experiences and insights of survivors of gun violence must be harnessed to develop appropriate and survivor-centered approaches to maximise recovery, restoration of function, and wellbeing. There is enormous potential for civil society organisations and the NGO community in particular, to work in a more targeted and collaborative manner to ensure that such an approach is integrated across the various sectors. The combined knowledge and experience of researchers, policy analysts, practitioners, survivors and activists across a variety of sectors such as public health, violence and injury prevention, gun control, rehabilitation and trauma care and disability rights, could result in an effective movement to ensure that South

Africa meet its obligations under the CRPD and realises more effective injury and violence prevention, in addition to survivors receiving the support to which they are entitled.

Contributors: Adèle Kirsten, independent consultant. **Cate Buchanan** and **Rebecca Peters** undertook drafting and editing. **Mireille Widmer** and **Emile LeBrun** provided additional editing.

Peer reviews were provided by **Christine Buchanan** (South Africa); **Timothy C. Hardcastle**, trauma surgeon, University of KwaZulu-Natal, President of the Trauma Society of South Africa and Deputy Director of the Trauma Unit at Inkosi Albert Luthuli Central Hospital, Durban (South Africa); **Shanaaz Mathews**, Special Scientist, South African Medical Research Council (South Africa); and **Garth Stevens**, Associate Professor and Clinical Psychologist, University of the Witwatersrand (South Africa).

References

[1] D. Bradshaw, N. Nannan, R. Laubscher, P. Groenewald, B. Nojilana, R. Norman, D. Pieterse and M. Schneider, *South African National Burden of Disease Study 2000* (Cape Town: South African Medical Research Council, 2004).

[2] M. Seedat, A. van Niekerk, R. Jewkes, S. Suffla and K. Ratele, "Violence and injuries in South Africa: prioritising an agenda for prevention," *The Lancet* 374/9694 (2009), p. 1011.

[3] M. Seedat, A. van Niekerk, R. Jewkes, S. Suffla and K. Ratele (2009), p. 1011.

[4] M. Schonteich and A. Louw, "Crime in South Africa: A country profile," *Institute for Security Studies Paper 49* (2001).

[5] A. Louw, "The Start of a 'Crime Wave'? The 2005/06 official crime statistics in context," *South African Crime Quarterly 18* (2006), pp. 1-8.

[6] South African Police Service, *Crime Report 2010/2011* (Pretoria: South African Police Service, 2011). See also United Nations Office on Drugs and Crime, *2011 Global Study on Homicide: Trends, Contexts, Data* (Vienna: UNODC, 2011), p. 46.

[7] M. Seedat, A. van Niekerk, R. Jewkes, S. Suffla and K. Ratele (2009), p. 1011.

[8] South African Police Service (2011).

[9] KwaZulu-Natal Department of Health, "Burden of Mortality in KwaZulu-Natal, KwaZulu-Natal," *Epidemiology Bulletin* Issue 14 (2006). This is consistent with the mortality data in the National Injury Mortality Surveillance System, *A profile of fatal injuries in South Africa. 9th Annual Report* (Cape Town: Medical Research Council/UNISA Crime, 2007).

[10] Centre for the Study of Violence and Reconciliation, *The violent nature of crime in South Africa—A concept paper prepared for the Justice, Crime Prevention and Security Cluster* (Johannesburg: CSVR, 2008).

[11] Several interviewees who expressed this view requested anonymity due to the sensitive nature of the issue.

[12] Telephone interview by Adele Kirsten with Thembani Dyule, Cape Town, 29 February 2012; Interview with Mark Roberts, Hanover Park, Cape Town, 22 February 2012.

[13] R. Jewkes, N. Abrahams and S. Mathews, "Preventing Rape and Violence in South Africa: Call for leadership in a New Agenda for Action," *Medical Research Council Policy Brief* (Cape Town: Medical Research Council, 2009).

[14] United Nations Office on Drugs and Crime (2011), p. 31 and p. 10. The Gini index or coefficient is the international standard for measuring the distribution of income and wealth in a country.

[15] J. Cock and L. Nathan (Eds), *War and society: The militarisation of South Africa* (Cape Town: David Philip, 1989). In the 1980s black police officers were issued with personal side arms

for self-defence purposes as they were vulnerable to attack by the anti-apartheid forces; this also included several black businesspeople.

[16] These units were informal militia operating within townships across South Africa and loosely under the control of the African National Congress (self-defence units) and Inkatha (self-protection units).

[17] J. Cock and L. Nathan (1989).

[18] N. Abrahams, R. Jewkes and S. Mathews, "Guns and gender-based violence in South Africa," *South African Medical Journal* 100/9 (2010), pp. 586-588. Half of these female homicide victims were killed by their male intimate partners, with licensed firearms being the main risk factor. See also K. Ratele, "Watch your man: Young black males at risk of homicidal violence," *South African Crime Quarterly* 33 (2010), pp. 19-24; R. Morrell, *Changing men in Southern Africa* (Pietermaritzburg: University of KwaZulu-Natal Press, 2001); M. Langa and G. Eagle, "The intractability of militarized masculinity: interviews with former combatants in East Rand," *South African Journal of Psychology* 38/1 (2008), pp.152-178.

[19] United Nations Office on Drugs and Crime (2011). This view was supported in interviews by Adele Kirsten with health professional and senior police officers: Prof van As, Head of Trauma Unit, Red Cross Children's Hospital, Cape Town, and President Childsafe South Africa, 22 February 2012; Prof Andrew Nicol, Head of Trauma Unit, Groote Schuur Hospital, Cape Town, 23 February 2012; Dr Lorna Martin, Western Cape forensic pathologist, Cape Town, 21 February 2012; Richard Matzopoulos, epidemiologist and specialist researcher at the Medical Research Council of South Africa's Burden of Disease Research Unit, 12 January 2012; Lt. General Lamoer, Western Cape Provincial Police Commissioner, 23 February 2012; Dr Gilbert Lawrence, Head of Department, Department of Community Safety, Provincial Government of the Western Cape, Cape Town, 21 February 2012.

[20] *Firearms Control Act*, No. 60 of 2000. See www.acts.co.za/firearms_control_act_2000.htm Accessed 14 November 2012.

[21] 2000 *Firearms Control Act*: in particular Section 111, 112, and Section 121, Schedule 4.

[22] *Protocol on Control of Firearms, Ammunition and Other related Materials*.

[23] This is a ratio of 106 firearms for every 1000 persons. This figure is based on the 1999 mid-year estimate of 43 million in R. Chetty, *Firearm Use and Distribution in South Africa* (Pretoria: National Crime Prevention Centre, 2000), p. 32.

[24] Email correspondence from the Central Firearms Registry, 18 August 2011. These figures are approximates, as the Registry is unable to give exact data due to undergoing an overhaul of its implementation of the FCA as well as an incomplete renewals process. 2011 data are the most recent available at the end of 2012.

[25] A. Soutar, South African Arms and Ammunition Dealers Association, oral submission to the Portfolio Committee on Safety and Security on the Firearms Control Amendment Bill (B12-2006), 16 August 2006.

[26] A.B. van As, C.D. Parry and M. Bletcher, "The Alcohol Injury Fund," *South African Medical Journal* 93/11 (2003), pp. 828-829. Email correspondence with Prof Charles Parry, Director: Alcohol and Drug Abuse Research Unit, Medical Research Council, Cape Town, 26 March 2012; telephone interview with Richard Matzopoulos, epidemiologist and specialist researcher at the Medical Research Council of South Africa's Burden of Disease Research Unit, 14 August 2012.

[27] Interview by Adele Kirsten with Antony Altbeker, economist and consultant to the National Treasury, 2 May 2012; Also see South African Law Reform Commission, *A Compensation Scheme for Victims of Crime in South Africa* (Pretoria: SALRC, 2001), pp. 71-91; pp. 128-137, for discussion on calculating compensation.

[28] R. Matzopoulos, M. Prinsloo, J. Bopape, A. Butchart, M. Peden and C. Lombard, *Estimating the South African trauma caseload as a basis for injury surveillance* (Cape Town: South African Medical Research Council, 2000); D. Bradshaw, N. Nannan, R. Laubscher, P. Groenewald, B. Nojilana, R. Norman, D. Pieterse and M. Schneider, *South African National Burden of Disease Study 2000* (Cape Town: South African Medical Research Council, 2004).

[29] Northern Cape, Eastern Cape, Limpopo, North West, and Mpumalanga. Telephone interview with Dr Timothy Hardcastle, trauma surgeon, University of KwaZulu-Natal, President of the Trauma Society of South Africa and Deputy Director of the Trauma Unit at Inkosi Albert Luthuli Central Hospital, Durban (South Africa) 26 March 2012; all of these hospitals would

offer a range of rehabilitation services which includes specialist medical services such as neurology and orthopaedics, as well as physical, occupational and speech therapies.

30 There are some exceptions such as Milpark private hospital in Johannesburg. Interview with Prof Andrew Nicol.

31 Interviews with Prof van As; Prof Andrew Nicol; and telephone interview with Dr Timothy Hardcastle, 26 March 2012.

32 Telephone interview with Dr Timothy Hardcastle, 26 March 2012.

33 H. Coovadia, R. Jewkes, R. Barron, P. Sanders and D. McIntyre, "The health and health system of South Africa: Historical roots of current public health challenges," *Lancet* 374/9692 (2009), pp. 817-834; D. McIntyre, M. Thiede, M. Nkosi, V. Mutyambizi, M. Castillo-Riquelme, J. Goudge, L. Gilson and E. Erasmus, *A Critical Analysis of the Current South African Health System* (Cape Town: Health Economics Unit, University of Cape Town and Centre for Health Policy, University of the Witwatersrand, 2007); B. Harris, J. Goudge, J.E. Ataguba, D. McIntyre, N. Nxumalo, S. Jikwana and M. Chersich, "Inequities in access to health care in South Africa," *Journal of Public Health Policy* 32/S1 (2011), S102-S123.

34 H. Coovadia, R. Jewkes, R. Barron, P. Sanders and D. McIntyre (2009), pp. 817-834.

35 Interview by Adele Kirsten with Carol Bell, Cape Town, 17 January 2012.

36 Statistics South Africa, *General Household Survey 2010* (Pretoria: Stats SA, 2011). The data for the under-five age group was discarded due to concerns on accuracy.

37 Statistics South Africa, *Census 2001: Prevalence of disability in South Africa* (Pretoria: Stats SA, 2005).

38 T. Emmet, "Disability, poverty, gender and race," In B. Watermeyer, L. Swartz, T. Lorenzo, M. Schneider and M. Priestley (Eds), *Disability and social change: A South African agenda* (Cape Town: Human Sciences Research Council Press, 2006), pp. 207-233.

39 Interview with Jan Webster, Director, Comacare, Cape Town, 23 January 2012.

40 Comacare, internal document, not dated: *Training Unit for Families—a new concept in responsive, responsible health care for one of the five priority wellness areas of Western Cape government.*

41 Telephone interview with Dr Timothy Hardcastle, 26 March 2012.

42 Hanover Park is a middle-to-low income township on the Cape Flats with a history of gang violence.

43 Groote Schuur is a large provincial public hospital in Cape Town with a Level 1 trauma facility.

44 This is supported by the findings of B. Harris, J. Goudge, J.E. Ataguba, D. McIntyre, N. Nxumalo, S. Jikwana and M. Chersich, "Inequities in access to health care in South Africa," *Journal of Public Health Policy* 32/S1 (2011), S102-S123.

45 B. Harris et al (2011).

46 B. Harris et al (2011), S118.

47 B. Harris et al (2011), S118; World Health Organization, *The World Health Report—Health Systems Financing: The Path to Universal Coverage* (Geneva: WHO, 2010).

48 I. Fry and S. Brockerhoff, *The role of social security in alleviating the levels of poverty and inequality in South Africa,* Input Paper to the National Planning Commission (Johannesburg: Studies in Poverty and Inequality Institute, 2011), p. 2.

49 See the *Social Assistance Act,* No.59 of 1992 at www.dsd.gov.za/index.php?options=com_docman&task Accessed 28 May 2013.

50 Black Sash Trust, *You and Your Rights: Disability Grant.* See www.blacksash.org.za/index.php/your-rights/social-grants/item/disability-grant. Also see www.info.gov.za/documents/constitution.

51 South African Social Security Agency, *You and Your Grants 2010/11* (Pretoria: SASSA, 2010). The cash received is not conditional and can be spent on whatever the recipient deems necessary.

52 I. Fry and S. Brockerhoff (2011).

53 V. Taylor, *Social Protection in Africa: An Overview of the Challenges,* Research Report prepared for the African Union (Addis Ababa: AU, 2008).

54 This can lead to a situation whereby the person using the grant for anti-retroviral medication and improved nutrition grows stronger and therefore no longer qualifies for the grant. They then change behaviour which leads to poor compliance with their AIDS treatment regime, allowing them to qualify for the grant again.

55 Interviews with Margie Schneider, disability studies researcher, Johannesburg, 1 March 2012; Ratula Beukman, Black Sash Trust Advocacy Programme Manager, Cape Town, 23 February 2012; and telephone interview with Ari Seirlis, National Director of the QuadPara Association of South Africa, QASA, Durban, 12 March 2012.

56 Interview with Ratula Beukman, Black Sash Advocacy Programme Manager, Cape Town, 23 February 2012. Also see, M. Chennells and K. Hall, *Income poverty, unemployment and social grants* (Cape Town: Children's Institute, University of Cape Town, 2010).

57 Interview with Ratula Beukman, 23 February 2012.

58 This section is drawn from an interview with Margie Schneider; S. Rule, T. Lorenzo and M. Wolmarans, "Community-based rehabilitation: new challenges," In B. Watermeyer et al (2006), pp. 273-290; S, Mitra, "*Disability Cash Transfers in the Context of Poverty and Unemployment: the Case of South Africa,*" World Development 38/12 (2010), pp.1692-1709; I. Woolard and M. Leibbrandt, *The role of cash transfers in reducing poverty and inequality in South Africa over the post-apartheid period* (Cape Town: Southern Africa Labour and Development Research Unit, School of Economics, University of Cape Town, 2011).

59 These services are devolved from the national to the provincial, district and local level.

60 National Planning Commission, *National Development Plan—2030: Our future-make it work* (Pretoria: NPC, 2012), pp. 54-55.

61 National Planning Commission (2012), p. 55.

62 Interview with Margie Schneider; L. Swartz and M. Schneider, "Tough choices: disability and social security in South Africa," In B. Watermeyer et al (2006), pp. 234-244.

63 J. Rauch, *The 1996 National Crime Prevention Strategy* (Johannesburg: Centre for the Study of Violence and Reconciliation, 2001).

64 G. Simpson, "The fight against crime can no longer afford to ignore victims' rights," *The Sunday Independent* 21 July (1996). Available at: www.csvr.org.za/wits/articles/artcrimg.htm Accessed 20 November 2012.

65 Although adopted through the White Paper on Safety and Security in 1998, since about 2000, due to agency restructuring, in particular the downgrading of the function and authority of the police secretariats (a civilian oversight body at national and provincial level) and a lack of clarity on institutional mandates, it has had little sway. Ironically, the VEP is the only part of the NCPS that is being implemented in any way.

66 Telephone interview with Barbara Holtmann, gun violence survivor, process facilitator and violence prevention practitioner, Johannesburg, 20 August 2012; National Planning Commission, *National Development Plan—2030: Our future-make it work* (Pretoria: NPC, 2012).

67 Department of Social Development, *Integrated Victim Empowerment Policy. Fourth Draft* (Pretoria: DSD, 2007).

68 G. Simpson (1996).

69 The six government agencies are: Department of Social Development, Department of Health, Department of Correctional Services, Department of Justice and Constitutional Development, South African Police Services, and the National Prosecuting Authority.

70 See VEP Forum at www.dsd.gov.za/npo/VEP1/index.php?option=com_content&task=view&id=71 Page updated 20 May 2010. Accessed 20 November 2012.

71 Interview by Adele Kirsten with Nomfundo Mogapi, Programme Manager, Trauma and Transition Programme, Centre for the Study of Violence and Reconciliation, Johannesburg, 7 March 2012.

72 In terms of the *Police Act* it is mandatory for each police station to have a Community Police Forum.

73 Department of Social Development (2007), p. 24.

74 South African Police Service (2011), p. 63 reports 789 police stations (out of a total of 1146) have victim support rooms. Training was done by the South African Police as well as by a number of NGOs. Telephone interview by Adele Kirsten with Yvette Geyer, trainer, Institute for Democracy in Africa, 5 May 2012.

75 The most recent Victims of Crime Survey conducted by Statistics South Africa is available at www.statssa.gov.za/publication/PO341/PO3412011.pdf; also see www.issafrica.org/crimehub/page.php?page=1000034 Accessed 20 November 2012.

[76] Email correspondence between Adele Kirsten and Pam Crowsley, mother of Daniel, killed in an accidental shooting in 2004 at the age of 16. The firearm owner was charged with negligent use under Section 102 of the FCA only after the Crowsley's complained to the Central Firearms Registry.

[77] J. Watson, "Domestic Violence and the Victim Empowerment Programme" (PowerPoint), no date. Available at: www.boell.org.za/downloads/DVA_Joy_Watson.pdf Accessed 28 February 2012.

[78] K. Dey, J. Thorpe, A. Tilley and J. Williams, *The Road to Justice: Victim Empowerment Legislation in South Africa. Road Map Report* (Cape Town: Rape Crisis Cape Town Trust, 2011), p. 39.

[79] K. Dey, J. Thorpe, A. Tilley and J. Williams (2011), p. 40.

[80] Department of Social Development, UN Office Drugs and Crime and the European Union, *National Policy Guidelines for Victim Empowerment* (Pretoria: DSD, undated). Available at: www.info.gov.za/view/DownloadFileAction?id=111693 Accessed 28 February 2013.

[81] Department of Social Development (2007).

[82] The review process started in 2000 and the SA Law Reform Commission submitted its first report to the Department of Justice in 2004, but it was only released in April 2011; Also see South African Law Reform Commission (2001).

[83] South African Law Reform Commission (2001). See also South African Law Reform Commission, *Report: Sentencing (A Compensation Fund for Victims of Crime)*, (Pretoria: SALRC, 2004).

[84] South African Law Reform Commission (2004).

[85] K. Dey, J. Thorpe, A. Tilley and J. Williams (2011), p. 40.

[86] C. Frank, *Quality Services Guaranteed?,* Institute for Security Studies Monograph Series, No. 137 (Pretoria: ISS, 2007), p. 2.

[87] These Acts can be accessed at www.justice.gov.za/legislation; For the Child Care Act see www.acts.co.za/child_care/index.htm Accessed 28 May 2013.

[88] *Firearms Control Act*, 2000: Preamble xi

[89] C. Frank (2007), p. 3.

[90] C. Frank (2007), p. 22.

[91] Interview with Lisa Vetten, Director of Tswaranang Legal Advocacy Centre, Johannesburg, 12 August 2012. This view is also supported by C. Frank (2007), p. 23.

[92] C. Howell, S. Chalklen and T. Alberts, "A history of the disability rights movement in South Africa," In B. Watermeyer et al (2006), p. 65.

[93] S. Matsebula, M. Schneider and B. Watermeyer, "Integrating disability within government: the Office on the Status of Disabled Persons," In B. Watermeyer et al (2006), pp. 85-92.

[94] These Acts can be found (in order mentioned) at: www.justice.gov.za/acts/; and www.labour.gov.za/acts/

[95] *Constitution of the Republic of South Africa*, No 108 of 1996:Section 9 (3): the State may not unfairly discriminate directly or indirectly against anyone on one or more grounds, including race, gender, sex, [....], disability, language and birth; Section 12 (2): Everyone has the right to bodily and psychological integrity, which includes the right to security in and control over their body; Section 27 (c) Everyone has the right to social security, including if they are unable to support themselves and their dependents, appropriate social assistance.

[96] *Constitution of the Republic of South Africa*, No 108 of 1996: Section 184.

[97] In interviews with Shuaib Chalken, UN Special Rapporteur on Disability, Cape Town, 14 January 2012 and Margie Schneider, Johannesburg, 10 August 2012, both noted the leading role of South Africa in the CRPD negotiations.

[98] S. Matsebula, M. Schneider and B. Watermeyer (2006), p. 85.

[99] Statistics South Africa (2005), p. 5.

[100] Convention and Protocol signed on 30 March 2007 and ratified on 30 November 2007. The draft report was presented publicly by the Deputy Minister of Women, Children and People with Disabilities on 20 February 2013. In March it was submitted to the UN Committee. Available at: www.pmg.org.za/report/20130220-department-women-children-people-disabilities-country-report-un-conve Accessed 28 May 2013.

[101] The closure of the OSDP was not welcomed by the disability rights movement as it was concerned that it would dissipate the focus on people living with disability.
[102] Interview with a Chief Director in the Department of Women, Children and People with Disabilities, Pretoria, 30 March 2012.
[103] Interview with Shuaib Chalken; Interview with William Rowland, Patron of the South African National Council for the Blind and Chairperson of the International Disability Alliance CRPD Forum, Pretoria, 22 March 2012; and telephone interview with Ari Seirlis.
[104] National Planning Commission (2012), p. 56.

"My body from the breast down, I couldn't feel it.
Imagine just seeing shit in your bed without having felt it...
I wanted to kill myself... I promised myself that when I get discharged,
I would drink everyday. It was living hell...
I felt as if I'm alive above my tummy, downwards I felt dead.
I even burned my legs with cigarettes."

Erny, South Africa

Gun Free South Africa,
The physical, social and economic costs of gun violence,
Brief no. 5 (2005).

SPOTLIGHT SECTION
Ronnie Fakude (South Africa)

I'm a 50 year old paraplegic and have been awaiting trial [in Bloemfontein's Grootvlei Prison, South Africa] since my arrest on fraud charges in December 2011. I can't walk, I can't control my bowel or bladder and have to wear disposable baby nappies which my family buy for me. I can't feel a thing from my waist down. I'm paralysed from level four and don't have a wheelchair.

My co-accused all got bail. The main reason I never applied for bail was because I knew I couldn't afford it. My family have managed to raise some money now and I'm hoping for a hearing soon. Even my Rand 1,400 (USD152) disability grant, which I used for my seven year old daughter's schooling, has stopped. I asked a social worker here to help me renew it but she said she couldn't because I haven't been sentenced yet.

If I use my [crutches] I have to pull my legs and throw them to the front. That's how I walk. I was shot in my spinal cord, which was cut in the middle during a hijacking in the driveway of my house three years before my arrest. Before I was transferred here I was in Johannesburg prison, where the doctor prescribed a wheelchair for me. The doctor at Grootvlei says I must get a wheelchair from an outside hospital but hasn't referred me.

We are 88 men in this cell which is meant for 32. Sometimes there are more. Twelve people sleep in two bunks pushed together, that's six on the top and six on the bottom. I have my own bed on the bottom, which is a privilege. Luckily, I don't have to share because of my medical status. There are eight or ten people with TB [tuberculosis] in this cell and four or five we know are HIV-positive. A guy with multi-drug resistant TB sleeps on top of me. I feel vulnerable all the time. Not because I'm threatened physically; I'm always called names and treated like an alien. I got tuberculosis while I was in Joburg prison, prior to moving here. This means I have a compromised lung and am prone to infections. I'd rather die than be here.

I can't rely on other inmates for help because they change all the time. People come and go so I have to help myself. My upper body is very strong so I just pull my legs along the floor. There's only one toilet and one shower for this cell. It's so crowded people even sleep on sponges on the toilet floor. Sometimes there's no water in the toilet and it doesn't work. The smell and the flies are horrible. The food in the kitchen is also covered in flies.

It's a big mission for me to get food. It takes 30 minutes to drag my legs to the kitchen. That's why I don't have breakfast, I just drink water. I only go to the kitchen once a day for lunch, which is at 11am. The warders in the kitchen won't allow other prisoners to bring me food. They say I have to fetch it myself. I can't get the right diet here. Prison food is not good for me or anyone with special needs like mine. It gives me indigestion. When I asked for special food and complained about my diet, I was told DCS [the Department of Correctional Services] had to get recommendations from a dietician. Then I was told the prison budget was R11 (USD1.20) per prisoner a day—for three meals—and they couldn't afford to give me what I need.

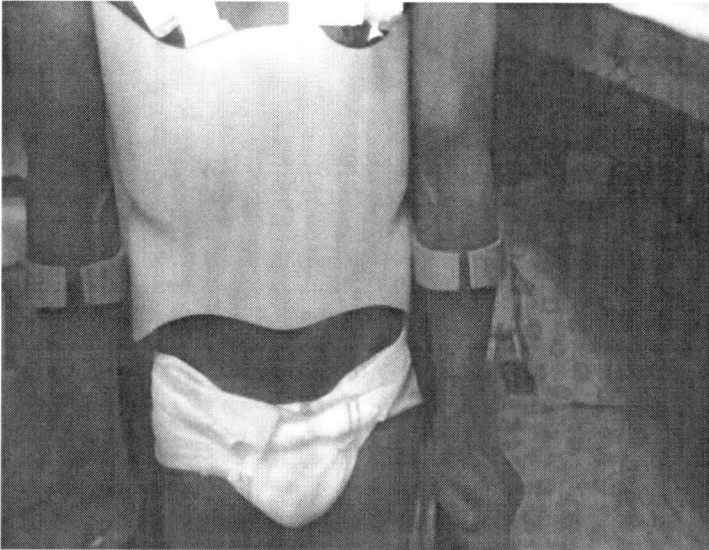

(Image: Courtesy of Carolyn Raphaely, 2013)

Paraplegics need special diets. I have indigestion because of the bad prison diet. I also have ulcers, which cause me terrible pain and make me shit blood. I have one kidney and my intestines are sutured because of injuries from my hijacking. I have pains and pins and needles throughout my body because I can't exercise or get physiotherapy.

Awaiting trial prisoners are only allowed non-contact visitors during the week. You have to speak to your family through a microphone from behind a glass and you get a maximum of 30 minutes. My family can only visit at weekends because of work. I made a special request for a visit [in March] which was granted. It was the first time my wife has visited me since 2011 because it's so expensive to come here from Joburg. It cost her R1,500 (USD163) for transport and she also brought me R500 (USD54) worth of food, nappies and medicine. The captain in charge said I wasn't allowed food, only nappies. When I complained, he cut my visit short. I saw my wife for about three minutes.

There's no proper prison hospital here and prisoners die in the cells because they can't get medical attention. When I had very bad indigestion and was shitting blood, it took a week for me to get to the prison hospital. I haven't been given any medication since getting here, not even a Brufen [headache/pain tablet].

I have to wash my pressure wounds and sores twice a day. I can't even get swabs or bandages. The last time I asked for Savlon, I was told to wash my wounds with salt water. I'm in constant pain. Sleep is the only escape. I've only seen a doctor here once, in September last year, and he prescribed medical shoes for me. I'm still waiting.

If you're sick today, you might see a doctor next week. If you need a painkiller you'll have to wait a week till the doctor comes. Then you won't get medicine. Not because the doctor doesn't want to give you medicine but because there isn't any.

The independent prison visitors of the Judicial Inspectorate do come here to take complaints, but then nothing happens. Some warders try to help me but others ask me why I think I'm so special and require different treatment. Living in these conditions means I've been sentenced before I am sentenced.[1]

Postscript:

The Wits Justice Project uncovered Fakude's dire situation in February 2013. Since the first article was published in the UK, progress was made to secure him medical attention and legal support. After appealing to the DCS to pay attention to this case, Fakude was moved to the prison hospital in mid-March and immediately placed on a drip by "medical staff". A doctor visits the prison only once a week. The National Council for Persons with Physical Disabilities heard about his plight and arranged for a private doctor to see him. The Free State Association for Physical Disabilities then donated a wheelchair. Whether the "hospital" is a better alternative to the cell is a moot point. "It's just a normal cell with single beds instead of bunks," Fakude said. "It is clean, has a tiled floor and isn't as crowded as a cell. That's the only difference. Actually, my cell bed is better than the hospital bed." Fakude's wife, Precious, points out that even if the "hospital" is less crowded than a conventional cell, if a paraplegic inmate is accommodated there indefinitely, there is the danger of exposure to infection, particularly for a person with a compromised immune system.

During the course of Fakude's April 2013 bail application, the prison doctor testified that she had seen Fakude walk. After a private doctor testified that he was indeed paraplegic, the magistrate sought a third opinion from an independent neuro-surgeon. This confirmed his permanent paraplegia and a lower motor neuron injury. Even so, his bail application was dismissed because of his previous record of fraud convictions.

There are about 46,000 people on remand in South Africa. The DCS does not keep centralised data on prisoners with disabilities. A fund has been set up for Ronnie Fakude under the auspices of the National Council for Persons with Physical Disabilities. People from all around the world have donated. You can too at: http://witsjusticeproject.com/prisoner-a-update-page/

References

[1]   As told to Carolyn Raphaely, Wits Justice Project, University of the Witwatersrand, South Africa February 19, 2013 and March 8, 2013. This text is drawn: C. Raphaely, "Oscar Pistorius case highlights plight of South Africa's disabled prisoners," *The Guardian* (UK) 22 February (2013), and the *Saturday Star* 23 February (2013); and, C. Raphaely, "Paraplegic's hellish ordeal in prison," *Mail and Guardian* 8 March (2013).

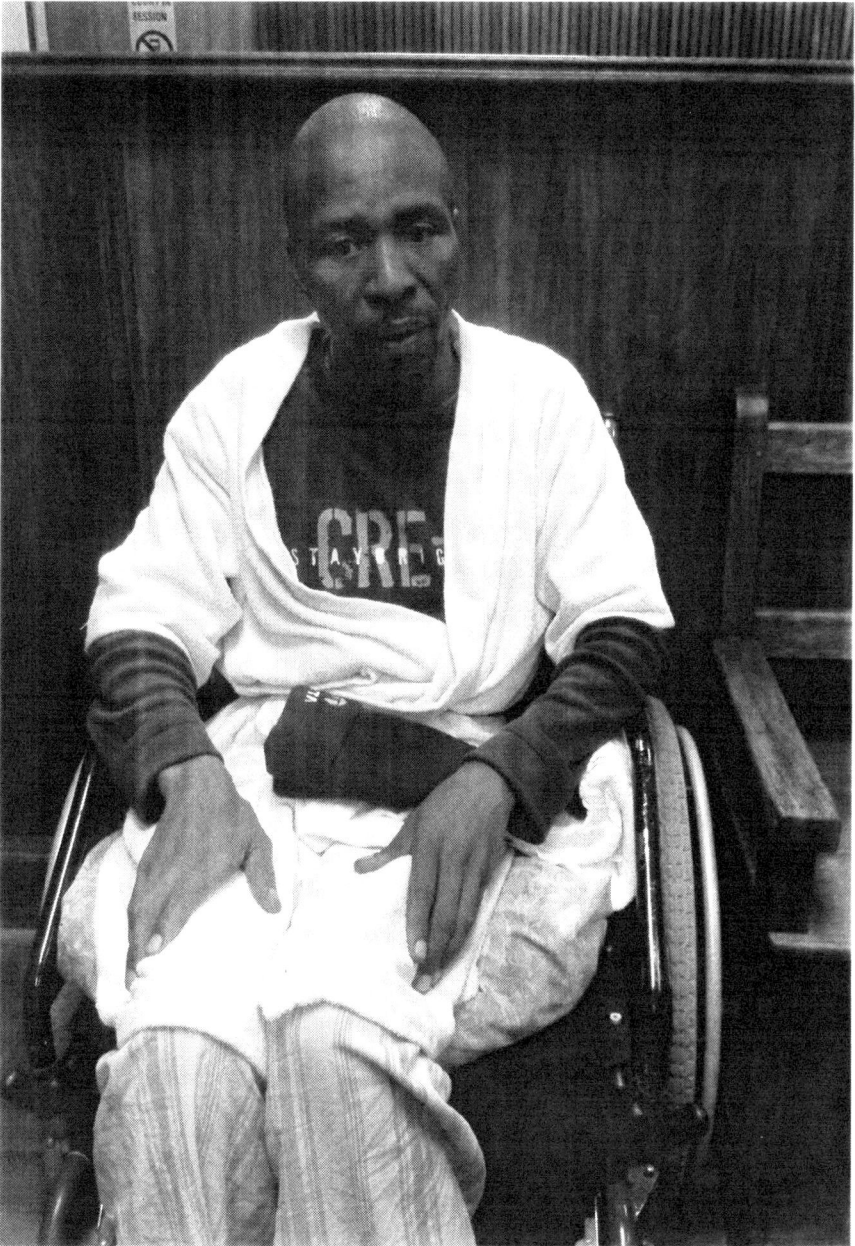

Ronnie Fakude at bail hearing in April 2013. (Image: Courtesy of Carolyn Raphaely)

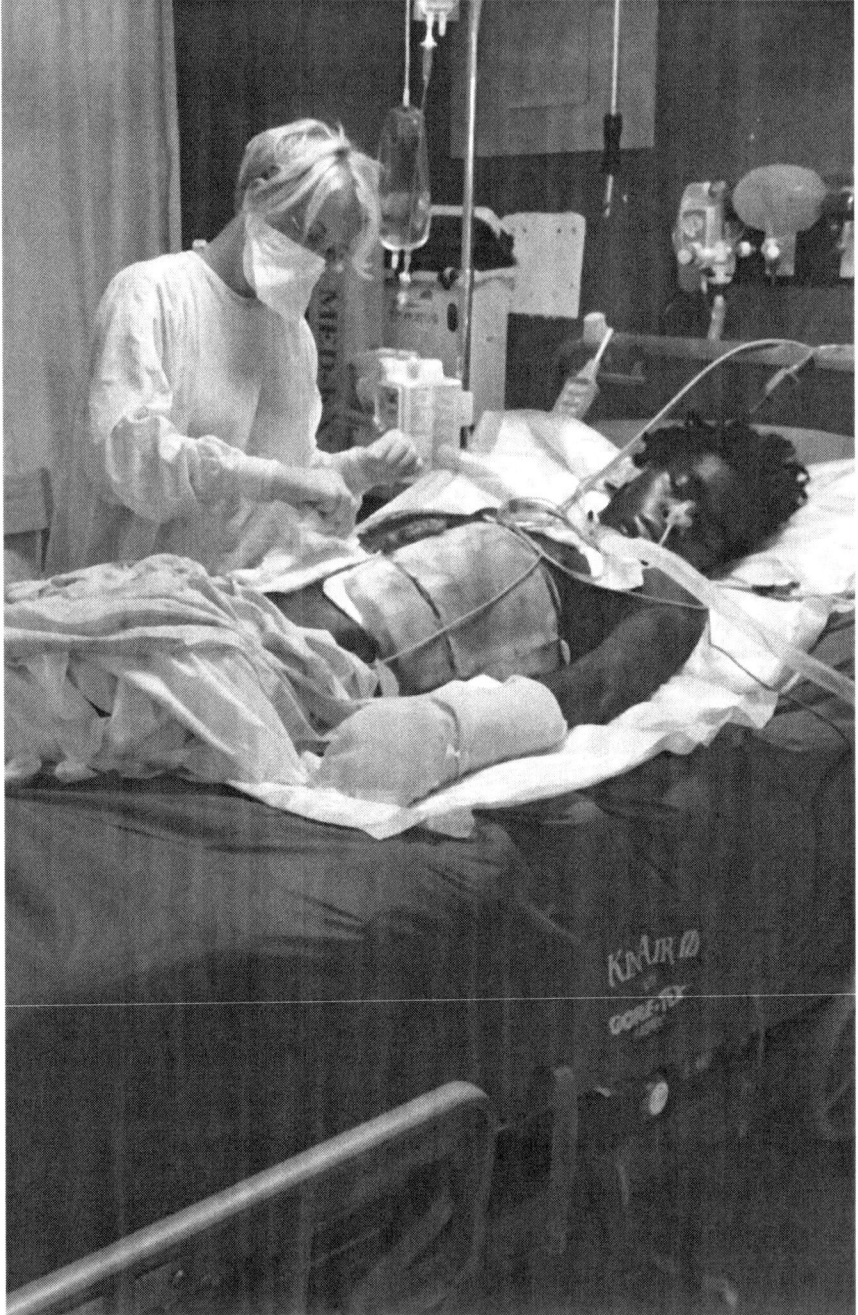

Shooting survivor Carlos McIntosh spent six weeks in the Critical Care Unit at Sunnybrook and Women's College Hospital, Toronto. Nurse Emily Lamothe dresses his numerous wounds in an isolation room due to an infection. (Image: Toronto Star/ GetStock.com, 2005)

9 Canada

Introduction
Gun violence levels in Canada are consistently low by international standards. Over the past three decades, they have declined to historic levels. Yet thousands of survivors still cope with the cumulative physical and psychological impacts of gun injuries and deaths. While Canada provides a range of services for crime victims through support programmes at a provincial level, the needs of many gun violence survivors remain poorly addressed. This chapter highlights some aspects of gun violence in Canada; current assistance available to victims of crimes; and caregiving challenges. As young black men are disproportionately injured and/or killed by guns, the chapter pays special attention to the experiences of black mothers who survive the loss of children to gun violence, especially those who do not meet the eligibility criteria for some victim support services such as compensation.

Section 1: Violence in Canada
The homicide rate in Canada has declined since 1980; in 2010, there were 554 homicides in a nation of 35 million people, a rate of 1.62 per 100,000 people.[1] Gun-related homicides have also declined over that period (see Figure 1). In 2010, 32% of homicides were committed with guns, though this varied by region. In cities, the proportion is higher. In Toronto, half of all homicides were committed with guns, followed by Vancouver (44%) and Montréal (33%). Most gun homicides involved handguns (64%), as opposed to rifles or shotguns (23%), and sawed-off shotguns or automatic firearms (13%).

Figure 1. Homicide rates by most common weapon type, Canada, 1980 2010

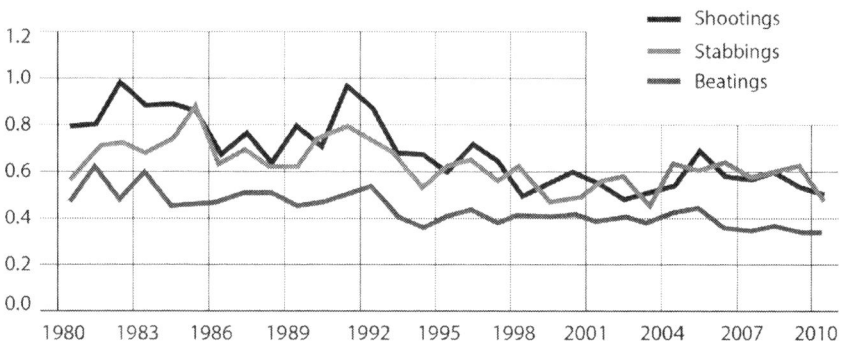

Source: T.H. Mahony, *Homicide in Canada 2010* (Ottawa: Statistics Canada, 2011).

In about three-quarters of firearm deaths the victims are males.[2] Young men aged 12-17 are more likely than adults to use a gun in a crime.[3] Non-fatal firearm injuries in Canada cannot be quantified because the State does not track or publish information on them.[4] However, a study based on National Trauma Registry data for 1999-2003 showed that 784 people across Canada were admitted to hospital with serious firearm injuries over that period. Of these injuries, 28% were self-inflicted; 60% were assaults; 6% were unintentional; and 6% were of unknown intent.[5] The study found that 94% of the injuries occurred among men, with the majority of victims being between 15 and 34 years old.

Gun violence: Sources, types and trends
In 1991 gunshot injuries cost Canada approximately CAD6.6 billion (USD6.7 billion), a per capita cost of CAD235 (USD237).[6] Of this, some CAD63 million (USD64 million) was spent on medical and mental health care and CAD10 million (USD11 million) on public services such as police investigation and transportation to the emergency department. Suicides and attempted suicides accounted for CAD4.7 billion (USD4.9 billion), while homicides and assaults cost CAD1.1 billion (USD1.3 billion). This analysis did not include the cost of long-term services for home care, post-traumatic stress disorder, or other essential support for survivors. This short-term focus reflects the nature of the services available, generally limited to the immediate emergency care.

Canada has about 400 youth gangs with approximately 7,000 active members from a range of cultural and ethnic backgrounds.[7] In metropolitan areas such as Toronto, they are predominantly young minority males residing in marginalised immigrant communities.

Poverty, prestige, and protection have been identified as the main factors underlying youth involvement in gang and gun violence in Canada.[8] Vulnerabilities linked to poverty, such as living in economically marginalised communities, are significant risk factors for violence, and a contributor to violent lifestyles in which firearms are considered necessary for protection.[9] As one mother who lost a son to gun violence states: "...money is what makes people get guns. If a person is poor and sees a way to make money and that making money is through drugs, they will... and when you are dealing with money you need protection. People use guns for protection and control."[10]

Gun regulation in Canada
Canada's national gun law was overhauled with the 1995 *Firearms Act* (Bill C-68), enacted after the murder of 14 female engineering students at the École Polytechnique in Montréal on 6 December 1989. The *Act* banned certain types of guns, and established an owner licensing and gun registration system. The federal Government contributes funds to provinces to administer aspects of the Act, such as processing licences and registration certificates. However not all provinces have opted to enter into arrangements with the federal Government.[11] In 2012 the *Act* was significantly altered by Bill C-19 (see below).

Candidates for a firearm license undergo criminal and background checks, and complete a weapons safety course. Two referees must review the application and confirm they do not know any reason why the applicant should not have a firearm.[12] The law requires current and ex-spouses (up to two years separated) to be notified of the applicant's intention to obtain a firearm license. Although spousal consent is not required for the license to be approved, any concern from a spouse will trigger a secondary review of the application. The spousal notification provision was created in response to the 1997 "Vernon Massacre", in which a man killed his estranged wife, eight members of her family, and then himself with his legally acquired gun.[13] The licensing and registration system is designed to maintain accountability and decrease the likelihood of misuse and unregulated person-to-person purchases. Firearm owners can only purchase ammunition for which they are licensed, by showing proof of a gun license. In Canada, guns and ammunition are subject to the same taxes as most other consumer products. The tax revenue is not earmarked for health or justice systems in particular.

There are three classes of firearms: Ordinary rifles, shotguns, and combination guns are generally classified as non-restricted; handguns are restricted; and fully automatic firearms, semi-automatic, converted automatics, short-barrelled and small calibre handguns are prohibited.[14] In 2012, the Royal Canadian Mounted Police (RCMP) reported 756,140 restricted and prohibited firearms.[15] Non-restricted firearms registration was not reported for 2012, although in 2011 they made up 91% of all registered firearms.[16] The latest data (from September 2012), indicates there are 1,927,693 valid firearm licenses.[17]

In April 2012 the national parliament passed Bill C-19, which discontinued the registration of rifles and shotguns (non-restricted firearms) and required the destruction of existing registration records. The new law did not affect registration requirements for restricted or prohibited firearms.[18] The Government argued that the gun registry was costly and its existence criminalised millions of "honest and law-abiding" hunters and farmers.[19] Licences to possess a firearm, as well as safety training and safe storage measures, remain requirements. The law passed despite strong opposition from victim advocates and gun control proponents.[20]

Section 2: Assistance for survivors

Information is scarce on pre-hospital care for gun violence survivors in Canada. Generally, trauma victims receive emergency response from an ambulance service, which transfers them to a local hospital, or to one of the country's 16 Level I and 16 Level II trauma centres. Trauma centres are primarily located in large urban areas.[21] Approximately 23% of Canadians reside more than one hour away from a Level I or Level II trauma centre, and en route death rates are higher in these areas.[22] Self-inflicted injuries, suicide attempts, and injuries at home have poorer outcomes because of the delay in the arrival of medical personnel—and because firearm suicide attempts frequently involve head injuries. Of the injuries resulting in fatalities at the hospital, 83% occur on the first day.[23]

The average length of hospital stay for gunshot survivors is 17.7 days, with more than 39% requiring surgery during hospitalisation.[24] Under the national health insurance programme (Medicare), medical care and immediate rehabilitation services are delivered without direct cost to qualifying Canadians. Each province has the responsibility to administer health services, with some variations in services coverage.[25] However, non-qualifying individuals (e.g. those without citizenship) are billed for their care.

Gunshot survivors, including those severely and/or permanently impaired, are usually discharged to another acute care hospital, home with or without support, or on to long term rehabilitation.[26] Long-term rehabilitation services provided out of hospital by health professionals (e.g. physiotherapists) are not covered by Medicare.[27] Financial support for long term disability services not covered by Medicare can be sought from the provincial or federal Government—e.g., the Ontario Disability Support Program[28] and Canada Pension Plan Disability.[29] However, some survivors interviewed claim that these programmes' burdensome paperwork and strict eligibility requirements limit applications and approvals. With no national or provincial disability insurance schemes to cover long-term rehabilitative care, survivors are left to seek financial and other forms of support from families, friends, or charities and faith-based organisations. An unusual compensation process, by the perpetrators, provided CAD2 million (USD2.2 million) restitution paid to Louise Russo (see Box 3) making it possible for her to afford long-term rehabilitation care.[30] This is however a rare outcome.

Services for survivors of violent crimes and grieving relatives of murder victims in Canada are provided by governments and non-governmental organisations, police services, and the private sector. At the federal level, the Correctional Service of Canada, Parole Board of Canada, Policy Centre for Victim Issues, and National Office for Victims provide pre—and post-trial services such as information about offenders and financial assistance for victims to attend court hearings.[31] (Limited financial assistance is also available to victims of serious violent crime suffered abroad.) The Canadian Resource Centre for Victims of Crime, a non-government agency in Ottawa, provides emotional support, information, and advocacy for victims and survivors of crimes.[32] Victim service programmes typically offer short-term counselling and emotional support, preparation for court, assistance with victim impact statements, and referrals to other services.

Since 1989, financial support for victim services has come from provincial and federal Victim Surcharges (i.e. portions of court fines). The Victim Surcharge is currently 30% of any fine imposed on offenders. In the absence of a fine, the surcharge is CAD100 (USD110) on summary conviction and CAD200 (USD215) on indictable offences. These funds are paid into the province or territory's victim assistance fund.[33] In addition, nine provinces have victim compensation programmes, such as the Criminal Injuries Compensation Board (CICB) in Ontario, providing financial compensation to survivors of violent crime and families of homicide victims.[34] Programmes vary but compensation can be awarded for pain and suffering, medical, rehabilitation, dental or eyewear costs, and income loss. Counselling costs, support for dependents, funeral and burial costs, and any other expenses identified by the Compensation Board as reasonably incurred are also covered.[35]

The 1992 *Correctional and Conditional Release Act* defines a victim as a "person who, as a result of the commission of a crime by another, suffers emotional or physical harm, loss of or damage to property or economic harm…" When a crime results in the death of a person, then the child, parent, dependant, or spouse of that person is defined as the victim.[36] Although this definition is consistent across provinces, there are variations in eligibility criteria and in the kinds of support offered. In Nova Scotia, financial compensation is not available; instead, the service pays for professional counselling once the investigation of the crime is over (and provided other criteria are met). Financial compensation for pain and suffering is only provided in Ontario and Prince Edward Island. Victim services are offered in Newfoundland, Labrador, Yukon, Nunavut, and the Northwest Territories, but these jurisdictions do not currently have compensation programmes.[37]

Even where the full range of services is offered, not all survivors are eligible for all compensation and other victim services. Families of homicide victims who were involved in activities deemed to have contributed to their own deaths may not receive victims' compensation.[38] This excludes many survivors in need of financial and psychological support. For example, young people injured during the course of gang activities in Toronto do not qualify for victims' compensation on the basis that their actions contributed to their harm. This population is arguably at greatest risk for reoffending, and neglecting them in services is an enormous lost opportunity.[39] Research from other contexts indicates that gang shootings (whether fatal or not) are often followed by retaliatory attacks.[40] Based on working with young people affected by gun violence in Toronto, Jabari Lindsay notes: "Every kid who is a survivor of gun violence becomes a potential shooter. When an older sibling gets shot, you can almost start to plot when they will pick up a gun and shoot somebody."[41]

The financial burdens experienced by survivors compound an already devastating emotional and life-changing trauma. Conversations with 48 black mothers in Toronto who lost children to gun violence revealed that 43 of them were denied victim compensation either because their children had criminal records (n=30) or because the mothers did not manifest medically diagnosed mental shock as a demonstration of their grief (n=13).[42] In Ontario, pain and suffering compensation is only given to survivors who have witnessed the murder of a loved one or came upon the body shortly after, and are deemed to have suffered an extreme psychological shock.[43] Some mothers who have been denied compensation based on this criterion feel that this is a punishment, stating that their grief is no less traumatic than others with different circumstances.

Official data on gun violence do not include information on the ethnicity or race of victims. However, research based on police sources found that the majority of young people who died from gun violence in Toronto were from ethnic minorities, primarily young black youth.[44] Consequently, many black mothers and siblings bear the social, emotional and financial burden of survivorship. Some of the Toronto mothers felt the rejection of their applications for compensation was discriminatory, and failed to consider the social circumstances connected to their children having a criminal record.[45]

Box 1. Profile: Julia Farquharson[46]

My son Segun was shot dead on 18 May 2001 in Toronto. He was 24 years old. During the murder he activated the voicemail on his cell phone, which captured the final moments of his life. Hearing that voicemail has been a source of continuing trauma for me. The death has impacted me both mentally and physically. At first I was numb. Over time I absorbed the entire trauma in my body, and it made me sick. In 2005, I was almost crippled, I couldn't walk. I had to crawl to the washroom. I couldn't bend down. The doctor told me that I had spinal stenosis [narrowing of the spine].

The loss affected my family members and me tremendously. One of my children was so affected that he got himself in trouble with the law. Unfortunately, people did not recognise that the trauma led him to act out of the ordinary. This situation traumatised the family all over again.

I have not been able to work since then. My mind tells me I can work, but my body won't allow me to. I am reduced to a disability pension. This is another strain. I was told that when a loved one dies from a criminal act, families are entitled to compensation. I applied for this compensation and was told that my son "caused his own death", and was denied. The funeral cost me CAD15,000 (USD16,000). I had to use all my savings and put the rest on my credit card. Being denied this compensation really troubled me. My son didn't commit suicide. How then could he have caused his own death? Why should I be penalised for his death? Criminal compensation should be what they say it is—exceptions shouldn't be in the fine print.

After the death of my son, I noticed that there were more young men being murdered. It didn't seem like anybody cared at all, except the mothers who lost their children. I wanted to do something. So I helped start a group called UMOVE—United Mothers Opposing Violence Everywhere. I wrote letters to politicians to complain about the lack of programs, recreations, employment, and education. These are all issues relating to gun violence. I spoke to schools and communities about my experience, because that's how we can impact societal systems and make social change.

I had to make my own resources. The only cushion that was there for me is my belief in God. He restored my soul and gave me strength. It's not a physical strength; it's a spiritual and mental strength. I cannot stop now. I have to do everything in my power to see that things resolve.

Addressing survivors' immediate needs is critical, as healthy recovery depends largely on early crisis intervention.[47] Such services in Canada are usually available within 24 hours to assist survivors with their interactions with the police, contacting family and friends, and helping to process emotions and deal with daily tasks (see Box 2, for an example). Survivors are also referred to psychologists, doctors and victim services agencies for ongoing mental health support.[48]

Box 2: Community Crisis Response Program[49]

The Community Crisis Response Program (CCRP) is a coordinated programme of municipal services, police, community organisations, faith communities, and residents in Toronto. CCRP responds to violent incidents (e.g. shootings, stabbings, assaults, and gang activities) in any neighbourhood by providing support and resources to assist community response and recovery. Within 24 hours of an incident, CCRP staff conducts a needs assessment, mobilises local resources, coordinates community debriefings, and arranges information sharing to address the needs of survivors, families, and the community in culturally appropriate ways.

The programme helps survivors of violence to obtain immediate counselling and financial support through a local government agency, Victim Services Toronto. This agency provides psychosocial support and partial support for funeral costs. Local legal clinics help with applications to the Criminal Injury Compensation Board. CCRP also works with survivors to identify their long term support needs. For example, if survivors feel they are in danger, CCRP can work with local organisations to develop safety plans; or coordinate support through the Attorney General's Victim/Witness Assistance Program.

CCRP works with local support services to identify community concerns and develop responses for residents affected by the ripple impacts of violence. This could include mobilising grief and trauma counsellors, educating the community about coping mechanisms, and identifying local sources of conflict. It can finance local memorials or resident-led initiatives to support healing; and it facilitates support for service providers who are also affected by traumatic incidents.

As an example of good service delivery in Toronto, CCRP aims for quick response times, comprehensiveness, and non-judgemental front line workers. However, a continual challenge for CCRP is ensuring the safety of the families of gang shooting victims, who may be at risk of intimidation in the aftermath. Supervisor Scott McKean explained that many survivors live in public housing where accommodation is scarce; transfers can take more than a year, and there is no way of knowing whether the new neighbourhood will keep people from further harm. Sometimes moving outside the city is the best solution, but inter-municipal transfers between public housing providers do not exist. McKean recommends that crisis intervention policies foster partnerships between municipal housing providers to facilitate emergency transfers.

Improving assistance for survivors

While Canada's victim assistance programmes are extensive compared to many other countries, important improvements are required. The development of advocacy groups among victims and survivors, initially fuelled by the raw emotions of personal experiences, can be important for improving services, systems, and policies.[50] In addition to the service disqualification criteria noted above, interviews with service providers highlighted a need for provision and/or improvement of services in the following areas:

Trauma-informed grief counselling

Several service providers interviewed feel there are insufficient grief support services for survivors of violent crime in general. Those that do exist often do not address the specific needs of gun violence survivors, whose trauma may be compounded by stigma, guilt, and self-blame. Reverend Sky Starr, a grief therapist working in a disadvantaged neighbourhood in Toronto, believes that grief counsellors need trauma-focused training to enhance recovery and healing processes; and that training should also be made accessible to teachers and healthcare professionals who interact with gun violence survivors. Making trauma-informed counselling available to survivors, however, "requires a shift at the national level in recognising grief as a mental health issue."[51]

Support groups for gun violence-specific trauma

Various interviewees stressed the importance of available and accessible peer support groups. Survivors of violent crimes can benefit from support, assistance, and understanding in groups of others who have had similar experiences.[52] Most effective support groups create a safe space for survivors to tell their stories and express their grief openly and extensively without feeling judged.[53] Lorraine Small, whose 15 year old son Jordan Manners was murdered in the stairwell of his high school, reflected: "At the funeral there were hundreds of people, but I was alone the next day and even years later... a support group with other mothers who truly cared would make a world of difference to me."[54] Jabari Lindsay agreed: "I have worked with communities that suffer loss to gun violence and have realized that the creation of a safe space through support groups is important. However, it needs to be a community space and the community needs to be the designer."[55]

Assistance in dealing with police and the criminal justice system
Several survivors reported that their dealings with police left them feeling powerless and defeated. Black mothers felt devalued, and many felt that the police's actions were influenced by racial prejudice. One mother cried uncontrollably as she recalled: "the police ransacked my home, spoke down to me, refused to answer my questions and had the nerve to ask if the drug money paid for my house... I have worked three jobs since I came to this country."[56] Studies have found that survivors' interaction with the criminal justice system can increase their stress and intensify their sense of violation—what is termed 'secondary victimisation'.[57] Avoiding this requires crisis intervention teams, mental health care providers, and/or support groups to prepare people for processes such as police interviews and criminal investigations. Steve Sullivan, Executive Director of Ottawa Victim Services, puts it succinctly, "Justice is not just how you treat the offender but how you treat the survivors."[58]

Funding for survivor-led community groups
While counselling and other psychological services are available through government victim services, survivors deemed ineligible for these services must turn to free community-based support (and to private services if they can afford them). Community-based survivor-led services can significantly assist the recovery process of injured individuals as well as grieving family members.[59] However, several interviewees commented that a lack of sustained funding has led to the closure of many of these programmes and that funding opportunities available tend to focus on specific areas of victimisation such as violence against women, or on short-term interventions. As Audette Shephard, Chair of the anti-violence advocacy group UMOVE, points out: "Helping survivors move from victim to survivor to thriver requires a balance of programmes and services to help them along the way... grief is long term, 5-10 counselling sessions are just not enough. We need to always have access to services for post-traumatic triggers."[60]

Scott McKean of CCRP (see Box 2) noted that many agencies are committed to meeting the needs of survivors in a sustainable way but current funding models limit where and how they can provide support. Different agencies compete for the same funding. Although a competitive process does not preclude joint applications between agencies, McKean noted that, "current funding models do not allow for effective partnership development. Sometimes survivors use multiple services, but these service providers do not share information and develop collective service plans and delivery models because of policy and protocol restrictions. These policies not only threaten delivery of important community services for survivors, but also conflict with the public interest by limiting the capacity of service providers."[61]

Section 3: Caregiving, resiliency, and recovery
With limited access to specialised services, the burden of physical, emotional, logistical, and economic care of survivors falls to families. They not only take on caring duties, but also assume responsibilities previously held by the person who was shot. Louise Russo was paralysed in a drive-by shooting in Toronto (see Box 3). Prior to the shooting Louise was the primary caregiver for her severely impaired daughter, Jenna. Following her injury, her older children, elderly parents, husband, and hired help assumed the care of both Louise and Jenna. Every aspect of Louise's life has become more complicated. She lives with pain, spasms, and other physical complications.

Box 3. Profile: Louise Russo[62]

On 21 April 2004, at 45 years old, I went into a sandwich shop in Toronto and never imagined it would be the last time I would ever walk. I remember placing my sandwich order when I heard a loud sound. I could hear screaming and chairs moving, and before long I realised I was shot in my back and lying on the floor. That shooting left me paraplegic. I went through two months of hospitalisation and six months of rehabilitation. Now I live my life from a wheelchair.

This violent crime has altered and complicated every aspect of my life. The impact on my family is substantial. I have a severely disabled child who I was caring for prior to the shooting. I am no longer able to take care of her independently. This is probably the most difficult for me to cope with. My other daughter, who was with me that night and witnessed the shooting, became very withdrawn for a while. My husband did not work for two and a half years. My son who was 19 years old at the time has struggled significantly as well.

Trying to deal with a new body, a new life, and the effects of my disability on my family is intensely difficult. I have to find a new way of living. Even the simplest activities are difficult. My husband has to help me. I need help getting dressed. Making a simple meal has become complex. There are times I am angry, but I chose not to become bitter inside. I am a victim but I refuse to be victimised over and over again. I refuse to be a prisoner in my own body. I value and appreciate friendships and life so much more. My personal vision is to be as independent as possible and to continue moving forward.

I have come to understand that I can't take the little things for granted. It has been quite a remarkable journey but I was determined to turn this horrible tragedy into something positive. I started Working Against Violence Everyday (WAVE), an organisation that recognises individuals who stand against violence in their communities by upholding Respect, Responsibility, and the Role of leadership (3Rs).[63] WAVE recognises young people aged 9–19 who are making a difference in violence prevention in their schools and communities.

The first annual Walk Against Violence Everywhere (WAVE). The 2.5-kilometre route ended in a park renamed the Louise Russo Park. (Image: Carlos Osorio/ GetStock.com, 29 May 2006)

Stress and resilience factors among surviving relatives

Traumatic stress can also disrupt the psychological and social stability of people whose loved ones are shot dead. In a study of black mothers in Canada who lost a child to gun violence, the factors that contributed most to traumatic stress were changes in financial status due to job loss, changes in social activities, and changes in their regular routines. Some mothers experience strained relationships with friends and families, difficulty eating and sleeping, and onset of chronic illnesses such as hypertension. Many are single parents living in marginalised communities and have other children to care for. Sustaining their normal responsibilities while coping with grief and stigma is difficult. Some hold on to the cultural identity of the "Strong Black Woman", maintaining the appearance of coping effectively, which they may privately regard as a facade.[64]

Many secondary survivors lack the social and psychological resources needed for the caregiving responsibilities that are thrust upon them. Mothers who lose children to gun violence often experience significant mental health problems that affect their ability to care for themselves and other family members. As one mother puts it, "caregiving is an essential part of surviving, but how can I care for anyone when I cannot care for myself?"[65]

Several mothers highlighted gaps in community based services assisting with childcare, job losses, family breakdown, and housing following their loss. Such programmes can help grieving relatives move through their stress and trauma. It took Julia Farquharson almost a year to begin mourning her son. "I was too numb to cry. I didn't believe that it was my son, although I bathed and dressed his dead body myself... After the burial I roamed the city and spoke to everyone who would listen. On Segun's first death anniversary, the tears started to flow like a flood."[66] This is not an uncommon pattern of grieving. It signals the need for sustained community supports for survivors like Julia who have minimal access to resources (see Box 1).

If gun violence survivors are provided with appropriate formal and informal support, they have the potential to become change agents in society. Devastated by the loss of her son, Audette Shephard reflected: "I could have taken my own life; I had no idea how I would continue living without that child."[67] Now, as Chair of UMOVE, Shephard campaigns for policy changes and initiatives for victims of crime in Toronto. Similarly, after acquiring paraplegia from a stray bullet, Louise Russo has become a prominent advocate for violence reduction and disability rights. Both survivors attribute their empowerment to support from friends, family, and their spirituality.

The power of apology

Restorative justice facilitates face-to-face meetings between survivors of crime and violence and the offender. It can be one strategy for contending with powerlessness, grief and loss.[68] Corrections Canada has a Restorative Opportunities Program in which victims and families can ask to meet offenders as part of a Restorative Justice dialogue. This process provides an opportunity for offenders to acknowledge and make reparation to victims of their crimes.[69]

For mothers whose children have been murdered, an apology from the perpetrator during a restorative process can contribute powerfully to healing. Joan Howard lost her 24 year old son Kempton in 2003. In 2007 during the criminal trial she received a letter of apology from the convicted perpetrator. "At first it didn't make a difference," she recalled. "I barely listened in court as he read it. I just kept thinking, this can't bring my son back. I wanted to lash out at him... but now, in 2010 I know I got something that a lot of mothers didn't get and it helps... I don't want to admit it... I feel I'm betraying Kempton... but... it helps."[70]

Section 4: Standards and normative frameworks

Canada has actively contributed to the development of regional and global norms regarding the trade in small arms, and impacts of armed violence.[71] Canada is one of the 40 members of the United Nations Commission on Crime Prevention and Criminal Justice, and acted as Chair in 2011-2012. States share good practices in tackling urban crime, gangs, and criminal justice reform. Canada ratified the 2000 UN *Convention against Transnational Organized Crime* in May 2002, signed the accompanying 2001 *Protocol against the Illicit Manufacturing of and Trafficking in Firearms, Their Parts and Components and Ammunition, supplementing the United Nations Convention against Transnational Organized Crime* (the Firearms Protocol) in March 2002, and ratified the 2003 UN *Convention against Corruption* in 2007.

However, as a result of the passing of Bill C-19, Canada may not be able to ratify two important regional and global agreements: the 1997 *Inter-American Convention against the Illicit Manufacturing of and Trafficking in Firearms, Ammunition, Explosives, and Other Related Materials*, signed in 1997, and the Firearms Protocol. Both agreements require record keeping on firearms transactions and information exchange, especially for international tracing processes. Bill C-19 eliminated registration of most firearms.[72] This will create significant challenges for Canada to meet its commitment to international cooperation on firearm accountability.

As mentioned, the interests of crime victims come under the mandates of several federal agencies, especially in relation to the criminal justice processing of offenders. The Policy Centre for Victim Issues, located in the Justice Department, takes the lead and aims to ensure that the perspectives of victims are fully considered in federal laws and policies, as well as raise awareness of victims' needs nationally and internationally.[73] A leading policy framework is the *Canadian Statement of Basic Principles of Justice for Victims of Crime*, adopted in 1988 and followed by a renewed version in 2003.[74] Based on the 1985 UN *Declaration of Basic Principles of Justice for Victims of Crime and Abuse of Power*, the Statement articulates a commitment to fair treatment for victims, particularly during criminal justice processes. The Principles include providing information, treating victims with courtesy and compassion, and considering the diversity of victims in the development and delivery of programmes and services, education and training. These Principles guide all federal, provincial, and territorial laws, policies, and procedures affecting victims.

In 2010, Canada ratified the 2006 UN *Convention on the Rights of Persons with Disabilities* (CRPD, for more detail, see Annex 1). During the development and negotiation of the CRPD, Canada was one of the most engaged delegations.[75] However, the Council of Canadians with Disabilities (CCD) has written to the UN Human Rights Council expressing concern at their country's failure to act on its commitments under the CRPD.[76] CCD's concerns include the failure to establish coordinating or monitoring mechanisms, and the very limited financial resources provided for CRPD implementation. In addition, proposed changes to the welfare system "will force persons with disabilities to live in poverty longer."[77] Canada has not signed the Optional Protocol to the CRPD, which provides a complaints procedure for individuals denied their rights. The federal Government is currently developing a National Disability Act.

Conclusion

Canada has seen a steady decline in gun deaths over the past three decades, and the gun homicide rate is comparably low among industrialised countries. Nevertheless, gun violence is a concern, particularly in major cities, where risk factors such as poverty and social marginalisation coexist. Survivors of gun violence continue to experience financial, psychological, social, and physical consequences and challenges; and many survivors' needs are not met due to gaps in the availability of services and inconsistencies among the provinces and territories. Social policy reform is essential to overcome disparities across the nation. This could be accomplished by establishing national standards for the programmes, resources, and services that are equitable to survivors across Canada; including those who fall short of current eligibility criteria for certain victim services. Crisis intervention programmes and community-based services should be strengthened through sustained government (provincial and federal) funding. Trauma-focused grief support services provided by trained professionals are also necessary to meet the specific mental health needs of gun violence survivors.

Contributors: Annette Bailey, Assistant Professor, Ryerson University Daphne Cockwell School of Nursing, Toronto, Canada. **Divine Velasco**, Registered Nurse in Complex Continuing and Acute Care, Brampton Civic Hospital, Toronto, Canada. **Cate Buchanan** and **Rebecca Peters** undertook drafting and editing. **Mireille Widmer** and **Emile LeBrun** provided additional editing.

Peer reviews were provided by **Terry Roswell**, Department of Sociology, Ryerson University (Canada); **Audette Shephard**, United Mothers Opposing Violence Everywhere (Canada); **Steve Sullivan**, Executive Director, Ottawa Victim Services (Canada); and **Reverend Sky Starr**, Out of Bounds Grief Support (Canada).

A Ryerson University Faculty of Community Services Seed Grant also supported the development of this chapter.

References

[1]   T.H. Mahony, *Homicide in Canada 2010* (Ottawa: Statistics Canada, 2011). Available at: www. statcan.gc.ca/pub/85-002-x/2011001/article/11561-eng.htm#a4 Accessed 16 November 2012.

[2]   R. Vaillancourt, *Gender differences in police-reported violent crime in Canada, 2008* (Ottawa: Statistics Canada, 2010). Available at: www.statcan.gc.ca/pub/85f0033m/85f0033m2010024-eng.htm Accessed 16 November 2012.

3 M. Dauvergne and L. De Socio, *"Firearms and violent crime,"* Juristat 28/2 (Ottawa: Statistics Canada, 2009). Available at: www.statcan.gc.ca/pub/85-002-x/2008002/article/10518-eng.htm Accessed 16 November 2012.

4 Department of Justice Canada, *Firearms, Accidental Deaths, Suicides and Violent Crime: An Updated Review of the Literature with Special References to the Canadian Situation* (Ottawa: DOJ, 2012). Available at: www.justice.gc.ca/eng/pi/rs/rep-rap/1998/wd98_4-dt98_4/p2.html Accessed 16 November 2012.

5 C.J. Finley, D. Hemenway, J. Clifton, D.R. Brown, R.K. Simons and S.M. Hameed, "The demographics of significant firearm injury in Canadian trauma centres and the associated predictors of in hospital mortality," *Canadian Journal of Surgery* 51/3 (2008), pp. 197-203.

6 T. Miller, "Costs associated with gunshot wounds in Canada in 1991," *Canadian Medical Association Journal* 9/153 (1995), pp. 1261-1268. Note: CAD-USD rates reflect March 2013 currency conversions. The amounts would have been higher in 1991.

7 G.E. Tita, E. Troshynski and M. Graves, *Strategies for Reducing Gun Violence: The Role of Gangs, Drugs and Firearm Accessibility*, Research report 2007-3 (Ottawa: Public Safety Canada, 2007). Available at: www.publicsafety.gc.ca/res/cp/res/gun-vlnce-eng.aspx Accessed 16 November 2012.

8 G.E. Tita et al (2007).

9 M.C. Chettleburgh, *Young thugs: Inside the dangerous world of Canadian street gangs* (Toronto: Harper Collins Publishers, 2007).

10 Interview by Annette Bailey with Julia Farquharson in Toronto, 20 February 2012.

11 Royal Canadian Mounted Police, *Canadian Firearms Program—Overview* (Ottawa: RCMP, 2010). Available at: www.rcmp-grc.gc.ca/pubs/fire-feu-eval/pg1-eng.htm Accessed 18 November 2012.

12 Royal Canadian Mounted Police, *History of firearms control in Canada: Up to and including the Firearms Act* (Ottawa: RCMP, 2009). Available at: www.rcmp-grc.gc.ca/cfp-pcaf/pol-leg/hist/con-eng.htm Accessed 15 November 2012.

13 Coalition for Gun Control, *Canada's Firearms Legislation: Overview of Firearms Legislation in Canada* (Toronto: CGC, 2006). Available at: www.prevention-violence.ca/English/PDFsEnglish/CanadasFirearmsLegislation.pdf Accessed 13 November 2012. See also D. Doherty and J. Hornosty, *Exploring the links: Firearms, family violence and animal abuse in rural communities* (Ottawa: Public Safety Canada, 2008), pp. 1-180. Available at: www.legal-info-legale.nb.ca/en/safer_families_safer_communities_publications Accessed 12 November 2012.

14 Royal Canadian Mounted Police, "Registration of firearms (individuals)," Canadian Firearms Program. Web page updated 23 July 2012. Available at: www.rcmp-grc.gc.ca/cfp-pcaf/online_en-ligne/reg_enr-eng.htm Accessed 16 November 2012.

15 Royal Canadian Mounted Police, "Facts and Figures (July - September 2012)," Canadian Firearms Program. Web page updated 24 October 2012. Available at: www.rcmp-grc.gc.ca/cfp-pcaf/facts-faits/archives/quick_facts/2012/se-eng.htm Accessed 18 November 2012. Note: Prohibited firearms include guns that individuals can no longer get a license to buy for various reasons (e.g. military style weapons). Those who already owned such guns before the law changed (and their family members) can however still own them, hence these are referred in the weapons holdings statistics. In Canada the classes of firearms are articulated in the Criminal Code, not the Firearms Act. Since the laws changed again in 2012, and the scrapping of the registration scheme there is no way to count the number of guns, of any type, in Canada.

16 Royal Canadian Mounted Police, "Facts and Figures (July - September 2011)," Canadian Firearms Program. Web page updated 14 July 2011. Available at: www.rcmp-grc.gc.ca/cfp-pcaf/facts-faits/archives/quick_facts/2011/se-eng.htm Accessed 18 November 2012.

17 Royal Canadian Mounted Police, "Facts and Figures (July - September 2012)".

18 Royal Canadian Mounted Police, "Changes to the Canadian Firearms Program". Web page updated 24 July 2012. Available at: www.rcmp-grc.gc.ca/cfp-pcaf/change-changement-eng.htm Accessed 18 November 2012. A court order issued by the Quebec Superior Court requires residents of Quebec to register non-restricted firearms with the RCMP until further notice.

19 CTV News, "MP vote to scrap long-gun registry," February 15 (2012). Available at: www.ctv.ca/CTVNews/TopStories/20120215/long-gun-registry-c-19-third-reading-vote-120215/ Accessed 10 November 2012.

20 See Coalition for Gun Control, www.guncontrol.ca/English/Home/C19.html Accessed 7 January, 2013.

21 J.B. Kortbeek and B. Buckley, "Trauma-care systems in Canada," *Injury* 39/5 (2003), pp. 658-663.

22 S.M. Hameed, N. Schuurman, T. Razek, D. Boone, R. Van Heest, T. Taulu, N. Lakha, D.C. Evans, D.R. Brown, A.W. Kirkpatrick, H.T. Stelfox, D. Dyer, M.V. Wijngaarden-Stephens, S. Logsetty, A.B. Nathans, T. Charyk-Stewart, S. Rizoli, L.N. Tremblay, F. Brenneman, N. Ahmed, E. Galbraith, N. Parry, M.J. Girotti, G. Pagliarello, N.Tze, K. Khwaja, N. Yanchar, J.N. Tallon, J.A.I. Trenholm, C. Tegart, O. Amran, M. Berube, U. Hameed and R.S. Simons, "Access to trauma systems in Canada," *Journal of Trauma, Injury, Infection and Critical Care* 69/6 (2010), pp. 1350-1361.

23 C.J. Finley et al (2008).

24 C.J. Finley et al (2008).

25 Health Canada, "Canada Health Act - Frequently asked questions". Web page updated 20 October 2011. Available at: www.hc-sc.gc.ca/hcs-sss/medi-assur/faq-eng.php#a5 Accessed 16 November 2012.

26 C.J. Finley et al (2008).

27 Health Canada, "Canada Health Act - Frequently asked questions".

28 See Ontario Disability Support Program at: www.mcss.gov.on.ca/en/mcss/programs/social/directives/directives/ODSPDirectives/income_support/1_2_ODSP_ISDirectives.aspx Web page updated 13 August 2012. Accessed 20 November 2012.

29 See Canada Pension Plan Disability Benefit at: www.servicecanada.gc.ca/eng/isp/cpp/disaben.shtml Web page updated 16 November 2012. Accessed 20 November 2012.

30 P. Edwards and J. Rankin, "Behind the scenes in Louise Russo sandwich shop shooting deal," *Star.com* 29 January (2011). Available at: www.thestar.com/news/insight/2011/01/29/behind_the_scenes_in_louise_russo_sandwich_shop_shooting_deal.html Accessed 7 February, 2013.

31 Office of the Federal Ombudsman for Victims of Crime, "Victim services in Canada," (Ottawa: Government of Canada, 2011). Available at: www.victimsfirst.gc.ca/serv/vsc-svc.html Accessed 12 October 2012. For analysis of victims' compensation in Canada see: I. Waller, *Rebalancing Justice: Rights for Victims of Crime* (United Kingdom: Rowman and Littlefield, 2011).

32 See Canadian Resource Centre for Victims of Crime at: http://crcvc.ca/ Accessed 12 October 2012.

33 Department of Justice Canada, "Backgrounder: Victim surcharge," April (2012). Web page updated 3 August 2012. Available at: www.justice.gc.ca/eng/news-nouv/nr-cp/2012/doc_32731.html Accessed 12 October 2012.

34 Victims of Violence, *An overview of victim services in Canada* (Ottawa: VoV, 2012a). Available at: www.victimsofviolence.on.ca/rev2/index.php?option=com_content&task=view&id=389&Itemid=267 Accessed 8 September 2012. CICBs operate in British Columbia, Alberta, Saskatchewan, Manitoba, Ontario, Quebec, New Brunswick, Nova Scotia, and Prince Edward Island. Compensation may be funded through surcharges, although the Ontario CICB is funded mainly from general tax revenue.

35 C. Munch, *Victim services in Canada, 2009/2010* (Ottawa: Statistics Canada, 2012). Available at: www.statcan.gc.ca/pub/85-002-x/2012001/article/11626-eng.pdf Accessed 12 February 2012.

36 1992 *Corrections and Conditional Release Act*. Available at: http://laws-lois.justice.gc.ca/PDF/C-44.6.pdf Accessed 3 November 2012.

37 Victims of Violence, *Research—criminal injuries compensation* (Ottawa: VoV, 2011). Available at: www.victimsofviolence.on.ca/rev2/index.php?option=com_content&task=view&id=333&Itemid=23#ontario Accessed 20 November 2012.

38 Victims of Violence (2011).

39 B.M. Huebner, S.P. Varano and T.S. Bynum, "Gangs, guns, and drugs: Recidivism among serious, young offenders," *Criminology and Public Policy* 6/2 (2007), pp. 187-197.

40 For example, see K. Ratele, "Watch your man: Young black males at risk of homicidal violence," *South African Crime Quarterly* 33 (2010), pp. 19-24; and C. Cooper, D. Eslinger and P. Stolley, "Hospital-based violence intervention programs work," *Journal of Trauma* 61 (2006), pp. 534-540.

41   Interview by Annette Bailey with Jabari Lindsay in Toronto, 1 March 2012.
42   Information derived from demographics data collected for dissertation research. See A. Bailey, *Traumatic stress, social support, cognitive appraisal, and resiliency among black women experiencing gun violence loss*, unpublished PhD thesis (2011).
43   Victims of Violence (2011).
44   I. Ezeonu, "Gun violence in Toronto: Perspectives from the Police," *The Howard Journal* 49/2 (2010), pp. 147-165.
45   See A. Bailey (2011).
46   As told to Annette Bailey on 20 February 2012.
47   A. Roberts, *Crisis intervention handbook: Assessment, treatment, and research* (Oxford: Oxford University Press, 2005), p. 845.
48   Victims of Violence, A *survivor's guide to homicide and grieving* (Ottawa: VoV, 2012b). Available at: www.victimsofviolence.on.ca/rev2/index.php?option=com_content&task=view&id=318&Itemid=66 Accessed 20 October 2012.
49   Email correspondence between Annette Bailey and Scott McKean, Supervisor of the Community Crisis Response in Toronto, 7 April 2012. See: www.toronto.ca/nan/about/crisisresponse.htm
50   K. Stanbridge and J. Kenny, "Emotions and the campaign for victims' rights in Canada," *Canadian Journal of Criminology and Criminal Justice* 4/51 (2009), pp. 473-509.
51   Rev. Sky Starr works at Out Of Bounds Grief Support, see: www.outofboundsjf.org
52   Victims of Violence (2012b).
53   K. Stanbridge and J. Kenny (2009).
54   Interview by Annette Bailey with Lorraine Small in Toronto, 25 July 2010 (as part of dissertation research).
55   Interview by Annette Bailey with Jabari Lindsay.
56   Interview by Annette Bailey in Toronto on 15 February 2012 with a mother who lost her 17-year-old son in an execution-style shooting. This mother wishes to remain anonymous because court proceedings are underway.
57   For example, see A. Amick-McMullan, D. Kilpatrick and H. Resnick, "Homicide as a risk factor for PTSD among surviving family members," *Behavior Modification* 15 (1991), pp. 545-559.
58   Interview by Annette Bailey with Steve Sullivan in Ottawa, 11 June 2012.
59   M.S. Umbreit, *Family Group Conferencing: Implications for Crime Victims*, Center for Restorative Justice and Peacemaking, University of Minnesota (Washington DC: US Department of Justice, 2000). Available at: www.ncjrs.gov/ovc_archives/reports/family_group/welcome.html Accessed 16 November 2012.
60   Interview by Annette Bailey with Audette Shephard in Toronto, 15 February 2012.
61   Email correspondence between Annette Bailey and Scott McKean, 6 April 2012.
62   As told to Annette Bailey in Toronto on 26 February 2012.
63   See http://louiserussowave.ca/
64   See A. Bailey (2011).
65   Interview by Annette Bailey with Nadia Beckles in Toronto, 15 March 2012.
66   Interview by Annette Bailey with Julia Farquharson.
67   Interview by Annette Bailey with Audette Shephard.
68   M. Umbreit and B. Vos, "Homicide survivors meet the offender prior to execution: restorative justice through dialogue," *Homicide Studies* 4/1 (2000), pp. 63-87. See also M.P. Armour, "Journey of family members of homicide victims: A qualitative study of their posthomicide experience," *American Journal of Orthopsychiatry* 72/3 (2002), pp. 372-82.
69   Correctional Service Canada, *Restorative Opportunities Program* (Ottawa: Restorative Justice Division, 2012). Web page updated 7 August 2012. Available at: www.csc-scc.gc.ca/text/rj/vom-eng.shtml Accessed 29 October 2012.
70   Interview conducted by Reverend Sky Starr in Toronto on 25 February 2011 with Joan Howard, who lost her son Kempton Howard to gun violence.
71   K. Epps, "Bill C-19 and Canada's international firearms commitments," Speaking notes for the Standing Committee on Public Safety and National Security, Project Ploughshares, 22 November (2011). Available at: http://ploughshares.ca/pl_publications/bill-c-19-and-canadas-international-firearms-commitments/ Accessed 2 November 2012.
72   K. Epps (2011).

[73] Department of Justice, Canada, "Policy Centre for Victim Issues." Web page updated 20 September 2012. Available at: www.justice.gc.ca/eng/pi/pcvi-cpcv/index.html Accessed 3 November 2012.

[74] Department of Justice, Canada, "Canadian statement of basic principles of justice for victims of crime 2003." Web page updated 3 August 2012. Available at: www.justice.gc.ca/eng/pi/pcvi-cpcv/pub/03/princ.html Accessed 13 November 2012.

[75] Council of Canadians with Disabilities and Canadian Association for Community Living, "UN Convention on the Rights of Persons with Disabilities: Making domestic implementation real and meaningful," CCD-CACL Working Paper (Winnipeg: CCD, 2011). Available at: www.ccdonline.ca/en/international/un/canada/making-domestic-implementation-real-and-meaningful-feb2011 Accessed 2 February 2013.

[76] Council of Canadians with Disabilities, "Renewed political commitment and leadership: An imperative for the realization of the human rights of Canadians with disabilities," CCD Submission to the United Nations Human Rights Council Universal Periodic Review of May 2013 (Winnipeg: CCD, 2012). Available at: www.ccdonline.ca/en/international/un/canada/upr-2012 Accessed 22 November 2012.

[77] Council of Canadians with Disabilities (2012), paragraph 16.

SPOTLIGHT SECTION
Surviving the Lusignan Massacre in Guyana

The "Lusignan massacre" occurred on 26 January 2008 when a group of armed men targeted a working-class section of the village with high-powered weapons, leaving hundreds of spent shells behind. Lusignan, whose population is mainly of East Indian descent, sits on the eastern coast of Guyana, a nation of some 751,000 people. Given the small size of Guyana, the impacts of such an event were widely felt. For 30 minutes the attackers fired on five properties in one street of Lusignan. The violence killed 11 people from five families: four men, two women and five children. Of the 13 survivors, three people sustained permanent physical impairments and one man lost his entire family; the whole community was traumatised. Officers from three police stations failed to respond promptly to calls from residents until an hour after the attack was over and the perpetrators had escaped. A more timely service delivery from first responders, including emergency medical care and the police, might have saved lives and reduced the impact of injuries.

Three men have been charged with the murders, but no one has been convicted.[1] The local community believes the Guyana Police Force has failed to conduct a proper investigation and has instead arrested previous offenders without evidence linking them to the crime scene. Survivors have been forced to testify at court hearings for the accused, retelling their stories without psychological support. The lack of confidence in the criminal proceedings—the length of time taken to charge people, the weak evidence produced in court and lengthy duration of the trials—has also proved an impediment to healing for many survivors. As one resident reflected: "this home is a reminder of loss... I have not thrown away the blood soaked mattress and sheets."[2] In the aftermath of the massacre a select number of children in the community were provided with immediate psychosocial therapy.

Five years on, several survivors are struggling with the unresolved nature of the massacre. Howard Thomas, then 19 years old, moved to the interior of the country to avoid the memories his home contains. He doubts his capacity to forgive: "...How can you forgive someone who killed your family? How? I can't, I just can't. I ain't there yet and I ain't think that coming soon."[3]

Moreover, the financial stability of survivors has been adversely affected, and even though monetary assistance was available, it did not compensate for the loss of the main "breadwinners". Women forced to seek jobs because the men in their households were killed or injured, have transitioned from subsistence farming to full-time self-employment in the poultry industry (farming chickens on their own land). This new type of work places a high demand on women's time so they are no longer able to care as comprehensively for their children or elderly relatives.

The initial assistance focussed on replacing household items that were damaged, and/or contributing toward funeral expenses. The next level of assistance from the state was psychosocial intervention for children attending public schools in the community. Children also benefited from school uniforms, textbooks and school supplies from the Red Cross and religious organisations. The Government approved an exceptional policy of providing social assistance for two years to the affected families through the Ministry of Human Services and Social Security. The general public, including the Diaspora, donated to a public fund initiated by a local businessperson, which raised some USD30,000. This was distributed equally among the families and mainly spent on renovations to repair the damages to homes and property.

The UN Development Programme (UNDP), with other international organisations and a local NGO, set up livelihood projects to respond to the changes in heads of households and the reduction in incomes. Most survivors were engaged in subsistence farming or cottage industries; they were encouraged to scale up to micro-businesses with the opportunity to apply for grants. The livelihood ventures included rearing poultry, making cement blocks, growing cash crops and small-scale vending. These projects lasted for four months under the supervision of UNDP, and were independently sustained for about three years.[4]

Those children who benefitted from educational support have been successful at school and others continue to make strides despite the painful memory of their deceased relatives that cannot be fully explained by their parents.

To memorialise the victims of the massacre, the Indian Arrival Committee, an NGO that promotes Indian culture and works within the Indo-Guyanese community, hosts an annual commemorative service. The Committee has promised to build a memorial to honour the deceased.

The survivors from the massacre could have benefitted from a well-structured integrated recovery package or plan. Although people received seed funding to transition into new livelihoods, most survivors except one individual were not able to sustain these ventures beyond three years. The lack of sustainability could be attributed to rising prices for materials, feed and transportation, livestock dying before they could be sold, the rise of competing stores offering lower prices and varying levels of organisation and capacity amongst the grantees. Another contributing factor was the lack an effective strategy for long-term monitoring and connecting small businesses with ready markets.

The second shortcoming in the response was in the provision of psychosocial support to the survivors. All of the survivors during recent interviews indicated the need for counselling to deal with the aftermath of the incident.[5] Some four years later, many said they are still unable to come to terms with their loss, and noted the daily struggle to cope with the emotional turmoil.

One 56 year old farmer, whose impairments have affected his mobility and ability to provide for his family, laments the challenge of finding new work at this stage of his life. Parents expressed concern and a sense of helplessness about providing for the emotional wellbeing of children who witnessed the killings. These are children excluded from the group of in-school children who benefitted from psychosocial support in the aftermath of the massacre because they are not enrolled in a public school. All the survivors were unhappy about the long delay in the construction of the promised memorial.

Contributors: Tomaisha Hendricks, Youth and Community Development Specialist with Partners for Peace and Development. **Roxanne Myers,** Co-chair of Partners for Peace and Development and social policy consultant who served as part of an intervention team in Lusignan. **Cate Buchanan** and **Rebecca Peters** further drafted and edited the text.

References

1 "Three committed to High Court for Lusignan massacre," *Kaieteur News Online* 2 May (2010). Available at: www.kaieteurnewsonline.com/2010/05/02/three-committed-to-high-court-for-lusignan-massacre/ Accessed 27 November 2012
2 Interviews conducted by Roxanne Myers and Tomaisha Hendricks with survivor in Lusignan during March and April 2012.
3 "Lusignan massacre trauma remains," *Stabroek News* 28 January (2013). Available at: www.stabroeknews.com/2013/news/stories/01/28/lusignan-massacre-trauma-remains/ Accessed 30 January 2013.
4 "UNDP Support Affected Communities to Rebuild After Lusignan and Bartica killings," *Press Release*, UN Development Programme, 16 May (2006). Available at: www.undp.org.gy/web/pdf/press%20releases/press_release_BTPFTI_signing_May08.pdf Accessed 29 November 2012.
5 Interviews conducted by Roxanne Myers and Tomaisha Hendricks with nine survivors in Lusignan during March and April 2012.

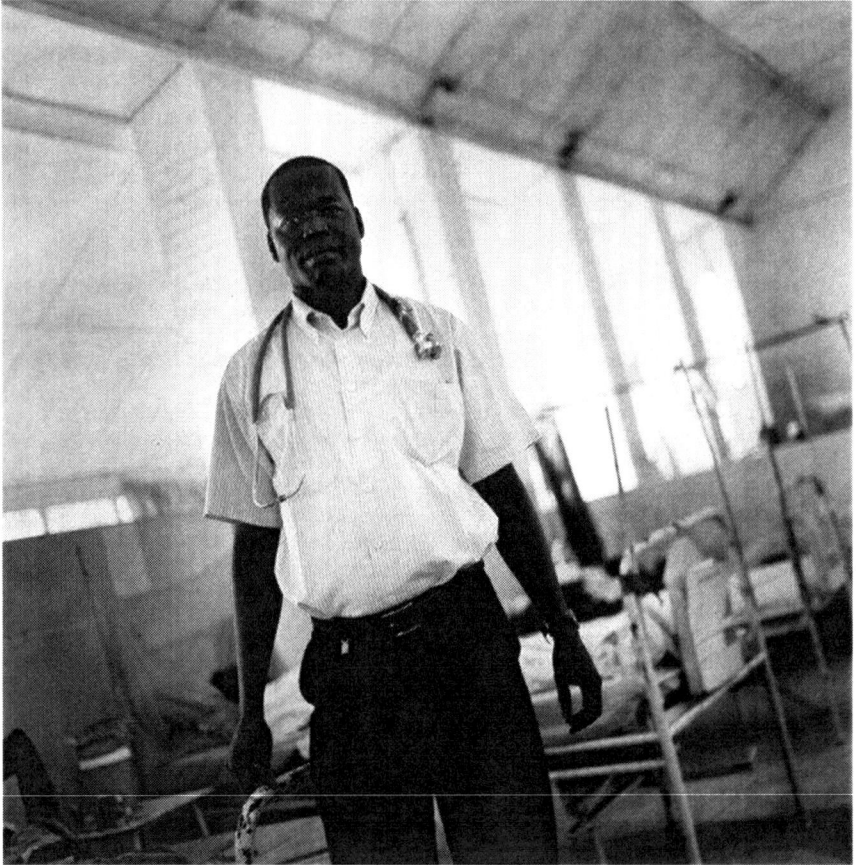

Dr. Dario, Head Surgeon, Juba Teaching Hospital, Sudan. Juba is the only surgical hospital in the whole of Equatoria. Post-signing of the 2003-2004 peace agreements roads opened up and people could travel more freely resulting in more people presenting for gunshot injury care. (Image: Kate Holt, March 2006. Image was part of the Centre for Humanitarian Dialogue exhibition, "Men and Guns")

SPOTLIGHT SECTION
Mental Illness Provisions in Gun Laws

My father didn't survive gun violence. He was shot in the head and chest five times with a .22 semiautomatic pistol from a distance of little more than a metre. After the first shot he tried to run but he was in a small unit in an inner city suburb of Sydney. There was nowhere to run and he died quickly.

The shooter was my sister, who had suffered from schizophrenia for more than ten years. She had paranoid delusions about our father and felt her life was in danger. She believed her only chance of survival was to kill him. For her it was an act of self-defence, despite the fact our father was a loving, peaceful and gentle man. Knowing her, how much she loved our Dad and understanding how her illness corrupted her mind, I can understand how she came to feel the way she did. What I cannot understand is how she came to be in possession of a loaded gun and how our supposedly protective systems could have failed so spectacularly.

The pistol was registered and belonged to a sporting shooters club where, earlier that day, she had been learning how to shoot. My sister had joined the club some weeks earlier. On the day of the shooting she practiced at the club then stole the pistol and returned home with it. The club eventually noticed the pistol was missing and called my sister at 14.21. She didn't answer. At 15.00 our father entered her apartment. At 15.12 the club captain called the police. At about that time my sister was shooting my father and minutes later she rang the police herself to tell them she had killed our father.

My sister had a long and well-documented history of mental illness, of which the police were aware. Yet she was able to join two gun clubs and learn how to shoot. How could someone so obviously unsuitable be given access to guns? All she had to do was fill in some paperwork. When it came to a question of whether she had a mental illness, she simply lied. There was no obligation on the club to check the truth of her answers and there were no background checks.

Australian gun laws
Guns laws in Australia were dramatically strengthened following a mass shooting in Tasmania in 1996.[1] State and territory laws were modified to produce a near-uniform national system of firearm regulation. The reforms led to the world's largest civilian weapons collection and destruction process and some 750,000 to a million guns removed from circulation.[2] These changes led to a decline in firearm homicide and suicide.[3] However, the last decade has seen state and territory governments slowly weaken the laws through amendments. Australians can no longer claim to have some of the strongest gun laws in the world.

In New South Wales (NSW), the gun lobby is strong—not because it enjoys wide support among the public, but because its political party, the Shooters and Fishers Party, holds the balance of power in one house of parliament. For several years this has enabled the party to make deals with the successive state governments, voting with the government in exchange for weaker gun laws.[4] In 2008 one such deal saw the gun laws amended to allow unlicensed individuals to shoot and receive training at firing ranges, as my sister did. The only requirement is that the individual fill in a form stating they do not suffer from mental illness, or have a previous conviction, or have a current apprehended violence order against them. Oversight is the responsibility of the NSW Firearms Registry, which has admitted that "generally no checks are undertaken."[5]

Lalin Fernando, 2008. (Image courtesy of Michelle Fernando)

Strengthening the NSW gun laws

The gun lobby wanted to make it easier to access guns for sport. They got what they wanted but at what cost to my family? My sister is still detained. I still have nightmares and panic attacks. My mother is still a widow, broken hearted and consumed with worry for her sick child. And nothing will bring my Dad back.

My family has been campaigning for an amendment to the law that enabled my sister to get access to a gun. This amendment would require individuals to be licensed before being able to shoot guns. The licensing process would involve background checks to screen out those unsuitable to be given access to firearms. This is far safer than the current system of self reporting. To date, two successive governments have failed to make that simple amendment.

Contributor: Michelle Fernando, Sydney, Australia.

References

[1] On 28 April 1996, a 28-year old man killed 35 people and wounded 23 more. He was sentenced to 35 life sentences. See: R. Peters, "Rational Firearm Regulation: Evidence based gun laws in Australia," In D. Webster and J. Vernick (Eds) *Reducing Gun Violence in America* (Baltimore: Johns Hopkins University Press, 2013), pp. 195-204. Available at: http://jhupress.files.wordpress.com/2013/01/1421411113_updf.pdf Accessed 4 June 2013.

[2] P. Alpers, "The Big Melt: How one democracy changed after scrapping a third of its firearms" In D. Webster and J. Vernick (2013), pp. 205-211. Available at: http://jhupress.files.wordpress.com/2013/01/1421411113_updf.pdf Accessed 4 June 2013.

[3] A. Leigh and C. Neill, "Do gun buybacks save lives? Evidence from panel data," *American Law and Economics Review* 12 (2010), pp. 462-508. Available at: http://aler.oxfordjournals.org/content/early/2010/08/20/aler.ahq013.short?rss=1 Accessed 4 June 2013.

[4] In April 2011 a new government came into power in NSW, one that is less dependent on the Shooters Party to pass legislation. However, the Party still holds considerable influence. In June 2012, the Government, Shooters Party and Christian Democrats Party struck a deal (in exchange for votes to privatise the energy sector) to enable shooting for sport in national parks. See: H. Aston, "Seasoned shooter joins opposition to hunting in state national parks," *The Sydney Morning Herald* 12 April (2013). Available at: www.smh.com.au/nsw/seasoned-shooter-joins-opposition-to-hunting-in-state-national-parks-20130411-2hokl.html#ixzz2TVGZGy4W Accessed 4 June 2013. Also see: http://nohunting.wildwalks.com/

[5] G. Jacobsen, "Gun death triggers battle to close pistol club and limit access to weapons," *The Sydney Morning Herald* 22 January (2011). Available at: www.smh.com.au/nsw/gun-death-triggers-battle-to-close-pistol-club-and-limit-access-to-weapons-20110121-19zzw.html#ixzz2SBGvadwt Accessed 4 June 2013.

Graffiti in the central plaza, Guatemala City. (Image: Heidi Schumann, 2006)

"May we come to see this garden cherish life for the sake of those who died
Cherish compassion for the sake of those who gave aid
Cherish peace for the sake of those in pain"

Words engraved in stone around a pool of remembrance at the site of
Australia's largest ever civilian gun massacre at the historical tourist site
Port Arthur in Tasmania. On 28 April 1996, a heavily armed young man
murdered 35 people, including children. Nineteen people were injured.
Twelve days later, spurred by public pressure, uniform national gun
laws were introduced by the Federal Government. This in turn led to the
world's largest civilian weapons buy back and destruction in history.

Border Security Force troops run for cover as they attempt to flush out two militants inside a house in Srinagar, Kashmir. (Ami Vitale/Panos, September 2002)

10 India

Introduction

Gun violence in India takes many forms: armed conflict, organised crime, electoral violence, caste clashes, interpersonal and gender-based violence. At present there is little accurate data on firearm fatalities; much less on people injured by gun violence. Sparse attention has been paid by Indian policymakers, advocates and researchers to firearm injuries and the needs and rights of those impaired by gun violence. Some survivor assistance policies have developed relatively recently, although they generally only provide compensation for people affected by armed conflict. These schemes take three forms: government initiatives, support from civil society organisations and state partnerships with NGOs. This chapter outlines these initiatives, and examines the challenges in assisting survivors at two levels: government policy and individual experiences based on survivor's perspectives.

Section 1: Violence in India

Violence in India is part of a broad range of challenges, which include landless peasants, development-induced displacement, gender-based violence, armed conflicts, poverty, discrimination based on caste, sex and religion, and trafficking in drugs and firearms. In 2009, criminal violence caused more than 14 times as many violent deaths as internal armed conflict.[1] However, as this chapter is a first effort to assess assistance to gun violence survivors in India it focuses specifically on gun violence related to armed conflict on this occasion.

Armed conflicts take place primarily in the north (in Jammu and Kashmir), northeast (spread over the states of Assam, Arunachal Pradesh, Manipur, Meghalaya, Mizoram, Nagaland and Tripura) and Naxal-affected regions (across the states of Chhattisgarh, West Bengal, Jharkhand and Orissa).[2] Data on India's armed conflicts are typically derived from two sources: a) the National Crime Records Bureau (NCRB), the police agency operating under the Ministry of Home Affairs (MHA); and b) the South Asia Terrorism Portal (SATP), an independent think tank that compiles data on terrorism and armed conflict from published news and government reports.

According to the NCRB national data, from 2001 to 2010 there were 9,517 civilian fatalities attributed to "terrorist and extremist" activity.[3] Importantly, data are limited by categories, and it does not indicate how many of these deaths were by gunshot.[4] The NCRB does have data on shootings by police: 3,716 civilians were injured and 2,615 killed in police shootings from 2001 to 2010. In terms of annual trends, the number of people shot dead by police decreased by 26%, from 309 in 2001 to 239 in 2010, while those wounded increased by 540%, from 110 to 713 over the same period (Figure 1).[5]

Figure 1. Persons killed and injured in police shootings 2001-2010

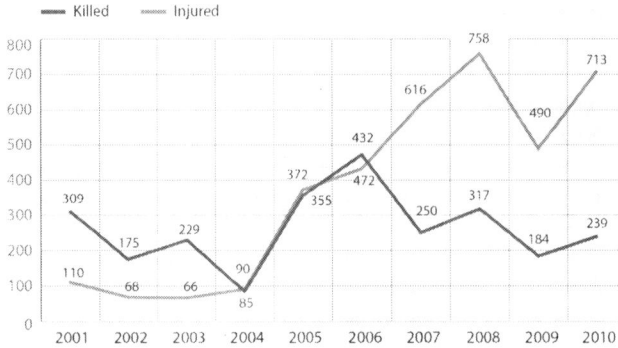

Source: National Crime Records Bureau, *Crime in India* (Delhi: NCRB, 2012). Data from: Table 14.2, Persons Killed Or Injured in Police Firing During 2001-2010, p. 564.

The NCRB data must be read with caution, due to underreporting, poor data collection practices, inconsistent data collection efforts across jurisdictions,[6] and suppression of information due to corruption.[7] These problems give rise to glaring discrepancies.[8]

For 2001 to 2010, the NCRB reported 86,181 gun-related homicides, suicides and unintentional deaths (Figure 2). Gun homicides decreased dramatically over the decade, from 8,019 to 3,064. Unintentional deaths have also decreased from 2,688 in 2001 to 1,688 in 2010, however there has been an increase from the minimum of 1,504 reported in 2009. In contrast, suicides have fluctuated between a minimum of 353 and a maximum of 752 in the same time period, with 666 reported suicides in 2010.[9] It is not possible to identify specific factors affecting the trends, since NCRB reports do not provide information on the circumstances of shootings.

Figure 2. Gun fatalities by intent: homicides, suicides, unintentional

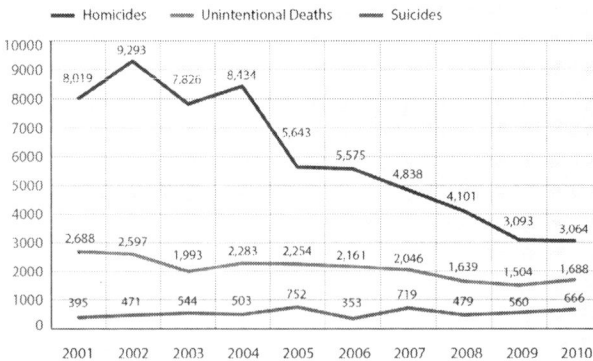

Source: National Crime Records Bureau, *Crime in India* (Delhi: NCRB, 2012). Data from: Table 3.7, Homicides, p. 340; National Crime Records Bureau, *Accidental Deaths and Suicides in India* (Delhi: NCRB, 2012). Data from: Table 1.11, Unintentional deaths—Number of Persons Injured & Died by Un-Natural Causes, p. 106 and Table 2.9, Suicides—Incidence of Suicides Categorised According to Means Adopted 2001-2010, p. 205.

India's gun death rate is not high by international standards—for example, 3,000 gun homicides is 0.25 per 100,000 people, roughly similar to most European countries. However, the national statistics conceal regional variations, which have implications for context-specific survivor assistance programmes. Again reliable data precludes clear disaggregation of injuries and deaths by type of violence. Table 1 however provides figures for the states with the highest gun homicide rates in 2010. Several of these states are affected by insurgencies and armed conflicts, others have high crime rates. In Kashmir, for example, one in ten people are estimated to have lost a member of their nuclear family in the conflict, and a third of the population reportedly has lost a member of their extended family.[10]

Table 1. States with the highest rates of gun homicides 2010

Ranking	State	Firearm homicide rate per 100,000 people
1	Manipur	1.48
2	Nagaland	0.76
3	Jharkhand	0.75
4	Bihar	0.71
5	Jammu and Kashmir	0.65
6	Haryana	0.58
7	Uttar Pradesh	0.45

Source: National Crime Records Bureau, *Crime in India* (Delhi: NCRB, 2012). Data from: Table 3.7, Number of victims murdered by use of firearms, 2001-2010, p. 340.

A 2005 study of 1,248 gun homicide victims from 1986-2003 by the Regional Institute of Medical Sciences (RIMS) in Imphal (Manipur) found that civilians comprised 53.8% of the total victims—28.3% killed by unknown groups or individuals, 21.2% by militants, and 4.3% by security forces. The victims were overwhelmingly male (98%). The largest age group (50.6%) was aged 21 to 30 years, followed by 20.5% aged 31 to 40 years.[11]

The significance of the above study is that it allows for a disaggregation of firearm violence in terms of victimisation. In aggregate terms, data from the Department of Forensic Medicine at RIMS concludes there were 3,599 fatalities caused by firearms from 1991 to 2009.[12] In the same time period there were 205 fatalities from explosive related incidents, 264 from sharp weapon injuries, and 532 from blunt weapon injuries.[13] The fact that firearm injuries constituted the highest number of cases being registered for autopsy at the Department is significant, as it outweighs all the other types of violent deaths. A more recent database found that there were 241 civilian fatalities and 104 injuries directly attributable to firearms between 2008 and 2009.[14] In the same two-year period there were 616 fatalities among suspected members of armed groups—of whom security forces killed 581 and other non-state actors killed 35. These fatalities have also been directly attributed to the use of firearms.[15]

Guns violence: Sources, types and trends

In 2006 (the most recent credible estimate), it was calculated that India had roughly 40 million civilian-owned firearms, of which about 6.3 million were licensed.[16] The regulation of civilian ownership of firearms began with the 1878 *Arms Act*, enacted by the British colonial government to restrict the carrying of arms following the mutiny of 1857.[17] The *Act* was replaced by the 1959 *Arms Act* and the 1962 *Arms Rules*, which currently regulate the acquisition, possession, manufacture, sale, import, export, and transport of arms and ammunition. Section 3(1) of the *Act* prohibits acquiring, possessing or carrying any firearms or ammunition without a license.[18] Applications are submitted through the police in each state and licenses are to be renewed every three years.[19] Critics argue that the *Act*'s provisions are outdated and inadequate to meet the realities of contemporary gun ownership, access and use in India.[20] In 2010, the central government introduced amendments to the gun control laws, expressing concern about the proliferation of firearms and ammunition (Box 1).[21]

NCRB data estimates the number of legal and illegal firearms reported in gun-related homicides from 2001-2010, with the latter used in up to 92% of recorded firearm homicides.[22] It is also common to read about incidents involving rudimentary craft weapons, whose inferior quality results in unintentional injuries (fatal and non-fatal). India has yet to create a national firearms database—or an injury surveillance system.

Box 1: Strengthening India's gun laws and the rise of the pro-gun lobby[23]

In August 2010, the then Minister for Home Affairs, Shri P. Chidambaram introduced the Arms (Amendment) Bill, which requires a police report before the granting of an arms licence. Under the existing law, if the police report is not received within the "prescribed time" (which remains undefined), the licensing authority has the discretionary power to issue the licence without the report. If and when the Bill becomes law, no licence will be granted without a police verification report, and police authorities will be held accountable for failure to furnish this report within 60 days. This also aims to prevent corruption in the licensing process. The onus will be on the police to ensure that a diligent verification process is undertaken and arms licences are granted only to people with appropriate identification and meeting existing criteria for weapons ownership.

The proposed changes spurred a highly visible mobilisation of gun control opponents, leading to the emergence of the National Association for Gun Rights India (NAGRI). NAGRI has demonstrated that it has influential supporters and access to policymakers. In August 2010, a delegation of parliamentarians from various political parties met with Prime Minister Singh to deliver a memorandum opposing the proposed changes.[24] It remains to be seen how strong and sustainable this gun lobby will be. A counterpoint to the gun lobby is the Control Arms Foundation of India (CAFI), established in 2004, and whom are active in advocating against small arms proliferation.

Section 2: Victims and survivors

Survivors of gun violence include combatants (state and non-state) and civilians. The two groups have different experiences in terms of care, assistance and survival. As previous research has helped establish concerns regarding recognised combatants, and because they are vastly outnumbered by affected civilians, this chapter focuses on civilian survivors.

Viewed as a health and human rights challenge, firearm-related injury and impairment is under-examined. For example, after two decades of violent conflict in Kashmir, more has been written about injuries from the 2005 Kashmir earthquake than about those from the violent conflict. This is significant, as injuries sustained in armed conflict tend to be far more serious than those of natural disasters. In Kashmir, injuries related to gunfire or explosions produce complex craniocerebral, chest, and diaphragmatic injuries. Inpatient mortality is 88%, with most victims dying within 30 minutes of hospital admission.[25] Medical supplies are expensive and only available intermittently; and, for security reasons, medical personnel are reluctant to practice in conflict areas. Health facilities are closed intermittently due to the risks posed by armed conflict in Manipur, Assam and Nagaland, resulting in displaced healthcare workers, and further undermining health service delivery.

Serious injuries have a large impact on the consumption of healthcare resources in the poorly funded Indian health system. A severely injured victim with gunshot wounds can consume an estimated INR38-51,000 (USD720-970) worth of transport, medical investigations, and aggressive treatment within the first hour following the injury.[26] The national government's health care budget in 2012-13 is USD6 billion, or USD4 per person in the Indian population.[27] As a comparison, USD40.4 billion was allocated for the military budget.[28]

Box 2. Profile: Javed Ahmad Tak

I am 38 years old, a Muslim male living in the Anantnag district of Jammu and Kashmir (J&K).

At the time of the injury, I was staying with my aunt and cousin while my uncle went to Delhi for cancer treatment. My cousin, affiliated to the then ruling party in J&K, the National Conference, was being targeted by militants for being a politician. Shortly after midnight, on 21 March 1997, I woke to the sound of strangers breaking into the house in an attempt to kidnap my cousin. In the ensuing melee and indiscriminate firing, I was shot at from close range. I was hit by a bullet in my spine, resulting in an injury which left me wheelchair-bound. I lost my right kidney, spleen, a part of my liver and intestine. At age 21, my life was changed forever. After the incident, no police or paramilitary force came to record the event or to help us. The police eventually closed my file for no clear reason. Even after I located the people who had shot me, and informed the police, they were unresponsive. I withdrew my complaint fearing for the safety of family members.

At the time of the injury, the family called a local doctor, who could provide only first aid. An ambulance arrived and I was driven to Shri Maharaja Hari Singh Hospital (Srinagar). At the time of my injury, there were no rehabilitation centres for spinal injuries. If I had accessed rehabilitation I may have been able to reduce some level of impairment, but the first time I got to have any rehabilitation was ten years later in New Delhi. In the meantime I suffered from pressure sores badly and lost further functioning in my feet. My right side hip joint was dislocated but it was too late to correct it.

I consulted many specialists in the private sector and went to the Indian Spinal Injuries Centre in New Delhi, where a large amount was charged for my personal rehabilitation treatment. My father had to pay for all my surgeries, selling our property in order to do so. After one year of treatment in Delhi, I returned to Srinagar and was unable to live normally or continue my treatment because there was no rehabilitation or counselling centres that could have trained me further to live independently. I remained confined to bed most of the time. My family assisted in my rehabilitation, even though they were not trained to do this. My parents were not ready to take me from hospital in Delhi, but hospital authorities forcibly discharged me and surprisingly the doctors did not advise any further rehabilitation. A correction in my hip joint, rehabilitation and counselling would have helped tremendously in my recovery, however after being discharged, the inconsistent treatment and lack of rehabilitation increased my disabilities.

After becoming physically disabled, my perceptions of society changed. As a person dealing with disability, I am deeply troubled by the constant social stigma and the obstacles we face in terms of right to employment, health care and education. The government assistance to which we are entitled is not provided on time. We have to go through several bureaucratic procedures to get the relevant certificates, in order to be eligible for government victim assistance programmes. People with disabilities often have to pay bribes to clerks and police for providing these verification certificates.

One of the biggest challenges disabled people face in J&K is having no source of steady income or employment. In Kashmir, a disabled person is given INR400 (USD7) per month as social security: INR200 (USD3.50) from the central government and an equal amount through the state Department of Social Welfare. In addition, the Ministry of Home Affairs helps victims of militancy, providing INR750 (USD13.50) per month under the National Communal Harmony programme. Given our costly ongoing medical expenses, we cannot sustain ourselves on this level of financial assistance. This is the main reason why disabled people are not accepted by society and are perceived as a burden, even by our families. We are not considered productive.

After the attack, to overcome my depression and distress, I started a new life from my bed, teaching children from poor families. After this, I found that society—and particularly my own community—was more accepting of me and needed me. This inspired me to continue my studies, initially distance courses in human rights and computing, and later a Master's degree in social work at Kashmir University.

In social work I learned different techniques to work for the welfare of people who are physically and mentally challenged. Since then I have fought continuously for the rights of the physically challenged. I filed a public interest lawsuit in J&K High Court, which led to the government services Recruitment Boards implement quotas for the physically challenged. There exists a 3% state quota for the employment of the people with physical impairments. Previously the J&K 1995 *Disability Act* was ignored by the recruiting agencies which were extremely discriminatory in this regard; however from 2001 the enforcement of the Act has been monitored.[29] In 2000, I founded the Humanity Welfare Organization (HELPline) working for the rights of persons with disabilities in J&K state.

In 2007, I opened a school, Zaiba Aapa Institute of Inclusive Education for disabled children—the first of its kind. This was possible due to the one-time payment of INR75,000 (USD1,370) I received from the J&K government. This is given to militancy victims who are regarded as having no links with militants. I refused it for six years on point of principle but eventually took it to establish the school.

While I was studying, I found that despite the *Disability Act*, universities and other educational institutions mostly ignored the needs of disabled students. At Kashmir University I organised the students to put pressure on the university authorities and claim their rights. Going around the university identifying peers was a great source of pleasure and an important part of my life; this enabled me to create bonds outside of my family for the first time. Our efforts paid off: for example, the university built ramps at the entrance of seven buildings. World Disability Day was celebrated at Kashmir University for the first time on 3 December 2005. The biggest achievement there is the opening of a special unit for the students with disabilities, motivating them towards higher education and research programmes. The unit is fully sponsored by University Grants Commission of India.

Widows and female caregivers

Violent conflict can change social structures, networks, and relations. During periods of conflict, female—and child-headed households increase, as adolescent and adult males have typically gone into exile, joined fighting forces, died, or disappeared.[30] In India these female heads of households confront not only economic difficulties but also difficult social circumstances: "their freedom of movement, ability to claim rights, justice and assert entitlements is socially constrained in societies where women without the 'protector' male are vulnerable; education and marriage plans are disrupted, and as the double burden is assumed, their own health is compromised."[31] Widowhood in South Asia very often leads to loss of dignity, identity and autonomy, since women become dependent on their relatives.[32] They are frequently denied inheritance and property rights, and are sexually harassed.

Many female survivors and caregivers are left out of government programmes for relief and rehabilitation in Indian conflict areas. For example, while relief is given to widows of men killed by militants in several states, there is little mention of assistance to wives, mothers or children of men who have disappeared. This has been the experience of Neena Ningombamin, a widow in Manipur (Box 5). Moreover, the needs of survivors of sexual violence are not specifically noted or included in the assistance available.[33]

Section 3: Standards and normative frameworks

Disability in India is defined by the 1995 *Persons with Disabilities (Equal Opportunities, Protection of Rights and Full Participation) Act* (PDA). The law defines a person living with disability as "a person suffering from not less than 40% of any disability as certified by a medical authority."[34] Thus, eligibility for disability-related legal protection is based on the medical model of disability and focused on impairment and functioning.

New Delhi, International Day of Persons with Disabilities. (Image: Courtesy of Disabled Rights Group, India, 3 December 2012)

It is estimated that between 55 and 90 million people in India are living with disability.[35] Besides the PDA, India has four additional relevant laws: the 1987 *Mental Health Act*; the 1992 *Rehabilitation Council of India Act*; and the 1999 *National Trust for Welfare of Persons with Autism, Cerebral Palsy, Mental Retardation* and the *Multiple Disabilities Act*. In principle, every *panchayat* (local government) is allocated government funding to build or amend public facilities for those with physical impairments; and 3% of all government jobs are reserved for people with impairment(s). However, 2006 government estimates (seemingly conservative) still put seven million people with impairments as seeking paid work.[36]

In 2007 India ratified the 2006 UN *Convention on the Rights of Persons with Disabilities* (CRPD). However, this did not include signature of the Optional Protocol enabling citizens to pursue complaints about breaches to the CRPD with the UN Committee charged with reviewing national reports and complaints from citizens once all domestic avenues have been exhausted (for more detail on the CRPD, see Annex 1). In theory there are several avenues for complaint in India, a leading one being through the National Human Rights Commission (NHRC), which also has a Special Rapporteur on Disability. This position has a national investigatory role and provides for the Rapporteur to submit recommendations to the NHRC, which can then direct states to take action to change laws and policies. Despite this, India's existing laws related to disability rights are regarded as poorly implemented, with weak accountability from official actors.[37]

There are however efforts underway to harmonise existing laws with CRPD obligations. In September 2012, the Ministry of Social Justice and Empowerment put forward the draft Rights of the Persons with Disabilities Bill which aims to replace the PDA.[38] It provides for further social and economic protection, and includes incentives in the form of tax breaks to private sector for employing people experiencing disability. If the Bill is passed, it will apply nationwide except in Jammu and Kashmir. The reason for the latter is unclear.[39]

Importantly, India's official victim assistance policies do not refer to any international standards such as the CRPD. They appear to be written in isolation from these standards and to ensure these policies reflect commitment to existing obligations is an area of future policymaking. There is no overarching victims' rights law, though efforts are underway to develop one in the coming years.[40]

While the literature on disability in developing countries is limited, a 2011 World Bank study found that people with severe impairments in India have limited access to healthcare, and spend 1.3 times more on healthcare than their able-bodied counterparts.[41] What seems particularly poorly understood in the Indian context (and seemingly elsewhere too) are the impacts of mental illness and disorders, particularly those related to violence and armed conflict. Protracted conflicts expose populations to mental health stressors for long periods.[42] Reflecting a desperate mental health situation, the casualty ward at the main hospital in Imphal received attempted suicide cases as 5.1% of all its patients between 2006 and 2009.[43] As an indicator of poor mental health, a 2006 study in Kashmir in two violence-affected, rural districts concluded that one-third of individuals thought about ending their life.[44] How this compares to other zones of conflict in India is unclear. What is known is that the NCRB reported the average rate of suicide in India is 11.4 per 100,000—yet in locations with insurgencies and ongoing violent conflict, rates are far higher, for example in Sikkim (45.9), Chhattisgarh (26.6), Tripura (20.1) and in West Bengal (17.8).[45]

Section 4: Assistance to survivors

Government agencies have a principal obligation to deliver long-term assistance and rehabilitation support across the country. However, they tend to have restrictive eligibility criteria, which exclude certain categories of survivors and caregivers. On the other hand, civil society initiatives are generally more inclusive, but funding shortages and limited organisational capacity often hampers their effectiveness. Examples are included in Box 3. Ideally the two sectors would increase cooperation (see Box 4). The following section describes and analyses examples of assistance available for survivors of gun violence.

Box 3: Examples of survivor assistance provided by central and state governments and NGOs

Some major policies and programmes illustrate some of the initiatives underway in India including:

National level:
In 2008 the MHA introduced its *Central Scheme for Assistance to civilian victims/family of victims of terrorist, communal and Naxal violence.*[46] It provides forms of social security to the families of people killed, and to survivors. Key provisions include:

- Family members are eligible for assistance in the event of death or permanent incapacitation, defined as "a disability of 50% and above suffered by the victim which is of permanent nature and there are no chances of variation in the degree of disability and the injury/disability renders the victim unfit for normal life for the rest of his [sic] life."
- INR300,000 (USD5,480) can be given to the family for each death or permanent incapacitation.
- Beneficiaries are allotted a health card by the district health society, entitling them to free medical treatment for life in respect of injuries and major illnesses caused by the violence.

The National Foundation for Communal Harmony is an autonomous body set up by the central government in 1992 to promote communal harmony and national integration.[47] It provides assistance for the physical and psychological rehabilitation of child victims of communal, caste, ethnic, or terrorist violence.

State level:
In 1995, the Jammu and Kashmir (J&K) government established a Rehabilitation Council with the aim of "providing assistance for the psychological and economic rehabilitation of widows, orphans, handicapped and the elderly who were victims of militancy and cross-border firing."[48] Two decades of violent conflict in the Kashmir Valley has led to a vast pool of affected individuals and families. One estimate, drawing on official data, calculates that between 1988 and 2009, the Kashmir conflict has led to the deaths of some 42,600 people.[49] It functions as an NGO but works closely with the state government with a budget of about INR21 crores (USD3.7 million). The Council provides one-off payments to the next-of-kin of people killed or injured in "militancy." Its development and welfare programmes can provide INR10,000 (USD190) in marriage assistance to young widows or a monthly pension for people with recognised injuries of INR500 (USD9.50).[50] The total number of beneficiaries assisted by the Council since 1995 is not known.

Government of Tripura policy on *Provision of assistance to victims of terrorist and communal violence* (2008).[51] Assistance is provided primarily in the form of monetary support to civilians and family members injured and killed by the violence.

Aashwas (the reassurance) programme organised by UNICEF with the Assam state police. This is a state-NGO partnership, set up in 2001, to assist children who are victims of violence and insurgency.[52]

Implemented at the state level since 2006 through the national MHA Naxal Management Division, for states affected by the Naxalite insurgency—Andhra Pradesh, Chhattisgarh, Maharashtra, Bihar, Jharkhand, Odisha, Uttar Pradesh, Madhya Pradesh and West Bengal. For example, the Security Related Expenditure (SRE) scheme provides a one-off payment of up to INR100,000 (USD1,811) to civilian victims and families in these states, in addition to the assistance provided by the central scheme above. SRE also provides funds for "rehabilitation of Left Wing Extremist cadres who surrender in accordance with the surrender and rehabilitation policy of the State Government concerned."[53]

Non-government level:
Rajiv Gandhi Foundation, through its Initiative to Educate, Rehabilitate and Assist Child Victims of Terrorism (INTERACT) programme, has been supporting children affected by armed conflict across the country since 1993.[54]

Manipur Women's Gun Survivors Network is a network of women affected by gun violence. It focuses on livelihood support for widows, psychosocial support and assistance with healthcare.[55]

Barriers to assistance

Several structural barriers affect government assistance programmes in India. First, the definition of "disability" varies broadly. Terms such as "handicapped", "impaired", "crippled", "deaf and dumb", and "challenged" are used interchangeably in policies and programmes for people living with disability. Related, policymakers appear to use different approaches (e.g. welfare or charity based vs. human rights based) to assess and address disability. These factors likely influence the ambiguous eligibility criteria of assistance schemes.

A second obstacle is the procedural requirements. An applicant for government assistance must furnish multiple documents to the district committee.[56] Such documents include a First Information Report, post-mortem certificate (in the event of death), and medical certificate (in case of permanent impairment).[57] If the victim is a minor, the birth certificate is required; in case of Naxal violence the district Superintendent of Police must issue an "eligibility certificate".[58] In conflict areas, with the collapse or dysfunction of governmental institutions, claimants may be unable to obtain these documents, and this affects their applications. Also, people from rural or poor backgrounds may not have any government registration or other proof of identity. Although most government procedures cater for illiteracy among applicants, there is a lack of awareness of assistance schemes and complicated bureaucratic procedures.

Figure 3. Procedural requirements for claiming survivor assistance from the central government

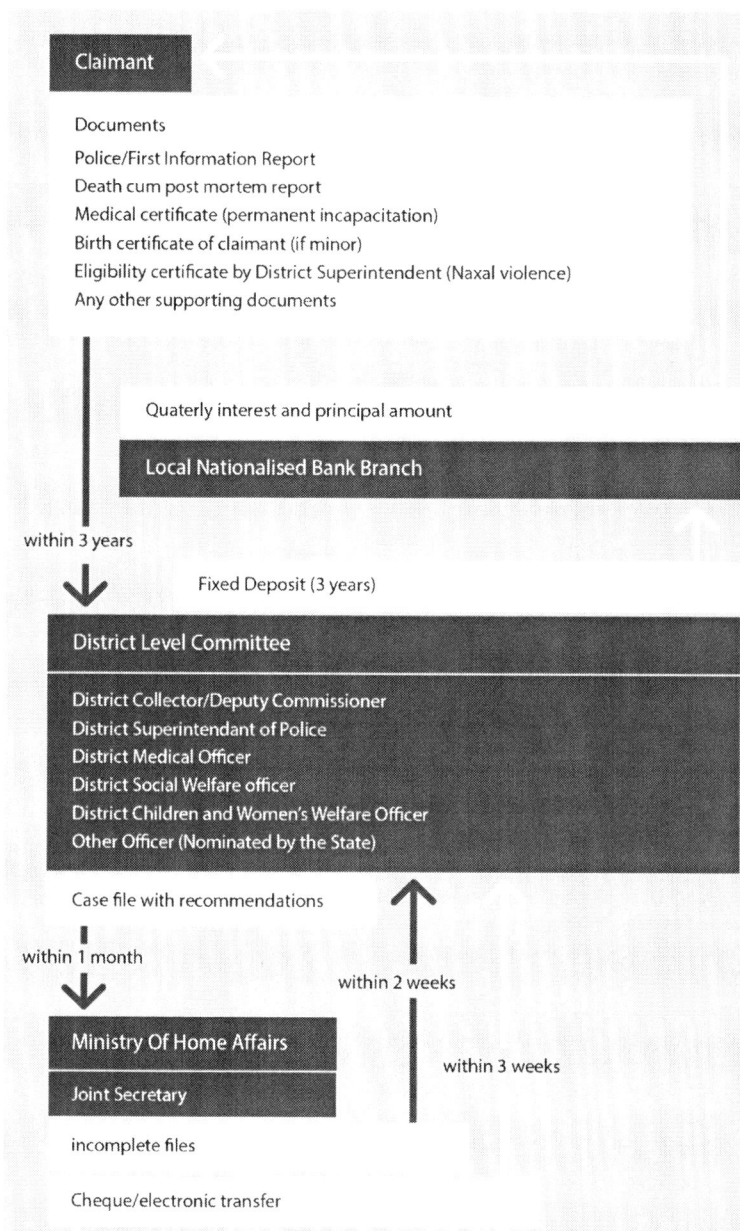

Claimant

Documents

Police/First Information Report
Death cum post mortem report
Medical certificate (permanent incapacitation)
Birth certificate of claimant (if minor)
Eligibility certificate by District Superintendent (Naxal violence)
Any other supporting documents

Quaterly interest and principal amount

Local Nationalised Bank Branch

within 3 years

Fixed Deposit (3 years)

District Level Committee

District Collector/Deputy Commissioner
District Superintendant of Police
District Medical Officer
District Social Welfare officer
District Children and Women's Welfare Officer
Other Officer (Nominated by the State)

Case file with recommendations

within 1 month

within 2 weeks

Ministry Of Home Affairs

Joint Secretary

within 3 weeks

incomplete files

Cheque/electronic transfer

Source: Ministry of Home Affairs, "Revised guidelines of 'Central scheme for assistance to civilians victims/family of victims of terrorist, communal and Naxal violence," (MHA: New Delhi, 2010). Schematic outline created by Siddharth David, Centre for Enquiry Into Health and Allied Themes, Mumbai.

Figure 3 provides an outline of the steps involved for claiming victim assistance from the central government scheme. The figure highlights the bureaucratic maze and procedural complexity faced by survivors trying to engage with the scheme. For instance, having the Superintendent of Police, District Commissioner, District Medical Officer and District Social Welfare Officer in a meeting together, even briefly, requires a high degree of protocol and a time-consuming process of negotiating appointments.

Medical care can also be provided to beneficiaries on a case by case basis as part of policies created by the national Ministry of Health and Family Welfare. For example, the Rashtriya Arogya Nidhi policy enables people to access specialist care at specific facilities for no additional cost.[59] What is not clear is how well these policies are known or utilised.

Throughout India, there is a lack of survivor assistance in the form of government support for the families of people killed or injured by security forces (see Neena Ningombam's story, Box 5). Such barriers to assistance raise serious questions about civilian access to justice, since security forces involved in extrajudicial killings can invoke immunity from prosecution under the *Armed Forces Special Powers Act* (AFSPA).[60] Where they do exist, there are also questions to be asked about the eligibility criteria. For example, government programmes do not assist individuals who are deemed to be "perpetrators"—i.e. insurgents, militants—nor members of their families. In communities affected by violence, many survivors of gun violence are also perpetrators, or related to perpetrators. Rehabilitation of perpetrators is distinct from victim assistance for survivors, and there is very little information on the specifics of these policies in India. This is an important area requiring research, since many perpetrators of gun violence live in the same communities as their victims.

Box 4. Practitioner's perspective: Gajendra K. Goswami

The Indian criminal justice system is mainly accused-oriented; it does not focus on the survivors, and the concept of victim assistance is not recognised or understood. In general, the rights of victims tend to be overlooked, and immediate assistance depends upon the discretionary powers of the person in uniform at that point in time and place. When violent incidents occur, the government tends to recognise primarily the territorial threat to the State. The resulting negative impacts on civilians and those injured do not receive the attention they deserve.

Government provisions for financial assistance focus solely on those affected by acts of terrorism, Naxalism and communal violence. They exclude other prevalent and lethal forms of violence such as organised crime, non-conflict armed violence and caste clashes. Moreover, there is no statutory scheme recognising the rehabilitative needs of such survivors or perpetrators.

The central government's initiative for victims of terrorism, Naxalism and communalism is a step in the right direction to assist families and communities affected by violence, but its actual execution is yet to be achieved. Such initiatives will not have a widespread impact till they are more well known, both at government level and also by the victims, their families and communities, who are not even aware that assistance is legally owed to them, and thus do not ask for it.

Some state governments have schemes offering financial compensation to victims, but this as a one-time handshake, with no long-term responsibility from the state's end towards its citizen.

The only non-monetary provision is the offer of government jobs, with the added criterion that "no other person in the family is in the government sector… Otherwise he/she will receive approximately INR150,000 (USD2,850)."[61] Such types of initiatives are not always sustainable or effective. For example, an elderly person may require other forms of support to even make use of their financial compensation. Also, for someone severely injured from violence, a one-time monetary grant is not a durable solution. Instead they need gainful employment or vocational training to allow them to be partially independent and contribute productively towards society; that should be the goal.

Both NGOs and government(s) have their strengths and weaknesses. NGOs have limited capacity and reach, and in general are not immediately trusted by civilians. However, overall, they are more trained and responsive to the needs of those injured, broken families and widows. On the other hand, government representatives, including members of the security forces, often lack empathy, are insensitive, lack affinity to the community and are less concerned about the needs of local people. However, they have more capacity, such as human resources already in place. If NGOs and government work together more systematically, they will be in a better position to provide immediate assistance and care to survivors, which is very poor across India, except in the cities. This can help save many lives, as many die due to lack of transport, distant hospitals, waiting for many hours to get medical aid. In remote and isolated places emergency help is just not available! As long as assistance programmes continue to work in isolation, the people who need help will suffer.

Practical steps to increase awareness could include training and sensitisation on survivor assistance for:

- District and sub-division police and administrative officers;
- Public representatives, including parliamentarians, the legislative assembly and *gram pradhans* (village heads);
- Journalists, who are in a position to generate immense awareness and to report on cases of malpractice, insensitiveness and ineffectiveness of policies.[62]

Assistance by civil society

A major difference between civil society and government support to gun violence survivors is that most civil society initiatives offer assistance to those victimised by both state and non-state actors. Also, such programmes tend to have a higher public profile. Civil society assistance takes two forms: partnerships with government (a hybrid model) or more commonly, independent initiatives.

One such significant organisation is Extrajudicial Execution Victims' Families Association in Manipur (EEVFAM), created in 2009 by women whose husbands were killed by security forces (Box 5). This type of organisation helps women who may not have any other avenues of official assistance. A similar organisation in the same state is Manipur Women Gun Survivors Network (see Box 3).

Box 5. Profile: Neena Ningombam[63]

At 35, Neena Ningombam is a widowed mother of two young sons. Her husband Michael was killed by government soldiers who later claimed he had belonged to a terrorist organisation. Such "fake encounters" are common in Manipur, northeast India.[64] Neena has been unable to secure any financial support from the central government, which does not recognise the violence perpetrated by its own forces. Assisted by the NGO Human Rights Alert, she has launched a lawsuit against the government, seeking financial support, and prosecution of those who killed her husband.

"The fact that Michael was branded as a terrorist is something that weighs heavily against my future and that of my children," she said. "The Department of Social Welfare rejects any support of children and spouses of militant rebels. For attacks by underground groups, the government comes up with compensation for surviving relatives and offers jobs that would otherwise be much more difficult to get. And we are not eligible for these things either. The National Foundation for Communal Harmony has a fund to help young children of victims of armed conflict to go to school. One of the most important documents you have to include to apply is the police report. In my case, that automatically means 'Application denied.' Nor am I eligible for a widow's pension, simply because there is no pension scheme for women under 40. But most gun widows are under 40! Apart from our lawsuit, what it now comes down to, not only for me but for all women in my situation, is finding our way through the bureaucratic maze of government facilities and welfare programmes."

Ranjeeta Sadokpam from Human Rights Alert explains: "You run up against corruption. The officials distribute public funds to family, friends and 'quid pro quo' networks wherever possible. The last thing the local government does is offer any transparency into its own programmes and policy. That is a constant in Manipur. When someone from an insurgency group is killed in a firefight with police or paramilitaries, the rebel leaders are sometimes willing to pay surviving relatives compensation. It is a very flawed and dubious form of life insurance, but not even this is an option for Neena because Michael had no connection whatsoever with any militant group. She has no one to turn to. She is turned away by literally every party and institution."

After Michael's death, his family helped Neena get an administrative job at a driving school. The management allows Neena to take her youngest son to work when she has no childcare, which is often the case. She earns INR2000 (USD37) per month.

The struggle with bureaucratic institutions drove widows like Neena to establish Extrajudicial Execution Victims Families Manipur (EEVFAM). "In EEVFAM, gun widows combine their strength. We are creating our own fund. This is excruciatingly slow, because nearly all our members are women from poor families. But we are supporting each other psychologically, socially and financially, and we are organising our legal support by working with local human rights organisations. To my knowledge, no gun widow has yet won a case. But the more cases surviving families start, the greater the legal pressure and the greater the chance that we will win a case somewhere down the road."

Neena further notes: "In Manipur, there are now scores of government programmes for AIDS patients, and for AIDS orphans and widows. This is necessary and it is good. It is something that governments anywhere in the world, including India, can find money for. And for victims of terrorists, there is always attention and lots of money available. But victims and survivors of fake encounters and state terror have nowhere to turn. The subject is politically taboo, the widows are stigmatised and anyone who makes waves risks terrible consequences. This is why local organisations like EEVFAM are so important."

Conclusion

Gun violence in India exists in many forms. This chapter focussed on the civilian survivors of armed conflict, and addressed the recent development of policies created to assist survivors and their families. Present assistance schemes take three forms: government initiatives, civil society programmes, and state partnerships with NGOs. These initiatives, however, are better on paper than in practice: scale remains small and access is impeded by lack of timely implementation of holistic support to survivors.

A key finding of this chapter is that the lack of reliable data inhibits focussed analysis and discussion. Assessing and responding to the needs of gun violence survivors requires reliable evidence to design and implement effective assistance programmes and policies. Due in part to this lack of evidence, and in part to a limited understanding and weak institutional responses, survivors face a daunting series of challenges in accessing the assistance they are entitled to and deserve.

Recognising this as a topic for detailed investigation and systematic action is a crucial policy step for the central and state governments. There is also a need to look beyond armed conflict at other forms of gun violence prevalent in India—especially violence related to crime and interpersonal violence—in order to more holistically address the needs and rights of all gun violence survivors.

Contributors: **Sonal Marwah**, Project Coordinator, India Armed Violence Assessment of the Small Arms Survey, Switzerland. **Nobhojit Roy**, visiting Professor of Public Health, Tata Institute of Social Sciences and Chief of Surgery at BARC Hospital in Mumbai, India. **Samrat Sinha**, Assistant Professor and Assistant Director, Centre for Study of Political Violence, Jindal School of International Affairs, India. **Ouseph Tharakan**, Project Officer, Centre for Humanitarian Dialogue in Singapore, writing in his personal capacity. **Cate Buchanan** and **Rebecca Peters** undertook drafting, fact checking and editing. **Mireille Widmer** and **Emile LeBrun** provided additional editing.

Box contributors: **Gajendra K. Goswami**, Deputy Inspector of Police and Operation Chief of Anti-Terrorist Squad in Uttar Pradesh. Currently working at the United Nations Office on Drugs and Crime's Regional Office for South Asia; **Javed Tak**, Humanity Welfare Organization, Jammu and Kashmir (India).

Peer reviews were provided by **Aaron Karp**, Small Arms Survey (USA); **K. Jaishankar**, Department of Criminology and Criminal Justice, Manonmaniam Sundaranar University, Tamil Nadu and President of the South Asian Society of Criminology and Victimology (India); **Anil Kohli**, Department of Forensic Medicine, University College of Medical Sciences (India); and **Javed Tak**, Humanity Welfare Organization, Jammu and Kashmir (India). Additional thanks to: **Bina Lakshmi Nepram** of the Manipur Women's Gun Violence Survivors Network (India); and **Dorodi Sharma** and **Javed Abidi**, Director of the National Centre for Promotion of Employment for Disabled People and Chairperson of Disabled People's International (India).

References

[1] Small Arms Survey, "India's States of Armed Violence: Assessing the Human Cost and Political Priorities," *India Armed Violence Assessment*, Issue Brief, No 1, September (Geneva: SAS, 2011 a).

[2] Naxalites or Naxalism is named after a village in West Bengal where peasants rose up against landlords in 1967, rejecting existing communist parties in the process of establishing a new vision for communist ideology. For further background see, J. Harriss, *The Naxalite/Maoist Movement in India: A Review of Recent Literature*, ISAS Working Paper, No. 109, 8 July (2010). Also see: Centre for Humanitarian Dialogue and the Delhi Policy Group, "Case Study One: Talks between Maoists and the Government in Andhra Pradesh in 2004," In *Conflict resolution: Learning lessons from dialogue processes in India* (Geneva: HD Centre, 2011), pp. 8-20.

[3] National Crime Records Bureau armed conflicts data is included under extremist and terrorist violence. National Crime Records Bureau, *Crime in India* (Delhi: NCRB, 2012 a). Data from: Table 3.2, Motives Of Murder And Culpable Homicide Not Amounting To Murder 2001-2010, p. 330.

[4] Only four categories exist in the NCRB data: Riot control, 'other', anti-dacoity operations and operations against terrorist and extremists. See: http://ncrb.nic.in/cii2010/cii-2010/Table%2014.2.pdf Accessed 20 November 2012.

[5] National Crime Records Bureau (2012 a). Data from: Table 14.2, Persons Killed Or Injured in Police Firing, recorded under 'Against extremist and terrorists 2001-2010,' p. 564.

[6] Regarding data collection, the NCRB's central database relies on statistics reported by all state and city police agencies, and the quality of data collection varies amongst the different police stations.

[7] Small Arms Survey (2011 a).

[8] Small Arms Survey, "A Heavy Hand—The Use of Force by India's Police," *India Armed Violence Assessment*, Issue Brief No.3 (Geneva: SAS, 2012).

[9] National Crime Records Bureau, *Accidental Deaths and Suicides in India* (Delhi: NCRB, 2012 b). Data from: Table 1.11, Number of Persons Injured or Killed by Un-natural causes, p. 106 and Table 2.9, Distribution of Suicides by Means adopted during 2010, p. 205.

[10] K. de Jong, N. Ford, S van de Kam, K. Lokuge, S. Fromm, R. van Galen, B. Reilley and R. Kleber, "Conflict in the Indian Kashmir Valley I: Exposure to violence," *Conflict and Health* 2/11 (2008), p. 10.

[11] K. Pradipkumar, F. Marak, S. Keisham, M. Phom and A. Momonchand, "Homicidal fatal firearm injuries," *Journal of Indian Academy of Forensic Medicine* 27/4 (2005), pp. 222-225. Note: The RIMS study is exclusively a summary of post-mortem reports of firearm injury victims. The reports attempt to record the type of incident however robbery or a fight is regarded as a "motivation" and not recorded in the medical report. For this information police data would be the source of information and need to be matched up to the post-mortem report.

[12] Display Board, Department of Forensic Medicine, Regional Institute of Medical Sciences (RIMS), Imphal. Data collected in November 2010 as part of the research process, *Manipur Conflict Risk, Vulnerability and Impact Project*, conducted from 2010 to 2012.

[13] Display Board, Department of Forensic Medicine, RIMS, Imphal (2010).

[14] The Manipur Micro Level Insurgency Database 2008-2009 was developed by the Jamsetji Tata Centre for Disaster Management and the Centre for Study of Political Violence. See, S. Sinha and N. Roy, *The Burden of Armed Conflict and Insecurity: A Case Study of Conflict Dynamics in the State of Manipur (2008-2009)*, Unpublished report (2011).

[15] S. Sinha and N. Roy (2011).

[16] Small Arms Survey, "Mapping Murder - The Geography of Indian Firearm Fatalities," *India Armed Violence Assessment*, Issue Brief No.2 (Geneva: SAS, 2012), p.3.

[17] The mutiny in 1857 by Indian soldiers of the British East India Company's army led to rebellion against British rule across large parts of northern and central India. Following the mutiny, governance of India was taken over by the British crown which then undertook a range of military, administrative and legal reforms to tighten their rule over India. The

1878 *Arms Act* was introduced as part of this process. It required Indians to have a licence to possess firearms but exempted Europeans and some categories of government officials from this provision.

18   Ministry of Home Affairs, *Arms and Ammunition Policy for Individuals* (Delhi: MHA, n.d), p. 2, para 4. Available at: www.mha.nic.in/pdfs/AaAPolicyInd-080410.pdf Accessed 20 November 2012.

19   Licences are generally granted only to individuals facing threats to their lives, for protection of properties, and to sportspersons. Licence fees vary depending on the type of weapon.

20   "Citizens have right to possess arms and weapons: Madras high court," *Daily News and Analysis* 19 June (2011). Available at: www.dnaindia.com/india/report_citizens-have-right-to-possess-arms-and-weapons-madras-high-court_1560414 Accessed 28 January 2013.

21   Ministry of Home Affairs (n.d).

22   National Crime Records Bureau (2012 a). Data from: Table 3.7, Number of victims murdered by use of firearms, 2001-2010, p. 340. This was a similar finding in Small Arms Survey (2011 b).

23   Ouseph Tharakan, independent analyst, contributed this box as well as other information in Section 1.

24   "Digvijay attacks MHA for amendments to Arms Act," *Indian Express* August 18 (2010). Available at: www.indianexpress.com/news/digvijay-attacks-mha-for-amendments-to-arms-act/662037/0 Accessed 20 November 2012.

25   B. Rashid, M. Wani, A. Kirmani, T. Raina and U. Altaf, "Analysis of 3794 civilian craniocerebral missile injuries—Results from 20 years of Kashmir conflict," *Pan Arab Journal of Neurosurgery* 14/1 (2010), pp. 24-25.

26   Cost estimation is based on Dr. Nobhojit Roy's personal experience of treating trauma victims in India. This is an estimate of average costs of serious gunshot injuries at a public hospital in Mumbai.

27   "Budget 2012: Health sector gets 34,488 crore, up by 13.24%," *The Economic Times* 16 March (2012). Available at: http://articles.economictimes.indiatimes.com/2012-03-16/news/31201457_1_budget-estimates-plan-outlay-railway-budget Accessed 20 November 2012.

28   L.K. Behera, *India's Defence Budget 2012-13*, Institute for Defence Studies and Analyses. Available at: www.idsa.in/idsacomments/IndiasDefenceBudget2012-13_LaxmanBehera_200312 Accessed 20 November 2012.

29   *Jammu and Kashmir Persons with Disabilities (Equal Opportunities Protection of rights and Full Participation) Act* (1998). Available at: http://india.gov.in/allimpfrms/allacts/3183.pdf.

30   United Nations, *Women, Peace and Security* (New York: UN, 2002), pp. 22-24. Available at: www.un.org/womenwatch/daw/public/eWPS.pdf Accessed 11 November 2012.

31   Interview by Sonal Marwah with Rita Manchanda, South Asian Forum on Human Rights in New Delhi, 4 June 2012.

32   A.D. Shrestha and R. Thapa, "Introduction: Historical background: The nature of conflict in modern South Asia," In A.D. Shrestha and R. Thapa (Eds), *The impacts of armed conflict on women in South Asia* (Colombo: Regional Centre for Strategic Studies, 2007).

33   Interview by Sonal Marwah with Anuradha Chenoy, Professor at School of International Studies, Jawaharlal Nehru University New Delhi in New Delhi, 30 May 2012.

34   International Disability Rights Monitor, *International Disability Rights Monitor: Regional Report of Asia 2005* (Chicago: International Disability Network, 2005), p. 40. Available at: http://idrmnet.org/pdfs/CIR_IDRM_Asia_05.pdf Accessed 11 November 2012.

35   World Bank, *People with Disabilities in India: From Commitment to Outcomes*, Human Development Unit, South Asia Region (Washington DC: The World Bank, 2009).

36   World Bank (2009).

37   Interview by Sonal Marwah with Javed Abidi, Director of the National Centre for Promotion of Employment for Disabled People in India, and founder of the Disability Rights Group, New Delhi, 31 May 2012.

38   An interesting account of some of the efforts and challenges in a document from the NHRC (no date) to the UN Office of the High Commissioner for Human Rights, *Relevant inputs from NHRC, India for the preparation of thematic study by OHCHR in relation to Convention on the Rights of Persons with Disabilities (CRPD) and its optional protocol*. Available at: www2.ohchr.org/english/issues/disability/docs/study/NHRCIndia.doc Accessed 29 November 2012.

39   Ministry of Social Justice and Empowerment, *The Draft Rights of Persons with Disabilities Bill, 2012*, Department of Disability Affairs, September (2012). Available at: http://socialjustice.nic.in/pdf/draftpwd12.pdf Accessed 12 November 2012.

40   A useful overview of standards and key challenges in the area of crime victim support is to be found in K. Chockalingam, *Measures for crime victims in the Indian criminal justice system*, Resource Material Series No. 081, The 144th International Senior Seminar, Visiting Experts Papers (United Nations Asia and Far East Institute for the Prevention of Crime and the Treatment of Offenders, 2010). Available at: www.unafei.or.jp/english/pdf/RS_No81/No81_11VE_Chockalingam.pdf Accessed 28 March 2013.

41   S. Mitra, A. Posarac and B. Vick, *Disability and Poverty in Developing Countries: A Snapshot from the World Health Survey*, Social Protection Discussion Paper No. 1109 (Washington DC: The World Bank, 2011), p. 14. Available at: http://siteresources.worldbank.org/SOCIALPROTECTION/Resources/SP-Discussion-papers/Disability-DP/1109.pdf Accessed 11 November 2012.

42   World Bank, "Conflict Prevention and Reconstruction," *Mental Health and Conflict*, Social Development Notes 13 (Washington DC: The World Bank, 2003).

43   Death Register RIMS Hospital Data collected by Armed Conflict Research and Documentation project, Tata Institute in Mumbai. Data was collected in July 2010.

44   510 semi-structured interviews were conducted. See, Médecins Sans Frontières, *Kashmir: Violence and Health: A quantitative assessment on violence, the psychosocial and general health status of the Indian Kashmiri population* (Netherlands: MSF, 2006). Available at: www.artsenzondergrenzen.nl/pdf/KASHMIRFINALVERSION221106.pdf Accessed 11 November 2012.

45   National Crime Records Bureau, *Crime in India* (Delhi: NCRB, 2012). Table 2.2, Accidents and Suicides in India, Incidence and Rate of Suicides—2010, pp. 191-192.

46   Ministry of Home Affairs, *Revised guidelines of 'Central scheme for assistance to civilians victims / family of victims of terrorist, communal and Naxal violence* (MHA: New Delhi, 2010). Available at: http://mha.nic.in/pdfs/T-Guide141008.pdf Accessed 26 November 2012. This scheme uses the term "terrorism" for militancy and insurgency-related violence and specifically for acts defined in Section 15 of the 1967 *Unlawful Activities (Prevention) Act* (UAPA). Communal violence refers to "planned and organised acts of violence by members of one community against members of another community with the intent of creating or expressing ill-will or hatred and leading to loss of life or injuries to people." Naxal violence refers to "planned and organised acts of violence by members of the Communist Party of India (Maoists), all its formations and front organisations - who have been declared a terrorist organisation and banned under the UAPA".

47   National Foundation for Communal Harmony - Communal Harmony Awards. Available at www.prd.kerala.gov.in/nfch.pdf Accessed 1 June 2012.

48   Ministry of Home Affairs, *Annual Report 2006-07, Departments of Internal Security, States, Home, Jammu and Kashmir Affairs and Border Management* (New Delhi: MHA, 2007), pp. 13-14. Available at: http://mha.nic.in/pdfs/ar0607-Eng.pdf Accessed 11 November 2012. See also: Government of Jammu and Kashmir, Home Department, *Memo on Rehabilitation Policy*, 31 January (2004). Available at: http://mha.nic.in/pdfs/JK-RehabilitationPolicy.pdf Accessed 11 November 2012.

49   P. Mishra, "Kashmir: The World's Most Dangerous Place," *New York Review of Books* 4 March (2010). For further discussion on data issues related to Kashmir, also see Small Arms Survey (2011 a).

50   "Rehabilitation Council Plays Godmother to Militancy Victims," *Himalayan Affairs* 31 December (2009). Available at: www.himalayanaffairs.org/article.aspx?id=33 Accessed 24 November 2012.

51   Government of Tripura, Home Department, *Memorandum on Provision of assistance to victims of terrorist and communal violence*, No. F 1(64)-PD/2007, 16 December 2008. Available at: http://india.gov.in/allimpfrms/alldocs/12507.pdf Accessed 11 November 2012.

52   Aashwas website, Assam Police. Available at: www.assampolice.gov.in/aashwas/index.html Accessed 24 November 2012.

53   Ministry of Home Affairs, Naxal Management Division, *Important schemes for LWE affected states* (MHA: New Delhi, n.d). Available at: http://mha.nic.in/uniquepage.asp?Id_Pk=540 Page updated 15 January 2013. Accessed 18 February 2013.

54 INTERACT also offers a 'Young Scholars Leadership Initiative' which is an effort to support these communities to rebuild their future. Though the scholarship programme provides financial and counselling support to all age groups, the focus is on children age 12-18. Information provided by Sreeja, Chief Operating Officer, Rajiv Gandhi Foundation to Sonal Marwah in New Delhi on 10 April 2012. See: www.rgfindia.com/core_edu_prog.htm

55 See www.womensurvivorsnetwork.org

56 The District Committee, which is under the supervision of the District Magistrate, is composed of the District Superintendent of Police, District Medical Officer, and District Social Welfare Officer, District Children's and Women's Development Officer and an officer nominated by the state government.

57 First Information Report is a document prepared by the police when they receive information about the commission of an offence that does not require a warrant to investigate. It is one of the first documents created as part of a criminal investigation. See S. S. Chatterjee, *First Person Information Report & You* (Commonwealth Human Rights Initiative, n.d.) Available at: www.humanrightsinitiative.org/publications/police/fir.pdf Accessed 26 November 2012.

58 Ministry of Home Affairs (2010), p. 5.

59 The Rashtriya Arogya Nidhi is a policy established in 1997 by the Ministry of Health and Family Welfare to provide "financial assistance to patients, living below poverty line who is suffering from major life threatening diseases, to receive medical treatment at any of the super specialty hospitals/institutes or other Govt. hospitals." See: http://india.gov.in/sectors/health_family/index.php?id=15 Page updated 10 February 2011. Accessed 26 November 2012.

60 The AFSPA, enacted in 1958, extends full powers to security forces including the right to fire upon suspects, arrest without warrant any person against whom a reasonable suspicion exists, enter and search any premises without warrant. It is active in Manipur, Nagaland, Assam, Tripura, Meghalaya and the Tirap district of Arunachal Pradesh. Anyone exercising the powers conferred by this Act is protected from legal prosecution. Critics contend that the AFSPA amounts to a licence to kill, detain and harass without restraint and with full impunity. For further background see: Centre for Humanitarian Dialogue and the Delhi Policy Group, *Conflict resolution: Learning lessons from dialogue processes in India* (Geneva: HD Centre, 2011).

61 See Ministry of Home Affairs (2010).

62 As told to Sonal Marwah in New Delhi on 16 March 2012.

63 Adapted with permission by Rebecca Peters of the Surviving Gun Violence Project from F. van Lierde, *We Widows of the Gun* (The Hague: Cordaid, 2011), pp. 102-105.

64 "Fake encounters" are incidents when suspected criminals, terrorists, insurgents or other individuals are shot dead by the police, and those killed are then portrayed as the aggressors who opened fire, so the police escape legal sanction. See: United Nations, *Press Statement - Country Mission to India* [by] *Christof Heyns*, United Nations Special Rapporteur on extrajudicial, summary or arbitrary executions (19-30 March, 2012). Available at: www.ohchr.org/en/NewsEvents/Pages/DisplayNews.aspx?NewsID=12029&LangID=E Accessed 26 November 2012.

SPOTLIGHT SECTION
Suela Lala (Albania)

In 1997, after the fall of the Ponzi schemes, Albania went through political and economic turmoil. Armouries were looted and civilians became heavily armed. Anarchy followed. At 14 years of age I was accidentally shot in my home from external fire. This resulted in quadriplegia. I have therefore lived most of my life with a disability caused by gun violence. However, even living in Albania, a country where armed violence is still very present today and where little has been done to improve the situation, I find myself more connected to the disability rights movement. This is because the disability movement is a big group of people, who experience disability as a result of different impairments or causes, coming together to fight for common interests such as accessibility, the right to education, employment, etc.

Before I joined the Control Arms Coalition and began lobbying for an Arms Trade Treaty in 2011, I had put aside the episode that led to my injury; and to some degree I had been not paying attention to the armed violence still going on in my country. This is probably because the struggle for disability rights is so large, and we have so much to do.

I identified myself as a survivor of armed violence in the early years after the injury. Back then, the need for psychological support and proper rehabilitation was more immediate. Unfortunately, at that time you are very vulnerable and focused on survival, rather than taking part in activity pushing for improvements in the system.

In Albania there is still no psychological support or proper rehabilitation for those experiencing armed violence. But today I and many others find it easier to identify ourselves as persons living with disability. I have gone through the immediate need for help and being vulnerable, and now have a more pragmatic, forward—looking attitude which goes well with disability activism.

Some things persist. For persons with spinal cord injury, rehabilitation is a crucial element even after the initial difficult time has passed. Fifteen years since my injury, Albania has still not established a holistic spinal cord injury rehabilitation unit. After the clinical stage and some fragmented physical therapy services provided in the public hospital, a person experiencing spinal cord injury is left at a loss as how to deal with their new life. She or he doesn't get any information how to manage their day to day care and support on how to use equipment. The luckiest ones might get some rehabilitation programme abroad.

Because of this lesson, there is a need for all those who have experienced armed violence in Albania to join forces, to policies for prevention in the first place, but also to improve services for people already affected by armed violence.

Contributor: Suela Lala, lawyer and disability rights activist, Albania.

Suela Lala, 2013. (Image: Courtesy of Suela Lala)

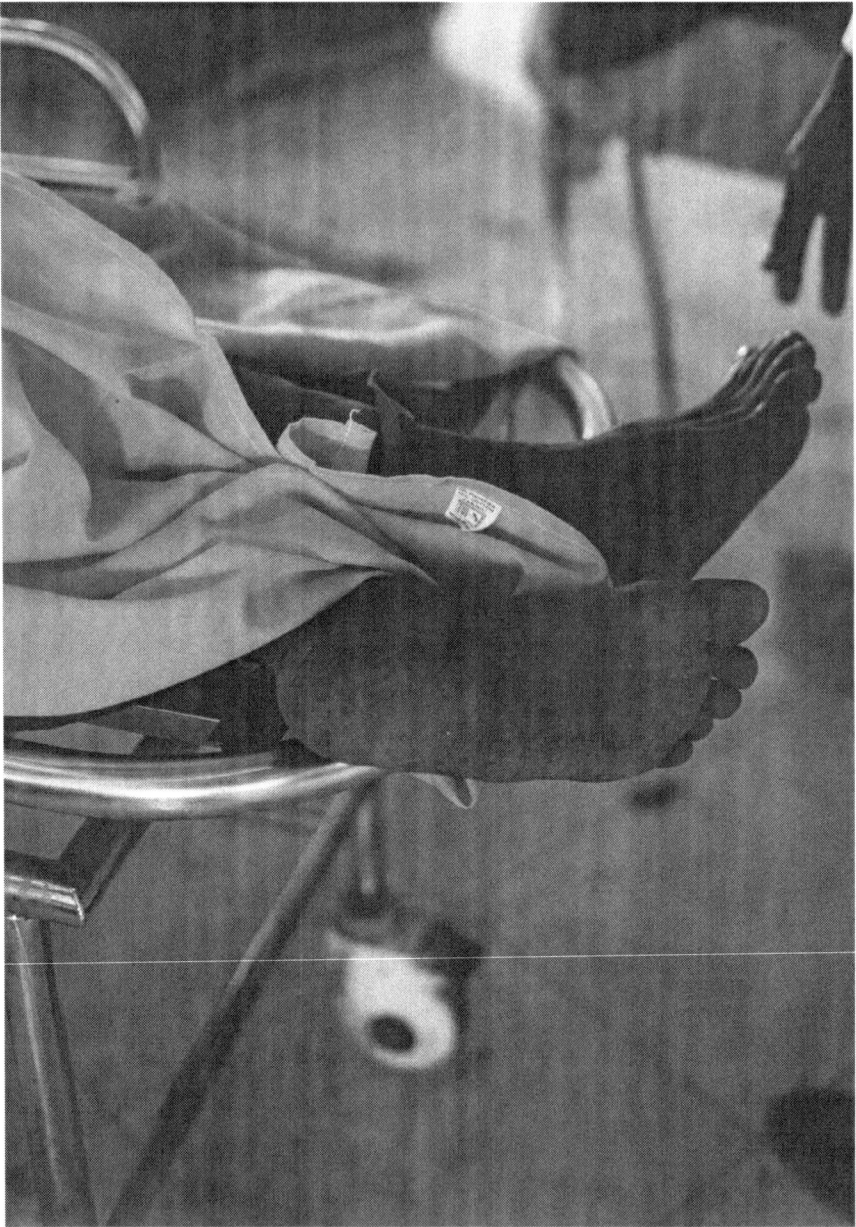

A man is wheeled into a recovery room at Bor hospital after undergoing an operation following a gunshot wound in Jonglei state, South Sudan. Clashes between rival ethnic groups erupted in eastern Jonglei state, caused 144 wounded people to be evacuated to the hospital. (Image: Mackenzie Knowles- Coursin/IRIN, 15 July 2013)

11 Conclusion and Recommendations

Gun Violence, Disability and Recovery has sought to challenge assumptions and provide fresh perspectives and ideas on how to fulfil our collective obligations to survivors and carers. Meaningful support to survivors of gun violence is both a moral imperative and a fundamental human right. It is also an investment in breaking cycles of violence.

We conclude with a set of recommendations drawing on the wealth of contributions reflected in this volume.[1] Most are directed at governments at various levels (national, provincial/state, local), where legislators and officials have the primary responsibility for adopting adequate laws and regulations, allocating budgets, and providing oversight and coordination. However, many points are also relevant for civil society and NGOs, as well as international and regional organisations. A wide range of actors are in a position to advance standards and good practice, including the fundamental principle of including survivors in all aspects of policy and programming, from design through to evaluation.

These suggestions are broad, in order to reach a wide set of stakeholders—including those in countries and regions not covered in the country-specific studies or the thematic chapters. The recommendations provide a starting point for readers to review their own policies, services, and practices, and to identify the most pressing needs and gaps to be filled.

1. Trauma and emergency care
All trauma care networks, whatever their level of sophistication, can be improved. Trauma care should be affordable, accessible (geographically and financially), and of high quality. Two important elements for reaching these goals are: minimum standards of care for medical and non-medical personnel, and a coordinated response to violent events across agencies and services. Improvements to quality of care begin with audits to assess gaps in systems and services, and the development of training standards and protocols. Professional associations have an important role to play in this regard; this includes first responder training and strategies for police and other non-medical personnel. Training should cover awareness of measures to reduce levels of impairment, as risks and levels of loss of function can often be reduced earlier; and mental health, to ensure psychological trauma does not go undetected and untreated. The WHO Global Campaign for Violence Prevention is an important reference point in these areas.[2] Additionally, health personnel should be educated and sensitised not to discriminate between presumed "innocent" and "guilty" victims. Priorities include:

- Audits of trauma care systems—including transport to medical facilities, care received, morbidity and mortality rates, and mental health support.

- Inclusion of a focus on violence, injuries, impairments, and disability awareness in health professional education and training curricula.
- First responder training and support in communities with violent "hot spots" or neighbourhoods.

2. Rehabilitation and psychosocial support

Few States are able to provide the full range of rehabilitation support needed to address short—and long-term physical impairments and/or psychological trauma from violence. Understandings of disability are moving increasingly beyond the medical model—viewed in terms of deficits in functionality—to more holistic approaches that consider the interactions of an individual with her or his environment (built, social, political), also referred to as the social determinants of health. The move toward community-based rehabilitation (CBR) is consistent with this positive trend; good quality CBR can also contribute to reducing the costs of care. Better training and standards for rehabilitation professionals and community workers dealing with violent injuries, traumatic stress disorders, and grief are also essential to improving services. Priorities include:

- Evidence-based procedures to detect and respond to trauma, grief, and mental health on a continuum in hospital settings, the criminal justice system, and the community.
- Providing rehabilitation services that begin in hospital immediately post-injury and continue through to life in the community.
- Adaptations of the built environment including homes, public buildings, schools, libraries, and other spaces, particularly in low income settings.
- Inclusion of community-based rehabilitation in armed violence prevention and reduction planning and programming.

3. Peer support initiatives

Survivors of violently acquired injury or trauma have been effective in providing therapeutic assistance/support to other survivors. Whether one-on-one or in group settings, harnessing survivors' leadership in peer support programmes can be a low-cost way to help the newly victimised with advice and counselling on health management, self-care, identity changes, access to resources, and legal processes. Peer support groups are often "grassroots" initiatives that struggle to find sustainable funding; yet they can make an important contribution to breaking cycles of violence. Programmes based on peer support can also help the wider community affected by vicarious post-violence trauma. Priorities include:

- Inclusion of peer support initiatives in programming to reduce gun violence.
- Sustainable funding for peer support initiatives for gun violence survivors.
- Connecting hospitals with local peer support initiatives to assist individuals post-discharge.
- Evaluation of peer support efforts to gather evidence on good practice. This would also provide solid affirmation of their value to funding agencies.

4. Caregiving

After an individual is released from hospital, most of the burden of care falls on her or his family and other volunteers. This work is often performed by women and girls because of gendered social norms that regard caregiving as "women's work". It is often undervalued, unpaid or underpaid, and unrecognised; yet caregiving has clear economic, health, and human rights implications for both the recipient and the carer. Sustainable caregiving is instrumental to good outcomes for survivors of gun violence, and an important link between health systems and social protection. However many caregivers, particularly in low income settings, suffer economically because they are not able to work outside the home or participate in education or training.[3] To protect caregivers' health and wellbeing, caregiving should be linked to the health system, from primary through to tertiary care. Ideally, compensation or income support should be available for caregivers. Beyond financial considerations, caregiving can lead to vicarious trauma; carers themselves should have access to psychosocial assistance and respite care. Priorities include:

- Creation of a "carer's pension" in social protection systems to provide some degree of recognition and compensation.
- Policy-relevant research on the consequences for caregivers, particularly women and girls, and on household and community economies.
- Ensuring that caregiving is fully included in estimates on the cost of armed violence; this requires expertise to ensure that unpaid or underpaid domestic labour, particularly by women and girls, is appropriately valued.

5. Social protection/assistance

Social protection programmes assist in sustaining the livelihoods of survivors who are unable—temporarily or permanently—to earn an income. In some countries the government provides little or no social protection; or benefits can only be accessed by individuals who previously contributed to the scheme, namely people in the formal labour market. However, survivors of gun violence are frequently unemployed, underemployed, or employed in the informal sector. They often come from low income, marginalised, or even unrecognised communities. Social protection systems should be inclusive, and eligibility criteria must be carefully weighed to avoid excluding individuals with legitimate needs. Social assistance must account for the full cost of care, including increased health costs over time, caregiving, and equipment replacement. Particularly in low income settings, benefits must be distributed with accessibility in mind. This may mean accounting for difficulties faced by some recipients in using public transport or finding information. Finally, while return-to-work programmes are often valuable, they must be designed to avoid poverty traps, in which beneficiaries are effectively worse off if they manage to earn some income. Priorities include:

- Policy-relevant research on modes and mechanisms for social protection/ assistance that may be relevant in disadvantaged communities where many people are informally or under-employed.
- Consideration of no-fault disability insurance schemes as a mechanism for increasing resources for disability services.

6. Conflict and post-war interventions
Post-war or conflict survivor assistance is particularly challenging due to high levels of need, service delivery disruptions, dilapidated infrastructure, scarce resources, and the low priority assigned to human rights when a State is fragile or in transition. In such contexts, international actors often step in to provide essential services. Peace agreements are also one mechanism for framing assistance policy and programmes. Recommendations on trauma and emergency services remain valid here, particularly in relation to preventing long-term impairments and ensuring that all sides have access to services. Equally important, though certainly more challenging, are timely, comprehensive, and inclusive rehabilitation and recovery services, including psychosocial support. Formal disarmament, demobilisation and reintegration (DDR) programmes often miss opportunities to improve services for all survivors of violence, regardless of whether they have served in direct combat. When "emergencies" drag on for years, humanitarian support must not only deliver immediate services but also plan for and help build the long-term development of health and social systems, in concert with relevant government agencies and civil society. At all levels, survivors and their supporters should be involved in programme design, implementation, and monitoring. Priorities include:

- Inclusion of a specific module on trauma, disability and recovery in the United Nations Integrated DDR Standards.
- Guidance for negotiators and mediators on language and principles to consider when drafting peace agreements or implementation strategies.[4]
- Inclusion of mental health services, which are culturally appropriate and gender-sensitive, in relief and recovery efforts.

7. Twin-track approach and non-discrimination
The established concept of a "twin-track approach" to disability rights and development is directly relevant to gun violence survivors.[5] Physical and psychological trauma may require specific parallel paths of action, concurrent to existing justice and health system capacity, to expedite or strengthen policies and services. At the same time, many of the concerns of gun violence survivors echo those of broader communities experiencing disadvantage or denial of basic rights and services, such as crime victims, former combatants, women associated with fighting forces, and people encountering disability discrimination. No particular group should be privileged at the expense of another. Attention to non-discrimination has, for example, grown to become a core principle of victim assistance programming related to the Anti-Personnel Mine Ban Treaty and *Convention on Cluster Munitions*. This is a right that demands elaboration in the area of gun violence survival. The test of good policy or service development is that in addition to filling a gap for survivors of gun violence, it also improves conditions for people experiencing disability or disadvantage more broadly. Priorities include:

- Harmonising services for all victims of armed violence and identifying unintentional discrimination in programmes and policies.
- Including a disability-specific focus as well as attention to violence issues in development planning, or plans to address health and violence.[6] Other relevant processes include Poverty Reduction Strategy Papers, formal DDR, and security system reform.

8. Victim and survivor responsive policing and justice systems

In many places, victims' rights are not yet enshrined in criminal law. Such laws should specify procedures, timeframes, responsible agencies, and areas for input from victims and survivors, and their families. They should also include explicit commitments to prevent secondary victimisation, ensuring that relevant personnel will work to promote the dignity of survivors and victims of conflict, crime, and violence, act in a non-discriminatory manner, and avoid re-traumatising individuals and families through insensitive or unnecessary requests, demands, or behaviour. Fulfilling these commitments requires that security and justice personnel be sensitised to the psychological trauma of survivors and the risks of discrimination. Pointers for strengthening policy and practice are offered in the chapter on Victims' Rights and International Standards (Box 4).

Survivors can also benefit greatly from simplified and more accessible procedures—such as the Road to Justice Card proposed by the South African Rape Crisis Cape Town Trust—enabling people to track their cases through the justice system. Strengthening services laws and is a challenge, especially in places where health, security, and justice systems are weak or pressured. In some contexts it may be too challenging to develop integrated services; but at the very least, policy should be coordinated across various agencies and sectors.[7] Strategic development of victims' services should be included in armed violence mapping and prevention efforts, security system reform, 'health and violence' national plans, and other relevant processes. Priorities include:

- Case tracking systems for survivors and their families to improve accountability from the criminal justice system.
- Developing or updating codes of practice or victim-specific laws in line with relevant international obligations, in particular the 1985 UN *Declaration of Basic Principles of Justice for Victims of Crime and Abuse of Power.*[8]
- Developing compensation or funding schemes that support practical disability-inclusive services for survivors of conflict, violence, and crime.

9. Perpetrators

Survivors of gun violence who are associated with armed opposition forces, gangs, criminal or "subversive" groups are routinely denied assistance and support by government policies and programmes. In some high-violence areas, this may include many or most gun violence victims and their families. This challenging area of public policy demands debate and discussion. Denial of support to this population group can reinforce marginalisation, alienation, political instability, and make breaking cycles of violence even more difficult. It also contributes to poor health outcomes. It may be controversial to recognise that many perpetrators of violence have been influenced by adverse political, social, and economic conditions, and to make rehabilitation available to them. However, their rehabilitation is necessary as an investment in violence prevention and long-term stabilisation. Eligibility criteria for compensation schemes should be reviewed to avoid unfairly punishing the surviving relatives of deceased victims. Clarity on what constitutes good practice in the area of restorative justice for the perpetration of armed violence should also be synthesised for those engaged in policy and programming. Priorities include:

- Developing protocols for programmes targeting perpetrators of armed violence, ensuring that such guidance includes a focus on disability and gender concerns.
- Evaluating existing initiatives in this area, to build an evidence base for future policy and programming.
- Clarifying laws and policies on access to compensation or services for people accused or convicted of crime, as well as their families and other dependants. Such information could be included in armed violence mapping exercises.

10. Research, analysis, and advocacy

There is a deficit of research and policy-relevant analysis on survivors' needs and realities, as well as on the effectiveness of short—vs long-term interventions and mechanisms. Action-oriented, robust research that is accessible to policymakers is therefore a leading priority. Longitudinal studies tracking trends in experiences, impacts, and outcomes are required to identify needs, inform policy and service provision objectives. Attention to trauma systems, rehabilitation services, mental health programmes, judicial procedures, and the overall status of disability issues in a country remain missing in efforts to map armed violence. This broadened scope is necessary so that armed violence reduction and crime prevention efforts can be linked to disability rights advocacy and policy. Gun violence survivors must be meaningfully and deliberately included in research, advocacy, and programme and policy development. The disability rights clarion call, "nothing about us, without us" must be taken seriously by those investigating armed violence.[9] Engaged participation can take many forms and is one way to implement Article 4.3 of the CRPD, which calls for the active consultation and involvement of people living with disability in processes relevant to them. Sustainability of programming is another under-researched area, and a challenge for those providing direct services for survivors of violence, crime, and conflict.[10] Priorities include:

- Engaging and including survivors in armed violence research and programming.
- Developing a strategic research agenda in which diverse sectors (health, human rights, justice, security, disability, armed violence etc.) collaborate.
- Developing mixed method (longitudinal, quantitative, and qualitative) studies to break the data impasse and provide policymakers with detailed and reliable analysis. Including standardised violence-related items in population-level health and social surveys will enable benchmarking and international comparisons over time.

11. Creative approaches to funding services and policy development

Many States lack the capacity to provide services for gun violence survivors due to current limitations in resource allocation. This volume provides examples of programming in low and middle income countries, illustrating that low cost does not necessarily mean low impact. Creative funding schemes can be found, for example, using court fines to support victim services, or using taxes from gun sales or gun registration and licencing fees to fund programmes in the health and criminal justice systems. The focus on El Salvador in this volume highlighted how it is already leading the way in this regard. In 2013 an overwhelming majority of States voted in favour of the *Arms Trade Treaty*; its preamble, at least, recognises the needs and challenges of victims of armed conflict.[11] Thus the ATT provides States with a mandate and an opportunity to explore assistance to survivors of armed violence. Noting the urgency of stimulating better services and policy for survivors of armed violence generally, and specifically gun violence which has to date not enjoyed the same level of funding or attention as other conventional weapons victim assistance processes such as anti-personnel landmines or cluster munitions, it is time for the international community to commit to a Global Fund for Survivors of Armed Violence. A global fund would significantly assist in channelling direct support to innovative service providers and those at the cutting edge of policy development and action-oriented research. It ought to be time-limited in keeping with the principle of non-discrimination and to avoid institutionalising bias between those who suffer violently acquired impairments against those with experiencing disability from other means or sources.[12] A fund can also reduce the transaction costs of donors having multiple funding streams and enable ordinary citizens to donate.[13] Becoming operational in 2015 would be a symbolic and practical way to remedy the exclusion of disability and violence from the Millennium Development Goals, due for renewal that year. Priorities include:

- Donor agencies and private philanthropists contributing to a Global Fund for Survivors of Armed Violence with a 2015 start date.
- A definitive international study to assess innovations and blockages that may exist in relation to funding streams across governments, UN funds, and foundations to assist survivors of armed violence.

12. Strengthen normative frameworks and policies
Global standards, legally and politically binding, need to be translated into national legislation and policy. States should ensure national accession and implementation of relevant key instruments (summarised in Annex 1). These standards should guide the development of national laws. However, good legislation is not enough: adequate implementation mechanisms and resources must be provided. Implementation is best done in partnership with non-government actors, particularly survivors groups. It is therefore important that such groups also participate in developing policies and laws as well as monitor their implementation. Priorities include:

- Identifying synergies among international instruments to address gaps and inconsistencies in global normative frameworks.
- Policy guidance for States on implementing relevant international standards into national policies and laws.
- Supporting the emergence and operation of survivor groups to input into legislative and policy developments.

13. Gun control and survivor-sensitive gun laws
The best strategy to reduce the suffering associated with surviving gun violence is to prevent gun violence in the first place. Strategies to achieve this at national, regional, or global levels have been clearly articulated.[14] To begin with, the trade, use, possession, storage, and destruction of arms must be strictly regulated. Global evidence suggests that civilian access to firearms should be strictly managed, and some weapons entirely prohibited. All arms sales, commercial and private, should be subject to regulation, including a high standard of screening and a robust,

computer-based system of firearm registration. Confiscated and surplus guns should be destroyed, not donated or sold. Gun laws should be linked to victims' rights laws as well as laws on violence against women, given the role of guns in perpetrating intimate partner and family violence. A survivor focus should also be included in gun control laws, with linkages to obligations under the CRPD. These laws should articulate funding strategies to ensure that taxes on gun sales (or other mechanisms) channel funds into services for survivors. Priorities include:

- Reviewing existing gun laws to recognise obligations towards survivors of gun violence, affirming their rights to services and support.
- Considering how gun sales taxes or a portion of license and registration fees can be dedicated to strengthening or creating services in the health and justice systems.
- Linking gun laws to other relevant laws (e.g. victims' rights charters/codes, laws addressing violence against women).

Conclusion

These recommendations are a first effort to map out a policy agenda related to surviving gun violence. States, communities, and service delivery organisations will determine their priorities based on local circumstances and what policies and programmes are already in place. Many people and organisations working to reduce armed violence, promote development, human rights, social inclusion, and gender justice do not see this topic as part of their mandate. The first fundamental change is to adjust our collective perspectives and priorities to include a focus on survivors of gun violence, in order to do justice to the millions of people injured and traumatised every year.

References

[1] The recommendations were written by Cate Buchanan and Mireille Widmer. Additional input was received from Emile LeBrun and Rebecca Peters. The text was peer reviewed, with suggestions and feedback received from: Annette Bailey, Assistant Professor with Ryerson University Daphne Cockwell School of Nursing (Canada); Sheree Bailey, independent disability rights and victim assistance adviser (Australia); Nerina Cevra, Action on Armed Violence (England); Vanessa Farr, independent gender expert (South Africa); Jasmin Galace, Philippines Action Network on Small Arms; Timothy Hardcastle, trauma surgeon, University of KwaZulu-Natal, President of the Trauma Society of South Africa and Deputy Director of the Trauma Unit at Inkosi Albert Luthuli Central Hospital, Durban (South Africa); Sara Hylton, formerly of the Danish Demining Group (Kenya); Thilo Kroll, Co-Director of the Social Dimensions of Health Institute of the Universities of Dundee and St Andrews (Scotland); Suela Lala, disability rights activist (Albania); Sonal Marwah, India Armed Violence Assessment, Small Arms Survey (India); James Mercy, US Centers for Disease Control and Prevention (USA); Charles Mock, Professor of Surgery and Epidemiology, Harborview Injury Prevention and Research Center, University of Washington (USA); Daniel Mont, Senior Research Fellow at the Leonard Cheshire Disability and Inclusive Development Centre (England); Noam Ostrander, Associate Professor and director of the Masters of Social Work Program, DePaul University, Chicago (USA); Andres M. Rubiano, Chief of Trauma and Emergency Services at Neiva University Hospital in Huila (Colombia); Christian Holmboe Ruge, Director, Humanitarian Disarmament Programme at the International Law and Policy

Institute (Norway); Aleema Shivji, independent consultant (England); Reverend Sky Starr, Out of Bounds Grief Support (Canada); Fiona Stephenson, Haiti Spinal Cord Injury Database Co-ordinator (Haiti); Lilu Thapa, Danish Demining Group (Kenya).

2 The WHO Global Campaign for Violence Prevention is based on the recommendations in the 2002 *World Report on Violence and Health*. Goal five is: "Strengthen responses for victims of violence." WHO proposes four practical country-level recommendations in this regard: advocate for improvements in the quality of services; conduct a policy audit and situational analysis; improve emergency medical services and trauma care; and involve the community in the design of specialised services. See, A. Butchart, A. Phinney, P. Check and A. Villaveces, *Preventing Violence: A Guide to Implementing the Recommendations of the World Report on Violence and Health* (Geneva: World Health Organization, 2004), p. 65.

3 See the WHO Long-Term Care Policy Initiative and its various outputs including: J. Brodsky, J. Habib and M. Hirschfeld (Eds), *Long-term care in developing countries: Ten case studies* (Geneva: World Health Organization, 2003); J. Brodsky, J. Habib and M. Hirschfeld (Eds), *Key policy issues in long-term care* (Geneva: World Health Organization, 2003). Also see, E. Esplen, *Gender and Care: Overview Report*, BRIDGE, Institute of Development Studies (Brighton: BRIDGE, 2009).

4 The Surviving Gun Violence Project aims to generate such guidance in 2014 and welcomes input.

5 UK Department for International Development, *Disability, poverty and development* (London: DFID, 2000).

6 Some 30 States have developed these plans thus far including but not limited to: Australia, Belgium, Costa Rica, France, Jordan, Macedonia, Malaysia, Mexico, Mongolia, Nepal, Romania, Russia, South Africa, Sri Lanka, Thailand and the United Kingdom. Email communication between Cate Buchanan and Chris Mikton, World Health Organization, Violence and Injury Prevention team, 7 March 2013.

7 A. Butchart, A. Phinney, P. Check and A. Villaveces (2004), p. 64.

8 Waller provides a model law for policymakers. See: I. Waller, *Rebalancing Justice: Rights for Victims of Crime* (United Kingdom: Rowman and Littlefield, 2011).

9 The phrase has its origins in Central Europe: *Nihil novi nisi commune consensu,* "Nothing new without the common consent". See http://en.wikipedia.org/wiki/Nihil_novi. It came into use in English in the disability rights movement during the 1990s. See, J. Charlton, *Nothing About Us Without Us, Disability, Oppression and Empowerment* (Berkley: University of California Press, 2000).

10 The Sustaining Ability site provides a good starting point for learning more: www.sustainingability.org.

11 Available at: www.un.org/disarmament/ATT/. There are substantive clauses, with a prevention focus, on the links between gender-based violence and lax arms export control. Article 7.4 states that arms exporters "shall take into account the risk of [weapons] being used to commit or facilitate serious acts of gender based violence or serious acts of violence against women and children." For further background see Women's International League for Peace and Freedom, Web page, "Gender and the Arms Trade Treaty". Available at: www.peacewomen.org/pages/att Accessed 17 April 2013.

12 The point of such a fund would be to stimulate much needed services and provide a "bridge" for organisations to transition to accessing longer term or permanent funding sources that are more broadly focussed on human rights, violence, gender justice and victims' rights. A time-limited fund (e.g. 15 years) would provide the necessary financial support to improve services, generate applicable research and policy, and most importantly enable grant recipients a decent timeframe to establish or refine existing programmes that could be evaluated for efficacy, impact and reach.

13 The Disability Rights Fund (DRF) offers a good example of how such an initiative could operate, taking a strategic approach to developing capacity, services, and evidence at a country level, and how private and public donors can come tog`ether to maximise resources, reduce bureaucracy, refine impact and share a strategic vision. Donors include the Australian Agency for International Development, the American Jewish World Service, the Leir Foundation, the Open Society Foundations, Sigrid Rausing Trust, and the UK Department for International Development. The DRF also works to shape policy coherence

amongst donors in this area. See for example: Disability Rights Fund, *Beyond Charity: A Donor's Guide to Inclusion—Disability funding in the era of the UN Convention on the Rights of Persons with Disabilities* (Boston: DRF, 2011).

[14] The work of Frank Zimring remains a touchstone for coherent policy in this area: F. Zimring, "Firearms, violence and public policy," *Scientific American* November (1991), pp. 24-30. For detailed guidance see United Nations, *International Small Arms Control Standards*, various modules at www.smallarmsstandards.org; Centre for Humanitarian Dialogue and Inter-Parliamentary Union, *Missing Pieces: A Guide for Reducing Gun Violence Through Parliamentary Action* (Geneva: HD Centre, 2007). Available in various languages at http://survivinggunviolence.org/topic/armed-violence/gun-violence/missing-pieces-directions-for-reducing-gun-violence-through-the-un-process-on-small-arms-control/; D. Hemenway, *Private Guns, Public Health* (Ann Arbor: University of Michigan Press, 2004); UN Development Programme, *How to guide: Small arms and light weapons legislation* (New York: UNDP, 2008). Available at: www.poaiss.org/CASAUpload/Members/Documents/9@SALWGuide_Legislation.pdf

"There are two ways of spreading light:
to be the candle or the mirror that reflects it."

Edith Wharton

"Vesalius in Zante (1564),"
North American Review, No. 175 (1902).

A bullet hole in the window of a district security office in Kaabong town serves as a reminder of Karamoja's recent and more insecure past. (Image: Khristopher Carlson/IRIN)

Annex 1
International Standards Relevant to Survivors of Gun Violence

This document presents a broad but not exhaustive selection of international instruments important for coherent policymaking related to services and normative standards for survivors of gun violence. It includes both legally binding as well as politically binding instruments, as both forms contribute to policy and legal developments.[1] Only global documents are referenced here; regional agreements of benefit to survivors of gun violence also exist—for example the 1999 *Inter-American Convention on the Elimination of All Forms of Discrimination Against Persons With Disabilities,*[2] or the 2012 European Union Directive establishing minimum standards on the rights, support and protection of victims of crime—but are not the focus of this document.[3]

In the first section, the instruments have been broadly classified into six categories: 1) human rights; 2) war and armed conflict; 3) social protection and livelihoods; 4) criminal justice systems, including standards on the rights of victims of crime; 5) crime prevention; and 6) disarmament and weapons control. Categories have been selected to correspond to existing policy communities, as the representatives of States called upon to negotiate and implement weapons control and disarmament instruments, for example, will not necessarily be the same ones responsible for victims' rights concerns. Needless to say there is considerable overlap among these categories. In the second section, a table presents all instruments in chronological order, highlighting which issues they cover among a selection of 22 key themes. Finally, the third section provides a brief summary of each of the instruments covered highlighting the relevance for survivors of gun violence.

Section 1: Thematic categories

Theme 1: Human rights
Global human rights instruments build on the International Bill of Human Rights, comprised of the 1948 *Universal Declaration of Human Rights* and the two 1966 Covenants.[4] From there, thematic instruments have articulated the rights of people in particular situations or categories: women, children, persons with disabilities, refugees and internally displaced people, amongst others. The United Nations Human Rights Council and treaty enforcement bodies provide various procedures for receiving complaints from individuals and considering patterns of violations of human rights and fundamental freedoms. So-called "special procedures"— Special Rapporteurs, working groups or independent experts—also monitor the implementation of human rights instruments. There are for example Special Rapporteurs on adequate housing, right to education, eradicating extreme poverty,

right to food, physical and mental health, and the promotion of truth, justice, reparations and guarantees of non-recurrence.[5] Specialised United Nations (UN) agencies often guide normative development, including in national legislation—e.g. the World Health Organization for the right to health, the High Commissioner for Refugees for displaced persons, the High Commissioner for Human Rights to press for disability rights or UNICEF for children's rights. Such processes are important for recognition and enforcement of the rights of survivors of gun violence, including health, non-discrimination, participation, redress and general social protection. The following is not a comprehensive list of human rights instruments, but rather a list of those most relevant for survivors of gun violence:

Legally binding:
- 1948 Universal Declaration of Human Rights[6]
- 1951 Convention and 1967 Protocol relating to the Status of Refugees
- 1966 International Covenant on Economic, Social and Cultural Rights
- 1966 International Covenant on Civil and Political Rights
- 1979 Convention on the Elimination of All Forms of Discrimination Against Women
- 1984 Convention Against Torture and other Cruel, Inhuman or Degrading Treatment or Punishment
- 1989 Convention on the Rights of the Child
- 2002 Optional Protocol to the Convention Against Torture and Other Cruel, Inhuman or Degrading Treatment or Punishment
- 2006 Convention on the Rights of Persons with Disabilities

Politically binding:
- 1982 World Programme of Action Concerning Disabled Persons
- 1989 Principles on the Effective Prevention and Investigation of Extra-Legal, Arbitrary and Summary Executions
- 1990 Basic Principles on the Use of Force and Firearms by Law Enforcement Officials
- 1993 UN Standard Rules on the Equalisation of Opportunities for Persons with Disabilities
- 1998 UN Guiding Principles on Internal Displacement
- 1990 Basic Principles on the Use of Force and Firearms by Law Enforcement Officials
- 2000 UN Economic and Social Council (ECOSOC) General Comment No. 14: The right to the highest attainable standard of health
- 2005 World Health Assembly Resolution 58.23: Disability, including prevention, management and rehabilitation
- 2006 Principles for the Prevention of Human Rights Violations Committed with Small Arms and Light Weapons
- 2007 World Health Assembly Resolution 60.22: Health systems: emergency care systems
- 2012 General Comment 3 of the Committee Against Torture on the right to redress
- 2013 UN Human Rights Council Resolution 22/21—Torture and other cruel, inhuman or degrading treatment or punishment: rehabilitation of torture victims
- 2013 World Health Assembly Resolution 66.9: Disability

Theme 2: War and armed conflict

The laws of war, or International Humanitarian Law (IHL), are based, in part, on the four Geneva Conventions of 1949, complemented by two additional protocols in 1977. In addition, a substantial body of IHL relates to limiting the means and methods of warfare. While some human rights guarantees can be suspended in times of war, IHL remains in force. The International Criminal Court (ICC) can prosecute the most serious breaches of IHL. The body of law known as International Criminal Law (ICL) provides rights in times of armed conflict for individual civilians and combatants. These rights include not only rehabilitation but also justice: the pursuit of criminal sanctions against the perpetrators of armed violence. Relevant instruments include:

Legally binding:
- 1949 Geneva Conventions on wounded and sick combatants on land (I), at sea (II), prisoners of war (III), and civilians (IV)
- 1977 Additional Protocols to the Geneva Conventions on protection of victims in international armed conflict (I) and non-international armed conflict (II)[7]
- 1998 Rome Statute of the International Criminal Court
- 2000 Optional Protocol to the Convention on the Rights of the Child on the Involvement of Children in Armed Conflict

Politically binding:
- 2005 Basic Principles and Guidelines on the Right to a Remedy and Reparation for Victims of Gross Violations of International Human Rights Law and Serious Violations of International Humanitarian Law

Theme 3: Social protection and livelihoods

Building on the International Covenant on Economic, Social and Cultural Rights, the International Labour Organization (ILO) promotes and develops labour rights, including social protection and disability rights. It has produced a large number of "technical conventions" offering guidance for States to ensure economic and social rights. This body of law and the associated policy community are important to secure the livelihoods of people living with disability. However the main conventions are several decades-old, and do not adequately address contemporary concerns such as recognising caregiving duties, or improving social protection for people employed in the informal market. Relevant instruments include:

Legally binding:
- 1952 ILO Social Security (Minimum Standards) Convention No. 102
- 1958 ILO Discrimination (Employment and Occupation) Convention No. 111
- 1964 ILO Employment Injury Benefits Convention No. 121
- 1967 ILO Invalidity, Old-Age and Survivors' Benefits Convention No. 128
- 1969 ILO Medical Care and Sickness Benefits Convention No. 130
- 1983 ILO Vocational Rehabilitation and Employment (Disabled Persons) Convention No. 159

Politically binding:
- 1955 ILO Vocational Rehabilitation (Disabled) Recommendation No. 99
- 1983 ILO Vocational Rehabilitation and Employment (Disabled Persons) Recommendation No. 168

Theme 4: Criminal justice systems including the rights of victims of crime

International standards for criminal justice systems have been largely developed through the UN Commission on Crime Prevention and Criminal Justice (CCPCJ) and the UN Office on Drugs and Crime (UNODC). This body of instruments spells out a number of victims' rights standards, protections for witnesses and perpetrators, and specific reference to the rights and needs of juveniles.[8] Relevant instruments include:

Legally binding:
- 2003 Convention against Corruption

Politically binding:
- 1955 UN Standard Minimum Rules for the Treatment of Prisoners
- 1985 UN Standard Minimum Rules for the Administration of Juvenile Justice
- 1985 UN Declaration of Basic Principles of Justice for Victims of Crime and Abuse of Power
- 1990 UN Rules for the Protection of Juveniles Deprived of their Liberty
- 1997 UN Guidelines for Action on Children in the Criminal Justice System
- 2000 UN Basic Principles on the Use of Restorative Justice Programmes in Criminal Matters
- 2005 UN ECOSOC Guidelines on Justice Matters involving Child Victims and Witnesses of Crime

Theme 5: Crime prevention

The CCPCJ and the UNODC have also developed principles to assist States prevent crime, recognising that criminal justice processes should be accompanied by preventive measures. The norms underpinning these principles can assist survivors by preventing reoffending and repeat victimisation. Relevant instruments include:

Legally binding:
- 2000 Convention against Transnational Organized Crime and its three protocols:
- 2000 Protocol to Prevent, Suppress and Punish Trafficking in Persons, Especially Women and Children
- 2000 Protocol against the Smuggling of Migrants by Land, Sea and Air
- 2001 Protocol against the Illicit Manufacturing of and Trafficking in Firearms, Their Parts and Components and Ammunition

Politically binding:
- 1995 UN Guidelines for Cooperation and Technical Assistance in the Field of Urban Crime Prevention
- 2002 UN ECOSOC Resolution on Action to Promote Effective Crime Prevention

Theme 6: Disarmament and weapons control

Some multilateral agreements on disarmament and conventional weapons control have relevant provisions or make specific reference to survivors (generally referred to in treaty text as "victims"). This creates some degree of accountability on States, though progress has been slow. Some are included for their relevance for future policymaking in the area of victim assistance. The Anti-Personnel Mine Ban Convention offers a case in point. Agreed with brief reference to affected individuals, a dedicated policy process has since emerged from the treaty process focused on "victim assistance", resulting in normative change, dedicated programming and targeted services. Relevant instruments include:

Legally binding:
- 1997 Convention on the Prohibition of the Use, Stockpiling, Production and Transfer of Anti-Personnel Mines and on their Destruction
- 2003 Protocol on Explosive Remnants of War (Protocol V to the 1980 Convention on Prohibitions or Restrictions on the Use of Certain Conventional Weapons which may be deemed to be Excessively Injurious or to have Indiscriminate Effects)
- 2008 Convention on Cluster Munitions
- 2013 Arms Trade Treaty

Politically binding:
- 2001 UN Programme of Action to Prevent, Combat and Eradicate the Illicit Trade in Small Arms and Light Weapons in All Its Aspects

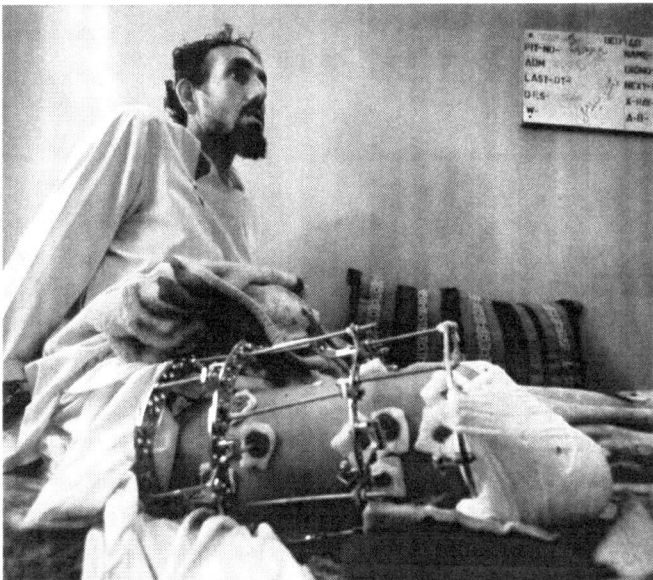

A survivor of a drive-by shooting by insurgents in Mirwais Hospital in Kandahar, Afghanistan. He is back in hospital with an infection after having his leg amputated at the knee. He had to travel to Karachi, Pakistan for the amputation. (Image: Kate Holt, 18 March 2011)

Section 2: Thematic table

Table 1 lists all these instruments chronologically, identifying the issues covered wholly or in part. Twenty-two issues have been identified that are of relevance to survivors of gun violence, from medical assistance to access to justice, social and economic rehabilitation, and participation. After the table, each instrument is again presented, in the thematic order above, with a short narrative highlighting its relevance to survivors.

● Covered
○ Indirectly or partly covered

Treaty or instrument	Universal Declaration of Human Rights	Geneva Convention for the Amelioration of the Condition of the Wounded and Sick in Armed Forces in the Field (Convention I)	Geneva Convention for the Amelioration of the Condition of the Wounded, Sick and Shipwrecked Members of Armed Forces at Sea (Convention II)	Geneva Convention relative to the Treatment of Prisoners of War (Convention III)	Geneva Convention relative to the Protection of Civilian Persons in Time of War (Convention IV)	Convention and 1967 Protocol relating to the Status of Refugees	ILO Social Security (Minimum Standards) Convention (No. 102)
Year	1948	1949	1949	1949	1949	1951	1952
Violence prevention							
Non-discrimination	●				●	●	
Social protection	●				○	○	
Right to work	●				●	●	
Community involvement							
Housing support	○					○	
Education support	○				○		
Mobility, prosthetic devices							○
Rehabilitation support							
Children's rights	●				●		
Disability rights							
Women's rights		●	●	●	●		
Detention conditions					●		
Restorative justice							
Witness protection							
Reparation, compensation							
Access to justice	●				○	●	
Support for caregiving							
Psychological support							
Right to health	●	●	●	●	●		●
Participation	○				○		
Legally binding	●	●	●	●	●	●	●

Treaty or instrument	UN Standard Minimum Rules for the Treatment of Prisoners	ILO Vocational Rehabilitation (Disabled) Recommendation (No. 99)	ILO Discrimination (Employment and Occupation) Convention (No. 111)	ILO Employment Injury Benefits Convention (No. 121)	International Covenant on Economic, Social and Cultural Rights	International Covenant on Civil and Political Rights	ILO Invalidity, Old-Age and Survivors' Benefits Convention (No. 128)	ILO Medical Care and Sickness Benefits Convention (No. 130)
Violence prevention								
Non-discrimination	●		●		●	●		
Social protection		○		●	●		●	●
Right to work			●		●			●
Community involvement								
Housing support					○			
Education support	●	●			○			
Mobility, prosthetic devices		●						●
Rehabilitation support		●					●	●
Children's rights	●	●			●	●		
Disability rights		●		○	○	○		●
Women's rights	●					○		
Detention conditions	●					●		
Restorative justice								
Witness protection								
Reparation, compensation								
Access to justice						●		
Support for caregiving				○				
Psychological support	●				●			
Right to health	●				●			
Participation					○	○		
Legally binding			●	●	●	●	●	●
Year	1955	1955	1958	1964	1966	1966	1967	1969

Year	Treaty or instrument	1977 — Protocol Additional to the Geneva Conventions of 12 August 1949, and relating to the Protection of Victims of International Armed Conflicts (Protocol I)	1977 — Protocol Additional to the Geneva Conventions of 12 August 1949, and relating to the Protection of Victims of Non-International Armed Conflicts (Protocol II)	1979 — Convention on the Elimination of All Forms of Discrimination against Women	1982 — World Programme of Action Concerning Disabled Persons	1983 — ILO Vocational Rehabilitation and Employment (Disabled Persons) Convention (No. 159)	1983 — ILO Vocational Rehabilitation and Employment (Disabled Persons) Recommendation (No. 168)
	Violence prevention						
	Non-discrimination	●	●	●		○	
	Social protection				●	●	
	Right to work				●	●	●
	Community involvement				●		●
	Housing support				●		
	Education support			○	●		
	Mobility, prosthetic devices				●		●
	Rehabilitation support					●	●
	Children's rights	●	●				
	Disability rights			●	●		●
	Women's rights	●		●			
	Detention conditions	○	●				
	Restorative justice						
	Witness protection						
	Reparation, compensation						
	Access to justice	○	○	●			
	Support for caregiving						
	Psychological support	○			●		
	Right to health	●	●	●	●		
	Participation				●		●
	Legally binding	●	●	●		●	●

Treaty or instrument	Convention Against Torture and other Cruel, Inhuman or Degrading Treatment or Punishment	UN Declaration of Basic Principles of Justice for Victims of Crime and Abuse of Power	UN Standard Minimum Rules for the Administration of Juvenile Justice (The Beijing Rules)	Principles on the Effective Prevention and Investigation of Extra-Legal, Arbitrary and Summary Executions	Convention on the Rights of the Child	Basic Principles on the Use of Force and Firearms by Law Enforcement Officials	UN Rules for the Protection of Juveniles Deprived of their Liberty (The Havana Rules)	UN Standard Rules on the Equalization of Opportunities for Persons with Disabilities
Violence prevention	●			●		●		
Non-discrimination	●	●	●		●		●	○
Social protection	●				●			●
Right to work							●	●
Community involvement		●	●					●
Housing support					●			
Education support			●		●		●	●
Mobility, prosthetic devices								●
Rehabilitation support	○				●		○	●
Children's rights			●		●		●	●
Disability rights					●		○	●
Women's rights								
Detention conditions			●		●		●	
Restorative justice		●						
Witness protection	●							
Reparation, compensation	●	●		●				
Access to justice	●	●	○	●	●	●	○	
Support for caregiving								●
Psychological support		●	●		●	●	●	
Right to health		●	●		●		●	●
Participation					●			●
Legally binding	●				●			
Year	1984	1985	1985	1989	1989	1990	1990	1993

Treaty or instrument	UN Guidelines for Cooperation and Technical Assistance in the Field of Urban Crime Prevention	UN Guidelines for Action on Children in the Criminal Justice System	Convention on the Prohibition of the Use, Stockpiling, Production and Transfer of Anti-Personnel Mines and on their Destruction	Rome Statute of the International Criminal Court	UN Guiding Principles on Internal Displacement	Optional Protocol to the Convention on the Rights of the Child on the Involvement of Children in Armed Conflict	Convention against Transnational Organized Crime; Protocol to Prevent, Suppress and Punish Trafficking in Persons, Especially Women and Children; Protocol against the Smuggling of Migrants by Land, Sea and Air
Violence prevention	●		●				●
Non-discrimination					●		
Social protection		●			○		
Right to work					●		
Community involvement	○	●					
Housing support					●		
Education support					●		
Mobility, prosthetic devices							
Rehabilitation support		●	●				
Children's rights		●					○
Disability rights		○			○		
Women's rights					●		○
Detention conditions		●					
Restorative justice		●					
Witness protection		●		●			●
Reparation, compensation		●		●			
Access to justice	○	●		●			○
Support for caregiving							
Psychological support		●			●		
Right to health		●	●		●		
Participation				●	○		
Legally binding			●	●		●	●
Year	1995	1997	1997	1998	1998	2000	2000

Treaty or instrument	UN Basic Principles on the Use of Restorative Justice Programmes in Criminal Matters	UN ECOSOC General Comment No. 14: The right to the highest attainable standard of health	Protocol against the Illicit Manufacturing of and Trafficking in Firearms, Their Parts and Components and Ammunition, supplementing the United Nations Convention against Transnational Organized Crime	UN Programme of Action to Prevent, Combat and Eradicate the Illicit Trade in Small Arms and Light Weapons in All Its Aspects	UN ECOSOC Resolution on Action to Promote Effective Crime Prevention	Optional Protocol to the Convention Against Torture
Violence prevention			●	●	●	
Non-discrimination		●				●
Social protection						
Right to work						
Community involvement	○					
Housing support						
Education support						
Mobility, prosthetic devices						
Rehabilitation support						
Children's rights		●				
Disability rights		●				
Women's rights		●				
Detention conditions						○
Restorative justice	●					
Witness protection						●
Reparation, compensation						
Access to justice						○
Support for caregiving						
Psychological support		●				
Right to health		●				
Participation						○
Legally binding			●			●
Year	2000	2000	2001	2001	2002	2002

Treaty or instrument	Convention against Corruption	Protocol on Explosive Remnants of War (Protocol V to the 1980 Convention on Prohibitions or Restrictions on the Use of Certain Conventional Weapons which may be deemed to be Excessively Injurious or to have Indiscriminate Effects)	UN ECOSOC Guidelines on Justice in Matters involving Child Victims and Witnesses of Crime	Basic Principles and Guidelines on the Right to a Remedy and Reparation for Victims of Gross Violations of International Human Rights Law and Serious Violations of International Humanitarian Law	World Health Assembly Resolution 58.23: Disability, including prevention, management and rehabilitation	Principles for the Prevention of Human Rights Violations Committed with Small Arms and Light Weapons
Violence prevention		●				●
Non-discrimination			●	●		
Social protection						
Right to work						
Community involvement					●	
Housing support						
Education support						
Mobility, prosthetic devices					●	
Rehabilitation support			●	●		
Children's rights			●			
Disability rights					●	
Women's rights					○	
Detention conditions						
Restorative justice				○		
Witness protection	●					
Reparation, compensation			●	●		
Access to justice			●	●		
Support for caregiving						
Psychological support			●	○	○	
Right to health			●		●	
Participation						
Legally binding	●	●				
Year	2003	2003	2005	2005	2005	2006

	2006 — Convention on the Rights of Persons with Disabilities	2006 — Optional Protocol to the Convention on the Rights of Persons with Disabilities	2007 — World Health Assembly Resolution 60.22: Health systems: emergency care systems	2008 — Convention on Cluster Munitions	2012 — General Comment 3 of the Committee Against Torture on the right to redress	2013 — Arms Trade Treaty	2013 — Human Rights Council Resolution 22/21—Torture and other cruel, inhuman or degrading treatment or punishment: rehabilitation of torture victims	2013 — World Health Assembly Resolution 66.9: Disability
Violence prevention				●	●	●		●
Non-discrimination	●			●	●		●	●
Social protection	●				●		●	●
Right to work	●			○				
Community involvement			○					○
Housing support	●							
Education support	●							
Mobility, prosthetic devices	●							●
Rehabilitation support	●			●	●		●	●
Children's rights	●			○				○
Disability rights	●	●	○	○	●		○	●
Women's rights	●			○				
Detention conditions	○				●			
Restorative justice					●		●	
Witness protection					●			
Reparation, compensation					●		●	
Access to justice	●				●		●	
Support for caregiving	○							●
Psychological support				●	●		○	●
Right to health	●		●	●	○			●
Participation				●	●		●	●
Legally binding	●	●		●		●		

Section 3: Summary of instruments and standards

Theme 1: Human rights related
1948 *Universal Declaration of Human Rights* (UDHR)[9]
The first global expression of human rights standards, the UDHR was adopted in 1948 by the UN General Assembly.[10] It recognises a number of rights that are essential for survivors of gun violence: non-discrimination, access to justice, political participation, the right to work (including just remuneration), a standard of living adequate for the health and wellbeing of self and family (including medical care and social services), and specific protections for children. Although adopted as a non-binding instrument, it is now widely regarded as having the status of customary international law.

1951 *Convention and 1967 Protocol relating to the Status of Refugees* [11]
The Refugee Convention sets out important protections for persons who have obtained the status of refugee—implying they have crossed an international border and could demonstrate a well-founded fear of persecution. The protections include non-discrimination, freedom of religion, right to personal status, property, association, access to courts, and labour rights, housing, social protection and so on—on a par with the general population. The Convention was originally restricted to European refugees fleeing events having occurred prior to 1951, but the 1967 Protocol changed this into universal coverage.

1966 *International Covenant on Economic, Social and Cultural Rights* (ICESCR)[12]
The ICESCR came into force in 1976. It was one of two legally-binding covenants adopted by UN Member States in 1966 to elaborate the norms in the UDHR. Rights provided in the ICESCR include non-discrimination, health (including mental health), work and social protection. The references to education, housing and participation can also be helpful to survivors of gun violence. The general non-discrimination clause can be interpreted to include disability issues, particularly access to services.

1966 *International Covenant on Civil and Political Rights* (ICCPR)[13]
The ICCPR was the second covenant adopted in 1966; it also came into force in 1976. The ICCPR covers areas such as non-discrimination, access to justice, conditions of detention, and specific protections for children; it also refers to women's rights and equal rights of political participation. Its first Optional Protocol, adopted at the same time, allows the UN Human Rights Committee to receive and consider individual complaints.

1979 *Convention on the Elimination of All Forms of Discrimination against Women* (CEDAW)[14]
CEDAW entered into force in 1981. In addition to an overall focus on the legal status and rights of women, two articles are particularly important to survivors of gun violence. Article 12 obligates State parties to "eliminate discrimination against women in the field of health care" to ensure access to equal services. Articles 11.1d and 11.1e establish women's rights to "equal remuneration, including benefits" and to social security during and after employment.

1982 *World Programme of Action concerning Disabled Persons* (WPA)[15]

The WPA was an outcome of the International Year of Disabled Persons (1981). It was adopted by General Assembly Resolution 37/52 on 3 December 1982, and the anniversary of that date is celebrated as the International Day of Persons with Disabilities. A lengthy (and now somewhat outdated) document, the WPA was a global strategy to enhance disability prevention, rehabilitation and equalisation of opportunities, by approaching disability from a human rights perspective. It featured many recommendations for national action which remain relevant.

1984 *Convention Against Torture and Other Cruel, Inhuman or Degrading Treatment or Punishment* (CAT)[16]

The CAT was adopted by the United Nations General Assembly and entered into force in 1987. It was the first legally-binding international instrument exclusively dedicated to prohibiting torture and ill-treatment. The CAT was negotiated after the adoption of the 1975 *Declaration on the Protection of All Persons from Being Subjected to Torture and Other Cruel, Inhuman or Degrading Treatment or Punishment*. Article 2 of the Convention obliges each State party to "take effective legislative, administrative, judicial or other measures to prevent acts of torture." Article 14 requires every State party to "ensure in its legal system that the victim of an act of torture obtains redress and has an enforceable right to fair and adequate compensation." In 2012 a General Comment was issued by the UN CAT Committee to clarify the scope and substance of Article 14. In 2013 this was further affirmed in a UN Human Rights Council Resolution (both summarised below).

1989 *Convention on the Rights of the Child* (CRC)[17]

The CRC entered into force in 1990. It enshrines four major principles: non-discrimination; the best interests of the child; the right to life, survival and development; and respect for the views of the child. The CRC consolidated international recognition that children are direct holders of rights and have legal identities distinct from their parents', and that childhood should be afforded dedicated protection under law. Articles 23, 38 and 39 have particular relevance for survivors of gun violence. Article 23 obligates States to ensure that children with impairment(s) "enjoy a full and decent life" and specifically affirms their rights to access and services in education, rehabilitation, family assistance, and health care (paras. 1, 2, 3). Article 38 requires States to ensure that international humanitarian law applies to children, drawing attention to the overlap of international humanitarian law and human rights law. Article 39 relates to States' obligation to promote "physical and psychological recovery and social reintegration" of child victims of exploitation and abuse, including in armed conflicts.

1989 *Principles on the Effective Prevention and Investigation of Extra-Legal, Arbitrary and Summary Executions*[18]

The Principles call for measures to prevent, investigate and prosecute cases of extra-legal, arbitrary and summary executions. They are of relevance for the surviving relatives of victims of executions through the legal protections the Principles afford them, as well as the right to compensation. They also spell out measures to prevent the misuse of force by State officials.

1990 *Basic Principles on the Use of Force and Firearms by Law Enforcement Officials*[19]
The Basic Principles were adopted at the Eighth UN Congress on the Prevention of Crime and the Treatment of Offenders. They commit States to restrain and regulate the use of guns by police and other law enforcement officials. Under Principle 5, an official who shoots someone is required to: "Minimize damage and injury, and respect and preserve human life; ensure that assistance and medical aid are rendered to any injured or affected persons at the earliest possible moment; [and] Ensure that relatives or close friends of the injured or affected person are notified at the earliest possible moment." Persons affected by the official use of guns are entitled to an independent review process of the incident, and arbitrary or abusive use of firearms by law enforcement officials should be punished as a criminal offence.

1993 *UN Standard Rules on the Equalization of Opportunities for Persons with Disabilities* (Standard Rules)[20]
Adopted by General Assembly Resolution 48/96, the Standard Rules are a set of guidelines and principles for States to develop policies and laws to address disability-based discrimination. They are grounded in the recognition that disability is a function of the relationship between a person and their environment. (This concept was further developed in the 2006 *Convention on the Rights of Persons with Disabilities*, which defined disability as a social and political phenomenon, not solely a medical concern.) The Standard Rules highlight principles of the major human rights treaties (at that time), including non-discrimination, special protection and equity. They identify a State's obligations in areas such as medical care, rehabilitation and support services. They stress gender sensitivity and the elimination of gender-based discrimination (including violence) in disability-specific policies and services. They promote community-based rehabilitation and call for a disability component to be included in national health policies and priorities. Provisions for family members of people living with disability are relevant to secondary survivors of gun violence as well as caregivers. The Standard Rules provide for a Special Rapporteur who reports annually to the Commission for Social Development (part of the UN Economic and Social Council).[21]

1998 *UN Guiding Principles on Internal Displacement*[22]
These Principles are an annex to the 1998 report submitted to the UN Human Rights Commission by the Representative of the Secretary-General on internally displaced persons (IDPs). They are particularly relevant for survivors who have fled armed conflict. Under Principle 19.1, "All wounded and sick internally displaced persons as well as those with disabilities shall receive to the fullest extent practicable and with the least possible delay, the medical care and attention they require, without distinction on any grounds other than medical ones. When necessary, internally displaced persons shall have access to psychological and social services." Principle 19.2 calls for specific attention to the health needs of women, particularly if they are survivors of sexual violence.

2000 *UN ECOSOC General Comment No. 14: The right to the highest attainable standard of health* (GC14)[23]
GC14 expands on Article 12 of the ICESCR pertaining to the "right to the highest attainable standard of health." GC14 asserts that this "a right to the enjoyment of a variety of facilities, goods, services and conditions necessary for the realization

of the highest attainable standard of health" (para. 9). Essential elements of health care systems are listed, including availability, accessibility (non-discrimination, physical accessibility, affordability, and information accessibility), acceptability and quality. It emphasises important elements such as community-level treatment, mental health, and health insurance. GC14 re-affirms the rights of people experiencing disability, stressing the need for both public and private health services to avoid discrimination (para. 26). It reminds States of their "core obligation" to "adopt and implement a national public health strategy and plan of action" (para. 43f). Finally, it specifies conditions upon which States may find themselves in violation of the right to health (Part III).

2002 *Optional Protocol to the Convention Against Torture and Other Cruel, Inhuman or Degrading, Treatment or Punishment* (OPCAT)[24]

The OPCAT entered into force in 2006 and establishes a "system of regular visits undertaken by independent international and national bodies to places where people are deprived of their liberty, in order to prevent torture and other cruel, inhuman or degrading treatment or punishment" (Article 1). A Sub-Committee of independent experts undertake country visits to examine the condition of detention facilities (including police stations, prisons, pre-trial, juvenile and immigration detention centres, mental health and social care institutions). The visits require the permission of the State in question. Each visit concludes with a confidential report to the State. If the State does not engage with, or improve conditions on the basis of the report, the Sub-Committee may request the CAT Committee to publish the report.

2005 *World Health Assembly Resolution 58.23: Disability, including prevention, management and rehabilitation*[25]

The preamble of Resolution 58.23 mentions war and violence among the causes of injury and disability. The operative provisions address several issues relevant to survivors of gun violence, including training and employment, community-based rehabilitation, and access to adequate and effective medical care as well as "prostheses, wheelchairs, driving aids and other devices." The Resolution calls for better national policies and programmes to implement the 1993 Standard Rules. It foreshadows the first *World Report on Disability* (released in 2011);[26] as well as the CRPD.

2006 *Principles for the Prevention of Human Rights Violations Committed with Small Arms and Light Weapons*[27]

The Principles articulate standards for state and non-state actors to prevent human rights violations with small arms and light weapons. The UN Special Rapporteur on Human Rights and Small Arms (at the time), Barbara Frey, noted that under international human rights law, States are required to exercise due diligence to protect people within their territories from abuse, even those committed by private actors. The Principles reiterate the significance of other instruments related to the use of force and firearms (see above, 1990 Principles) and established human rights law. The Principles compel States to take effective measures to minimise violence by not only criminalising acts of armed violence and enforcing criminal sanctions, but by preventing small arms from getting into the hands of those who are likely to misuse them by, for instance, adopting and enforcing minimum licensing requirements. The State itself may be liable if it fails to investigate and prosecute massacres or take reasonable steps to regulate guns in order to protect citizens from homicides, suicides, accidents, a pattern of intimate partner or family violence, and/ or organised crime.

2006 *Convention on the Rights of Persons with Disabilities* (CRPD)[28]

The CRPD entered into force in 2008. It is the definitive treaty protecting and promoting the rights of persons with disabilities. The CRPD does not introduce any new rights, but rather sets out the State's obligations to meet existing civil, cultural, economic, political and social rights in the specific context of people living with disability discrimination. A number of its articles are particularly relevant to survivors of gun violence. Article 16 recognises that people living with disability are at higher risk of violence, injury and abuse, and calls on States to take appropriate legal measures to "promote the physical, cognitive and psychological recovery, rehabilitation and social reintegration of persons with disabilities who become victims of any form of exploitation, violence or abuse, including through the provision of protection services." Article 25 asserts the need for the "highest attainable standard" of health services, noting the need for gender-sensitive design and implementation. Article 26 emphasises habilitation and rehabilitation, and Article 27 focuses on work and employment. Article 29 and 30 focus on participation, the former in political and public life (including in NGOs) and the latter in cultural life, recreation, leisure and sports. "Full and effective participation and inclusion" is also a basic principle of the Convention and therefore permeates all its provisions. Article 32 includes a requirement for inclusive international cooperation and development programmes. This places an obligation on States providing development assistance.

The CRPD benefits from a dedicated implementation apparatus including the Conference of Parties, national reporting, the Committee on the Rights of Persons with Disabilities[29] with experts to oversee implementation and review national reports, and expert group meetings. Many States are complying with its provisions through the development or refinement of national disability laws and action plans.[30]

2006 *Optional Protocol to the Convention on the Rights of Persons with Disabilities*[31]

The CRPD Optional Protocol came into force in 2008. It provides an avenue for individuals to seek redress for human rights violations that have not been resolved through national mechanisms, or because there were not institutions or processes in place to seek redress. It enables the CRPD UN Committee to receive and consider communications from, or on behalf of, individuals who claim to have been victims of a violation of the CRPD. The Committee can take action on "grave or systematic violations" (Article 6) by requesting that the State in question explain the circumstances and report on actions it took to address violations. The Committee may conduct an inquiry or, with the consent of the State, visit that country and meet with relevant individuals and organisations. Failing approval to visit, the State shall respond within six months to the Committee.

2007 *World Health Assembly Resolution 60.22: Health systems: emergency care systems*[32]

Resolution 60.22 represents the highest level of international attention ever devoted to emergency care systems. It urges States to assess their pre-hospital and emergency care context, and provides guidance for what constitutes an adequate response, including coordination, training, a universal access number, monitoring and data collection. WHO is asked to support States, for example by developing standardised tools and techniques. The Global Alliance for Care of the Injured was launched in 2013 as part of implementing this resolution.[33]

2012 *General Comment 3 of the Committee Against Torture on the right to redress* (GC3)[34]

GC3 expands upon the right to redress as outlined in Article 14 of the *Convention Against Torture*. It elaborates, in particular, on the right to rehabilitation which it states "should be holistic and include medical and psychological care as well as legal and social services" (para. 11) and not be dependent on survivors being involved in formal justice processes (para. 15). It affirms the 2005 *Basic Principles and Guidelines on the Right to a Remedy and Reparation for Victims of Gross Violations of International Human Rights Law and Serious Violations of International Humanitarian Law* (explained in theme 2) and notes that the right to redress under the CAT extends not only to survivors of torture, but also to survivors of ill-treatment, and ensures that all individuals have a right to redress, not just those who were subjected to violations within the territory of the State party. GC3 defines "victim" using the 1985 *Declaration of Basic Principles of Justice for Victims of Crime and Abuse of Power* definition (explained in theme 4) and also refers to the use of the term "survivors" as preferable in some contexts. The Comment refers to redress as containing five core elements, articulated in the Basic Principles: restitution, compensation, rehabilitation, satisfaction, and guarantees of non-repetition.

2013 *UN Human Rights Council Resolution 22/21—Torture and other cruel, inhuman or degrading treatment or punishment: rehabilitation of torture victims*[35]

Resolution 22/21 addresses the right to redress with a specific focus on rehabilitation for victims of torture and ill-treatment. The Resolution "encourages States to adopt a victim-oriented approach and to put victims and their individual needs at the centre of redress procedures including by implementing procedures for the effective participation of victims in the redress process", without discrimination. It also "stresses that national legal systems must ensure that victims obtain redress without suffering any reprisals for bringing complaints or giving evidence." The Resolution affirms what was stipulated in GC3 to the CAT. Resolution 22/21 is the most prominent reference to date by the Human Rights Council to the right and need for rehabilitation services as part of States' obligations to provide redress to victims of torture and ill-treatment.

2013 *World Health Assembly Resolution 66.9: Disability*[36]

Resolution 66.9 urges States to implement the *Convention on the Rights of Persons with Disabilities*, develop a national disability strategy and plan of action, and improve data collection. States are also encouraged to ensure that mainstream health services are inclusive of persons living with disability and provide more support to informal caregivers. The Resolution also tasks the WHO "to prepare... a comprehensive WHO action plan with measurable outcomes, based on the evidence in the World report on disability", which was published in 2011.

Theme 2: War and armed conflict related

1949 *Geneva Convention for the Amelioration of the Condition of the Wounded and Sick in Armed Forces in the Field* (GCI)[37]

GCI spells out the specific protections to be afforded to wounded and sick combatants, principally the right to health, with due regards to the needs of women, safety of the person, and non-discrimination (Article 12). The Convention also affords much consideration to the protection of medical personnel and facilities, an obvious concern in times of war. Along with its sibling Conventions II to IV, GCI only applies in the case of armed conflicts of an international character, although common Article 3 enumerates a set of minimum provisions in a non-international armed conflict. The limitations in scope, addressing only international armed conflicts conducted by regular armies, is addressed with the 1977 Additional Protocols I and II (see below), to which more than 160 States are party.

1949 *Geneva Convention for the Amelioration of the Condition of the Wounded, Sick and Shipwrecked Members of Armed Forces at Sea* (GCII)[38]

GCII offers similar protections to combatants at sea who have been incapacitated: the right to health, again with due regards to the specific needs of women, safety of the person, and non-discrimination (Article 12). It continues by spelling out the protections to be afforded to medical personnel and facilities.

1949 *Geneva Convention relative to the Treatment of Prisoners of War* (GCIII)[39]

GCIII takes a strong stance on the humane treatment of prisoners of war and obligates their captors (the Detaining Power) to respect their right to life and to health. Detaining powers cannot deny medical treatment to prisoners of war and must provide special facilities for the care of injured and impaired prisoners, and their rehabilitation, pending repatriation (Article 30). The Convention also demands regular medical inspections in detention areas (Article 31) and for relief organisations to be allowed to assist prisoners of war (Article 125).

1949 *Geneva Convention relative to the Protection of Civilian Persons in Time of War* (GCIV)[40]

GCIV applies to populations of occupied territories, internees, soldiers who have surrendered or been taken out of conflict due to injury, and aliens in territories involved in conflict. Article 14 allows parties to a conflict to create and recognise "safety zones and localities" to protect people who experience acute vulnerability including those who are wounded or sick. Articles 18-22 also protect Red Cross/Red Crescent workers and provide for medical treatment and safety of persons who are wounded. While the Convention applies only to armed conflicts between two or more parties, its provisions apply to occupied territory of an entity not recognised as a State.

1977 *Protocol Additional to the Geneva Conventions of 12 August 1949, and relating to the Protection of Victims of International Armed Conflicts* (Protocol I)[41]

Protocol I to the Geneva Conventions strengthens the protections afforded to humanitarian workers and organisations (Articles 17 and 81) to attend to victims of war, and expands protections for women and children affected by violent conflict (Articles 76-78). Protocol I recognises the need to protect both physical and mental health (Articles 11 and 75); an important expansion of global norms in the understanding of health.

1977 *Protocol Additional to the Geneva Conventions of 12 August 1949, and relating to the Protection of Victims of Non-International Armed Conflicts* (Protocol II)[42]

Protocol II to the Geneva Conventions focuses on non-international (internal) armed conflicts, which the Geneva Conventions address briefly in common Article 3. Protocol II contains many important provisions for survivors of gun violence, particularly protections for children affected by violent conflict. Article 4.3.c prohibits children under the age of 15 being recruited into armed forces or groups or allowed to take any part in the hostilities. Article 4.3.d. affords the same protections to children under 15 who have participated in hostilities. This rule is important for child combatants who lay down arms or are captured: in spite of their role in hostilities, they are still protected as children first. Protocol II also provides for the care of individuals who have become sick or wounded during armed conflict, whether they are civilians or combatants (Article 7), including their right to treatment. Like Protocol I, it also recognises the need to protect both physical and mental health (Articles 4 and 5).

1998 *Rome Statute of the International Criminal Court*[43]

The Rome Statute was adopted in 1998. It entered into force in 2002, and can only prosecute crimes committed after the date of entry into force (1 July) and where domestic efforts to pursue prosecution have been exhausted, or are not possible. Universal jurisdiction was limited in the Statute negotiation process to include only nationals of a State party; alleged crimes committed in the territory of a State party; or situations referred to the International Criminal Court (ICC) by the UN Security Council (Articles 12 and 13). The Rome Statute covers four types of crimes for the ICC to prosecute: genocide, crimes against humanity, war crimes, and crimes of aggression.

The first set of arrest warrants were issued in mid-2005 (related to the Lord's Resistance Army in Uganda), and since then a further seven situations resulted in indictments by the court (related to the Democratic Republic of the Congo, Darfur/ Sudan, Kenya, Central African Republic, Libya, Côte d'Ivoire and Mali).[44] The ICC has established important innovations in the area of the involvement of victims in court processes, specifically to enable direct, rather than passive, participation in court proceedings. This is facilitated by a Victims Participation and Reparations Section. Article 75 outlines that the Court can order a convicted individual to pay reparations to individuals including property confiscation from perpetrators—a first in international law. Collective reparations are also possible which may be funnelled through the Trust Fund for Victims established in 2002. This Section is also mandated by the rules of the Court Registry to keep applicants informed on the progress of their submission and court process. A Victims and Witnesses Unit offers counselling, security arrangements, support during testifying and forms of witness protection.

2000 *Optional Protocol to the Convention on the Rights of the Child on the Involvement of Children in Armed Conflict*[45]

The Optional Protocol entered into force in 2002. It specifies that ratifying States can accept volunteers under the aged of 18 into their armed services, but cannot conscript them. This also applies to non-state actors and insurgent forces. Of additional relevance to survivors of armed violence is Article 6.3 which reaffirms the obligation of States to provide "all appropriate assistance" for the physical and psychological recovery and social reintegration of children involved in armed conflict as combatants, sex slaves, porters, camp workers, etc.

2005 *Basic Principles and Guidelines on the Right to a Remedy and Reparation for Victims of Gross Violations of International Human Rights Law and Serious Violations of International Humanitarian Law* (Basic Principles)[46]

The Basic Principles were adopted by consensus in General Assembly Resolution 60/147. They developed from a 1989 UN resolution to produce uniform international standards on the right to restitution, compensation and rehabilitation for victims of gross/serious violations of international human rights and humanitarian law.[47] Victims are defined individually and collectively, encompassing immediate family members, dependants, and also unrelated persons who were harmed while intervening to assist victims (Principle 8). The definition is drawn from the 1985 UN *Declaration of Basic Principles of Justice for Victims of Crime and Abuse of Power* (see below in Criminal Justice section). "Harm" is defined expansively, including "physical or mental injury, emotional suffering, economic loss or substantial impairment of their [victims'] fundamental rights." The obligations of States are to prevent violations; investigate, prosecute and punish perpetrators; provide effective access to justice; and give full reparation to victims (Principle 3). Reparations should be "proportional to the gravity of the violations and harm suffered", and include five elements: restitution, compensation, rehabilitation, satisfaction and guarantees of non-repetition (Principle 15).

Theme 3: Social protection and livelihoods

1952 *ILO Social Security (Minimum Standards) Convention (No. 102)* (C102)[48]

C102 came into force in 1955. It covers a wide range of social security topics, from medical care to benefits in case of sickness, unemployment, old age, employment injury, maternity, invalidity and "survivors"—which in this case refers to widow/widowers and children of a deceased primary earner. It commits States to ensure that medical care is available to "protected persons" (including certain percentages of a country's employees, its economically-active population and residents overall). Such care should include general practitioner and specialist care, hospitalisation and prosthetic appliances (Article 34). Health services should cooperate with vocational rehabilitation services, "with a view to the re-establishment of handicapped persons in suitable work" (Article 35). Invalidity benefits take over when sickness benefits are exhausted and the person has diminished capacity for paid work.

1955 *ILO Vocational Rehabilitation (Disabled) Recommendation (No. 99)*[49]

ILO No. 99 represents a unanimous and historic decision by the International Labour Conference, recommending that vocational rehabilitation services be provided to anyone with an impairment who has reasonable prospects of working. The agreement describes the process for identifying vocational guidance needs. It recommends that users of rehabilitation services be reimbursed for transportation costs, board and lodging, and any prosthetic or other necessary appliances. Close cooperation between rehabilitation and medical services is called for, and the emphasis is placed on equal opportunity. Other suggested measures include the creation of preferential employment opportunities for people living with disability.

1958 *ILO Discrimination (Employment and Occupation) Convention (No. 111)* (C111)[50]

C111 came into force in 1960. It expands on other anti-discrimination provisions in international law, such as Article 23 in the UDHR. Article 1.3 of C111 defines employment and occupation as including access to vocational training, access to employment and to particular occupations, as well as terms and conditions of employment. C111 recognises "disablement" may require special protection or assistance in employment (Article 5.2). This provision paves the way for affirmative action for people experiencing disability discrimination, such as some survivors of gun violence. On the other hand, C111 allows discrimination based on the "inherent requirements" of a particular job. This provision could be used to bar people with impairments from types of work which the employer assumes they are unable to perform, such as manual labour.

1964 ILO Employment Injury Benefits Convention (No. 121) (C121)[51]
C121 entered into force in 1967. It applies in cases of "industrial accidents and occupational diseases." This means it can assist people who were shot in the course of their work, such as bus drivers or private security guards. State parties commit to providing injured employees with medical care (including prosthetic appliances) and cash benefits (Article 10). A further commitment is to provide rehabilitation services "designed to prepare a disabled person wherever possible for the resumption of his [sic] previous activity, or, if this is not possible, the most suitable alternative gainful activity, having regard to his [sic] aptitudes and capacity" (Article 26).

1967 ILO Invalidity, Old-Age and Survivors' Benefits Convention (No. 128) (C128)[52]
C128 came into force in 1969 as a revision of several other Conventions from 1933. States may ratify all or part of C128, and may also decide to exclude sections of the population from its coverage—for example, people in casual employment (Article 37). States adopting the provisions on invalidity benefits also undertake to provide rehabilitation services (Article 13). Part 3 covers benefits for "survivors", a term used for widows and widowers and children of deceased primary earners.

1969 ILO Medical Care and Sickness Benefits Convention (No. 130) (C130)[53]
C130 entered into force in 1972. It commits States to offer medical insurance to large parts of their population (defined in Article 10). The insurance should cover: a) general practitioner care, including home visits; b) specialist care in and outside of hospitals; c) pharmaceutical supplies; d) hospitalisation where necessary; e) dental care; and, f) medical rehabilitation, including the supply, maintenance and renewal of prosthetic and orthopaedic appliances (Article 13). C130 also provides for sickness benefits (Articles 18-27). As with most ILO Conventions, exceptions are provided for low-income countries (Article 2).

1983 ILO Vocational Rehabilitation and Employment (Disabled Persons) Convention (No. 159) (C159)[54]
C159 entered into force in 1985, establishing basic principles of equal opportunity and non-discrimination in employment for people living with disability. The most significant contribution of C159 is the requirement that countries institute laws and policies on vocational rehabilitation and employment. The treaty is equally applicable to people with physical and mental impairment(s) and conditions. It includes important provisions for gender equity in employment and the creation of "special positive measures" to promote equality of opportunity and treatment between workers of varying abilities (Article 4).

1983 ILO Vocational Rehabilitation and Employment (Disabled Persons) Recommendation (No. 168)[55]

ILO No. 168 supplements Convention No. 159. It defines a person living with disability as "an individual whose prospects of securing, retaining and advancing in suitable employment are substantially reduced as a result of a duly recognised physical or mental impairment" (para. 1). The Recommendation spells out a number of elements that could only be inferred in the Convention. For example, it recommends community participation for vocational rehabilitation services (Part III), and recognises the role of organisations representing persons living with disability (para. 17). It moves away from the medical model of disability by recommending for example the "elimination, by stages if necessary, of physical, communication and architectural barriers and obstacles affecting transport and access to and free movement in premises for the training and employment of disabled persons; appropriate standards should be taken into account for new public buildings and facilities" (para. 11.g).

Theme 4: Criminal justice systems including the rights of victims of crime

1955 UN Standard Minimum Rules for the Treatment of Prisoners (SMR)[56]

The SMR were adopted by the First UN Congress on the Prevention of Crime and the Treatment of Offenders in 1955.[57] The SMR are relevant to survivors of gun violence who are thought or found to be perpetrators and therefore kept in custody. The first principle is non-discrimination, though disability and health status are not included in the specific grounds of discrimination listed. The SMR requires that accommodation "meet all requirements of health" (Article 10), and that medical care be provided for physical and mental health (Articles 22-26), including transfer of sick prisoners to hospital in case of need. Rehabilitation is mentioned, but only in relation to prisoners' status as offenders with a remedial understanding in mind.

1985 UN Standard Minimum Rules for the Administration of Juvenile Justice (Beijing Rules)[58]

The Beijing Rules were adopted by General Assembly Resolution 40/33. They set out a model for justice systems for juvenile offenders, based on the promotion of young people's wellbeing and proportionality of their offences.[59] The Rules apply to many young survivors of gun violence by articulating uniform standards for how juvenile offenders are to be treated in the justice system. They mandate separate living spaces from adult offenders in prisons (Rule 26.3) and require that juveniles in institutions receive "care, protection and all necessary assistance—social, educational, vocational, psychological, medical and physical—that they may require because of their age, sex and personality and in the interest of their wholesome development" (Rule 26.2).

1985 UN Declaration of Basic Principles of Justice for Victims of Crime and Abuse of Power (Declaration)[60]

Adopted by General Assembly Resolution 40/34, the Declaration provides guidance on the rights of victims' as well as actions to punish offenders. "Victims" are defined individually and collectively, making the Declaration applicable to survivors of mass crimes (such as genocide, forced displacement or ethnic cleansing) as well as individual or isolated crimes. The definition includes people victimised by their family members (Principle 2), as well as those victimised by State officials who violate criminal law or otherwise abuse their power (Principles 1, 11 and 18).

The rights enumerated include access to justice, restitution, compensation and assistance. If compensation is not available from the offender, the State should try to provide financial compensation to people who sustained "significant bodily injury or impairment of physical or mental health", or to their families in case of death or physical or mental incapacitation (Principle 12). Apart from financial compensation, victims are entitled to "the necessary material, medical, psychological and social assistance," which can be provided from government, voluntary or community-based sources (Principle 14). Police, health and other officials should receive training to sensitise them to the needs of victims, as well as guidelines to ensure "proper and prompt aid" (Principle 16). Significantly for people with gun-related injuries or trauma, Principle 17 requires attention for "those who have special needs because of the nature of the harm inflicted."

1990 *UN Rules for the Protection of Juveniles Deprived of their Liberty* (Havana Rules)[61]
The Havana Rules were developed at the Eighth UN Congress on the Prevention of Crime and the Treatment of Offenders, and adopted by General Assembly Resolution 45/113. Like the 1985 Beijing Rules, the Havana Rules are relevant for young survivors of gun violence who are identified as offenders by the justice system. The first Havana Rule states that "the juvenile justice system should uphold the rights and safety and promote the physical and mental well-being of juveniles." Health features in several other rules; for example, Rule 28 requires conditions of detention to take full account of the particular needs, status and special requirements of juveniles, based on factors including mental and physical health. Disability is mentioned once, in Rule 4 on non-discrimination.

1997 *UN Guidelines for Action on Children in the Criminal Justice System*[62]
Adopted by ECOSOC Resolution 1997/30, these Guidelines spell out detailed protections for children, whether they are victims, witnesses, or perpetrators of criminal acts. Part II of the document reinforces previous agreements on children identified as perpetrators, but additionally recognises the needs of those suffering particular disadvantage (as many gun violence survivors do). Guideline 17 says: "Appropriate action should be ensured to alleviate the problem of children in need of special protection measures, such as children working or living on the streets or children permanently deprived of a family environment, children with disabilities, children of minorities, immigrants and indigenous peoples and other vulnerable groups of children." Part III deals with protections for child victims and witnesses. A child surviving gun violence who is identified as a victim is entitled to "access to assistance that meets their needs, such as advocacy, protection, economic assistance, counselling, health and social services, social reintegration and physical and psychological recovery services. Special assistance should be given to those children who are disabled or ill. Emphasis should be placed upon family—and community-based rehabilitation rather than institutionalization" (Guideline 46).

2000 *UN Basic Principles on the Use of Restorative Justice Programmes in Criminal Matters*[63]
These Principles were adopted by ECOSOC Resolution 2002/12. They encourage States to adopt and standardise restorative justice processes, in which a victim and an offender (and sometimes other people affected by the crime) "participate together actively in the resolution of matters arising from the crime, generally with

the help of a facilitator."[64] Restorative outcomes can include apology, reparation, restitution and community service.

2003 *Convention Against Corruption*[65]

This Convention entered into force in 2005. It seeks to combat corruption through international cooperation—legal assistance, joint investigations, asset recovery—as well as technical assistance. It deals with both prevention and repression (criminalisation and law enforcement). For the latter, detailed provisions cover the protection of witnesses, experts and victims involved in the prosecution of corruption cases.

2005 *Guidelines on Justice in Matters involving Child Victims and Witnesses of Crime*[66]

These Guidelines were adopted by ECOSOC Resolution 2005/20, building on the 1997 *Guidelines for Action on Children in the Criminal Justice System*. The 2005 Guidelines recognise that "children who are victims and witnesses may suffer additional hardship if mistakenly viewed as offenders when they are in fact victims and witnesses" (para. II.7.e); a problem encountered by some young survivors of gun violence. Particular emphasis is placed on the principle of non-discrimination (Section VI).

Theme 5: Crime prevention

1995 *UN Guidelines for Cooperation and Technical Assistance in the Field of Urban Crime Prevention*[67]

Adopted by ECOSOC Resolution 1995/9, these Guidelines support the design and implementation of action plans for community-based crime prevention. The document addresses primary prevention of crime as well as prevention of reoffending through rehabilitation of offenders—a relevant topic for survivors of gun violence who are also perpetrators. It also recommends the protection of victims, including through systems of victim assistance.

2000 *UN Convention against Transnational Organized Crime* (UNTOC); *Protocol to Prevent, Suppress and Punish Trafficking in Persons Especially Women and Children; Protocol against the Smuggling of Migrants by Land, Sea and Air*[68]

The UNTOC came into force in 2003, covering the criminalisation of transnational organised crime, money laundering, corruption, and obstruction of justice in the investigation of such crimes. It focusses on mutual legal assistance among States to prosecute and punish these crimes, but also contains provisions on protection of witnesses and victims. The first Protocol to the UNTOC, dealing with trafficking in persons, came into force in 2003. Like the Convention itself, the Protocol is primarily devoted to investigation and prosecution; however, a secondary objective is to protect and assist the victims of trafficking, which may include some survivors of gun violence. The second Protocol, dealing with the smuggling of migrants, came into effect in 2004. It calls for protection and assistance of people who have been smuggled, but does not specify what form that assistance should take.

2001 *Protocol against the Illicit Manufacturing of and Trafficking in Firearms, Their Parts and Components and Ammunition, supplementing the United Nations Convention against Transnational Organized Crime* (Firearms Protocol)[69]

The Firearms Protocol came into force in 2005. This third UNTOC Protocol was the first legally binding global instrument on small arms. States undertake to criminalise trafficking, regulate manufacturing, and mark firearms so they can be traced. There is no mention of victims or survivors, but is included in this document because by tackling one aspect of the arms trade, it stands to contribute over the long term to reducing gun violence—ideally in conjunction with other measures to reduce the supply, demand and misuse of weapons.

2002 *ECOSOC Resolution on Action to Promote Effective Crime Prevention*[70]
These Guidelines were adopted by ECOSOC Resolution 2002/13, building on the 1995 *Guidelines for Cooperation and Technical Assistance in the Field of Urban Crime Prevention*. Drawing on good practices, the 2002 document elaborates on four approaches to crime prevention: social development, community or locally-based crime prevention, situational prevention (including provision of assistance and information to potential and actual victims), and reintegration of offenders. The latter two strategies aim to prevent repeat victimisation. An implementation handbook was published in 2010.[71]

Theme 6: Disarmament and weapons control
1997 *Convention on the Prohibition of the Use, Stockpiling, Production and Transfer of Anti-Personnel Mines and on their Destruction* (Anti-Personnel Mine Ban Convention)[72]
The Anti-Personnel Mine Ban Convention entered into force in 1999. It was the first disarmament instrument to include a provision to assist affected individuals as an integral part of controlling a class of weapons. Article 6.3 notes: "Each State Party in a position to do so shall provide assistance for the care and rehabilitation, and social and economic reintegration, of mine victims and for mine awareness programs." This was included against significant opposition from several States. Since adoption however, assisting survivors has become a solid focus. The norm has been reinforced through the adoption of principles and understandings by States to guide their victim assistance efforts and through the adoption of successive five-year action plans: the Nairobi Action Plan 2004-2009 and the Cartagena Action Plan 2009-2014.[73] Common to both plans is the principle of non-discrimination, a focus on a rights-based approach, and increased access to services for health care, rehabilitation, and economic and social inclusion.

2001 *UN Programme of Action to Prevent, Combat and Eradicate the Illicit Trade in Small Arms and Light Weapons in All Its Aspects* (PoA)[74]
Adopted at the 2001 UN Conference on Small Arms, this agreement is politically binding. Its focus is predominantly on the prevention, and investigation of, illicit arms trafficking, with only the preamble mentioning the people killed, injured and displaced by gun violence. However the title element "in all its aspects" suggests wider interpretations are possible. At the Review Conferences in 2006 and 2012, civil society and some States attempted to introduce new commitments into the PoA to incorporate a focus on survivors. These efforts produced a modest result in the Outcome Document of the 2012 Conference.[75] In Part I, "understanding" of the needs of survivors is called for: "We remain gravely concerned about the negative impact of the illicit trade in small arms and light weapons on women, men, children, youth, the elderly and persons with disabilities and call for improved understanding of the different concerns and needs of these groups" (para. 14). Part II contains a stronger commitment by States, "to explore means to eliminate the negative impact of the illicit trade in small arms and light weapons on women" (para. 2(i)) and "to address the special needs of children affected by armed conflict" (para. 2(j)).

2003 *Protocol on Explosive Remnants of War (Protocol V to the 1980 Convention on Prohibitions or Restrictions on the Use of Certain Conventional Weapons which may be deemed to be Excessively Injurious or to have Indiscriminate Effects)* **(ERW Protocol)**[76]
The ERW Protocol entered into force in 2006. It extends the 1980 *Convention on Certain Conventional Weapons* (CCW) to cover unexploded and abandoned artillery shells, mortar shells, hand grenades, cluster munitions and bombs which imperil the safety of civilians and communities after war. The Protocol includes specific reference to rehabilitation and assistance to survivors (Article 8.2 and 8.3). In 2008, a Plan of Action on Victim Assistance was adopted.[77]

2008 *Convention on Cluster Munitions* **(CCM)**[78]
The CCM entered into force in 2010 and provides the most comprehensive legal obligations to assist the victims of any weapons control instrument. Article 2.1 defines cluster munition survivors to include both those directly injured or affected and those indirectly affected, such as families and communities. Article 5 obligates States with survivors in their territory to "adequately provide age—and gender-sensitive assistance, including medical care, rehabilitation and psychological support, as well as provide for their social and economic inclusion." A further requirement is to develop laws, policies and national action plans for assistance, and to "closely consult with and actively involve cluster munition victims and their representative organisations." This direct support is the responsibility of the countries where survivors live. However, other States, if they are able to do so, are required to help through financial assistance and cooperation (Article 6.7). Article 7 requires States to make "every effort to collect reliable relevant data with respect to cluster munition victims", and to report annually on the progress made.

2013 *Arms Trade Treaty* **(ATT)**[79]
Adopted by the General Assembly in April 2013 and opened for signature in June of that year. It will enter into force once ratified by 50 States. The ATT regulates international sales of conventional weapons, from battle tanks and combat aircraft to guns. Unlike the landmine and cluster munitions treaties, the ATT contains no commitments to assist the people injured by the weapons it covers. However, it is the first multilateral treaty to note the needs of victims of armed violence generally. The preamble recognises the "security, social, economic and humanitarian consequences of the illicit and unregulated trade in conventional arms... that civilians, particularly women and children, account for the vast majority of those adversely affected by armed conflict and armed violence... the challenges faced by victims of armed conflict and their need for adequate care, rehabilitation and social and economic inclusion." An important preventive focus, in the legally binding clauses of the treaty, is recognition of the links between gender-based violence and lax arms export controls, stating that arms exporters "shall take into account the risk of"... weapons..."being used to commit or facilitate serious acts of gender based violence or serious acts of violence against women and children" (Article 7.4).

Contributors: Cate Buchanan, Rachel Garaghty, Rebecca Peters and **Mireille Widmer** of the Surviving Gun Violence Project developed the Annex. **Helaine Boyd** assisted with fact-checking and drafting.

Peer reviews were provided by **Sheree Bailey,** independent disability and victim assistance adviser (Australia); **Shuaib Chalklen,** UN Special Rapporteur on the Standard Rules on the Equalization of Opportunities for Persons with Disabilities (South Africa); **Barbara A. Frey,** Director, Human Rights Program, University of Minnesota (USA) and UN Special Rapporteur on the prevention of human rights violations committed with small arms and light weapons (2002-2006); **Janet E. Lord,** Burton Blatt Institute, Syracuse University and the Harvard Law School Project on Disability (USA); **Daniel Mont,** Principal Research Associate, University College London and Senior Research Fellow, Leonard Cheshire Disability and Inclusive Development Centre (UK); **Sarah Parker,** Senior Researcher, Small Arms Survey (Switzerland); and **Christian Holmboe Ruge,** Director, Humanitarian Disarmament Programme, International Law and Policy Institute (Norway).

References

[1]   "Politically binding" reflects a commitment made by States to implement the instrument or standard. Such documents do not create legal obligations for the States signing up to them, but do signify a certain level of political commitment to implementation. "Legally-binding" implies that non-respect of a provision can be challenged before an international court, although instruments generally specify dispute-resolution mechanisms and the strength of verification and enforcement procedures varies.

[2]   Treaty and ratification status available at: www.oas.org/juridico/english/sigs/a-65.html Accessed 8 August 2013.

[3]   Directive 2012/29/EU of the European Parliament and of the Council of 25 October 2012 establishing minimum standards on the rights, support and protection of victims of crime, and replacing Council Framework Decision 2001/220/JHA. Available at: http://eurlex.europa.eu/LexUriServ/LexUriServ.do?uri=OJ:L:2012:315:0057:0073:EN:PDF Accessed 8 August 2013.

[4]   *International Covenant on Civil and Political Rights*, and *International Covenant on Economic, Social and Cultural Rights*.

[5]   See www.ohchr.org/EN/HRBodies/SP/Pages/Themes.aspx for the complete list of thematic mandates. In addition, country-specific special procedures also exist.

[6]   The 1948 UDHR is not legally binding, but is universally accepted and has the status of customary international law, providing the foundational principles for all later legally binding instruments on human rights.

[7]   Full titles for Conventions and Protocols: *Convention (I) for the Amelioration of the Condition of the Wounded and Sick in Armed Forces in the Field.* Geneva, 12 August 1949; *Convention (II) for the Amelioration of the Condition of Wounded, Sick and Shipwrecked Members of Armed Forces at Sea.* Geneva, 12 August 1949; *Convention (III) relative to the Treatment of Prisoners of War.* Geneva, 12 August 1949; *Convention (IV) relative to the Protection of Civilian Persons in Time of War.* Geneva, 12 August 1949; *Protocol Additional to the Geneva Conventions of 12 August 1949, and relating to the Protection of Victims of International Armed Conflicts* (Protocol I), 8 June 1977; *Protocol Additional to the Geneva Conventions of 12 August 1949, and relating to the Protection of Victims of Non-International Armed Conflicts* (Protocol II), 8 June 1977. Available at: www.icrc.org/eng/war-and-law/treaties-customary-law/geneva-conventions/index.jsp Accessed 6 August 2013.

8   While the CCPJ standard minimum rules are not legally binding on States they are recognised to be of significance as universally accepted non-legal standards. See: www.unodc.org/unodc/commissions/CCPCJ/

9   Available at: www.un.org/en/documents/udhr Accessed 6 August 2013.

10 Resolution 217 A (III).

11 Available at: www.unhcr.org/3b66c2aa10.html Accessed 7 August 2013. At 7 August 2013: 146 ratifications. Source: http://treaties.un.org/Pages/ViewDetails.aspx?src=TREATY&mtdsg_no=V-5&chapter=5&lang=en

12 Available at: www.ohchr.org/EN/ProfessionalInterest/Pages/CESCR.aspx Accessed 6 August 2013. At 6 August 2013: 160 ratifications and 70 signatories. Source: http://treaties.un.org/Pages/ViewDetails.aspx?mtdsg_no=IV-3&chapter=4&lang=en

13 Available at: www.ohchr.org/EN/ProfessionalInterest/Pages/CCPR.aspx Accessed 6 August 2013. At 6 August 2013: 167 ratifications and 74 signatories. Source: http://treaties.un.org/Pages/ViewDetails.aspx?mtdsg_no=IV-4&chapter=4&lang=en%23EndDec

14 Available at: www.ohchr.org/Documents/ProfessionalInterest/cedaw.pdf Accessed 6 August 2013. At 6 August 2013: 187 ratifications and 99 signatories. Source: http://treaties.un.org/Pages/ViewDetails.aspx?src=TREATY&mtdsg_no=IV-8&chapter=4&lang=en

15 Available at: www.un.org/documents/ga/res/37/a37r052.htm Accessed 6 August 2013.

16 Available at: www.hrweb.org/legal/cat.html Accessed 12 August 2013. At 12 August 2013: 153 ratifications and 78 signatories. Source: http://treaties.un.org/Pages/ViewDetails.aspx?mtdsg_no=IV-9&chapter=4&lang=en

17 Available at: http://www.ohchr.org/EN/ProfessionalInterest/Pages/CRC.aspx Accessed 6 August 2013. At 6 August 2013: 193 ratifications and 140 signatories. Source: http://treaties.un.org/Pages/ViewDetails.aspx?mtdsg_no=IV-11&chapter=4&lang=en

18 Available at: www.ohchr.org/Documents/ProfessionalInterest/executions.pdf Accessed 6 August 2013.

19 Available at: www.unrol.org/files/BASICP~3.PDF Accessed 6 August 2013.

20 Available at: www.un.org/documents/ga/res/48/a48r096.htm Accessed 6 August 2013.

21 Shuaib Chalklen of South Africa has been in the position since 2009. See *The Special Rapporteur's Global Survey on the implementation of the Standard Rules* (New York: UN Enable, 2006). Available at: www.un.org/esa/socdev/enable/rapporteur.htm Accessed 6 August 2013.

22 Available at: www.unhchr.ch/Huridocda/Huridoca.nsf/0/d2e008c61b70263ec125661e0036f36e Accessed 6 August 2013.

23 Available at: www.unhchr.ch/tbs/doc.nsf/(symbol)/E.C.12.2000.4.En Accessed 6 August 2013.

24 Available at: www.ohchr.org/EN/ProfessionalInterest/Pages/OPCAT.aspx Accessed 12 August 2013. At 12 August 2013: 69 ratifications and 72 signatories. Source: http://treaties.un.org/Pages/ViewDetails.aspx?mtdsg_no=IV-9-b&chapter=4&lang=en

25 Available at: www.who.int/disabilities/WHA5823_resolution_en.pdf Accessed 6 August 2013.

26 World Health Organization and World Bank, *World Report on Disability* (Geneva: WHO, 2011).

27 Final report submitted by Barbara Frey, Special Rapporteur, in accordance with Sub-Commission resolution 2002/25 (A/HRC/Sub.1/58/27), endorsed by Sub-Com. res. 2006/22, UN Doc A/HRC/Sub.1/58/L.11/Add.1 at 3. Available at: www1.umn.edu/humanrts/instree/smallarmsprinciples.html Accessed 6 August 2013.

28 Available at: www.ohchr.org/EN/HRBodies/CRPD/Pages/ConventionRightsPersonsWithDisabilities.aspx Accessed 6 August 2013. At 6 August 2013: 133 ratifications and 156 signatories. Source: http://treaties.un.org/Pages/ViewDetails.aspx?mtdsg_no=IV-15&chapter=4&lang=en

29 The Committee consists of 18 members who act in an individual capacity for four year terms; 50% of the Committee is renewed every two years. The Chairperson is Ron McCallum, Professor of law at the University of Sydney. It meets twice a year. National reports, including shadow reports from NGOs, can be accessed at www.ohchr.org/en/hrbodies/crpd/pages/crpdindex.aspx

30 In July 2013 Cate Buchanan and Sheree Bailey estimated some 84 States have specific law/s in place to promote disability rights. This was drawn from data at: UN Enable reporting on CRPD ratifications into domestic laws and the Country Laws Index of the Disability Rights Education and Defense Fund available at: http://dredf.org/international/lawindex.shtml Accessed 31 July 2013. Thanks to Marianne Schulze for her assistance. Related to including

a focus on disability in poverty reduction strategies see, for example, the work of Handicap International and CBM at www.making-prsp-inclusive.org Accessed 16 August 2013.

[31] Available at: www.ohchr.org/EN/HRBodies/CRPD/Pages/OptionalProtocolRightsPersons WithDisabilities.aspx Accessed 6 August 2013. At 6 August 2013: 77 ratifications and 91 signatories. Source: http://treaties.un.org/Pages/ViewDetails.aspx?mtdsg_no=IV-15-a&chapter=4&lang=en

[32] Available at: www.wpro.who.int/mnh/A60_R22-en.pdf Accessed 6 August 2013.

[33] See: www.who.int/violence_injury_prevention/services/gaci/en/index.html Accessed 16 August 2013.

[34] Available at: www2.ohchr.org/english/bodies/cat/docs/GC/CAT-C-GC-3_en.pdf Accessed 8 August 2013.

[35] Available at: http://ap.ohchr.org/documents/alldocs.aspx?doc_id=21560 Accessed 20 August 2013.

[36] Available at: http://apps.who.int/gb/ebwha/pdf_files/WHA66/A66_R9-en.pdf Accessed 8 August 2013.

[37] Available at: www1.umn.edu/humanrts/instree/y1gcacws.htm Accessed 7 August 2013. At 7 August 2013: 195 ratifications. Source: www.icrc.org/ihl/INTRO/365

[38] Available at: www1.umn.edu/humanrts/instree/y2gcacws.htm Accessed 7 August 2013. At 7 August 2013: 195 ratifications. Source: www.icrc.org/ihl/INTRO/370

[39] Available at: www1.umn.edu/humanrts/instree/1929c.htm Accessed 6 August 2013. At 6 August 2013: 195 ratifications. Source: www.icrc.org/ihl/INTRO/375

[40] Available at: www.un-documents.net/gc-4.htm Accessed 6 August 2013. At 6 August 2013: 195 ratifications. Source: www.icrc.org/ihl/INTRO/380

[41] Available at: http://treaties.un.org/doc/Publication/UNTS/Volume%201125/volume-1125-I-17512-English.pdf Accessed 6 August 2013. At 6 August 2013: 173 ratifications. Source: www.icrc.org/ihl/INTRO/470

[42] Available at: http://treaties.un.org/doc/Publication/UNTS/Volume 1125/volume-1125-I-17513-English.pdf Accessed 6 August 2013. At 6 August 2013: 167 ratifications Source: www.icrc.org/ihl/INTRO/475

[43] Available at: http://untreaty.un.org/cod/icc/statute/romefra.htm Accessed 6 August 2013.

[44] International Criminal Court Web page, "Situations and cases". Available at: www.icc-cpi.int/en_menus/icc/situations%20and%20cases/Pages/situations%20and%20cases.aspx Accessed 16 August 2013.

[45] Available at: www.ohchr.org/EN/ProfessionalInterest/Pages/OPACCRC.aspx Accessed 6 August 2013. At 6 August 2013: 152 ratifications and 129 signatories. Source: http://treaties.un.org/Pages/ViewDetails.aspx?mtdsg_no=IV-11-b&chapter=4&lang=en

[46] Available at: www.ohchr.org/EN/ProfessionalInterest/Pages/RemedyAndReparation.aspx Accessed 6 August 2013.

[47] T. Van Boven, *Basic Principles and Guidelines on the Right to a Remedy and Reparation for Victims of Gross Violations of International Human Rights Law and Serious Violations of International Humanitarian Law* (United Nations Audiovisual Library of International Law, 2010). Available at: http://untreaty.un.org/cod/avl/pdf/ha/ga_60-147/ga_60-147_e.pdf Accessed 16 August 2013.

[48] Available at: www.ilo.org/dyn/normlex/en/f?p=1000:12100:0::NO::P12100_ILO_CODE:C102 Accessed 6 August 2013. At 6 August 2013: 49 ratifications. Source: www.ilo.org/dyn/normlex/en/f?p=NORMLEXPUB:11300:0::NO:11300:P11300_INSTRUMENT_ID:312247:NO

[49] Available at: www.ilo.org/dyn/normlex/en/f?p=NORMLEXPUB:12100:0::NO:12100:P12100_ILO_CODE:R099 Accessed 6 August 2013.

[50] Available at: www.actrav.itcilo.org/english/common/C111.html Accessed 6 August 2013. At 6 August 2013: 172 ratifications. Source: www.ilo.org/dyn/normlex/en/f?p=NORMLEXPUB:1 1300:0::NO:11300:P11300_INSTRUMENT_ID:312256:NO

[51] Available at: www.ilo.org/dyn/normlex/en/f?p=1000:12100:0::NO::P12100_ILO_CODE:C121 Accessed 6 August 2013. At 6 August 2013: 24 ratifications. Source: http://webfusion.ilo.org/public/applis/appl-byconv.cfm?conv=C121&lang=EN

[52] Available at: www.ilo.org/dyn/normlex/en/f?p=1000:12100:0::NO::P12100_ILO_CODE:C128 Accessed 6 August 2013. At 6 August 2013: 16 ratifications. Source: http://webfusion.ilo.org/public/applis/appl-byconv.cfm?conv=C128&lang=EN

53 Available at: www.ilo.org/dyn/normlex/en/f?p=1000:12100:0::NO::P12100_ILO_CODE:C130 Accessed 6 August 2013. At 6 August 2013: 15 ratifications. Source: http://webfusion.ilo. org/public/applis/appl-byconv.cfm?conv=C130&lang=EN

54 Available at: www.ilo.org/dyn/normlex/en/f?p=1000:12100:0::NO::P12100_ILO_CODE:C159 Accessed 6 August 2013. At 6 August 2013: 82 ratifications. Source: http://webfusion.ilo. org/public/applis/appl-byconv.cfm?conv=C159&lang=EN

55 Available at: www.ilo.org/dyn/normlex/en/f?p=1000:12100:0::NO::P12100_INSTRUMENT_ ID:312506 Accessed 6 August 2013.

56 Available at: www.ohchr.org/EN/ProfessionalInterest/Pages/TreatmentOfPrisoners.aspx Accessed 6 August 2013.

57 They were approved by ECOSOC Resolutions 663 C (XXIV) of 1957 and 2076 (LXII) of 1977.

58 Available at: www.un.org/documents/ga/res/40/a40r033.htm Accessed 6 August 2013.

59 Defence for Children International, web slide show, *Beijing Rules*. Available at: www. child-abuse.com/childhouse/childrens_rights/dci_bei1.html Accessed 16 August 2013.

60 Available at: www.un.org/documents/ga/res/40/a40r034.htm Accessed 6 August 2013. Also see: United Nations Office for Drug Control and Crime Prevention and the Centre for International Crime Prevention, *Handbook on Justice for Victims of Crime: On the use and application of the Declaration of Basic Principles of Justice for Victims of Crime and Abuse of Power* (New York: UN, 1999). Available at: www.uncjin.org/Standards/9857854.pdf Accessed 16 August 2013.

61 Available at: www.un.org/documents/ga/res/45/a45r113.htm Accessed 6 August 2013.

62 Available at: www.ohchr.org/EN/ProfessionalInterest/Pages/CriminalJusticeSystem.aspx Accessed 6 August 2013.

63 Available at: www.un.org/en/ecosoc/docs/2002/resolution%202002-12.pdf Accessed 6 August 2013.

64 United Nations Office on Drugs and Crime, *Handbook on Restorative Justice Programmes*, Criminal Justice Handbook Series (New York: UNODC, 2006).

65 Available at: www.unodc.org/documents/treaties/UNCAC/Publications/Convention/ 08-50026_E.pdf Accessed 6 August 2013. At 6 August 2013: 167 ratifications and 140 signatories. Source: http://treaties.un.org/Pages/ViewDetails.aspx?mtdsg_no=XVIII-14& chapter=18&lang=en

66 Available at: www.un.org/en/pseataskforce/docs/guidelines_on_justice_in_matters_ involving_child_victims_and.pdf Accessed 6 August 2013.

67 Available at: www.unodc.org/pdf/compendium/compendium_2006_part_03_01.pdf Accessed 6 August 2013.

68 Available at: www.unodc.org/documents/treaties/UNTOC/Publications/TOC%20Conven tion/TOCebook-e.pdf Accessed 6 August 2013. At 6 August 2013: 177 ratifications and 147 signatories (UNTOC); 157 ratifications and 117 signatories (first Protocol); 137 ratifications and 112 signatories (second Protocol). Sources: UNTOC—http://treaties.un.org/Pages/ ViewDetails.aspx?mtdsg_no=XVIII-12&chapter=18&lang=en Protocol on trafficking— http://treaties.un.org/Pages/ViewDetails.aspx?mtdsg_no=XVIII-12-a&chapter= 18&lang=en Protocol on smuggling—http://treaties.un.org/Pages/ViewDetails.aspx?mtdsg _no=XVIII-12-b&chapter=18&lang=en

69 Available at: www1.umn.edu/humanrts/instree/illicitfirearms.html Accessed 6 August 2013. At 6 August 2013: 101 ratifications and 53 signatories. Source: http://treaties.un.org/ Pages/ViewDetails.aspx?mtdsg_no=XVIII-12-c&chapter=18&lang=en

70 Available at: www.unodc.org/documents/justice-and-prison-reform/crimeprevention/ resolution_2002-13.pdf Accessed 6 August 2013.

71 United Nations Office on Drugs and Crime and the International Center for the Prevention of Crime, *Handbook on the Crime Prevention Guidelines: Making them work*, Criminal Justice Handbook Series (New York: UNODC, 2010). Available at: www.unodc.org/documents/justice- and-prison-reform/crimeprevention/10-52410_Guidelines_eBook.pdf Accessed 6 August 2013.

72 Also known as the Ottawa Convention. Available at: www.apminebanconvention. org/overview-and-convention-text Accessed 6 August 2013. At 6 August 2013: 161 ratifications and 133 signatories. Source: http://treaties.un.org/Pages/ViewDetails. aspx?src=TREATY&mtdsg_no=XXVI-5&chapter=26&lang=en

73 Both action plans are available at: www.apminebanconvention.org/review-conferences Accessed 12 August 2013.

[74] Available at: www.un.org/events/smallarms2006/pdf/No150720.pdf Accessed 6 August 2013.

[75] Available at: http://www.poa-iss.org/RevCon2/documents/RevCon-DOC/Outcome/PoA-Rev Con2-Outcome-E.pdf Accessed 6 August 2013.

[76] Available at: disarmament.un.org/treaties/t/ccwc_p5/text Accessed 6 August 2013. At 6 August 2013: 82 ratifications. Source: www.icrc.org/ihl/INTRO/610

[77] Available at: www.unog.ch/80256EDD006B8954/(httpAssets)/13BF73112AB2D03AC12579C 3004D2DD8/$file/VA_PoA_OfficialDoc_Eng.pdf Accessed 6 August 2013.

[78] Available at: www.clusterconvention.org/files/2011/01/Convention-ENG.pdf Accessed 6 August 2013. At 6 August 2013: 83 ratifications and 108 signatories. Source: http://treaties. un.org/Pages/ViewDetails.aspx?src=TREATY&mtdsg_no=XXVI-6&chapter=26&lang=en

[79] Available at: www.un.org/disarmament/ATT Accessed 6 August 2013. At 6 August 2013: 2 ratifications and 81 signatories. Source: http://treaties.un.org/Pages/ViewDetails. aspx?src=TREATY&mtdsg_no=XXVI-8&chapter=26&lang=en

Lightning Source UK Ltd.
Milton Keynes UK
UKOW05f2358220714

235594UK00002B/99/P